Lecture Notes in Computer Science   5030

Commenced Publication in 1973
Founding and Former Series Editors:
Gerhard Goos, Juris Hartmanis, and Jan van Leeuw

T0237793

Editorial Board

David Hutchison
  Lancaster University, UK
Takeo Kanade
  Carnegie Mellon University, Pittsburgh, PA, USA
Josef Kittler
  University of Surrey, Guildford, UK
Jon M. Kleinberg
  Cornell University, Ithaca, NY, USA
Alfred Kobsa
  University of California, Irvine, CA, USA
Friedemann Mattern
  ETH Zurich, Switzerland
John C. Mitchell
  Stanford University, CA, USA
Moni Naor
  Weizmann Institute of Science, Rehovot, Israel
Oscar Nierstrasz
  University of Bern, Switzerland
C. Pandu Rangan
  Indian Institute of Technology, Madras, India
Bernhard Steffen
  University of Dortmund, Germany
Madhu Sudan
  Massachusetts Institute of Technology, MA, USA
Demetri Terzopoulos
  University of California, Los Angeles, CA, USA
Doug Tygar
  University of California, Berkeley, CA, USA
Gerhard Weikum
  Max-Planck Institute of Computer Science, Saarbruecken, Germany

Hong Mei (Ed.)

High Confidence
Software Reuse
in Large Systems

10th International Conference on Software Reuse, ICSR 2008
Beijing, China, May 25-29, 2008
Proceedings

 Springer

Volume Editor

Hong Mei
Peking University
Institute of Software
School of Electronics Engineering and Computer Science
Beijing 100871, China
E-mail: meih@pku.edu.cn

Library of Congress Control Number: 2008926386

CR Subject Classification (1998): D.2, K.6, D.1, J.1

LNCS Sublibrary: SL 2 – Programming and Software Engineering

ISSN	0302-9743
ISBN-10	3-540-68062-4 Springer Berlin Heidelberg New York
ISBN-13	978-3-540-68062-8 Springer Berlin Heidelberg New York

Springer is a part of Springer Science+Business Media

springer.com

© Springer-Verlag Berlin Heidelberg 2008

Typesetting: Camera-ready by author, data conversion by Scientific Publishing Services, Chennai, India
Printed on acid-free paper   SPIN: 12270422   06/3180   5 4 3 2 1 0

Preface

Software reuse depicts a great vision for the software industry. It has been widely viewed as a promising way to improve both the productivity and quality of software development. However, despite of the successes we have achieved, there are still many issues that have limited the promotion of software reuse in the real world. Therefore, software reuse has remained an important hotspot of research. ICSR is the premier international conference in the field of software reuse. It has been an important venue for presenting advances and improvements within the software reuse domain, and a powerful driving force in promoting the interaction between researchers and practitioners.

The theme of ICSR 10 was "High Confidence Software Reuse in Large Systems." A high confidence system is one that behaves in a well-understood and predictable fashion. Today's trends towards widespread use of commercial off-the-shelf (COTS) technology, increased integration, continuous evolution, and larger scale are yielding more complex software systems. So, the problem of how to build high confidence complex systems and how to reuse software with a high level of confidence has become a new attractive topic for research. Furthermore, high-level software asset reuse has been a goal for the last 20–30 years, and it can still be considered an unsolved question. Components-based development, MDA-MDE-MDD, extreme programming, and other techniques or methods are promising approaches to software reuse that still need more research.

These proceedings report on the current state of the art in software reuse. The topics covered in the proceedings include software architecture, software components, high confidence technology, domain engineering, product line approaches, service-oriented engineering, model-based approaches and several other aspects of software reuse.

May 2008   Hong Mei

Organization

Organizing Committee

General Chair	Juan Llorens, University Carlos III of Madrid, Spain
Program Chair	Hong Mei, Peking University, China
Workshops Chair	Jianjun Zhao, Shanghai Jiao Tong University, China
Tutorial Chair	Jeff Poulin, Lockheed Martin Systems Integration-Owego, USA
Doctoral Symposium Chair	Gregory Kulczycki, Virginia Tech, USA
Tools Demo Chair	Jose Luis Barros, Unversidad de Vigo, Spain
Local Arrangements Chair	Bing Xie, Peking University, China
Publicity Co-chairs	Bill Frakes, Virginia Tech, USA
	Ge Li, Peking University, China
Finance Chair	Chuck Lillie, ISASE, USA
	Wei Zhang, Peking University, China
Web Chair	Donggang Cao, Peking University, China

Program Committee

Sidney Bailin	Knowledge Evolution, USA
Jose Luis Barros	Unversidad de Vigo, Spain
Ted Biggerstaff	SoftwareGenerators.com, USA
Sholom Cohen	Software Engineering Institute, USA
Reidar Conradi	Norwegian University of Science and Technology, Norway
Hakan Erdogmus	NRC Institute for Information Technology, Canada
John Favaro	Consulenza Informatica, Italy
Robert Feldt	Blekinge Institute of Technology, Sweden
Bill Frakes	Virginia Tech, USA
Cristina Gacek	University of Newcastle upon Tyne, UK
Gonzalo Genova	Universidad Carlos III Madrid, Spain
Birgit Geppert	Avaya Labs, USA
Hassan Gomaa	George Mason University, USA
Yanxiang He	Wuhan University, China
Zhi Jin	Institute of Mathematics Chinese Academy of Sciences, China
Merijn de Jonge	Philips, Netherlands
Kyo Kang, Postech	Korea
Gregory Kulczycki	Virginia Tech, USA

Patricia Lago	Vrije Universiteit Amsterdam, Netherlands
Filippo Lanubile	Universitàdi Bari, Italy
Xuandong Li	Nanjing University, China
Chuck Lillie	ISASE, USA
Chao Liu	Beihang Universtiy, China
Juan Llorens	Universidad Carlos III Madrid, Spain
Mike Mannion	Glasgow Caledonian University, UK
Masao Matsumoto	Kyushu Sangyo University, Japan
Hong Mei	Peking University, China
Ali Mili	New Jersey Institute of Technology, USA
Maurizio Morisio	Polytechnic of Turin, Italy
Markku Oivo	University of Oulu, Finland
Rob van Ommering	Philips Research Laboratory, Netherlands
Witold Pedrycz	University of Alberta, Canada
Jeff Poulin	Lockheed Martin Systems Integration- Owego, USA
Wolfgang Pree	University of Salzburg, Austria
Ruben Prieto-Diaz	James Madison University, USA
Klaus Schmid	University of Hildesheim, Germany
Alberto Sillitti	Free University of Bolzano/Bozen, Italy
Ioannis Stamelos	Aristotle University of Thessaloniki, Greece
Claudia Werner	University of Rio de Janeiro, Brazil
Jianjun Zhao	Shanghai Jiao Tong University, China
Wenyun Zhao	Fudan University, China

Sponsors

Corporate Technology, Siemens Ltd., China.

Table of Contents

Product Line

Domain Models and Analysis

Service Oriented Environment

Components and Services

Reuse Approaches and Pattern

Reuse Approaches and Frameworks

Reuse Approaches and Methods

Introducing Architecture-Centric Reuse into a Small Development Organization*

Hans-Jörg Beyer[1], Dirk Hein[1], Clemens Schitter[1],
Jens Knodel[2], Dirk Muthig[2], and Matthias Naab[2]

[1] WIKON Kommunikationstechnik GmbH
Luxemburger Str. 1-3, 67657 Kaiserslautern, Germany
{hjb,dhe,csc}@wikon.de
[2] Fraunhofer Institute for Experimental Software Engineering (IESE)
Fraunhofer-Platz 1, 67663 Kaiserslautern, Germany
{jens.knodel,dirk.muthig,matthias.naab}@iese.fraunhofer.de

Abstract. Reuse promises cost-effective development and maintenance of software systems. Profiting from reuse, however, requires an upfront investment into creating building blocks to be reused by applications. When therefore required resources are limited, creating reusable building blocks practically often means migrating existing software assets into reusable components while concurrently realizing new developments. This pragmatic approach, which is especially often found in small organizations, often frustrates the vision of successful reuse across similar products.

This paper, however, presents a success story of iteratively introducing architecture-centric development at Wikon GmbH. This small German company develops remote monitoring and controlling devices with a small team of three engineers only. The presented approach for adopting systematic reuse eventually reduced effort for development and testing by more than 35% without any decline in quality.

Keywords: Architecture-centric development, architecture compliance checking, embedded systems, reuse, software architecture, technology transfer.

1 Introduction

Reuse has been generally accepted as one promising way of tackling the challenges of software development organizations. It reduces development time and cost, as well as effort spent on assuring the quality of the resulting product. Hence, reuse frees resources in a development organization that then can focus on new or special functionality and thus, leads eventually to more attractive products. Profiting from reuse, however, requires an upfront investment into creating assets to be reused later. To perform this task successfully, experts are needed, as desperately as for the ongoing

---

* This work was performed as part of the project ArQuE (**Ar**chitecture-Centric **Qu**ality Engineering), which is partially funded by the German Ministry of Education and Research (BMBF) under grant number 01 IS F14.

H. Mei (Ed.): ICSR 2008, LNCS 5030, pp. 1–13, 2008.

product developments that typically cannot be delayed. Consequently, creating reusable assets in practice often means transforming existing software pieces into reusable components while concurrently realizing new developments. This combination is hard to implement successfully in practice and thus organizations often end up in trying ad-hoc reuse (e.g., by "copy & paste") and typically fail.

In this paper, however, we present a success story in establishing an architecture-centric approach at a small development organization, Wikon GmbH. We applied product line engineering concepts to achieve reuse at a higher level of abstraction than source code. Iteratively, we evolved the development organization towards systematic reuse by introducing an architecture-centric strategy for product development. The Wikon products are embedded systems (measurement devices that monitor technical facilities remotely) developed by a team of three people: two developers and one person mainly responsible for quality assurance. Compared to the previous product generation, the new strategy of architecture-centric development saved 12 person-months of development time (from 32 to 20 person-months) and 3 person-months for quality assurance (mainly testing, from 8 to 5 person-months). At Wikon GmbH, the investment hurdle was overcome by the collaboration with Fraunhofer IESE in a joint research project. By means of this project, Wikon was convinced to start introducing new architecture-centric activities that eventually led to the achievement of the reuse gains mentioned above. However, the results show that an architecture-centric product line approach can be successfully scaled down to small organizations.

In Section 2, we discuss what we understand by the term architecture-centric development in general, while Section 3 presents how we instantiated it at Wikon. Furthermore, Section 3 presents an overview of architecting the Wikon products over more than one year. Then Section 4 compares the results to the previous product generation and presents the lessons learned from a non-technical, qualitative viewpoint. Finally, we provide some concluding remarks in Section 5.

2 Architecture-Centric Development

Software architecture is defined as the fundamental organization of a system embodied in its components, their relationships to each other and to the environment, and the principles guiding its design and evolution [8]. All software systems developed have an architecture, but not always it has been designed consciously, and there often exists no explicit documentation describing it. Architectures provide critical abstractions that make it possible to reason about and describe the structure and behavior of a system. They facilitate communication among several stakeholders of a system and enable discussions about the system characteristics. In our opinion, architectures are the means to express, negotiate, and resolve competing concerns of the various stakeholders of a system.

Ideally, the architecture would cover the different needs and concerns of the various stakeholders of the software system from just one perspective in a simple view. However, due to the inherent complexity of software systems, architectures are in practice complicated constructs, which cannot be captured in just one view. To completely describe architectures, the state-of-the-art in architecting (e.g., see [4], [5], [6], [7], [10], [13], [14]) proposes using several perspectives, which results in documentations consisting of multiple architectural views. Here, a view is a representation of a whole system from the perspective of a related set of concerns [8] and is based on a defined viewpoint. Thus, the viewpoint is a specification of the conventions for constructing and using a view [8]. Architectural views are typically customized for the development organization and tailored to the stakeholders' needs. In architecture-centric development, they are iteratively refined, adapted, and updated in each cycle. Such views serve as the central artifacts in system development for the following purposes: to communicate about the system and its characteristics, to make decisions regarding a number of activities such as project planning, quality engineering, and development processes, to define, plan, and monitor the work assignments realized by developers, and to monitor and control the achievement of development goals.

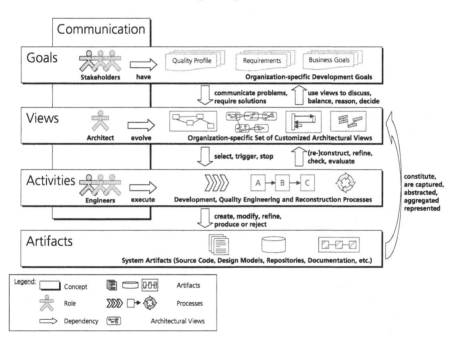

Fig. 1. Architecture-centric Development

Figure 1 depicts the main concepts of architecture-centric development. We abstracted this conceptual view from concrete architecture definition methods, development processes, or techniques. Architecture-centric development is a goal-oriented approach with three major roles: stakeholders, architects, and engineers. The **stakeholders** are the people (an individual, a team, or an organization or classes thereof, see [8]) working with software architectures or having an interest in or concerns with the software system. They use architectural views to ensure that the system's quality profile, the functional requirements, and the business goals are achieved. In case of conflicting goals, they negotiate, balance, and decide about alternative solutions. The **architects** of a software system are the persons or teams who defined and constructed the architecture, supervise the creation of the system, and evolve the architecture during maintenance and evolution. They know about different views on the architecture and are responsible for providing the views to the stakeholders and for assigning these views to their respective concerns. The architects provide solution concepts documented in architectural views and trigger appropriate software engineering activities. These activities are conducted by the **engineers** and eventually result in system artifacts detailing and implementing the solution concepts. The engineers are technical persons who contribute to software development by executing development, quality engineering, or reconstruction processes resulting in artifacts other than the architecture itself. They realize the technical solutions sketched out by the architecture.

In short, the architecture is regarded as one of the most important artifacts in the lifecycle of a software system. Thus, architecture-centric development aligns all activities with the architecture and uses architectural views as communication vehicle.

3 Architecting at Wikon

This section gives an overview how we instantiated architecture-centric development at Wikon. The Wikon GmbH has been a manufacturer of remote control systems (hardware and software) for more than 15 years. Currently, the company consists of about 25 employees. One of their main applications are battery-powered remote control systems (the XENON series) for the energy sector (e.g., water, gas, heat, or liquid gas meters). The systems collect data from different meter types (e.g., different protocol interfaces, pulse outputs) and transmit the data in regular intervals to the Wikon Internet server platform, called WatchMyHome, using a GSM modem. Customers can access the WatchMyHome server and view the measurement data remotely. If necessary, customers can trigger activities based on the measurement data in order to control the facility monitored (e.g., refill a tank, plan the visits of technical service personnel, etc.). The scope of the work presented in this paper addresses only the embedded system – the family of measurement device called the XENON series. The XENON series is implemented in the programming language C (except for about 1% lines of code written in Assembler). The XENON variants can be distinguished by the measurement sensor, the underlying hardware, the measurement protocol (when and how often are values measured and transmitted), and the GSM message format. The development team for XENON comprises three persons, one acting mainly as quality engineer and architect, the other two acting as developers. However, due to the fact that the development organization is rather small, the roles are not strict. The main effort is spent on software development and maintenance; however the three engineers are as well responsible for hardware engineering of the device.

3.1 Iterative Development of the XENON8 Platform

Architecting as an explicit activity was started at Wikon when the software for the XENON8 series of measurement devices was developed. In contrast to its ancestor – the XENON7 series – this new platform comprised a new microcontroller and a changed hardware configuration. While XENON7 offered a FlashRom with 32kByte program memory, XENON8 had a FlashRom with 64 KByte. The new hardware enabled the implementation of new functionality like firmware update over the air, an extended set of SMS commands, extended size for data logging. Formerly, the XENON7 platform had been developed and maintained in an implementation-centric way with ad-hoc reuse (i.e., by copy & paste of source code fragments); there was no architectural documentation available. The introduction of architecting at Wikon was supported by Fraunhofer IESE researchers. In particular, they enabled the technology and knowledge transfer on architecting, provided support for architecture compliance checking, and acted as external reviewers of design and implementation.

Figure 2 gives an overview of the Wikon product map, iterations in architecting, and other development activities that were selected and executed in an architecture-centric manner. The development of the XENON8 platform was started in mid 2006 with the first architecting activities aimed at systematic, strategic reuse. Four iterations of architecting have been conducted so far. (1) We documented an initial set of architectural views and started code restructurings accordingly. (2) The architecture was refined based on compliance checking results. These two iterations mainly addressed reuse aspects. (3) We extended the view set for better support of reuse aspects and populated these views. (4) This iteration is currently ongoing (dashed line represents the point in time when we prepared this paper) and deals with variability management. The main business goals for the design of the Wikon architecture were to increase flexibility towards customer requirements and to reduce time to market for new product variants. To achieve these goals, the main design driver was to turn the monolithic implementation into explicit components, and to separate the application-specific parts from (potentially) reusable core components.

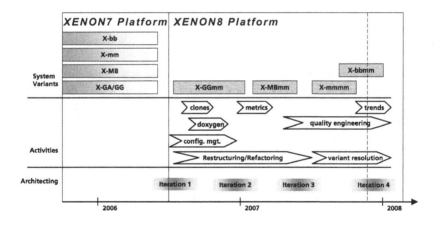

Fig. 2. Architecture-centric Development at Wikon

Iteration 1: The first architecting activity we conducted was to define the architecture of the XENON8 platform. To learn about the variability, we analyzed two variants of the ancestor platform XENON7 (X-GG and X-GA). For the architecture definition, we applied the architecting module of Fraunhofer PuLSE® (Product Line Software and System Engineering, please refer to [3] for details)[1] methodology, which resulted in four architectural views, namely conceptual view (see Figure 3), structural view

---

[1] PuLSE is a registered trademark of the Fraunhofer Institute for Experimental Software Engineering (IESE) in Kaiserslautern, Germany.

(see Figure 4), behavioral view (see Figure 5), and implementation view[2]. This initial documentation of the implemented architecture was partially reconstructed based on the analysis of the XENON7 platform. It enabled efficient discussions and reasoning on the abstraction level of the software architecture. Hence, the architectural views were used as a communication vehicle and served as a foundation for making.

The conceptual view (see Figure 3) is the most abstract architectural view used for describing the Wikon architecture. This view captures the application domain by mapping the functionality of the system to conceptual components and showing conceptual interfaces. It also depicts the interplay and relationships among the various elements. The conceptual view is interesting for all stakeholders (however, especially suited for everyone interested in a high-level overview of the system).The conceptual components are described by their responsibilities: An event is initiated at regular time intervals, by interrupts or by incoming external messages. Events are handled by an **EventManager**. The event activates the measurement devices and results in a set of activities: The measurement device executes an **Processing** of sensor data, composes messages, and transfers them via a built-in **GSM Modem** sending text messages (**SMS**, Short Message Service) or data messages (**PDU**, Protocol Data Unit). The **Protocol** defines the format and syntax for accessing and reading **Sensor** values. The **Configuration** prescribes how the measurement device reacts to events.

The structural view (see Figure 4) describes the functional decomposition of the system and captures the static structure of a system in terms of layers and subsystems, and the relationships between the various elements. The structural view depicts the top-level subsystems (see Figure 4a and b) and consists of two complementing parts. Figure 4a depicts how subsystems are logically grouped into layers, while Figure 4b describes the data and control flow from incoming sensor values to outgoing messages. The behavioral view (see Figure 5) illustrates how the architectural elements defined in the structural view interact with each other and realize the required behavior. For that purpose, execution scenarios are used (i.e., short textual descriptions of anticipated usages of a system) represented in UML-based collaboration diagrams. The implementation view maps the elements of the structural view to the source code. It is therefore especially interesting for technical stakeholders like developers.

Furthermore, we conducted static architecture compliance checking (see [9], [12] for related work on architecture compliance checking) to measure the distance of the intended target architecture and the existing implementations X-GA and X-GG. In total, 54% of the dependencies (i.e., includes, calls, or variable accesses) among subsystems violated the intended target architecture.

Activities derived from iteration 1: Based on the documentation of the architecture, several activities were derived as support and improvement of the overall development: First, we introduced the configuration management system *Subversion* and aligned the storage of the implementation with the documented architecture. Previously, versions of the products could only be archived on the full code basis. This made tracking changes across multiple products very time-consuming and error-prone. Second, the implementation was restructured as prescribed in the structural view. Previously, all source code files had been stored in one flat directory. Traceability was ensured between the corresponding artifacts at the architecture level, the implementation level. In some

---

[2] Due to confidentiality reasons we will not describe the architectural views in detail.

cases, functionality was relocated during restructuring to remove architecture violations and achieve higher cohesion inside subsystems and lower coupling among subsystems. Third, clone detection was applied to identify and remove duplicates in the code at the implementation level. With this activity, we took a first step towards reuse by avoiding the multiple existence of equal or similar code and appropriately locating the respective functions. Fourth, the code documentation was improved by introducing the *doxygen* tool.

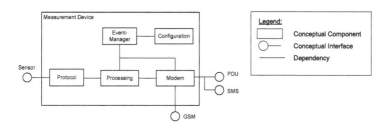

Fig. 3. The Wikon Architecture – Conceptual View

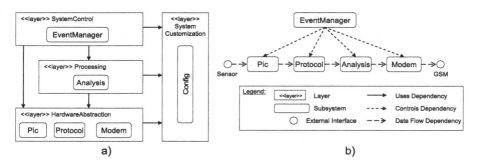

Fig. 4. The Wikon Architecture – Structural Views

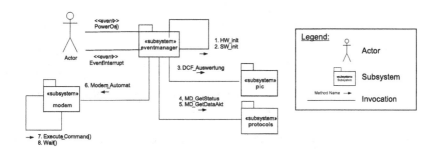

Fig. 5. The Wikon Architecture – Behavioral View: Event-Driven Measurement Loop

Iteration 2: After the implementation was restructured as described before, the compliance between the initially intended architecture and the implemented architecture was checked. This time, only few architecture violations were discovered. Due to the intended restructuring and some technical constraints, it was partially necessary to update the architectural views to represent the architecture consistently. The subsystems that were discovered to be common to all products were prepared for improved reuse. To achieve this, variable parts were extracted as far as possible into the subsystem *config*. Thus, it became possible to concentrate the biggest portion of the adaptation effort for a new product on two subsystems only: *config* and *main*. *Config* is a specific subsystem that was introduced to capture the major variability; *main* is the central startup subsystem that also represents some variability.

Activities derived from iteration 2: The refinement of the architecture and the restructuring to improve reuse led to another adaptation of the implementation. Further, a measurement program was defined to reveal potential disadvantages and risks of the restructuring for reuse. These metrics mainly focused on the resulting dependencies among the subsystems. If the principle of high cohesion and low coupling had been violated, there might be an adverse impact on quality attributes like maintainability. However, no potential problems were discovered in this step.

Iteration 3: The third iteration of architecting started with a check of architecture compliance as described before. This was done to make sure that the changes to the architecture and implementation in iteration 2 and the subsequent activities would not lead to inconsistencies. During the elicitation of the most important quality attributes for Wikon, flexibility was highly prioritized. Based on this selection, architecture evolution scenarios [6] were defined that capture the exact nature of flexibility as expected by Wikon. Focusing on such concrete scenarios allows for an explicit treatment of the quality attribute at the architectural level. Therefore, we applied an organization-specific customization to the set of architectural views. The first architectural viewpoint we defined was the *"Estimated impact viewpoint"*. It represents an estimation by the Wikon experts on the impact of the individual evolution scenarios on the single subsystems. Through this viewpoint, the estimated effort of potential evolutions can be controlled better. Adding the knowledge about the likelihood of certain evolution scenarios, decisions can be derived on how to adapt the architecture in order to decrease the overall effort for evolution. For one specific scenario, the introduction of a new external hardware device, another viewpoint was defined. It investigates the encapsulation of hardware elements with respect to their usage by external subsystems. The better the internals of the devices are encapsulated, the lower the estimated impact of a replacement will be.

Activities derived from iteration 3: After iteration 3, quality engineering was emphasized as an additional activity. Thus, the resulting code was reviewed by Fraunhofer IESE to assure high quality of the realization and adherence to the proposed concepts. Based on the introduced separation of common reusable parts and product specifics, benefits for the testing process were realized. That is, the common parts were thoroughly tested separately and only the specifics were tested for every product. Although the earlier restructuring for reusable subsystems had achieved its goal to a large extent, some minor variations were still there. They were tackled in a further step dealing by the introduction of distinct preprocessor commands to resolve the variants.

Iteration 4: This iteration of architecting is currently ongoing. It explicitly addresses and visualizes the comparison of multiple variants at the implementation level.

4   Discussion – Platform Comparison XENON7 vs. XENON8

To discuss the achievements of architecture-centric development with systematic, strategic reuse, we compare the products of the XENON8 platform to its predecessor platform, namely XENON7. Although the platform and the products are not equal (e.g., XENON8 offers to connect four sensors instead of two), we think that the two platforms can be compared. On top of both platforms, four distinct variants have been derived. For both platforms, all products are derived from the base variant (X-GG/GA and X-GGmm). Table 1 lists the reuse degree for the derived variants. The reuse degree percentage indicates the amount of code of the respective base variant being reused: for XENON7 through ad-hoc reuse and for XENON8 through systematic reuse. It can be observed that the extent of reuse more than doubled for XENON8. Table 1 lists further the effort spent on development and testing of the product. The Wikon expectation was that product development for XENON8 would at least consume similar effort as that for XENON7. The basis for this assumption was the fact that XENON8 is more complex to develop due to the increased number of sensors and changed hardware. Table 1 shows that, due to systematic reuse and architecture-centric development, 12 person-months of development time could be saved. The overall effort for testing was reduced by 3 person-months because of the increased extent of reuse (i.e., core subsystems did not require new testing in other variants).

Despite the reduced time to market and the reduced development and testing time, no increased vulnerability to errors could be detected in the first field releases of XENON8 variants. Table 2 shows the aggregated number of field defects reported by Wikon customers. For both platforms, only the first 6 months after the release of the base variant have been considered as reporting period (since more data for XENON8 variants were not yet available). The overall product quality seems to be at least on an equal level. However, sound statement with respect to the product quality can only be made when more variants have been released to the market.

At the implementation level, the following observation can be made using source code metrics. Table 3 compares the base variant of XENON7 (X-GA) with the base variant of the XENON8 platform (X-GGmm) capturing the snapshot after the restructuring phase was completed. The code size of the base variant X-GGmm increased because of the reusable components and the enhanced functionality. Accordingly, the total number of files and functions increased. A fine-grained analysis of the added lines of code revealed that the new code is, to a very large extent, responsible for the new functionality. Due to the introduction of *doxygen*, the number of commented lines almost doubled. Since Wikon enabled variants managed by preprocessor statements (e.g., #ifdef), the number of inactive lines increased significantly, too. A positive effect can be observed when analyzing code complexity. Both maximum nesting of control structures (e.g., switch, do, while, if and for statements) and cyclomatic complexity as defined by McCabe [11] decreased.

Because of the limited amount of available resources the resource consumption of the final product is another important comparison criterion in the embedded system domain. At Wikon, we measured the resource consumption of an embedded system by the usage of ROM (i.e., the size of the binary program code). The mere restructuring and refactoring of the source code had virtually no adverse impact on the resources consumption. Table 4 shows that the resource consumption for the XENON8 platform was increased for the most part by enhanced functionality.

Table 1. Platform Comparison – Reuse, Development Effort, and Testing Effort

Platform	Product	Reuse Degree	Development Effort	Testing Effort
XENON7	X-GG/GA	–	10 person-months	2.5 person-months
	X-MB	approx. 25%	10 person-months	2.5 person-months
	X-mm	approx. 25%	6 person-months	1.5 person-months
	X-bb	approx. 20%	6 person-months	1.5 person-months
XENON8	X-GGmm	–	6 person-months	1.5 person-months
	X-MBmm	approx. 60-70%	6 person-months	1.5 person-months
	X-mmmm	approx. 60-70%	4 person-months	1 person-month
	X-bbmm	approx. 60-70%	4 person-months	1 person-month

Table 2. Platform Comparison – Aggregated Field Defect Data after 6 Months[3]

Platform	Field Defects Reported	Software-caused Defects (in %)
XENON7	4	50%
XENON8	2	0%

Table 3. Platform Comparison – Source Code Metrics

Metric	X-GGmm	X-GA	Comparison X-GGmm to X-GA
Total Number of Files (Code/Header)	55 (23/22)	45 (21/24)	22% (10%/-8%)
Total Number Lines of Code (active/inactive/commented)	41.071 (9.287/1.6742/9.732)	22.695 (7.734/5.996/5.877)	81% (20%/179%/66%)
Number of Functions	198	153	29%
File Size in LOC (max/avg)	5.104/747	2.782/504	83%/48%
Function Size in LOC (max/avg)	1.153/91	947/75	22%/22%
Maximal Cyclomatic Complexity	71	97	**-27%**
Maximal Nesting	5	8	**-38%**

Table 4. Platform Comparison – Resource Consumption

Platform	Program Memory	Usage
XENON7	32 KByte	96-97 %
XENON8 (porting of XENON7 code)	64 KByte	48 %
XENON8 (restructuring, minimal enhancements)	64 KByte	52 %
XENON8 (enhanced functionality)	64 KByte	74 %

Shifting the development towards an architecture-centric paradigm with reuse and introducing derived activities like configuration management are an organizational investment. In case of Wikon, this investment hurdle could be overcome due to the joint research project. Without this project, Wikon as a small development organization would not have been convinced to dedicate resources and effort to architecture-centric

---

[3] Note that the explanatory power of Table 2 is still preliminary due to less delivered products.

development. However, the experiences made provide evidence that deciding in favor of architecture-centric development is positive. This approach paid off for Wikon, and we believe that it is worthwhile to apply a product line approach for small development organizations (even without external funding). However, it has to be scaled-down and customized to the small organization. The iterative strategy (e.g., tailoring activities, migrating one part after the other, and refining the architecture in several increments) was the key to success since it allowed us to apply the small amount of available effort very effectively.

From an organizational point of view, the most significant change is that the role of the architect at Wikon became an active one. The tasks and responsibilities of the architect are now clearly defined and architecting has a clear impact on product development (as opposed to the situation when developing the XENON7 series). Another lesson learned is that architecting requires customizations to the development organization. All activities have to be tailored to the business goals, the organization and the engineers. In our opinion, finding the right customization is most crucial when introducing change into a development organization. The tool-supported analyses by the Fraunhofer SAVE tool (Software Architecture Visualization and Evaluation, see [9]) – an Eclipse plug-in for conducting architecture analyses – helped to reduce the effort for redocumentation of the implemented architecture, architecture compliance checking, and controlling the evolution of the system.

In short, the main lesson learned is that strategic reuse anchored on an architectural level is a worthwhile goal for small development organizations. The investments paid off, and the results are perceived as successful by the Wikon engineers.

5 Conclusions and Outlook

Successfully transferring new ideas and concepts from research into industrial practice is a challenge. In this experience report, we discuss our lessons learned in introducing architecture-centric development at Wikon. The results show that investments into reuse and architecting are worthwhile, even for small development organizations and without external funding. The shift of the development paradigm from ad-hoc reuse towards pro-active, systematic reuse can be considered as successful. For the first product generation developed, the architecture-centric development saved 12 person-months of development time and 3 person-months (both approx. 37%) for quality assurance (compared to the previous product generation). At the same time, no decrease in the quality was observed for the first products in the field. So far, the architecture-centric development with reuse has supported the construction of four measurement devices.

The main challenges when introducing architecture-centric development were, on the one hand, to find the appropriate customization of software architecture practices proposed by literature. On the other hand (and this is especially true for small development organizations), the initial investment hurdle has to be overcome. At Wikon, we were able to break this barrier due to a joint research project and due to the definition of an iterative strategy. For us, the results achieved are hints that investment in architecture-centric development and reuse pays off in general. We think that an iterative, architecture-centric product line approach can be scaled down to small development organizations.

The evolution and maintenance across these variants over time is the next challenge to be addressed by Wikon. Due to reduced time to market and increased flexibility, it is expected that the number of variants supported will increase over time. One open issue here is the management of variability. Up to now, no explicit variation points have been introduced, and there are no feature models or decision models at the moment. The variant resolution is purely manual. The introduction of (semi-) automated variant management (ideally tool-supported) remains a challenge. Furthermore, more variants mean higher system complexity. The architecture has to be iteratively refined and updated with respect to the new variants. An even stronger split between product-specific and reusable components is one of Wikon's design goals. To ensure the reuse benefits, architecture compliance checking will be applied regularly in the future. Detected violations are reviewed and, if critical, be removed. The next steps at Wikon will address the introduction of explicit variability management and the definition of an architectural view that captures the set of multiple, implemented variants and allows their comparison on an architectural level.

Further ongoing and future work aims at sustaining architecture-centric development at Wikon. To monitor the success of architecture-centric development with strategic reuse, a measurement strategy applying the quality improvement paradigm (QIP, see [1]) and the goal question metric paradigm (GQM, see [2]) has to be defined. This measurement strategy is ideally an automated early-warning system for quality decays. Fraunhofer IESE will generalize the experiences made in establishing reuse in small development organizations.

References

1. Basili, V., Caldiera, G., Rombach, H.D.: The Experience Factory. In: Marciniak, J. (ed.) Encyclopedia of Software Engineering, vol. 1, pp. 469–476. John Wiley Sons, Chichester (1994)
2. Basili, V., Caldiera, G., Rombach, H.D.: The Goal/Question/Metric Paradigm. In: Marciniak, J. (ed.) Encyclopedia of Sofware Engineering, vol. 1, pp. 528–532. John Wiley & Sons, Chichester (1994)
3. Bayer, J., Flege, O., Knauber, P., Laqua, R., Muthig, D., Schmid, K., Widen, T., DeBaud, J.-M.: PuLSE: A Methodology to Develop Software Product Lines. In: Proceedings of the Fifth ACM SIGSOFT Symposium on Software Reusability (SSR 1999), pp. 122–131 (1999)
4. Bosch, J.: Design and Use of Software Architectures. Addison-Wesley, Reading (2000)
5. Clements, P., Bachmann, F., Bass, L., Garlan, D., Ivers, J., Little, R., Nord, R., Stafford, J.: Documenting Software Architectures. Views and Beyond. Addison-Wesley, Reading (2003)
6. Clements, P., Kazman, R., Klein, M.: Evaluating Software Architectures. Methods and Case Studies. Addison-Wesley, Reading (2002)
7. Hofmeister, C., Nord, R., Soni, D.: Applied software architecture. Addison-Wesley Longman Publishing Co., Inc., Amsterdam (2000)
8. IEEE Computer Society, IEEE Recommended Practice for Architectural Descriptions of Software-Intensive Systems, IEEE Std-1471-2000 (2000)

9. Knodel, J., Popescu, D.: A Comparison of Architecture Compliance Checking Approaches. In: 6th IEEE/IFIP Working Conference on Software Architecture, Mumbai, India (January 2007)

10. Kruchten, P.: The 4+1 View Model of Architecture. IEEE Softw. 12(6), 42–50 (1995)

11. McCabe, T.: A Complexity Measure. IEEE Transactions on Software Engineering 2(4), 308–320 (1976)

12. Murphy, G.C., Notkin, D., Sullivan, K.J.: Software Reflexion Models: Bridging the Gap between Design and Implementation. IEEE Transaction on Software Engineering 27(4), 364–380 (2001)

13. Shaw, M., Garlan, D.: Software Architecture: Perspectives on an Emerging Discipline. Prentice-Hall, Englewood Cliffs (1996)

14. Zachman, J.A.: A framework for information systems architecture. IBM Systems Journal 26(3), 277–293 (1987)

An Architectural Style for Data-Driven Systems

Reza Mahjourian

Department of Computer and Information Science and Engineering
University of Florida
Gainesville, FL 32611, USA
rezam@ufl.edu

Abstract. Data-driven systems and applications are specialized software solutions for acquisition, management, and presentation of information. These systems are usually developed using the same software tools, technologies, and processes used for creating any other type of software. Not only is this approach inefficient, but also it results in extreme redundancies due to the inherently repetitive nature of these applications. However, data-driven systems exhibit characteristics which can be exploited for extensive reuse across a single application or a family of applications. In this paper, we present XPage, an architectural style which is especially designed for building data-driven systems. We also provide several case studies from real-world deployments of XPage to help evaluate its efficiency and flexibility for developing real-world solutions.

1 Introduction

Data-driven systems are software solutions for information and data management. The two primary functions of these systems are acquisition and presentation of information. Information acquisition is typically performed using data entry forms or via interfacing with external data sources. Information presentation is concerned with retrieval and display of stored information to the user with appropriate navigation and querying facilities. Data-driven systems are also characterized by requiring intensive user interaction both for acquisition and retrieval of information. They are beyond doubt among the most common types of customized software systems in use today. University registration systems, e-commerce applications, content management systems, financial and accounting applications, a personal address book, and an online photo album are a few examples of data-driven applications.

Despite the existence of a consistent demand for development of new data-driven systems, they are mostly developed as one-off projects, with little reuse taking place beyond what is offered by the development technologies and programming languages used. Recently, the software industry has introduced some development frameworks which offer higher-level programming libraries to help with rapid development of data-driven applications. However, these frameworks are not high-level enough to prevent the repetitive nature of data-driven systems from showing up in the final programs as repetitions of nearly identical code segments or constructs. Moreover, none of these industrial frameworks offer an explicit software architecture, and the software engineering decisions behind their designs are buried in their implementations.

H. Mei (Ed.): ICSR 2008, LNCS 5030, pp. 14–25, 2008.

Academic research on producing agile techniques or methods for developing data-driven systems is severely lacking as well. Software engineering researchers consider data-driven applications to be in the realm of database research, because of their concentration on information management tasks. In addition, the seemingly primitive nature of "reading and writing structured data" appears to be lacking the necessary complexity to qualify as an interesting software research problem. On the other hand, database researchers have little interest in solving the software engineering challenges involved in streamlining development and managing complexity of software systems. In spite of that, it is quite surprising to know that the very little work done in this area comes from the database research community, and not from the software research community.

In this paper, we present an architectural style [1,2], which is specifically designed for creating and maintaining data-driven systems. This architectural style has been extracted from a software framework we developed in 2001 and gradually extended afterwards. We have dubbed the architectural style *XPage*, following the name of the original framework.

Before discussing the XPage style in detail, we are going to review the related work in Sect. 2. Section 3 presents the architectural style and its key components and connectors. Section 4 provides three cases studies from real-world applications developed based on this style. Finally, Sect. 5 wraps up the paper with conclusions.

2   Related Work

A comprehensive framework for developing data-driven applications should address a wide array of concerns, from providing efficient data storage and retrieval mechanisms, to handling complex user interactions in the presentation and view layer. To our best knowledge, no other architectural style has been proposed to support development of data-driven systems to this extent. However, there are some solutions proposed by the database research community which focus on related problems.

The most notable example in this category is WebML [3,4]. WebML is a product which provides a model-based development environment with a database-oriented view. The core of the application is created with a "structural model" which outlines the data model. Special-purpose data-aware "units" or "operations" are provided for data presentation or manipulation tasks. A program is created by associating these special units with the objects defined in the structural model. A "navigation model" is used to establish the links between different pages and content units.

In [5,6], Vigna proposes a solution based on developing the entire application out of the Extended *ER* (Entity Relationship) model [7]. In their solution, the cardinality constraints on entity relationships in the ER model are used to decide an appropriate presentation and navigation model for the application. Based on an augmented ER model, their software generates SQL statements for creating the required tables. The developer is expected to execute these statements to create the underlying database. User interface forms are also automatically created based on the ER model. Afterwards, the application can be customized directly by modifying the generated forms.

Even though the organization of data-driven applications is mostly influenced by the structure of their underlying data repositories, ER models lack the required expressive power to specify the structure and behavior of an entire application. In any data-driven system, a key factor in deciding the appropriate navigation and presentation model is the predefined flow of information according to its underlying business processes. This information is not captured in the ER model. A flexible software development framework requires mechanisms for specifying the business logic and view organization of an application independently of its underlying data model. Another undesirable side-effect of using ER models is that since Relational Databases Management Systems (RDBMS) are not directly based on ER models, the ER-based development tools have to assume responsibility for creating and managing the relational database as well. However, this is inflexible and counter-productive, since in many real-world situations there are database experts who prefer to design and fine tune the database independently. A requirement for working with legacy databases poses a similar problem.

Recently, we have witnessed introduction of some industrial software development frameworks which enable web developers to create data-driven applications more efficiently and rapidly. Examples of these frameworks include Ruby on Rails and CakePHP. The core of these frameworks is based on the concept of *Active Records*, which provide a two-way mapping between object classes and database tables. Any instantiation or modification of Active Records is directly reflected on their associated tables. Foreign key relationships are exposed in Active Records by linking attributes of one object to the instances of the referred objects. To implement the logic of an application, these frameworks recommend developers to write "controllers", which are service entry points for user defined operations on the data. However, they do not offer any higher-level components for the view layer of an application. The *scaffolding* technique can be used to rapidly create the view layer code out of the structure of the Active Records. However, the produced artifact is low-level code and the relationship between this code and the original Active Record can be lost with subsequent modifications to the either artifacts. Another source of inefficiency with these frameworks is that the standard mechanism for retrieving data from Active Records involves traversing them row by row to reach individual data objects. This suggests a low-level programming style, which for many data-driven scenarios can be entirely abandoned for a high-level view of the "whole data set".

None of these solutions address the software engineering side of the problem. Although they facilitate implementation of data-driven applications, their lack of an explicit architectural design makes it difficult to analyze these solutions with regard to issues of interest to the software engineering community. Moreover, since the relationship between implementation-level constructs and the architectural components and connectors is not clear, it is not easy to determine their potential for reuse across different domains. Nor can one try to formalize a process for designing, implementing, and maintaining the components needed for these solutions.

Another class of solutions which are extensively employed in creating data-driven systems are various middle-ware technologies such as Enterprise Java Beans [8]. These middle-ware technologies offer standardized interfaces for accessing and manipulating data sources, and include basic services such as concurrency, distribution, security, and component naming and registry. Such technologies can provide the platform for handling the data storage and retrieval tasks in data-driven systems, and thereby answer one side of the problem. However, they do not offer specialized solutions for the view layer. Another shortcoming of these technologies is that they do not suggest any particular architecture on their surrounding system. The assumption is that developers use "glue" code to instantiate, utilize and maintain these objects whenever necessary. Despite being flexible, this is less in line with the spirit of software architectures, which advocate reuse by formalizing exemplification of good engineering solutions.

In [9,10] Mattmann et al. present the OODT reference architecture, which is a solution for locating remote data sources and aggregating data from distributed data providers. OODT components and connectors provide the services of data source registry, identification, and querying on top of the industrial middle-ware technologies. Although OODT components and connectors can be employed for creating data-driven systems, like middle-ware technologies, OODT does not offer any solution for the view layer of these systems, mainly because its focus is on a different problem. Abstracting and modeling the interactions in the view layer of data-driven applications is much more complex than modeling the data layer operations, which more or less exhibit a linear input-output model. Lastly, like middle-ware technologies, OODT's solution is "programmer-intensive" [9] as it does not employ a high-level description language.

3   The Architectural Style

In this section, we introduce the XPage architectural style and its accompanying development framework. First we provide an overview of the style and its key characteristics. We then proceed to introduce some of the individual components and connectors.

3.1   Overview

Overall Architecture. An XPage application is comprised of a set of interconnected *View Pages*. A View Page can be regarded as an abstraction of a web page, or a desktop form. Each View Page, in turn, contains one or more *View Forms*. The View Forms are data-aware components which can directly interact with the end-user. XPage offers different types of View Forms for common information acquisition, manipulations, and presentation tasks. Each View Form is connected to one or more *Data Sources*. A Data Source abstracts the data model of the underlying data source or destination. Data Sources, in turn, are associated with *Data Adapters*, which are connectors whose function is to provide a consistent interface over different types of data repositories available to the application. View Pages and View Forms constitute the view layer of an XPage application, while Data Sources and Data Adapters constitute its data layer. Figure 1 shows the overall architecture of XPage and its key components and connectors.

XPage components and connectors rely on a predefined initialization and launch protocol for their operation. Upon receiving a request for a specific View Page from the end-user, a *Coordinator* connector locates the corresponding XML file and instantiates the View Page component. This process is repeated for the View Forms in the loaded View Page and for any other components and connectors referenced in them. Once the component and connector hierarchy is loaded, a sequence of events are propagated in the hierarchy starting at the root View Page component. Some of the key events are

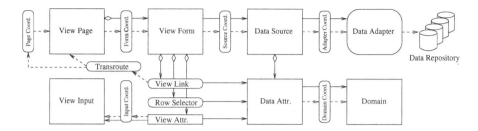

Fig. 1. The overall XPage architecture

load, init, register, process_read, process_write, and *commit*. User input and preferences are also passed to the components in the form of *Message* objects at various points in this sequence. Depending on its function, each component and connector may do a different task upon receiving the events.

Component and Connector Granularity. The components and connectors of XPage are divided into two distinct groups, based on their granularity. The *coarse-grained* components and connectors, are first-level players in the architecture of an application. They bundle considerable amount of functionality to make them capable of handling significant data-driven responsibilities in a data-driven system. However, the XPage style defines these coarse-grained components and connectors in terms of a number of common *fine-grained* components and connectors. The fine-grained components and connectors are generalizations of the common structural and behavioral elements which constitute the coarse-grained components.

Communication. In the data layer, components communicate with direct synchronous messages. In the view layer, communications take place by sending asynchronous messages which are carried by *Message* objects. Some particular interactions are so frequently used in data-driven systems that they demand for special treatment. For instance, in many cases, components rely on receiving foreign key parameters to determine what data item to display or manipulate. On a data entry form, a foreign key parameter must be received to establish a relationship between the newly created entity and its related entities in the database. Other frequent scenarios include requesting particular sort orders or filters on the presented information. In order to facilitate these interactions, XPage offers a Message type hierarchy, which covers various user interface events as well as inter-component communications.

Messages can be private or global. Private Messages have a particular recipient address, while Global Messages carry parameter-like values and are available to the entire component hierarchy. The private and global messages allow components to implement "push-", or "pull-"based communications, which are both handy in data-driven systems. In the view layer, all Messages are handled by a universal connector called the *Transroute* connector, which locates message recipients by their registered addresses. The Transroute connector is also responsible for processing user interface transitions such as submission of forms or loading of a new View Page.

The XPage Language. All the coarse-grained and fine-grained components of XPage are configured using an XML-based domain-specific language. A set of all such XML files is enough to describe an XPage application. At run time, XML files are loaded to instantiate and initialize the components and connectors upon request. The XPage framework employs an object caching mechanism to increase the performance of the application.

Extensibility. Clearly, complex applications have requirements which cannot be satisfied with the generic functionalities embedded in XPage components and connectors. Most components and connectors feature a number of *extension points* to let developers customize their behavior. The extension points are usually associated with the predefined events. There are two extension points for every event. For example, corresponding to the *process_write* event, there are two extension points called *before_process_write* and *after_process_write*. Developers can plug in custom code in these extension points to directly control the behavior of the components. For example, a data entry form can use the *before_process_write* extension to perform additional validations and potentially prevent the component from storing the data by canceling the *process_write* event.

In the following sections, we describe the XPage components and connectors in more detail.

3.2 Data Layer

Data Adapter. This coarse-grained connector is used to abstract away the heterogeneous interfaces of different types of data repositories. Whether the data repository is an RDBMS, an XML file, or a gateway to a remote web service, appropriate Data Adapters make them available to the application through a consistent interface which allows for data retrieval and data manipulation. Data Adapters translate the service requests into a language understandable by the underlying data repository. For instance, a request can be translated into a SQL query, an XPath query, or a web service invocation message. Data Adapters also offer transactional services to maintain the integrity of data repositories when multiple components need to collaborate for a single data operation.

Data Source. This coarse-grained component works on top of a Data Adapter. Data Sources are used to elevate the flat interface provided by Data Adapters to a hierarchical object model suitable for complicated interactions that view layer components need. Like Data Adapters, Data Sources provide data retrieval and manipulation interfaces, however in a more structured manner. Users of a Data Source work with individual *Data Attributes* which correspond to the columns in its data source or target. In addition, Data Sources can enforce various integrity constraints by collaborating with other Data Sources on related entities.

Data Attribute. In its simplest form, this fine-grained component corresponds to a column in a query definition. Data Attributes are associated with Data Sources. When the Data Source is retrieving data, its Data Attributes receive values for the corresponding columns. After a user requests the Data Source to retrieve a row of data, he is expected to contact its Data Attributes to get the retrieved values. Likewise, for storing and manipulating data, the user is expected to populate the Data Attributes with desired values before asking the Data Source to perform the operation. In addition, Data Attributes respond to a number of Messages for filtering the data source or requesting a particular sort order. They pass these requests up to their parent Data Source.

Data Attributes have a type hierarchy which determines their features and capabilities. Two of the important Data Attribute types are *Primary Key Data Attribute*, and *Foreign Key Data Attribute*. Primary Key and Foreign Key Data Attributes are required for data operations like create, update and delete. They let the Data Source know which set of the data values populated in the Data Attributes should be used to locate the affected data items, and which set should be used to provide the new or updated data. They also guide the Data Source to enforce various integrity constraints. The type of a Data Attribute also determines to which requests that Data Attributes can respond. For example, it determines whether the attribute is updateable or searchable. More complex Data Attributes like the *Derived Data Attribute* can interface with auxiliary Data Sources to automatically calculate derived and aggregated values.

Domain. This fine-grained component is used to help guarantee the validity of data handled by Data Attributes. If a Data Attribute is associated with a particular Domain component, all requests for writing to or reading from that Data Attribute pass through the associated Domain component for validation. Each Domain component provides two services of *read* and *write*. In addition to checking validity of values, these two services can also convert between internal and view-level representations of data values. For example, thousands separators can be automatically added and removed for numbers upon reading and writing of the data.

Figure 2 depicts the exchanged messages for an example data retrieval scenario. An external entity first configures the Data Attributes of a Data Source and then retrieves one row of information. Some internal messages are not shown.

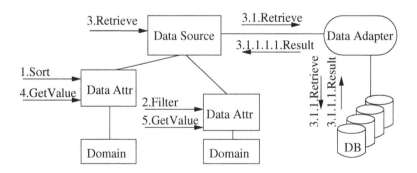

Fig. 2. Example data layer interaction

3.3 View Layer

View Page. An XPage application is implemented as a set of View Pages, which are coarse-grained components. View Pages contain the data-aware View Forms, as well as some presentation-only components like *Icons* and *Headers*.

View Form. View Forms are coarse-grained components with specialized functionalities, yet similar architectures. Typically, each View Form is associated with a Data Source which serves as the source and/or destination of data. Currently, there are five types of View Forms, corresponding to the five primitive operations on data: *Create Form, Read Form, Update Form, Delete Form,* and *Search Form.* These components are packed with common services which are usually required in implementing a data-driven application. For example a Read Form can automatically present the data in an underlying Data Source in grid format or itemized format. It can paginate the data rows, and automatically change the sort order if the end-user clicks on one of the grid columns. It also allows users to download its data set as a file. A Search Form can present the end-user with a data entry form for specifying filter criteria and then pass the filters to an associated Read Form for displaying the search results. A Create Form can automatically validate user input and warn the user if required entries are missing or invalid. A Delete Form can consult the integrity constraints in the data model to check for validity of a delete operation before attempting it. All these services are either provided by default or specified in configuration files at the conceptual level. These services are realized by collaboration of a number of common finer-grained components in the View Forms, which are described below.

View Attribute. These fine-grained components correspond to the individual data-aware "element types" on a View Form. Each View Form has a number of View Attributes. Typically, each View Attributes is connected to some Data Attribute from the View Form's associated Data Source. The connection between View Attributes and Data Attributes is established during component initialization. The type of collaboration between the View Attribute and the Data Attribute depends in part on the containing View Form. For example, on a Read Form, View Attributes receive the retrieved data from corresponding Data Attributes, but on a Create Form, View Attributes send user input value to Data Attributes for storage. View Attributes also respond to some specific Messages. For example, upon receiving a Filter Message, the View Attribute sends a filter request to its associated Data Attribute, which in turn is routed to its parent Data Source. Although View Attributes are more concerned with the logic of data operation, they also carry some presentational semantics based on their types. For instance, on a Read Form, View Attributes end up appearing as the header of data columns in the data grid shown to the user.

View Cell. These are fine-grained components which represent the individual data-aware elements. A View Cell may represent an individual data entry field on a form, or an individual value in a grid of displayed data. View Cells are not defined in the configuration files. Rather they are produced at run time during the operation of the View Forms. For example, on a Read Form, for each retrieved data row the View Attributes instantiate new View Cells. After retrieving all the rows, a grid of View Cells is formed which is displayed to the end-user. On data entry and manipulation forms, View Cells are instantiated during component initialization and are represented as individual data entry fields on the GUI. All View Cells maintain links to the original View Attributes that instantiated them to pass the messages they receive.

View Input. These are fine-grained components which represent the user interface widgets. Every View Cell which represents a data entry input is associated with a View Input. The type of View Input determines how that View Cell is represented on the user interface. Example View Inputs are text fields, multi-line text fields, drop down lists, checkboxes, etc. Since drop downs are heavily used in data-driven applications, they receive special treatment in the XPage style. By default, any View Attributes linked to a Foreign Key Data Attribute is represented as a drop down input on the user interface. As its parameter, the drop down View Input receives the Data Source component matching the target entity of the foreign key relationship. This enables the drop down input to display appropriate values from the referenced entity.

View Row Selector. View Row Selectors are fine-grained connectors whose purpose is to receive special filter requests via *Select Messages* and relay the filter to their associated Data Attribute. Any View Form can have a number of Row Selectors in addition to its View Attributes. The effect of sending a Select Message to a Row Selector is almost the same as sending a Filter Message to an ordinary View Attribute. They both result in limiting the data rows which are retrieved, or manipulated. However, the semantic difference is that Row Selectors are used when the View Form's operation relies on receiving the message. For example, an Update Form usually needs to work with an individual data row and refuses to operate if it does not receive a proper Select Message, because otherwise it may affect unintended data rows.

View Link. View Links are fine-grained connectors which link different View Pages in an XPage application. Depending on the containing View Form, a View Link may appear as a hyperlink taking the user from one page to the other, or as a form submit button. In either case, each View Link carries a number of Message objects. All communications between components on different View Pages take place through View Links, and are routed by the Transroute connector. For example, in a book list page, a View Link can be placed next to each row to allow the end-user to go to a book update page to modify that book. In this case, a foreign key value is sent to a target Row Selector in the book update page.

Figure 3 shows some of the view components and connectors involved in this example. Notice how the same View Attributes, View Cells, and View Links take different forms on the two types of View Forms. The View Link appears as a hyperlink on the Read Form, and as a submit button on the Update Form. When the View Link is on a data entry form, it also automatically carries the user input as a number of *Input Messages*.

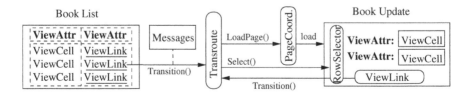

Fig. 3. Example view layer interaction

View Template. Contrary to what their name suggests, none of the view layer components and connectors mentioned so far are concerned with their presentation. Instead, each visible XPage component or connector is associated with some View Template component, which is able to "draw" it on the user interface. Standard View Templates are provided in the XPage framework for all coarse-grained and fine-grained components. Developers can customize the presentation of an individual component without having to provide custom presentations for its contained elements.

3.4 Support Components

Coordinator connectors are responsible for locating and loading other components during initialization of the component hierarchy. Based on the type of the requested components, Coordinators can decide intelligently whether they can reuse previously loaded components or not. This is particularly important for sharing Data Adapters for ensuring transactional integrity, as in order to successfully rollback transactions all related operations on a View Page must be handled by a single Data Adapter. Coordinators can also facilitate deploying the XPage style in a distributed environment, as they can transparently return stubs for remote components and connectors. Other XPage components facilitate user authentication, access authorization, navigation, and internationalization.

4 Case Studies

In this section, we briefly discuss some real-world deployments of the XPage style.

4.1 Squash

In [11], Esfahbod et al. use XPage to implement a web-based front-end for configuring an organizational gateway, which gives users controlled access to a set of internally administered infobases. The front-end allows the end-user to define available infobases together with a hierarchy of organizational users in different levels and groups. Access rights can be assigned to individual users or to organizational levels. From the information gathered in the database, appropriate configuration files are generated for a squid web proxy, which acts as the gateway to the actual infobases.

Despite unfamiliarity of this group with the XPage architecture and its framework, it took their three member team only six person-days to implement Squash. At that time they used an earlier version of XPage. In that version only the Create Forms offered drop down View Inputs, and this form of user input was not available in Search Forms. Since they needed such a feature on their search forms, and they did not want to bother modifying the XPage framework, they used the extension points as a workaround. They used a Create Form in place of the Search Form, however they overrode the *before_process_write* extension to cancel the create operation and instead route the user input messages to the Search Form for being processed as filter criteria.

4.2 BibIS

In 2006, XPage was used to develop a Bibliographic database for the Database Research Group at the Department of Computer Science at University of Florida. The core functionality of BibIS is to manage bibliographic data on publications. It allows end-users to manage publication types, enter publication information, and optionally upload article files. In addition to browsing and searching the publications, BiBIS allows users to generate BibTeX entries for any set of selected publications. Up to this point, the requirements could be satisfied using nothing but default XPage components and connectors.

However, the interesting requirement in BibIS was that all the publication attributes and publication types needed to be dynamically definable by the end-user. We used the extension points to satisfy this requirement. For the publication entity, an "empty" Data Source was defined with no Data Attributes. In the *before_load* extension point of this Data Source, we included custom code to load an auxiliary Data Source on the table containing publication meta-data. The custom code dynamically added Data Attributes to the publication Data Source to match the stored meta-data. Using this approach greatly reduced the complexity of this solution, since all other View Forms which worked with the publication entity were developed as if the publication table was a static table. Other extension points were used to update the structure of the actual publication table as the end-users updated the publication meta-data attributes.

4.3   Ringtone Vending Website

Our last case study is from the deployment of XPage on an Internet website for selling cell phone ringtones and logos. This system worked on three geographically distributed servers. A catalog server on the content provider's site offered web services for getting information on available content for sale. The web server presented the catalog to the Internet users and accepted orders. Received orders were sent to a GSM server, which communicated with the content provider to get the ringtone and then send it to end-user's cell phone.

Although there is no intrinsic support for web services in XPage, we used the extension points on two virtual Data Sources to provide the connection from the web server to the catalog server and the GSM server. The first virtual Data Source made a web service request to the catalog server upon a read request to get the catalog information. The second virtual Data Source was used as if it was saving user orders. However, instead it activated local scripts which sent order parameters to the remote GSM server.

A common theme that is seen in all the above experiences is an invariable need for extensibility in the architectural style. All these systems had requirements which were not predicted when XPage was designed. This confirms the importance of extensibility as a key requirement for such a generic software engineering solution.

5   Conclusions

We have presented the XPage architectural style for creating data-driven systems. XPage facilitates reuse at the code level by offering a conceptual domain-specific language. However, more importantly, it facilitates reuse at the architectural level by providing an efficient break down of responsibilities in the generic coarse-grained and fine-grained components. As part of future work, we are looking forward to presenting the software engineering challenges that we faced when designing XPage and the guidelines that we followed to address them.

Our successful experience with XPage shows that it is possible to streamline many activities involved in design and development of data-driven systems. However, we believe data-driven systems have much more capacity for reuse and we are looking forward to seeing more research devoted to discovering techniques and methods for exploiting this potential.

References

1. Perry, D.E., Wolf, A.L.: Foundation for the study of software architecture. Software Engineering Notes 17(2), 40–52 (1992)
2. Garlan, D., Shaw, M.: An introduction to software architecture. Advances in Software Engineering and Knowledge Engineering 2, 1–39 (1993)
3. Ceri, S., Fraternali, P., Bongio, A.: Web modeling language (webml): a modeling language for designing web sites. In: Proceedings of the 9th international World Wide Web conference, pp. 137–157 (2000)
4. Ceri, S., Fraternali, P., Matera, M.: Conceptual modeling of data-intensive web applications. IEEE Internet Computing 6(4), 20–30 (2002)
5. Vigna, S.: Erw: Entities and relationships on the web. In: Poster Proc. of Eleventh International World Wide Web Conference (2002)
6. Vigna, S.: Automatic generation of content management systems from eer-based specifications. ASE 00, 259 (2003)
7. Chen, P.P.S.S.: The entity-relationship model: Toward a unified view of data. ACM Transactions on Database Systems 1(1), 9–36 (1976)
8. Sun-Microsystems: Enterprise java beans, http://java.sun.com/ejb/
9. Mattmann, C.A., Crichton, D.J., Hughes, J.S., Kelly, S.C., Ramirez, P.M.: Software architecture for large-scale, distributed, data-intensive systems. In: WICSA 2004, p. 255 (2004)
10. Mattmann, C.A., Crichton, D.J., Medvidovic, N., Hughes, S.: A software architecture-based framework for highly distributed and data intensive scientific applications. In: ICSE 2006, pp. 721–730 (2006)
11. Esfahbod, B., Safy-Allah, H.: Squash: Design and implementation of a large scale http gateway and masqurader. Internet draft (2003),
http://behdad.org/download/Publications/squashdoc/squash.pdf

Architectural Analysis Approaches: A Component-Based System Development Perspective

Novia Admodisastro and Gerald Kotonya

Computing Department, Lancaster University,
Lancaster LA1 4WA, UK
{admodisa,gerald}@comp.lancs.ac.uk

Abstract. Component-based system development (CBD) relies on the integration of existing software components to compose systems. These are often black-box components whose functionality and configuration may not match the "ideal" system context. Systematic architectural analysis can ensure that risks resulting from architectural adaptations and trade-offs do not adversely affect critical system qualities (e.g. cost, dependability and system resource constraints). The analysis is likely to reveal not only how well an architecture satisfies a particular system context, but also how change might affect critical system attributes. However, current architectural analysis techniques differ widely in their analytical capabilities and support for reuse-driven development making it difficult for developers to assess their effectiveness in CBD. This paper proposes an evaluation framework based on the design challenges in CBD and uses it to review existing architectural analysis techniques.

Keywords: Component-Based Systems, Architectural Analysis, System Design.

1 Introduction

The importance of architecture in reuse-driven development is widely recognized [1,2,3]. Architecture provides a framework for establishing a match between available components and the system context. It is a key part of the system documentation; enforces the integrity of component composition and provides a basis for managing change. However, one of the most difficult problems in component-based system development (CBD) is ensuring that the software architecture provides an acceptable match with its intended application, business and evolutionary context. Unlike custom development where architectural design relies solely on detailed requirements specification and where deficiencies in application context can be corrected by 'tweaking' the source code, in component-based system development the typical unit of development is often a blackbox component whose source code is inaccessible to the developer. Getting the architecture right is therefore key to ensuring quality in a component-based system.

Architectural analysis in CBD provides the developer with a means to expose interface mismatches, assess configurations with respect to specific structural and behavioural constraints and to verify the adequacy of compositions with respect to quality constraints. Architectural analysis can also provide a basis for developing "what-if" scenarios to explore the implications of evolving a system [4,5]. However, current

H. Mei (Ed.): ICSR 2008, LNCS 5030, pp. 26–38, 2008.
© Springer-Verlag Berlin Heidelberg 2008

architectural analysis approaches differ widely with respect to their underlying models, analytical capabilities and ability to support CBD making it difficult for developers to ascertain their effectiveness in different application contexts [6,7].

This paper builds on the survey by Dobrica in 2002 [5], Babar in 2004 [10,11] and Kazman in 2005 [12] which focused largely on architectural analysis for custom development, to review methods and techniques for reuse-driven development. Our objective is two-fold: First, to provide the component-based system designer with a practical means of assessing the efficacy of existing architectural analysis techniques for CBD, and secondly, to provide the architectural analysis method developer with a set of key requirements for CBD. Our assessment framework comprises six necessary requirements for an architectural analysis approach in CBD and is derived from the design challenges in CBD.

The rest of this paper is organized as follows; section 2 discusses design challenges in CBD and identifies the necessary requirements for architectural analysis approaches. Section 3 reviews five existing architectural analysis approaches that support CBD. Section 4 provides a discussion of the results and a table summary. Section 5 provides some concluding thoughts.

2 Design Challenges in CBD

A typical component-based system architecture comprises a set of components that have been purposefully designed and structured to ensure that they have "pluggable" interfaces and an acceptable match with a defined system context. However, the blackbox nature of many software components means there is never a clean match between system specifications and concrete software components.

The Fig. 1 shows how the design process fits into a typical component-based system development process [13,16]. The architectural design stage partitions required functionality (i.e. services and constraints) into logical components, which can be composed using off-the-shelf components and services. The Discovery and verification phase is intended to ensure that there is an acceptable match between available software components and the system being built. The negotiation and planning phase implements the necessary mechanisms for resolving conflicting system attributes and sets out the development agenda. In our view, the principle challenge in developing component-based systems is to formulate efficient engineering models that can balance aspects of requirements and business concerns with the assumptions and capabilities embodied in software components. The design challenges in CBD can be summarized thus:

- *Component documentation*: 3rd party software components are often delivered with limited documentation. In addition, the components may have hidden design assumptions. This has serious implications for exception handling and overall system quality. The design challenge here is twofold: First, to devise ways to help the system developer to formulate appropriate analysis scenarios to understand the extent of problem, and secondly to help the developer identify and design appropriate safe-guards to minimise unforeseen side effects in the system [2,14].

- *Pluggability*. Blackbox components are generally not tailorable or "plug and play". This has implications for the system evolution and its life-cycle planning [4,15]. The design challenge here is to provide a cost-efficient means of exposing structural and behavioural mismatches and ways of developing tailored adapters.
- *Conflicting quality requirements*. Service quality constraints vary and conflict amongst themselves, and with system constraints. This makes them difficult to track and resolve. The challenge for the design process is to provide ways of assessing and addressing the adequacy of logical component configurations with respect to service, business organisation and system constraints [8,16]. Support for negotiation in the design process is essential.
- *Evolution*. Third party software components are subject to frequent upgrades. This often leads to a disparity in customer-vendor evolution cycles and may result in unplanned upgrades being forced on the customer. The design challenge here is to provide ways to minimise the risks associated with change. System integrators need to understand how proposed changes may affect not only the quality of the system, but its lifecycle planning [17].

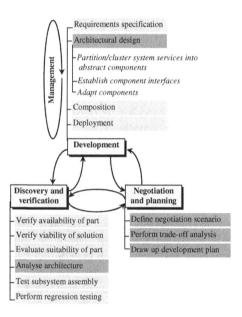

Fig. 1. Component-based system development

2.1 Necessary Requirements for Architectural Analysis

We have distilled the design challenges discussed in Section 2 into six key requirements that can used to design architectural analysis methods and assess their efficacy for CBD. We outline the requirements below:

1) *Pluggability*. A pluggable analysis allows the developer to adapt and tailor the design process to reflect the system context and to address domain specific needs (Fig. 2) [18, 19].

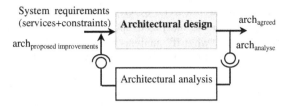

Fig. 2. Pluggable analysis

Fig. 3 illustrates the alternative embedded analysis. Because of its close binding with the design process, embedded analysis often poses problems where evaluation needs to be conducted for specific reasons such as safety analysis.

Fig. 3. Embedded analysis

2) *Negotiation.* Support for negotiation is essential in architectural design and analysis. As discussed in Section 2, there is never a clean match between system requirements and concrete software components. Different design trade-offs may be required in a system architecture to achieve desired quality attributes (Fig. 4).

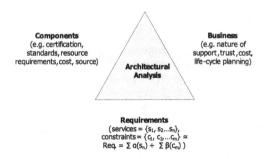

Fig. 4. Architectural analysis in CBD

3) *Formulating analysis scenarios.* Analysis scenarios are essential in helping the system developer understand how proposed designs and changes might affect not only the quality and operation of system, but also its life-cycle planning [10,20,21]. In summary, an analysis scenario should provide:
   - Support for standard/portable descriptions of the system architecture (e.g. UML and XML). Rami et al. [22] have highlighted ADLs as potential instrument to support software architecture evaluation.

- Support for augmenting architectural descriptions with specific constraints and other information to tailor the analysis to specific questions.
- Support for quantitative "what if" analysis (static and dynamic) under conditions of uncertainty that allow developers to describe scenarios to assess the impact of competing designs.

4) *Assessment.* Architectural assessment allows the developer to establish how well a proposed system design satisfies its application and business contexts. The result of the assessment process contributes towards regression testing, impact analysis and traceability activities that may be conducted later in the development process. There are several architecture assessment techniques including use-case scenarios, conformance to patterns, metrics and organization-specific assessment techniques. Use case scenarios provide information on system contexts and logical connections [23]. Design patterns and styles can be used to check if architectures and configurations conform to certain structural and behavioural characteristics [24]. Metrics provide useful quantitative information related to interface complexity, size, component dependency and other measurable system attributes. In summary, an ideal assessment technique should reveal:

- *Structural mismatches.* Incompatibilities in the data exchanged between components and verify architectural adherence to design heuristics and rules.
- *Quality mismatches.* Inconsistencies and mismatches between quality attributes and services and the system context. When we understand desired service and system qualities before a system is built, the likelihood of selecting or creating the right architecture is improved.
- *Behaviour mismatches.* Semantic mismatches between provided and required interfaces and defects in dynamic component interaction.

It is important that assessment techniques support both qualitative and quantitative analysis. *Qualitative* measurements provide a means for representing quality concerns in a subjective evaluation which allows logical reasoning, whilst *quantitative* analysis provides a mechanism to elicit subjective responses from the stakeholders that provide empirical and measurable values.

5) *Maturity.* Maturity indicates the state of readiness of architectural analysis approaches to be adopted in an organization. An important metric for measuring maturity is validation results [5,11]. We use a CMM-like [34] approach to categorize the maturity as follows: *initial* (approach has not being validated), *repeated* (validation through limited complexity and domains with consistent published results) and *defined* (validation through various complexity and domains with consistent published results).

6) *Tool support.* Architectural analysis is a complex activity that involves the planning, analysis, negotiation and assessment of large amounts of interrelated, often conflicting information. A tool should provide support for extracting architectural definition, storing architectural knowledge, analyzing architectural design decisions, identifying trade-offs and offering alternatives [11,18,25,26].

In the next section we use these requirements to assess architectural analysis approaches intended to support component-based development.

3 Architectural Analysis Approaches

3.1 ATAM

The Architecture Trade-off Analysis Method (ATAM) [9] is a pluggable scenario-based approach. ATAM focuses on multiple quality attributes (currently; modifiability, availability, security, and performance). It is aimed at locating and analyzing trade-off points for areas of highest risk in the architecture. Attribute-specific questions generated using scenarios of interest are used to identify possible architectural solutions to achieve desired system quality attributes. The analysis process derives three architectural decisions (i.e. sensitivity points, trade-off points and risks) that have marked effect on one or more quality attributes.

ATAM requires the participation and mutual cooperation of three groups of stakeholders: an evaluation team that is external to the project, project decision makers, and architecture stakeholders.

The approach requires the architect to walk through each high-priority attribute-specific scenario, showing how it affects the architecture (e.g. modifiability) and how the architecture responds to it (e.g. for quality attributes such as performance, security and availability). Along the way, the evaluation team documents the relevant architectural decisions, and identifies and catalogues their risk, non-risks, sensitivity points and trade-off. Sensitivity points are parameters in the architecture to which some measurable quality attribute is highly correlated. To find the trade-off, all important architectural elements with multiple sensitivities are located. For example the number of copies of a database might be a sensitivity point for both availability and performance. Fig. 5 shows how the ATAM activities are partitioned into four iterative phases. ATAM has been extensively evaluated in different application domains including embedded [9] and general information systems [1].

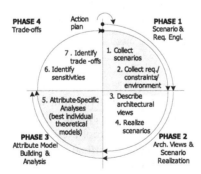

Fig. 5. ATAM activities [9]

3.2 i* Approach

REDEPEND-REACT is an architectural analysis tool that supports the i* approach which is represented in Strategic Dependency models (SD) [27,28]. i* is an actor modeling language that is used to represent software domains and actors (human, organization, hardware or other software). SD describes a network of dependency relationships amongst various actors in an organization context. Actors are represented by nodes; links between nodes represent dependencies between actors. The depending actor is called *Depender* and the actor who is depended upon is called the *Dependee*. The approach is shown in Fig. 6.

REDEPEND-REACT provides guidelines for formulating metrics over i* models that a developer can use to perform architectural analysis. The metrics are selected with respect to properties that are important to the system being modeled (e.g. security, efficiency or accuracy). Metrics are defined in terms of the actors and dependencies in the models, and the results of the evaluation are used to inform multiple component selection. Metric measurement is performed using a MS Excel[TM1] tool which allows the user to define additional metrics and to modify actor values interactively. As the values on the architectures are formulas based on these values, the results are automatically updated. REDEPEND-REACT has been successfully used to analyse several information management system case studies including; a Meeting Scheduler system, an e-Learning system and an e-Business system.

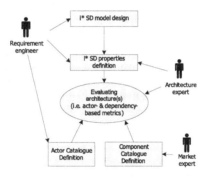

Fig. 6. i* architectural analysis process

3.3 ARGUS-I

ARGUS-I [29] is a specification-based analysis tool which uses the C2-style architecture description language [30] and augments it with component behaviour specification using Statecharts. The ARGUS-I tool performs analysis at *component* and *architectural* level. Component-level specification analysis allows for static (i.e. interface inconsistencies and component-Statechart inconsistencies) and dynamic analysis (i.e. enables the execution of component Statecharts). The analysis process is shown in Fig. 7.

Architecture-level specification checks are performed statically by verifying structural and behavioural dependencies among components, and dynamically by evaluating architecture configuration through simulation. The analysis capabilities of Argus-I have been illustrated using a medium-sized Elevator Control System example.

---

[1] MS Excel is a trademark of the Microsoft Corporation.

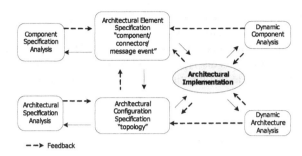

Fig. 7. ARGUS-I process

3.4 Odyssey-Adapt

Odyssey-Adapt is a plug-in for the Odyssey IDE [31] that is intended to support component adaptation and composition during development. Most of the analysis is focused on the component interface. The approach uses three design patterns (proxy, façade and adapter) to tackle component interface mismatches and structural complexity.

Fig. 8 shows the analysis process. The approach defines two types of dependencies between a provided and a required interface; *assembly connector* and *incompatibility* dependency. An assembly connector dependency represents the actual composition between two components through their interfaces. An incompatibility dependency shows the relationship between two components that require some kind of adaptation before their interface can be composed.

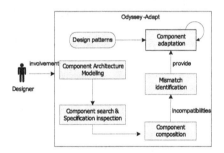

Fig. 8. Odyssey Adapt

Whenever a provided and a required interface are related, Odyssey-Adapt triggers the incompatibility detection function. Three types of incompatibilities are considered:

1. *Structural.* These are conflicts related to syntactic problems between a provided and required interface. These include interfaces with different names, interfaces with methods that differ in their signature, interfaces with different numbers of method, and any combination of these three. They are automatically discovered by a detection function that compares the specification of the interfaces.
2. *Behavioural.* These are semantic mismatches between the provided and required interface. This mismatch identification process is the responsibility of the designer,

which means that all conflicts are documented manually in an *incompatibilities note* and tagged with the provided interface.

3. *Hybrid.* These are mismatches that occur from combination of structural and behavioural incompatibility. This type of mismatch is automatically detected, provided that the behavioural incompatibility has been previously marked.

Odyssey-Adapt is a relatively new approach and has not been validated on a significant software system.

3.5 Engineering Framework

Becker et al. [32] have proposed an adaptation process for detecting and resolving component mismatches based on a taxonomy of design patterns. The adaptation process is applied during architectural design, whenever an analysis of the system indicates a mismatch between two constituent components. The taxonomy contains five distinct classes of component mismatches; *technical*, *signature*, *protocol*, *concept* and *quality*. These are associated with patterns that may overcome the mismatches. Fig. 9 shows the five steps in the adaptation process.

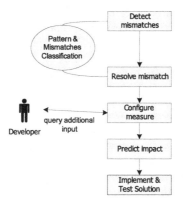

Fig. 9. The process of adapting a component

The Engineering Framework has been partially evaluated using a small case study of a water cooling system.

4 Methods Summary

The results of the assessment are summarised in Table 1. Briefly, ATAM is a maturing approach that is pluggable, supports greybox development and has extensive support for trade-off analysis (i.e. components, quality attributes and business concerns). It provides good help with formulating analysis scenarios but partial support for augmenting of architectural descriptions. However, it provides some support for experimentation. It is tool supported, and provides both qualitative and quantitative assessment for static and dynamic analysis.

Table 1. Comparison of architectural analysis approaches

REQUIREMENT	ANALYSIS APPROACH	ATAM	i* Approach	ARGUS-I	Odyssey-Adapt	Engineering Framework
System	Component type	◐ (Blk)	● (Blk)	● (Wht)	● (Wht)	● (Wht)
	Hybrid	○	○	○	○	○
Pluggability	Pluggable	●	○	●	○	●
	Embedded	○	●	○	●	○
	Guidance with negotiation	●	○	○	○	●
Negotiation	Stakeholder roles — Project Manager	●	○	○	○	○
	Stakeholder roles — Architect/ Designer	●	●	●	●	●
	Stakeholder roles — Evaluator	●	○	○	○	○
	Stakeholder roles — Market Expert	○	●	○	○	○
	Trade-off analysis — Quality attribute	●	●	○	○	●
	Trade-off analysis — Business concerns	●	○	●	●	●
	Trade-off analysis — Component	●	●	◐	●	◐
Defining analysis scenarios	Portable analysis	●	◐	○	●	●
	Architecture augmentation	●	○	●	●	●
	What-if analysis	●	●	○	○	●
Assessment	Structural	● (Ql, Qt)	● (Qt)	● (Qt, Ql.)	(Ql)	● (Ql)
	Behavioural	● (Ql, Qt)	○	● (Qt, Ql.)	○	● (Ql)
	Quality Attributes	●	●	○	○	○
Maturity		◐	◐	○	○	○
Tool support		◐	●	●	●	●

● Supported/ Defined   ◐ Partially Supported/ Repetition   ○ Not Supported/ Initial
Blk – Blackbox support   Wht – Whitebox support
Qt. – Quantitative assessment   Ql. – Qualitative assessment

The i* approach is a maturing, embedded approach that supports blackbox development. The approach provides strong support for negotiation. It also provides extensive help with formulating analysis scenarios and involves three different system stakeholders in the analysis. It is tool supported and provides good quantitative assessment for static analysis. It is significantly weak in dynamic analysis.

ARGUS-I is a new, pluggable approach that supports whitebox development and has poor support for negotiation. It provides limited help with formulating analysis scenarios. It is tool supported and provides good qualitative and quantitative assessment for static and dynamic analysis.

Odyssey-Adapt is a relatively new, embedded architectural analysis process for the Odyssey development environment. It supports whitebox development but provides poor support for negotiation. The analysis is largely structural and limited to component interface mismatches. There is no provision in the method for analysing non-functional properties. Limited support is provided in method for formulating analysis scenarios. The resulting assessment is a qualitative report detailing structural, behavioural and hybrid mismatches.

The Engineering framework is an immature, pluggable process that supports blackbox development. Its support for negotiation is limited to quality attributes. The framework provides limited support for both static and dynamic aspects of design. The resulting assessment is qualitative. In our view, the Engineering framework is still at an early stage of development. Its guidelines for component adaptation are very generic and it relies heavily on designer experience to achieve there's considerable reliance on designer experience as the steps above indicate.

5 Conclusions

Component-based software development is often promoted in literature as a rapid low-cost strategy for developing adaptable and extensible software systems. In reality the strategy carries significant risk throughout the system life cycle. The risks are related to: poor component documentation, the vulnerability risks associated with hidden design assumptions in blackbox components, interfaces mismatches and difficulties in mapping critical quality attributes to component architectures.

In this paper we have shown how architectural analysis can reveal not only how well a system satisfies a particular application context. We have also shown how systematic architectural analysis can help ensure that risks resulting architectural adaptations and trade-offs, and component changes do not adversely affect critical system qualities. The contexts in which third party components are used vary greatly. This means that the documentation supplied with the components is often incomplete or inadequate. Architectural analysis can help ensure that an acceptable solution is achieved, and mitigate situations where unforeseen user needs coincide with a component's undocumented design assumptions.

Unfortunately, current architectural analysis approaches for CBD vary widely with respect to their analytical capabilities and support for blackbox development making it difficult for developers to assess their efficacy in different application contexts. We have developed a CBD-sensitive framework for assessing architectural analysis approaches for CBD and used it to review five architectural analysis approaches. Our results show that there is significant disparity in the analytical capabilities and user validation of the approaches. Support for key component-based design issues is still patchy in most architectural analysis approaches. In particular the support for negotiation and defining analysis scenarios is lacking. While support for blackbox development is available in a number of approaches, these are relatively few. The role of stakeholder support in architectural analysis is largely left to the software architect. Critically, none of the approaches support hybrid reuse-driven development, even though, increasingly applications are being developed in which reusable components and services co-exist in the same system.

References

1. Bass, L., Clements, P., Kazman, R.: Software Architecture in Practice, 2nd edn. SEI Series in Soft. Eng. Addison-Wesley, Reading (2005)
2. Crnkovic, I., Larsson, M. (eds.): Building Reliable Component-Based Software Systems. Artech House Publisher (2002)
3. Medvidovic, N.: Moving Architectural Description from Under the Technology Lamppost. In: Proc. of the Euromicro Conf. on SEAA, pp. 2–3. IEEE Computer Society, Washington D.C. (2006)
4. Kotonya, G., Hutchinson, J.: Managing Change in COTS-Based Systems. In: Proc. of the IEEE Int. Conf. on Soft. Maintenance, pp. 69–78. IEEE Computer Society, Washington D.C. (2005)
5. Dobrica, L., Eila, N.: A Survey on Software Architecture Analysis Methods. IEEE Trans. on Soft. Eng. 28(7), 638–653 (2002)
6. Hutchinson, J., Kotonya, G.: Patterns and Component-Oriented System Development. In: Proc. of the Euromicro Conf. on SEAA, pp. 126–133. IEEE Computer Society, Washington D.C. (2005)
7. Abowd, G., Bass, L., Clements, P., Kazman, R., Northrop, L.: Recommended Best Industrial Practice for Software Architectural Evaluation. Tech. Report, CMU/SEI-96-TR-025 (1997)
8. Wallnau, K.C.: Volume III: A Technology for Predicable Assembly from Certifiable Components. Tech. Report, CMY/SEI-2003-TR-009 (2003)
9. Kazman, R., Klein, M., Barbacci, M., Longstaff, T., Lipson, H., Carriere, J.: The Architectural Tradeoff Analysis Method. In: Proc. of IEEE Int. Conf. on Eng. of Complex Comp. Syst., pp. 68–78 (1998)
10. Babar, M.A., Gorton, I.: Comparison of Scenario-Based Software Architecture Evaluation Methods. In: Proc. of the Asia-Pacific Soft. Eng., IEEE Computer Society, Washington D.C. (2004)
11. Babar, M.A., Zhu, L., Jeffery, R.: A Framework for Classifying and Comparing Software Architecture Evaluation Methods. In: Proc. of the 2004 Australian Soft. Engi. Conf., pp. 309–318. IEEE Computer Society, Los Alamitos (2004)
12. Kazman, R., Bass, L., Lattanze, T., Northrop, L.: A Basic for Analyzing Software Architecture Analysis Methods. J. Soft. Quality 13, 329–355 (2005)
13. Kotonya, G., Hutchinson, J., Bloin, B.: COMPOSE: A Method for Formulating and Architecting Component and Service–Oriented Systems. In: Stojanovic, Z., Dahanayake, A. (eds.) Service-Oriented Soft. Syst. Eng.: Challenges & Practices. Idea Group Inc. (2004)
14. Stafford, J., Wolf, A.: Software Architecture. In: Heineman, G.T., Council, W.T. (eds.) Component-Based Software Engineering: Putting the Pieces Together. Addison-Wesley, Reading (2001)

15. Sommerville, I.: Software Engineering, 8th edn. Addison-Wesley, Reading (2006)
16. Kotonya, G., Hutchinson, J.: A Service-Oriented Approach for specifying component-based systems. In: Franch, X., Port, D. (eds.) ICCBSS 2005. LNCS, vol. 3412, pp. 150–162. Springer, Heidelberg (2005)
17. Kotonya, G., Hutchinson, J.: Analysing the Impact of Change in COTS-Based Systems. In: Franch, X., Port, D. (eds.) ICCBSS 2005. LNCS, vol. 3412, pp. 212–222. Springer, Heidelberg (2005)
18. Obbink, H., Kruchten, P., Kozaczynski, W., Hilliard, R., Ran, A., Postema, H., Lutz, D., Kazman, R., Tracz, W., Kahane, E.: Report on Soft. Arch. Review and Assessment (SARA), http://philippe.kruchten.com/architecture/SARAv1.pdf
19. Klein, M., Kazman, R.: Attribute-Based Architectural Styles. Tech. report, CMU/SEI-99-TR-22. SEI (1999)
20. Ekstedt, M., Johnson, P.: Exploring Architectural Analysis Credibility from a Developer Perspective. In: Proc. on the Australasian Work. on Soft. and Syst. Arch., Sydney, Australia (2002)
21. Weiss, M.: Patterns and Non-Functional Requirements. Tech. paper. Carleton University (2001)
22. Rami, B., Wolfgang, E.: Evaluating Software Architectures: Development, Stability and Evolution. In: Proc. of ACS/IEEE Int. Conf. on Comp. Syst. and App., pp. 47–56. IEEE Computer Society Press, Los Alamitos (2003)
23. Jacobson, I., Griss, M., Jonsson, P.: Software Reuse: Architecture Process and Organization for Business Success. Addison-Wesley, Reading (1997)
24. Babar, M.A., Gordon, I.: A Tool for Managing Software Architecture Knowledge. In: Proc. of the Second Workshop on SHAring and Reusing architectural Knowledge Architecture, Rationale, and Design Intent, pp. 11–17. IEEE Computer Society, Los Alamitos (2007)
25. Kazman, R.: Tool Support for Architecture Analysis and Design. In: Proc. of Int. Conf. on Soft. Eng., pp. 94–97. ACM Press, New York (2002)
26. Bashroush, R., Spence, I, Kilpatrick P, Brown, T.J.: Towards and Automated Evaluation Process for Software Architectures. IASTED on Soft. Eng., 418, 182 (2004)
27. Grau, G., Franch, X., Maiden, N.A.M.: REDEPEND-REACT: an Architecture Analysis Tool. In: Proc. IEEE Int. Conf. on Req. Eng., pp. 455–456. IEEE Computer Society, Los Alamitos (2005)
28. The REDEPEND-REACT, http://www.lsi.upc.edu/~GESSI/REDEPEND-REACT/
29. Vieira, M.E.R., Dias, M.S., Richardson, D.J.: Analyzing Software Arch. with Argus-I. In: Proc. of the Int. Conf. Soft. Eng., pp. 758–761. ACM Press, New York (2000)
30. Medvidovic, N., Oreizy, P., Robbins, J.E., Taylor, R.N.: Using Object-Oriented Typing To Support Architectural Design in the C2 Style. In: Proc. of ACM SIGSOFT 1996. 4th Symposium on the Foundations of Soft. Eng., pp. 24–32. ACM Press, New York (1996)
31. Spagnoli, L., Almeida, I., Becker, K., Blois, A.P., Werner, C.: Adaptation and Composition within Component Architecture Specification. In: ICSR, vol. 3140, pp. 142–155. Springer, Heidelberg (2006)
32. Becker, S., Brogi, A., Gorton, I., Overhage, S., Romanovsky, A., Tivoli, M.: Towards an Engineering Approach to Component Adaptation. In: Reussner, R., Stafford, J.A., Szyperski, C.A. (eds.) Architecting Systems with Trustworthy Components. LNCS, vol. 3938, pp. 193–215. Springer, Heidelberg (2006)
33. Persse, J.R.: Implementing the Capability Maturity Model. Wiley, Chichester (2001)

Component-Based Abstraction and Refinement*

Juncao Li[1], Xiuli Sun[2], Fei Xie[1], and Xiaoyu Song[2]

[1] Dept. of Computer Science, Portland State University, Portland, OR 97207
[2] Dept. of ECE, Portland State University, Portland, OR 97207

Abstract. In this paper, we present a comprehensive approach to model checking component-based systems (including software, hardware, and embedded systems) through abstraction and refinement. This approach is based on assume-guarantee compositional reasoning and features two synergistic techniques: (1) an automatic algorithm to component-based abstraction and (2) a mechanized assistant for abstraction refinement. The key insight to the abstraction algorithm is that a verified property is a natural abstraction of a component. The abstraction algorithm automatically determines which component properties can be included in the abstraction for verifying a system property by determining whether the assumptions of the component properties hold in the context of the system. If the abstraction fails to establish the system property, the refinement assistant determines the causes of the failure, e.g., why a component property is not included, and provides automatic remedies or requests manual remedies. This approach has been applied in component-based hardware/software co-verification of embedded systems. Case studies have shown that this approach is very effective in abstracting component-based embedded systems and guiding abstraction refinement.

1 Introduction

A common trend in both hardware and software industries is component-based development (CBD): developing systems via assembly of components [1,2]. (In the hardware industry, CBD is also known as IP-based development [1].) Embedded systems are also increasingly component-based and include only the necessary hardware and software components for their missions, due to their diverse applications and often stringent physical constraints. CBD introduces compositional structures and standard component interfaces into systems and promotes reuse of design and development efforts. As verification becomes increasingly important, it is also desired to reuse verification efforts.

Reuse of verification efforts is further made possible by the increasing practice of assertion-based verification (ABV) [3]. ABV was initially developed for hardware verification, however, it is gaining popularity in software verification and embedded system verification. ABV requires component developers to specify temporal correctness properties of components as they are developed. Component properties are often specified in standard property specification languages such as the IEEE Property Specification Language (PSL) [4], which facilitates reuse of component properties.

---

* This research was supported by Semiconductor Research Corporation Contract 1356.001 and National Science Foundation Grant 0720546.

H. Mei (Ed.): ICSR 2008, LNCS 5030, pp. 39–51, 2008.

Model checking [5] is a formal verification method that has great potential in system verification. It provides exhaustive state space coverages for the systems being verified. A stumbling block to scalable application of model checking is its intrinsic complexity. The number of possible states and execution paths in a real-world system can be extremely large, which requires state space reduction. Compositional reasoning [6], as applied in model checking, is a powerful state space reduction algorithm and accomplishes verification of a property on a system by decomposing the system into modules, checking the module properties locally, and deriving the system property from the module properties. Compositional system structures introduced by CBD may greatly simplify application of compositional reasoning in system verification.

To leverage the collective effectiveness of CBD, ABV, model checking, and compositional reasoning in system verification, the following challenges need to be addressed:

- How to determine which component properties should be considered in deriving a system-level property? ABV tends to introduce a large number of component properties. Automation is needed in managing these properties and extracting the appropriate component properties for verifying a system-level property.
- How to determine which component properties can be used in verifying a system-level properties? Many properties have enabling assumptions. Automation is needed in determining whether a component property is *enabled*, i.e., whether its assumptions hold in the context of the system.
- How to determine the causes for a compositional reasoning failure, i.e., failure to derive a system property from component properties that have been established, and identify remedies for the problems? To address these problems, manual efforts are sometimes needed. It is desired to reduce the manual efforts when possible.

In this paper, we present a comprehensive approach to model checking component-based systems (including software, hardware, and embedded systems) through abstraction and refinement. This approach is based on assume-guarantee compositional reasoning [7,8,9,10,11,12,13] and features two synergistic techniques: (1) an automatic algorithm to component-based abstraction and (2) a mechanized assistant for abstraction refinement. The key insight to the abstraction algorithm is that a verified property is a natural abstraction of a component. This algorithm automatically determines which component properties should be considered in constructing the abstraction for verifying a system property by dependency analysis and which component properties can be included in the abstraction by determining whether the assumptions of these properties hold in the context of the system. If the abstraction fails to establish the system property, the refinement assistant determines the causes of the failure, e.g., why a component property is not included, and provides automatic remedies or requests manual remedies.

Our approach to component-based abstraction and refinement has been applied in hardware/software co-verification of embedded systems. Case studies have shown that this approach is very effective in abstracting component-based embedded systems and guiding abstraction refinement. In particular, this abstraction and refinement approach can be applied across the hardware/software boundaries smoothly.

The reminder of this paper is organized as follows. In Section 2, we provide the background of this work. In Section 3, we introduce the algorithm to component-based abstraction and the procedure for mechanizing abstraction refinement. In Section 4, we present application of component-based abstraction and refinement in hardware/ software co-verification and evaluate its effectiveness. In Section 5, we discuss related work. In Section 6, we conclude this paper and touch on future work.

2 Background

2.1 ω-Automaton Semantics

We adopt the L-process model of ω-automaton semantics, details of which can be found in [14]. Only the concepts necessary for this paper are given below. For an L-process, ω, its language, $\mathcal{L}(\omega)$, is the set of all infinite sequences accepted by ω. For L-processes, $\omega_1, \ldots, \omega_n$, their synchronous parallel composition, $\omega = \omega_1 \otimes \ldots \otimes \omega_n$, is an L-process and $\mathcal{L}(\omega) = \cap \mathcal{L}(\omega_i)$, and their Cartesian sum, $\omega' = \omega_1 \oplus \ldots \oplus \omega_n$, is also an L-process and $\mathcal{L}(\omega) = \cup \mathcal{L}(\omega_i)$. The safety closure $CL(\omega)$ of an L-process ω is an L-process whose language is the safety closure of the language of ω, $\mathcal{L}(CL(\omega)) = cl(\mathcal{L}(\omega))$. In [14], $cl(\mathcal{L})$ is termed as the smallest limit prefix-closed language containing $\mathcal{L}$. Given L-processes ω_1 and ω_2, ω_1 implements ω_2 (denoted by $\omega_1 \models \omega_2$) if $\mathcal{L}(\omega_1) \subseteq \mathcal{L}(\omega_2)$.

Under the ω-automaton semantics, model checking is reduced to checking L-process language containment. Suppose a system is modeled by the composition $\omega_1 \otimes \ldots \otimes \omega_n$ of L-processes, $\omega_1, \ldots, \omega_n$, and a property to be checked on the system is modeled by an L-processes, ω. The property holds on the system if and only if the language of $\omega_1 \otimes \ldots \otimes \omega_n$ is contained by the language of ω, $\mathcal{L}(\omega_1 \otimes \ldots \otimes \omega_n) \subseteq \mathcal{L}(\omega)$. A realization of the ω-automaton semantics is the S/R language [15]. S/R is the input formal language of the COSPAN model checker [15], which we utilize in this research.

2.2 Assume-Guarantee Compositional Reasoning

Assume-guarantee compositional reasoning, that each module guarantees certain properties based on properties of the other modules, was introduced by Chandy and Misra [7] and Jones [8] for analyzing safety properties. Abadi and Lamport [9], Alur and Henzinger [10], and McMillan [11] extended it to liveness properties. These extensions are incomplete, i.e., there exist properties of systems which are true but not provable using these extensions [12]. Amla, Emerson, Namjoshi, and Trefler proposed a sound and complete compositional reasoning rule for both safety and liveness properties [13]. This rule, Rule 1, has been realized in the ω-automaton semantics as shown below.

Rule 1. *For ω-automata P_1 and P_2 modeling two components of a system, and Q modeling a property of the system, to show that $P_1 \otimes P_2 \models Q$, find ω-automata Q_1 and Q_2 modeling the component properties such that the following conditions are satisfied.*

C0: $V^i(Q_1) \subseteq V^i(P_1)$ and Q_1 does not block P_2, and vice versa for Q_2
C1: $P_1 \otimes Q_2 \models Q_1$ and $P_2 \otimes Q_1 \models Q_2$
C2: $Q_1 \otimes Q_2 \models Q$
C3: Either $P_1 \otimes CL(Q) \models (Q \oplus Q_1 \oplus Q_2)$ or $P_2 \otimes CL(Q) \models (Q \oplus Q_1 \oplus Q_2)$

$V^i(P)$ is the set of interface variables of P. A process Q does not block process P iff (i) any initial state of P can be extended to an initial state of $P \otimes Q$, and (ii) for any reachable state of $P \otimes Q$, any transition of P from that state can be extended to a transition of $P \otimes Q$. An additional restriction on $P's$ and $Q's$, which is not shown in Rule 1, is that P_1 (or Q_1, respectively) and P_2 (or Q_2) modify disjoint sets of variables.

Note that checking Condition C3 is not needed if one of Q_1, Q_2, and Q is a safety property since its safety closure is itself. In [16], Rule 1 has also been extended to support compositional reasoning with components that have shared sub-components.

3   Component-Based Abstraction and Refinement

In this section, we first present a key observation that leads to our component-based approach to abstraction and refinement: verified properties of a component can serve as abstractions of the component if their assumptions are satisfied. Then, we introduce our automatic algorithm that constructs abstractions of a composite component (a system is a composite component) from verified properties of its sub-components. After that, we introduce a mechanized assistant to refinement of component-based abstraction.

3.1   Verified Properties as Component Abstractions

Once a property p is verified on a component C, we have $C \models p$, i.e., all behaviors that C exhibits are a subset of the behaviors allowed by p, and p is usually structurally less complex than C. Therefore, verified properties are natural abstractions of components. In the ω-automaton semantics, this is more appealing since systems, components, properties, and assumptions are modeled uniformly as ω-automata. In the rest of this paper, systems, components, properties, and assumptions are all modeled as ω-automata.

However, when verifying component properties, assumptions are often introduced due to the dependencies of a component to its environment. For instance, if p is verified on C under a set A(p) of assumptions, we have $A(p) \Rightarrow C \models p$. In this case, to utilize p as the abstraction of C, we must show that $A(p)$ can be satisfied. We introduce the concept of an *enabled* component property in a component composition as follows:

Definition 1. *Given a composition of components* $C = C_1 \otimes \ldots \otimes C_n$. *A property* $(p, A(p))$ *of* C_i, $1 \leq i \leq n$, *is enabled in* C *if and only if* $C_1 \otimes \ldots \otimes C_n \models A(p)$.

Checking whether p is enabled by checking $C_1 \otimes \ldots \otimes C_n \models A(p)$ is often as expensive as, if not more expensive than, directly checking $C_1 \otimes \ldots \otimes C_n \models p$. On the other hand, it is often the case that many other properties of $C_1, \ldots, C_n$ have already been verified. Therefore, it is desirable to determine whether $(p, A(p))$ is enabled, through analyzing the verified properties of $C_1, \ldots, C_n$.

Determining whether a sub-component property is enabled is further complicated by the fact that there may exist circular dependencies among the sub-component properties. It must be shown that these circular dependencies do not cause circular reasoning, before the sub-component properties can be deemed as enabled.

Not all enabled sub-component properties are necessary in verifying a property of the composition since properties are asserted on certain aspects of a component. Therefore, we only need to determine whether the sub-component properties related to the property of the composition are enabled. To ensure all the related sub-component properties are included, a straightforward approach is to apply cone-of-influence analysis [5] based on the component interfaces and their connections. This may bring in unnecessary properties. More accurate dependency analysis are needed to exclude such properties.

Based on the above discussion, we define an abstraction of a component as follows:

Definition 2. *Given a component $C = C_1 \otimes \ldots \otimes C_n$ and a property $(p, A(p))$ to be verified on C, an abstraction for checking $(p, A(p))$ is the composition of all verified properties of $C_1, \ldots, C_n$ that are related to p by dependency analysis and can be shown to be enabled through analyzing $A(p)$ and the verified properties of $C_1, \ldots, C_n$.*

The abstraction is conservative since each enabled property of a sub-component is a conservative abstraction of the sub-component. Composition of conservative abstractions is a conservative abstraction due to the language intersection property of ω-automata. Therefore, if $(p, A(p))$ holds on the abstraction, it also holds on C.

According to [17], properties can be categorized as safety properties, liveness properties, and their hybrids. (The same categorization is also applicable to assumptions.) Any property p can be represented as the intersection of a safety property and a liveness property. In the ω-automaton semantics, this is represented as $p \equiv CL(p) \wedge (\neg CL(p) \vee p)$ where $CL(p)$ is the safety closure [17] of p. In this study, we specify properties and assumptions using the ω-automata assertion templates in [16]. Based on these templates, it is easy to identify a safety or liveness assertion and decompose a hybrid assertion into its safety and liveness parts. Being able to identify safety and liveness assertions enables us to better determine whether circular dependencies among component properties can cause circular reasoning. We assume that the components and properties involved in component-based abstraction and refinement meet the restrictions imposed by Rule 1. Therefore, cycles with safety properties will not cause circular reasoning. We only need to consider pure liveness property cycles for possible circular reasoning.

3.2 Automatic Component-Based Abstraction

There are two major tasks for the component-based abstraction algorithm: (1) deciding which sub-component properties should be considered in constructing the abstraction for a composite component and (2) determining whether these sub-component properties are enabled. The efficiency and effectiveness of this algorithm lies in whether unnecessary properties can be excluded from the abstraction and necessary properties can be shown to be enabled as possible only by analyzing the sub-component properties.

Suppose that C is a composite component with sub-components $C_1, \ldots, C_n$. The interface I_i of C_i is a pair (V_i^I, V_i^O) where V_i^I is the set of variables C_i imports and V_i^O is the set of variables C_i exports. We assume all V_i^O's are disjoint. When C_i is composed with other components, the input variables in V_i^I are mapped to the output variables in V_i^O's of other components. P_i is a set of properties of C_i that are defined on I_i and has been verified. Each property in P_i is of the form $(p_{ij}, A(p_{ij})), 1 \leq j \leq m_i$ and m_i is the number of properties in P_i. Our abstraction algorithm constructs the abstraction for verifying $(p, A(p))$ on C from the sub-component properties, where $(p, A(p))$ is defined on the interface I of C and I is also a pair (V^I, V^O). To simplify the presentation of our algorithm, let $P = P_1 \cup \ldots \cup P_n \cup \{(true, p), (A(p), \emptyset)\}$, i.e., P

is the set of all sub-component properties with addition of $(true, p)$ and $(A(p), \emptyset)$ which are derived from $(p, A(p))$. $(A(p), \emptyset)$ is marked as enabled since $A(p)$ are assumptions on the environment of C. Our automatic abstraction algorithm is shown in Figure 1:

Inputs: $P = \{(true, \{p\}), (p_1, A(p_1)), \ldots, (p_s, A(p_s)), (A(p), \emptyset)\}$
           where s is the sum of the numbers of properties in $P_1, \ldots, P_n$
Outputs: "p holds" or "refinement needed"

Build the property dependency graph G from P;

foreach node $t \in G$ **do** /* via DFS or BFS */
    Find all nodes N in G that t depends on; /* via dependency arcs from t */
    if $!(P(N) \models A(t))$ **then** /* "!" representing logic negation */
        Mark t as DU (directly unsatisfied);
        enqueue (Que, t);
    endif
endfor

while !empty(Que) **do**
    t = dequeue (Que);
    Find all unmarked nodes N in G that depend on t; /* via arcs to t */
    foreach t' in N
        Find all unmarked nodes N' that t' depends on; /* via dependency arcs from t' */
        if $!(P(N') \models A(t'))$ then
            Mark t' as IU (indirectly unsatisfied);
            enqueue (Que, t');
        endif
    endfor
endwhile

if $(true, \{p\})$ is marked DU or IU **then return** "refinement needed";
else
    SCSs = {strong connected subgraphs of unmarked liveness properties};
    if !empty(SCSs) **then return** "refinement needed";
    else return "p holds";
    endif
endif

Fig. 1. Component-Based Abstraction Algorithm

Step 1: Build the property dependency graph G. To determine which sub-component properties should be considered in abstraction construction, we first construct a dependency graph based on the potential enabling relations among the sub-component properties. We initiate the graph with a single node $(true, p)$ and expand the graph from it. For each node $(p_g, A(p_g))$ in the graph, which has not been expanded, we first find all the sub-component properties $(p_h, A(p_h))$ based on the direct variable dependencies between $A(p_g)$ and p_h and then find all the sub-component properties $(p_k, A(p_k))$

based on the direct or indirect dependencies between p_h and p_k through examining only the property part (but not the assumption part) of each node along the dependency chain. If any $(p_h, A(p_h))$ or $(p_k, A(p_k))$ is not in the graph, include it in the graph, add a directed arc from $(p_g, A(p_g))$ to it, and put it in the queue for nodes to be expanded; otherwise, just add the arc.

Optimization based on ω-automata assertion templates. The above approach to building the property dependency graph may involve a lot of unnecessary component properties since it only considers variable dependencies. This may lead to significant overhead in abstraction construction and refinement. We optimize this approach using heuristics based on the semantic meanings of the ω-automata assertion templates in [16].

Example. Consider a system S with two components C_1 and C_2. C_1 outputs a variable a and inputs a variable b. C_2 outputs two variables b and c and inputs a variable a. The properties of C_1 and C_2 are shown in Figure 2. (Note that all assertions in a set, e.g., A_{12}, are conjunctive.) A system property to be verified is p: Repeatedly(c) with no assumption. The property dependency graph constructed for verifying p is in Figure 2.

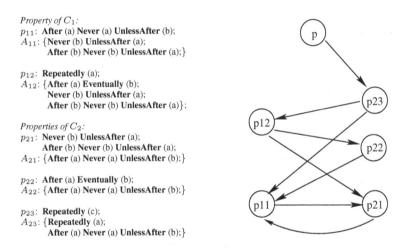

Fig. 2. Component Properties and Property Dependency Graph

Step 2: Determine enabled properties optimistically.

After the dependency graph is constructed, we determine, in an optimistic way, whether a sub-component property in the graph is enabled. It is optimistic since we assume, at this point, that dependency cycles do not cause circular reasoning. We will deal with these cycles in the next step.

We first conduct a breadth-first or depth-first search on the graph. For each node t in the graph, we find the set N of all nodes to which t has dependency arcs. We check $P(N) \models A(t)$, i.e., whether the property assertions from all the nodes in N can conjunctively satisfy the assumption assertions in $A(t)$. If no, we mark t as "directly unsatisfied", i.e., even if all the nodes in N are enabled, t will still not be enabled.

Starting from the set of nodes marked as "directly unsatisfied", we recursively identify nodes that are unsatisfied due to their dependencies to nodes that have been marked as unsatisfied. That an unmarked node t' has a dependency arc to an unsatisfied node t does not imply that t' is unsatisfied. We still need to check if the unmarked nodes which t' depends on can satisfy t'. This process terminates when there are no more unsatisfied properties to mark (assuming that dependency cycles do not cause circular reasoning). The unsatisfied nodes identified in this phase are marked "indirectly unsatisfied".

If $(true, p)$ is marked as unsatisfied, directly or indirectly, the abstraction algorithm returns and requests refinement; otherwise, the algorithm moves on to Step 3.

Step 3: Detect liveness circular dependencies. In this step, we detect the existence of circular dependencies among the unmarked liveness sub-component properties in the graph G. The circular dependency detection is by finding the strongly connected sub-graphs of the unmarked liveness sub-component properties. If there exist such sub-graphs in G, the abstraction algorithm returns and requests refinement.

Remarks: The component-based abstraction constructed by our algorithm includes all the sub-component properties which $(true, p)$ depends on and are identified as enabled. In this algorithm, we determine whether a node t can be satisfied by the nodes in N, by applying model checking, specifically, applying COSPAN with $P(N)$ as the system and $A(t)$ as the property to be checked. The complexity of such a check depends on the property and assumption assertions involved. Since we specify these assertions using the templates in [16], each assertion is simple and has only a few states. Therefore, the number of assertions is the deciding factor. The overall complexity of our algorithm also depends on the number of calls to COSPAN. The number of calls to COSPAN is, in the worst case, the sum of the number of nodes and the number of arcs in G. Other complexities of this algorithm include that of building the property dependency graph and that of detecting strongly connected sub-graphs of unmarked liveness properties.

3.3   Mechanized Abstraction Refinement

Our abstraction algorithm may fail to verify a property $(p, A(p))$ for the following two reasons: (1) the sub-component properties are insufficient to verify $(p, A(p))$ and (2) there exist liveness property dependency cycles that, before being validated to be free of circular reasoning, preclude inclusion of the involved sub-component properties in the abstraction. Below, we present our mechanized approaches to addressing the problems.

Insufficient sub-component properties. When our abstraction algorithm reports that it fails to establish $(p, A(p))$ due to insufficient sub-component properties, our refinement assistant conducts a breadth-first search through the dependency graph generated by the abstraction algorithm to identify all nodes that are marked "directly unsatisfied" and reachable from $(p, A(p))$ through only nodes marked "indirectly unsatisfied". For each such node, the assistant outputs the node, the nodes it depends on, and the error trace of the COSPAN call on this node. The user is asked to modify existing sub-component properties and introduce new sub-component properties. These modified or new sub-components properties need to be verified. If a sub-component is a primitive component, its modified or new properties are directly checked on the component; otherwise, the properties are checked again through component-based abstraction.

Liveness property circular dependencies. When our abstraction algorithm reports liveness property circular dependencies, our refinement assistant provides to the user all strongly connected sub-graphs of unmarked liveness properties. An automatic remedy the assistant can provide is to check the additional conditions (such as C3 in Rule 1) dictated by the rules in Sec 2.2, which, if established, can prevent circular reasoning. These conditions are essentially additional properties to be checked on the involved sub-components. If a sub-component is primitive, its additional property can be checked directly; otherwise, component-based abstraction is recursively applied. If these rules fail, the user needs to manually validate that the sub-graphs be free of circular reasoning using techniques such as temporal induction [11], modify the existing sub-component properties, or introduce new sub-component properties. (Note that modification of existing properties and introduction of new properties may lead to new circular dependencies.) If all sub-graphs are shown to be free of circular reasoning, $(p, A(p))$ holds.

Remarks: The abstraction/refinement loop terminates when $(p, A(p))$ is verified or the user aborts this loop. The user aborts this loop when an error is found or she has difficulty in modifying or introducing sub-component properties for verifying $(p, A(p))$. Errors in component composition are detected through the user examining the unsatisfied nodes in the dependency graph. Errors in sub-components are detected when verification of sub-component properties fails.

4   Application in Hardware/Software Co-verification

An Illustrative Example. We illustrate component-based abstraction and refinement with its application in hardware/software (HW/SW) co-verification of a sensor system as shown in Figure 3. Its software is partitioned into two components: software sensor (*S-SEN*) and software network (*S-NET*) and its hardware is partitioned into three components: hardware clock (*H-CLK*), hardware sensor (*H-SEN*), and hardware network (*H-NET*). The software components are specified in xUML [18] while the hardware components are specified in Verilog [19]. The software and hardware components are connected by bridge components (*B-SEN* and *B-NET*), which interact with the software components following the software semantics and with the hardware components

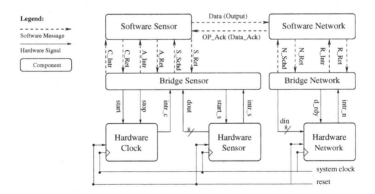

Fig. 3. Architecture of a sensor instance with software in xUML and hardware in Verilog

---

Repeated (H-NET.flag = true);   **Repeated** (H-NET.flag = false);

Fig. 4. Repeated transmission property

```
/* Properties of S-SEN */
Pss(1) → {PSN(1)}
Pss(2) → {PBS(1)}
Pss(3) → {PSN(4), PSN(1), PBS(1)}
Pss(4) → {PSN(4), PSN(1), PBS(3), PBS(2), PBS(1)}

/* Properties of S-NET */
PSN(1) → {Pss(1)}
PSN(2) → {PSN(1), Pss(1), PBN(1)}
PSN(3) → {PSN(1), Pss(1), PBN(1)}
PSN(4) → {PSN(1), Pss(1), PBN(1)}
PSN(5) → {PSN(1), Pss(4), Pss(1), PBN(2), PBN(1)}

/* Properties of B-SEN and B-NET */
PBS(1) → {Pss(2), PHS(1)}
PBS(2) → {Pss(3), Pss(2), PHS(2), PHS(1)}
PBS(3) → {Pss(3), Pss(2), PHC(1), PHS(2), PHS(1)}
PBN(1) → {PSN(2), PHN(1)}
PBN(2) → {PSN(3), PSN(2), PHN(2), PHN(1)}
PBN(3) → {PSN(5), PSN(3), PSN(2), PHN(2), PHN(1)}

/* Properties of H-NET */
PHN(3) → {PBN(3)}
```

Fig. 5. Dependencies among component properties

following the hardware semantics and propagate events such as software messages and hardware interrupts across the HW/SW boundary. A property to verify on this system is shown in Figure 4. This property asserts that the sensor system transmits on the network repeatedly. Repeated setting and clearing of a flag in *H_NET* indicates repeated transmission. (Space limitation precludes presentation of the component properties).

We apply component-based abstraction to verify the system property. The abstraction algorithm constructs an assume-guarantee dependency graph as shown in Figure 5. The abstraction algorithm is able to enable each property optimistically by ignoring dependency cycles. In this graph, there are only dependency cycles involving safety properties, there is no need to check for additional conditions and all these properties hold and they enable all other properties that depend on them. All the involved properties form the abstraction on which the system property is successfully verified.

To evaluate the effectiveness of our refinement assistant, we intentionally omit the properties $P_{BN}(3)$ and $P_{BS}(3)$ and their assumptions since these are properties of the bridge components that cannot be automatically generated from their designs. We then apply abstraction and refinement. The assistant reports that the property $P_{HN}(3)$ is not enabled since one of its assumptions is not satisfied due to the omission of $P_{BN}(3)$. When $P_{BN}(3)$ and its assumptions are introduced, the assistant then reports that the property $P_{SS}(4)$ is not enabled since one of its assumptions is not satisfied due to the omission of $P_{BS}(3)$. The key here is that the user is only notified when manual remedies are necessary. This refinement assistant is effective in locating unsatisfied assumptions and reports them to the user as hints for further property modification and introduction.

Table 1. Time and memory usage comparison

	Usages	Basic	Multi	Encrypting
TBCV	Time (Sec)	31272.8	-	-
TBCV	Memory (MB)	1660.62	Out of memory	Out of memory
Manual CBCV	Time (Sec)	41.89	10.34	0.77
Manual CBCV	Memory (MB)	9.11	6.05	3.57
Manual CBCV	# of COSPAN Calls	8	2	4
Automatic CBCV	Time (Sec)	205.93	10.45	12.97
Automatic CBCV	Memory (MB)	27.57	4.44	3.54
Automatic CBCV	# of COSPAN Calls	39	24	39

Experimental Results. Table 1 shows statistics from verification of the property in Figure 4 on three sensor systems of increasing complexity using three different approaches. The "Basic" system refers to the system discussed above. The "Multi" system and the "Encrypting" system are more complex than the "Basic" system. (See [20] for details of these systems.) TBCV denotes translation-based co-verification [21] which translates an entire system into S/R and then verifies the entire system with COSPAN. In the manual component-based co-verification (CBCV) approach [20], the component-based abstraction of a system is manually constructed. (Manually created abstractions serve as guidance in optimizing our automatic algorithm.) In the automatic CBCV approach, our automatic abstraction algorithm is applied to construct the abstraction. The time (or memory, respectively) usage of verifying a system using CBCV is the sum (or max) of the time (or memory) usages of verifying the new components and the abstraction. The component properties are verified by translating the properties and the corresponding components into S/R and applying COSPAN. (Translation of hardware components in Verilog utilizes FormalCheck [22] while translation of software components in xUML and bridge components utilizes ObjectCheck [23].) It can be observed that the time and memory usages of automatic CBCV are order-of-magnitude smaller than those of TBCV in verifying the first system and TBCV fails to verify the other systems due to out-of-memory while automatic CBCV finishes the verification using little time and memory (which include those for graph construction and strongly connected sub-graph detection). Although automatic CBCV uses more time and memory than manual CBCV, it is automatic and requires no manual effort in abstraction construction.

5   Related Work

Our approach builds on and extends compositional reasoning [6], in particular, assume-guarantee compositional reasoning [7,8,9,10,11,12,13]. It combines assume-guarantee compositional reasoning with abstraction/refinement [14] by utilizing component properties as abstractions. It integrates compositional reasoning and abstraction/refinement with component-based development and leverages assertion-based verification to address the component property formulation problem in application of compositional reasoning.

Abstraction techniques [5,14], as applied in model checking, reduce a system to a less complex system while preserving correctness of the property to be checked. Major approaches to abstraction that have been practically useful include (but are not limited to) localization reduction [14], data abstraction [5], and predicate abstraction [24]. In [11], McMillan integrated data abstraction, assume-guarantee compositional reasoning, and theorem proving techniques in the context of the Cadence SMV system [11]. Our approach, although more restricted compared to McMillan's approach, is more lightweight and is more closely integrated with component-based development.

6   Conclusions and Future Work

In this paper, we have presented a comprehensive approach to component-based abstraction and refinement. This approach is generally applicable although our implementation is based on the ω-automaton semantics and the COSPAN model checker, since its foundation is compositional reasoning. It advances compositional reasoning via integration with component-based development and assertion-based verification.

The accuracy and efficiency of our abstraction algorithm and refinement assistant is affected significantly by the dependency graphs that are constructed over component properties. The dependency graphs are conservative in that they do not omit any true dependency. However, there may be false dependencies introduced by dependency analysis. False dependencies may prevent the abstraction algorithm from including properties that should have been included in an abstraction and may also prevent the refinement assistant from providing an accurate description of the causes for a compositional reasoning failure. We will research better methods for removing false dependencies.

References

1. Jacome, M.F., Peixoto, H.P.: A survey of digital design reuse. IEEE Design and Test of Computers 18(3) (2001)
2. Szyperski, C.: Component Software - Beyond Object-Oriented Programming. Addison-Wesley, Reading (2002)
3. Maliniak, D.: Assertion-based verification smooths the road to IP reuse. Electronic Design (September 2002)
4. IEEE: IEEE Property Specification Language (PSL) (IEEE Std 1850-2005). IEEE (2005)
5. Clarke, E.M., Grumberg, O., Peled, D.: Model checking. MIT Press, Cambridge (1999)
6. de Roever, W.P., de Boer, F., Hanneman, U., Hooman, J., Lakhnech, Y., Poel, M., Zwiers, J.: Concurrency Verification: Introduction to Compositional and Non-compositional Proof Methods. Cambridge University Press, Cambridge (2001)
7. Chandy, K.M., Misra, J.: Proofs of networks of processes. IEEE Transaction on Software Engineering 7(4) (1981)
8. Jones, C.B.: Development methods for computer programs including a notion of interference. PhD thesis, Oxford University (1981)
9. Abadi, M., Lamport, L.: Conjoining specifications. TOPLAS 17(3) (1995)
10. Alur, R., Henzinger, T.: Reactive modules. FMSD 15(1) (1999)
11. McMillan, K.L.: A methodology for hardware verification using compositional model checking. Cadence Design Systems Technical Reports (1999)
12. Namjoshi, K.S., Trefler, R.J.: On the completeness of compositional reasoning. In: Emerson, E.A., Sistla, A.P. (eds.) CAV 2000. LNCS, vol. 1855. Springer, Heidelberg (2000)

13. Amla, N., Emerson, E.A., Namjoshi, K.S., Trefler, R.: Assume-guarantee based compositional reasoning for synchronous timing diagrams. In: Margaria, T., Yi, W. (eds.) ETAPS 2001 and TACAS 2001. LNCS, vol. 2031. Springer, Heidelberg (2001)
14. Kurshan, R.P.: Computer-Aided Verification of Coordinating Processes: The Automata-Theoretic Approach. Princeton University Press, Princeton (1994)
15. Hardin, R.H., Har'El, Z., Kurshan., R.P.: COSPAN. In: Alur, R., Henzinger, T.A. (eds.) CAV 1996. LNCS, vol. 1102. Springer, Heidelberg (1996)
16. Xie, F., Yang, G., Song, X.: Compositional reasoning for hardware/software co-verification. In: Graf, S., Zhang, W. (eds.) ATVA 2006. LNCS, vol. 4218. Springer, Heidelberg (2006)
17. Alpern, B., Schneider, F.: Defining liveness. Information Processing Letters 21(4) (1985)
18. Mellor, S.J., Balcer, M.J.: Executable UML: A Foundation for Model Driven Architecture. Addison-Wesley, Reading (2002)
19. IEEE: IEEE Standard for Verilog (IEEE Std 1364-2005). IEEE (2005)
20. Xie, F., Yang, G., Song, X.: Component-based hardware/software co-verification. In: Proc. of MEMOCODE (2006)
21. Xie, F., Song, X., Chung, H., Nandi, R.: Translation-based co-verification. In: Proc. of MEMOCODE (2005)
22. Kurshan, R.P.: FormalCheck User Manual. Cadence (1998)
23. Xie, F., Levin, V., Browne, J.C.: Objectcheck: A model checking tool for executable object-oriented software system designs. In: Kutsche, R.-D., Weber, H. (eds.) ETAPS 2002 and FASE 2002. LNCS, vol. 2306. Springer, Heidelberg (2002)
24. Graf, S., Saïdi, H.: Construction of abstract state graphs with PVS. In: Grumberg, O. (ed.) CAV 1997. LNCS, vol. 1254. Springer, Heidelberg (1997)

High Confidence Subsystem Modelling for Reuse

Birgit Penzenstadler and Dagmar Koss

Technische Universität München, Software & Systems Engineering
penzenst@in.tum.de, koss@in.tum.de

Abstract. Reuse of high confidence subsystems depends on their appropriate modelling and documentation. This paper discusses the different aspects that have to be considered when modelling a system and its subsystems. We propose a concrete artefact model for integrated reuse from requirements to technical architecture, which satisfies documentation demands with respect to functionality and the context assumed by the subsystem. Based on the artefact model, we describe the steps for conformity and compatibility checking at the development stage of subsystem integration and/or reuse.[1]

Keywords: Subsystem, artefact, reuse, conformity, compatibility.

1 Motivation

"How do we achieve reuse of high confidence software in large systems?" An answer to this question first requires an answer to the question "How do we build high confidence software?" To classify a software as deserving the predicate "high confidence", it has to be well-understood, predictable, and reliable: *Well-understood* requires a well documented requirements engineering and system's design, supported by a continuous modelling of the system. *Predictability* necessitates proper modelling with different, but consistent, interrelated views on the system to prevent modelling errors or architectural mismatches proactively. *Reliability* needs validation and verification of the modelled system.

Additionally, returning to the first question, we want the software to be reusable within large systems. Reuse is, inter alia, performed to reduce development costs. However, inappropriate or incomplete documentation sabotages this goal by increasing the effort for the (re)integration of an existing subsystem. Therefore it has to encompass clearly delimited and well documented subsystem borders.

We define a **subsystem border** as the *interface* of a subsystem *plus* the relevant surrounding *context* from the operational environment, the business domain, and organizational issues. To be able to model and document the subsystems in such a way, we need an adequate system requirements artefact model. A corresponding subsystem model with its artefacts and explicitly modelled subsystem border information allows the developer to extract such a subsystem,

---

[1] This work was partially funded by the German Federal Ministry of Education and Research (BMBF) in the framework of the REMsES project. The responsibility for this article lies with the authors.

H. Mei (Ed.): ICSR 2008, LNCS 5030, pp. 52–63, 2008.

including its documenting artefacts, and reuse it independent from the former environment within a new surrounding system.

Contribution: We present an approach for the explicit modelling of subsystem borders (interface plus context), thereby facilitating communication with subcontractors and reuse. We start with requirements engineering, go on to system's design and end with system (re-)integration. We present an artefact model, then discuss aspects of modelling subsystems for reuse, and propose concrete subsystem artefacts and explicit modelling of information about the subsystem borders. Finally we validate conformity and verify compatibility when reusing a subsystem. Our approach is useful for the development of high confidence COTS as well as all other types of high confidence software as soon as the system is complex enough to require decomposition into subsystems.

Related Work: There are some approaches that co-develop requirements and architecture, e.g. [23], and two that derive architecture from requirements, one for multi-agent systems [2] and an aspect-oriented method [21], but none that documents refinements of contextual issues within the subsystem.

Other work focuses on architecture design [26] and on the modelling of software libraries [12]. Close to the idea of software libraries is also software cartography [17], but without explicit consideration of compatibility and reuse. The composability and compatibility of services on the basis of components is discussed by [7] and [1].

Although the last ICSR [20] was concerned with COTS (components off-the-shelf), there was no work presented on either the representation of COTS borders with regard to ease reuse or concerning validation of conformity and verification of compatibility. The FLP component model [19] enhances systematic reuse by considering non-technical issues. However, there is no approach yet that explicitly models the borders of a subsystem.

Related work in terms of being able to make use of our ideas are the approaches to selecting adequate components for reuse, for example [18], who propose a systematic process for decision support in evaluating and ranking components, or [4], who focus on piecewise evaluation during component selection.

Outline: After introducing our background in Sec. 2, we start with our system requirements artefact model in Sec. 3 and explain subsystem border information documentation in Sec. 3.2. Then we give an example in Sec. 3.3 and present our steps for reuse in Sec. 4, before concluding with future work in Sec. 5.

2   Foundations

We follow an integrated approach of requirements engineering (RE) and system's design that develops a first sketch of the design during RE. This is based on an artefact-oriented requirements engineering reference model and a system architecture model with three abstraction layers.

The Requirements Engineering Reference Model. (REM [11]) classifies the artefacts of the individual requirements engineering process into three content categories and assigns documents for them building an integrated view by the use of quality gates (not further discussed here). The general *business needs* (later on referred to as *context*) incorporate general business objectives, return-on-investment analysis, high level system vision given by the stakeholder, and so on. The *requirements* specification includes the domain analysis, the functional analysis, and quality requirements and their dependencies. The *system concept* (later on referred to as *design*) comprises a detailed functional system concept and the system test criteria. This point of view is gained from industrial best practices while its content also includes aspects known from process driven frameworks and templates (e.g. using the Volere requirements specification templates [25] and the IEEE 830-1998 standard [13]).

Our System Architecture Model is based on the following three abstraction layers: the *usage layer* gives a specification of the system behaviour as it is perceived at the system border by the user (black box). It is represented as a hierarchy of services, which give a formal specification of parts of the system's behaviour, and lateral relationships between them. Next, the *logical architecture* is a realization of the services from the usage model defined in the layer above. It is modelled as a net of communicating (logical) components and can simulate the system's behaviour. Usually, there is an $n : m$-relationship between the services of the usage layer and the components of the logical architecture. The third layer, the *technical architecture*, comprises a software and a hardware view, linked via the deployment description. The software is modelled in tasks that are structured in clusters and those are mapped to the hardware units. The system architecture model is explained in detail in [6].

3   Artefact Model

According to [24] the quality criteria for requirements are, inter alia, to be complete, consistent, unambiguous, and traceable. These criteria are decideable and can be evaluated. Further discussion of that aspect is out of scope for this paper, instead we assume the requirements to have sufficient quality so we can concentrate on their appropriate documentation within the system's artefact model.

3.1   General System Artefact Model

We use the system artefact model depicted in Fig. 1. It features the three content categories context, requirements, and design, and orthogonally the three abstraction layers usage, logical architecture, and technical architecture. The mapping of artefacts to content category and abstraction layer is not always unique, but we have placed them according to their main focus. Some of the artefacts may appear refined on lower abstraction layers with an increased degree of detail.

The context artefacts are - ordered according to a decreasing level of abstraction - a domain model, the business context, the stakeholder context with a listing and the characteristics for each of them, an operational context includ-

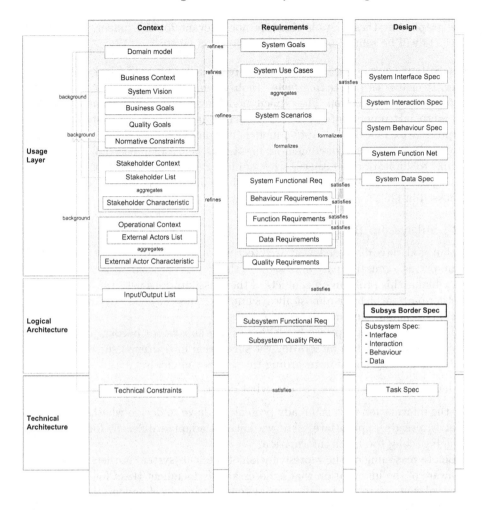

Fig. 1. Artefact model

ing a listing and characteristic of each external actor, an input/output list, and technical constraints. The business context can be further detailed into system vision, business goals, quality goals, and normative constraints.

The requirements artefacts are system goals, use cases and scenarios, functional requirements, and quality requirements. The functional requirements can be modelled as behavioural, functional, or data requirements according to the appropriateness for the system's design.

The design artefacts are interface, interaction, behaviour, and data specifications and a system's function net. The latter provides an intuitive functional overview of the system by depicting the interplay between the functions in form of a graph, but these details that are not relevant for this paper. The design artefacts will be refined on the lower abstraction layers.

The Subsystems. We are focusing on are modelled on the logical architecture layer. To enable a separate treatment of subsystems, there is an artefact called *subsystem border specification*. The explicit modelling and documentation of this artefact is crucial to enable integration or extraction and reuse of a subsystem. For that purpose we extract the subsystem model and complete it with the corresponding information required to document its borders as we detail in Sec. 3.3.

Due to limitations of space, we assume for the following that the system decomposition has been decided. The influencing criteria for this decision are discussed in [22].

3.2 Subsystem Borders

Garlan et al. have discussed, that architectural mismatch stems from mismatched assumptions a reusable part makes about the system structure it is to be part of. They blame this problem on conflicts of these assumptions with the assumptions of other parts, which are almost always implicit, thus they are extremely difficult to analyze before building the system [10].

Therefore the appropriate modelling of the subsystem borders is crucial to avoid mismatches when integrating the subsystem into a (new) surrounding system. The guiding question regarding the artefact model is:

"What information can we use and what do we have to add?"

For the information that is already present, we have to decide whether the given form is already appropriate, or if we have to adapt a different form to avoid dragging along too much information.

Before reasoning on the representation of the (sub)system borders, we have to be aware of the information that is necessary to document them for appropriate retrieval when searching for solutions by reuse during development: the **interface** and any corresponding **constraints**. As we are aware of the challenges which the idea of software libraries bring with them, we do not attempt to solve all their problems, but instead focus on the adequate documentation of subsystems. The latter includes a clear description of the functionality offered by the system and the functionality it requires from other system parts to perform at its optimum.

The constraints can roughly be divided into hardware and software constraints and then categorized as static or dynamic [15]. There is a great diversity of electrical and mechanical hardware constraints, but in this paper we consider only the ones that are related to software requirements.

The interface specification can be divided into a static (syntactic) and a dynamic (behavioural) part. The differentiation between static and dynamic specifications is cost-efficient, as verification of static specification usually requires less effort. So if the static specifications of the corresponding interfaces are compatible, the dynamic specifications are evaluated. A static interface specification includes:

Functions	name, header
Parameters	names and corresponding values (variable or object)
Data types	e.g. integers, strings, objects, ...
Type representation	e.g. volt, an email address,...
Value ranges	valid range for parameter
Stepping	maximum degree of increase or decrease
Pre-/postcond., invariants	e.g. voltage greater than zero
Communication	protocol and order of sent & received information

In the static specification there are some issues that, at a certain stage of development, could not be solved yet. For this reason, conditions and invariants have to appear in both listings, as some of them can be verified statically, but others only during runtime. The dynamic specification has to hold all information that can only be tested at runtime or (maybe) in a model simulation. Dynamic aspects, where compatibility has to be determined, are:

Message order	correct causal order as expected by receiver, including protocol communication messages
Message timing	e.g. message arrival within a certain time slot
Pre-/postcond., invariants	e.g. temporal logic formulae like $always(b < c)$
Ranges	conformance to limits
Stepping	conformance to min./max. in-/decrease

The constraints usually affect a greater part of the system or even the whole system, while the interface specifications described above normally apply only to the interfaces of components inside a system. Nevertheless, these constraints have to be refined for the subsystem and documented accordingly to have the complete relevant information available within the subsystem documentation. The constraints can also be categorized into static and dynamic parts and are imposed by the surrounding environment. The static constraints are for example:

Rules of conformity	e.g. standards, laws or business rules
Quality requirements	e.g. response time of database less than 20 seconds
Variability	optional parts within the subsystem

Note that laws or standards are to be considered as static in the sense of checking the conformity of the system to constraints they imply, because the internal system state at runtime does not take influence on whether the system is conform to a certain law or standard. However, on the other hand normative constraints do sometimes change during system development. This has to be taken care of by requirements evolution and change management, but the issue is independent from the here presented concerns about conformity. The dynamic constraints affect the whole system and can only be evaluated at runtime:

Ressources	the required processing speed, required memory space
Realtime conditions	overall response time of the system, system speed
Reliability	for example Mean Time To Failure

All of the listed information should ideally already be present in the artefact model defined above. This would reduce the task to extracting the information using the appropriate filter and feeding it into a template that features fields for the interface and the constraints listed above. We are aware that this is the theory while, in practise, it will be necessary to actively accumulate the required knowledge from different sources of information.

3.3 Subsystem Border Artefacts

The first idea of how the border modelling for subsytems should be documented is depicted in Fig. 2.

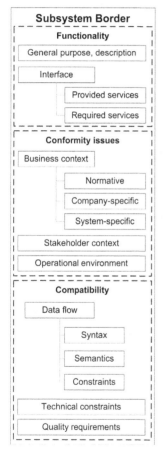

Fig. 2. Subsystem Border Modelling

Functionality: For the functionality of the subsystem we extract part of the system model with explicit interface documentation. To describe the general purpose of the subsystem, we use a textual form with a short version of a system vision. This can be seen as kind of "abstract" of the subsystem that shall give a concrete idea of what the system is built for and what functionality it offers. The explicit interface documentation already reflects the realization, as it lists the services provided by the subsystem (also known as *export interface* [5]) and the services required from other subsystems by the subsystem (also *import interface*).

Conformity Issues: These encapsulate contextual issues like laws, business rules, stakeholders, and operational environment. With regard to the three abstraction layers (Fig. 1) we can picture most of the content as imposed from "above", to say from the business needs and the context of the usage layer.

In detail, the business context contains normative, company-specific, and system-specific constraints. Normative constraints are implications from laws that have to be obeyed, e.g. data protection act, standards that the company wants to conform to, e.g. from ISO, and patents and licenses that are used.

Company-specific constraints are influences from business rules or information politics, e.g. servers may only be set up in countries with a special commercial agreement, and system-specific constraints derive from business goals, the system vision, and system goals, e.g. the system that shall achieve a 10% market share. Furthermore, we list implications from the stakeholder context, e.g. concerning reporting, and the operational environment, e.g. backup routines.

Compatibility: Compatibility issues contain descriptions of data flow, communication and technical constraints, and quality requirements. Most of the content in this section are implications from below with regard to the abstraction layers, to say from the software and hardware layer and the technical realization of the system. The data flow is characterized through its input and output, described through syntax, semantics, and further constraints imposed e.g. by value ranges or stepping. Communication and technical constraints are for example the message format that is used on the communication bus of the system. Quality requirements are usually the same as for the whole system. In some cases it may be possible to break them down, e.g. for response time.

Illustrating Example "Travel Booking System": A simple realization for the subsystem border documentation is depicted in Fig. 3 in form of a template. We use a travel booking system for illustration. The travel booking system includes all features related to travel booking, for example flight reservations and bookings, hotel bookings, check-in, reporting, accounting, and scheduling. It is designed as web service. The chosen subsystem is *flight reservation and booking.*

Subsystem Border Documentation	
Name of Subsystem	Flight booking
Purpose	The flight booking subsystem allows searching for flights and making reservations or bookings for listed results.
Interface	
Provided services	flight search, flight reservation, flight booking, cancelation
Required services	database query, user authentification, GUI
Conformity	
Business Context	Normative: data protection act
	Company-specific: only flights from XY are offered
	System-specific: store statistics on cancelations
Stakeholder Context	report cancelations to XY within 15 minutes
Operational Context	two redundant backup storage servers are running 24/7
Compatibility	
Data flow	Syntax: http request with search parameters w, x, y, and z
	Semantics: w: departure, x: destination, y: date, z: time
	Constraints: w ≠ x and y in future
Technical Constraints	requires SQL3 or higher
Quality Constraints	response time of database < 20 seconds

Fig. 3. Template for subsystem border documentation with example "Flight Booking"

4   Reuse of a Subsystem

For the reuse of a subsystem that has been documented in the way described above, we have to ensure matching functionality as well as both conformity and compatibility. We assume, we have listed all available subsystems in our software (reuse) library with the purpose description provided in the subsystem border documentation template, as described in the box entitled *Functionality* in Fig. 2 or in the example in Fig. 3. By performing a search on the software library, we have found a subsystem with the functionality that matches our demands. For the integration into a new surrounding system, we have to check for conformity and compatibility with the new environment.

4.1 Validation of Conformity

In order to validate the conformity of the proposed subsystem with regard to the new surrounding context, we consider a guided review as the most appropriate technique. When developing a system, we move downwards through the abstraction layers, enrichening each layer with more technical detail. After implementation, the integration process follows the reverse path through the abstraction layers. Thereby we have to validate on each level, that the system under construction is conform to the specification developed earlier. This is the only way to ensure that we developed "the right system". The review has to be performed manually by checking the different areas of context and comparing them to the context of the new surrounding system. The structure of the subsystem border documentation (Fig. 2) may serve as guidance for the review and the corresponding part of the example in Fig. 3 is the box titled *Conformity*.

4.2 Verification of Compatibility with (U)CML

Verification ensures that we developed "the system right", meaning that we verify that our implemented technical solution is compatible to the surrounding environment. Therefore we have to check the static (syntactic) as well as the dynamic (behavioural) fitting of a component with its environment. (U)CML - (Unified) Compatibility Modelling Language has been developed to solve static compatibility issues. (U)CML enables to model systems from scratch, specify the interfaces of the components, compare corresponding interfaces, and check their compatibility. It is also possible to verify the exchangeability of components. Referring to our example in Fig. 3, we can verify the box headed *Compatibility*. Similiar to interface automata [8], (U)CML takes an optimistic view on compatibility, that means, interfaces do not have to be a perfect match to be compatible, but in contrast to interface automata this is not achieved by finding an environment which is compatible (via the game theory). Instead, it is defined by applying compatibility rules to the in- and output to expand the compatibility matching range. Furthermore, interface automata are restricted to software, whereas (U)CML can also model hardware and electrical aspects of a system.

(U)CML Models. Consist of one system package on the highest level, which defines and capsules the system. It consists of packages (containers) and components. Packages can contain other packages and components, components cannot be decomposed any further.

Packages and components are connected via arrows and the endpoints on components are called plugs (in- and outputs). Arrows can only have one source and one destination point and cannot be recursive. For bi-directional communication there is a special communication-arrow. Information about the modelling objects is stored inside description fields. Description fields store structural information. Additionally, the component description field holds invariants and the plug de-

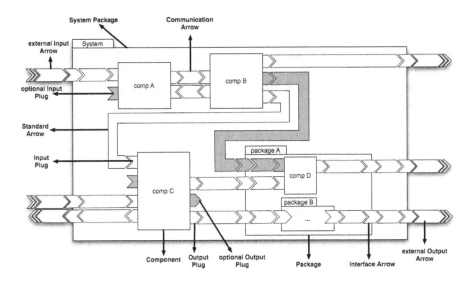

Fig. 4. A UCML model

scription field holds part of the interface specification for each in- and output of the component. This can be for example a type, a variable name, or a function. For a detailed introduction, see [16].

The two outstanding features are compatibility rules and optional in- and outputs. The latter is especially useful when using the same components in different systems. In- or outputs do not have to be connected necessarily, as the system still works without errors, and therefore the component is (re)usable for more than one system.

The other feature is the assignment of compatibility rules to the whole system or to a specific in- or output. Rules are, e.g., that an integer output can be matched to a long input or that a certain output value range corresponds to a certain input value range. With these rules it is possible to expand the compatibility check for corresponding out- an inputs. Rules can also be added as pre- or postconditions and invariants. They can be written in CCL, the Compatibility Constraint Language, which is similar to OCL [14].

Static Compatibility Tests: (U)CML allows two different kinds of compatibility tests. One is the structural correctness of the (U)CML model, for example, if every mandatory output plug is connected to a mandatory input plug, or if every component has at least one input and one output plug. The other one are compatibility tests, which are mainly performed by evaluating the corresponding description fields of the output- and input-plugs. If they match, the plugs are syntactically compatible, if they do not match, the compatibility rules have to be evaluated to check, whether they are compatible after applying the rules.

After the static checks, the dynamic checks have to be performed. This is currently being implemented in (U)CML by adding message sequence charts that model the behavior of the components [9].

5   Conclusions and Future Work

We have presented an approach to the explicit modelling of subsystem borders that facilitates communication with subcontractors and reuse. We have introduced a concrete artefact model for the integrated reuse from the requirements to the technical architecture. It provides for documentation demands with respect to functionality and the context assumed by the subsystem.

Based on that artefact model, we have described the steps for conformity and compatibility checking at the development stage of subsystem integration and/or reuse. The approach presented in this paper will be validated and applied more extensively to a case study within the REMsES research project [3].

Future work is to further detail the border documentation, as the proposed template is still scarce and needs to be extended with appropriate documentation techniques and tracing methods.

In parallel, we are currently working on an analysis of the criteria for the decomposition of systems, the influences and trade-offs between them, and the documentation of the rationale leading to such design decisions to further improve the trust for reuse of high confidence systems modeling.

Acknowledgements. We would like to thank Daniel Mendez-Fernandez, Felix von Ranke and the anonymous reviewers for their helpful comments and feedback on earlier versions of this paper.

References

[1] Attiogbé, C., André, P., Ardourel, G.: Checking component composability. In: Löwe, W., Südholt, M. (eds.) SC 2006. LNCS, vol. 4089, pp. 18–33. Springer, Heidelberg (2006)

[2] Bastos, L., Castro, J., Mylopoulos, J.: Deriving architectures from requirements. In: Requirements Engineering Conference. RE 2006. 14th IEEE International, pp. 332–333 (2006)

[3] Berghof Automationstechnik GmbH, DaimlerChrysler AG, SSE Universität Duisburg-Essen, and Software and Systems Engineering Technische Universität München. Project REMsES (2007), http://www.remses.org

[4] Bhuta, J., Boehm, B.: A method for compatible cots component selection. In: COTS-Based Software Systems (2005)

[5] Broy, M.: A core theory of interfaces and architecture and its impact on object orientation. In: Reussner, R., Stafford, J.A., Szyperski, C.A. (eds.) Architecting Systems with Trustworthy Components. LNCS, vol. 3938, pp. 26–47. Springer, Heidelberg (2006)

[6] Broy, M., Feilkas, M., Wild, D., Hartmann, J., Grünbauer, J., Gruler, A., Harhurin, A.: Umfassendes Architekturmodell für das Engineering eingebetteter software-intensiver Systeme. Technical report, Technische Universität München (to be published)

[7] Broy, M., Krüger, I., Meisinger, M.: A formal model of services. ACM Transactions on Software Engineering Methodology (TOSEM), 16(1) (2007), http://doi.acm.org/10.1145/1189748.1189753

[8] de Alfaro, L., Henzinger, T.A.: Interface automata. In: FSE 2001. Proceeding of the 9h Annual Symposium on Foundations of Software Engineering, pp. 109–120. ACM Press, New York (2001)

[9] Eckl, C.: Analysis and adaptation of MSCs for the examination of behavioral compatibility. Master's thesis, Technische Universität München (2007)

[10] Garlan, D., Allen, R., Ockerbloom, J.: Architectural mismatch: Why reuse is so hard. IEEE Software 12(6), 17–26 (1995)

[11] Geisberger, E., Broy, M., Berenbach, B., Kazmeier, J., Paulish, D., Rudorfer, A.: Requirements Engineering Reference Model (REM). Technical report, Technische Universität München (2006)

[12] Hunt, J., McGregor, J.: A model for software libraries. In: Institute, R.P. (ed.) Library-Centric Software Design (2005)

[13] The Institute of Electrical and Electronics Engineers, Inc., 345 East 47th Street, New York, NY 10017-2394, USA. IEEE Recommended Practice for Software Requirements Specifications (IEEE Std 830-1998), 10 (1998)

[14] Koss, D.: CCL reference (2007), http://www4.in.tum.de/~koss/da/compMSCAdapt.pdf

[15] Koss, D.: Kompatibilität und Kompatibilitätsmanagement. PhD thesis, Technische Universität München (to be published, 2008)

[16] Koss, D., Brandstätter, M.: (U)CML - a modeling language for modeling and testing compatibility. In: Proceedings: Software Engineering and Applications (2007)

[17] Lankes, J., Matthes, F., Wittenburg, A.: Architekturbeschreibung von anwendungslandschaften: Softwarekartographie und ieee std 1471-2000. In: Software-Engineering, Essen 2005, pp. 43–54 (2005)

[18] Lin, H., Lai, A., Ullrich, R., Kuca, M., McClelland, K., Shaffer-Gant, J., Pacheco, S., Dalton, K., Watkins, W.: Cots software selection process. In: Commercial-off-the-Shelf (COTS)-Based Software Systems, ICCBSS 2007. Sixth International IEEE Conference, February 26, 2007 - March 2 2007, vol. 2, pp. 114–122 (2007)

[19] Mei, H.: A component model for perspective management of enterprise software reuse. Ann. Software Eng. 11(1), 219–236 (2001)

[20] Morisio, M. (ed.): ICSR 2006. LNCS, vol. 4039. Springer, Heidelberg (2006)

[21] Navarro, E.: ATRIUM Architecture Traced from Requirements by Applying a Unified Methodology. PhD thesis, University of Castilla-La Mancha (2007)

[22] Penzenstadler, B., Mendez-Fernandez, D.: System decomposition for distributed development. In: ICSP 2008 (submitted, 2008)

[23] Pohl, K., Sikora, E.: COSMOD-RE: Supporting the co-design of requirements and architectural artifacts. RE 0, 258–261 (2007)

[24] Recknagel, M., Rupp, C.: Meßbare Qualität in Anforderungsdokumenten. Automotive Vertikal 2, 12–17 (2006)

[25] Robertson, J., Robertson, S.: Volere: Requirements specification template (2006), http://www.volere.co.uk/

[26] Wojcik, R., Bachmann, F., Bass, L., Clements, P., Merson, P., Nord, R., Wood, B.: Attribute-driven design (ADD). Technical Report CMU/SEI-2006-TR-023, CMU SEI Pittsburgh (2006)

A Trustable Brokerage Solution for Component and Service Markets

Colin Atkinson, Daniel Brenner, Oliver Hummel, and Dietmar Stoll

University of Mannheim, Chair of Software Engineering,
68159 Mannheim, Germany
{atkinson,hummel,stoll}@informatik.uni-mannheim.de,
dbrenner@uni-mannheim.de
http://swt.informatik.uni-mannheim.de

Abstract. As other engineering disciplines have often demonstrated, the costs and risks involved in developing new products are significantly reduced by the emergence of effective component markets. However, such markets have yet to appear in software engineering. In this paper we present an approach that addresses one of the main outstanding obstacles to software component markets – the overhead involved in establishing confidence in a component or service. The approach employs a new test definition metaphor which allows potential users to establish whether components do what they are supposed to do without giving them full access. We refer to this as the "black box brokerage" model for software markets which protects the interests of component providers as well as component users, and thus improves the economic motivation for reusing components. In the paper we also describe how a black box broker can be efficiently implemented, outline a new testing metaphor and explain its natural synergies with test-driven reuse.

1 Introduction

A long standing goal of software engineering has been to establish viable software markets that make it more cost effective to build new applications from third-party software components than to build them from scratch [1]. As other engineering domains have often demonstrated, the emergence of effective component markets is the key to driving down costs and making product development more a matter of routine assembly than of innovative design. The lack of such markets, at present, makes software engineering a highly-skilled and labor intensive activity and causes software to take up a disproportionate part of the cost of new systems and business processes. It follows that any technology or approach which removes some of the obstacles to third-party software reuse, and encourages the creation of viable software markets, will significantly boost the software industry's ability to enhance efficiency and competitiveness through more innovative applications.

In the early days of software engineering, when applications generally took the form of individual "programs" and components were mainly regarded as code modules (e.g. packages, classes etc.), the goal of establishing software markets was explored under the banner of "software reuse". As distributed architectures became ubiquitous,

H. Mei (Ed.): ICSR 2008, LNCS 5030, pp. 64–75, 2008.
© Springer-Verlag Berlin Heidelberg 2008

and applications started to take the form of Web-based, client-server systems, components became larger-grained and the goal of establishing markets revolved around developments in distributed object/component infrastructures (e.g. CORBA, J2EE, COM) [6] and web services[1][18]. Regardless of the specific technologies and concepts used, however, the basic challenges involved in establishing a viable software market have remained more or the less the same. The first major challenge is to set up and operate a repository with a sufficient number of software artifacts to make the effort of searching for suitable components worthwhile [8]. The second is to provide mechanisms by which developers of new applications/processes can find components "fit" for their purpose within these repositories. If the number of components is below a critical mass - making the likelihood of success too low - or if the effort involved in finding suitable components is too great, the economic balance will be unfavorable and developers will choose to "build" rather than "reuse" [3].

Significant progress has been made on the "component discovery" problem. Technologies for finding syntactically suitable artifacts within large software repositories have become more powerful in recent years [2], and public code search engines (such as Google Codesearch or Merobase) with millions of software assets provide a variety of syntactic search features ranging from specialized keywords corresponding to program concepts (e.g. method or class) to full interface-based searches. Finding syntactically suitable components is only half of the problem, however – it is also necessary to determine if components have the required semantics [7]. Unfortunately, the progress in syntactic search has not been matched by the progress in establishing whether software components are "fit for purpose". Formal approaches for describing software components are still complicated and thus not widely in use today. Furthermore the halting problem makes it impossible to assess whether a candidate component in a repository fulfills a given query specification, which makes formal descriptions impractical in the context of very large repositories. Thus, in practice, the only effective method of establishing whether a component does what it is required to do is to test it. However, from the point of view of establishing component markets, using current testing metaphors and technologies as the basis for assessing a component's fitness for purpose presents a fundamental dilemma - *the level of visibility or access needed to test a component is the same as that needed to use the component.*

Hence, the basic problem is to find a way of allowing potential customers to gain a sufficient level of confidence that a product meets their needs while protecting the supplier's right to be paid. When physical products are involved some kind of "right of return" is usually provided and suppliers are often rated according to their trustworthiness. When digital products are involved (which cannot be returned in a physical sense) some kind of usage restriction is usually applied. For example, in the case of music or video entertainment products, limited snippets of the products are made available (e.g. in the form of short trailers or music clips) so that potential customers can evaluate the product before purchasing it. Experience has shown that markets only flourish when the right kind of confidence building measures that balance the evaluation needs of consumers with the protection needs of providers are in place.

---

[1] The contributions we make in this paper are equally applicable for components and services although we will mostly mention only components for the sake of simplicity.

Of course, manufacturers of end-user software applications have struggled with this problem for years and have developed a variety of strategies for allowing users to evaluate software. These all involve issuing a special license key that allows the product to be used for a restricted period of time or in a restricted way [11]. However, these approaches to access control are not attractive in the context of software component markets because of the overhead involved. From the point of the view of potential component users, the overhead involved in first obtaining the necessary access key – which usually involves some form of registration – and in designing test software that properly handles the key and includes it in every invocation of the reused component, usually outweighs the potential benefits. It is likely that this issue will become even more pressing for future service markets where software agents are supposed to discover reasonable services automatically [17] and thus these overheads significantly tilt the balance towards the "build" end of the "build or buy" tradeoff.

From the point of view of component providers, the overhead involved in implementing an access control mechanism which is sufficiently secure against IT specialists – as opposed to the lay-people who use finished software applications – is usually too high. At the time of writing we are not aware of any fully-secure licensing mechanisms for traditional software components that are embedded as code within new applications, while for online services that are accessed over the Internet, there is the difficulty of distinguishing genuine new users from repeat users.

Finding a non-abusable and efficient way of establishing confidence in a component is thus one of the main outstanding obstacles to establishing viable software markets and thus to the evolution of software development into a mature engineering discipline. In this paper we propose a new way of addressing this dilemma. In the following section we describe the idea of our so-called black box brokerage approach. Section 3 then introduces our new platform-independent testing metaphor and section 4 discusses how it is integrated into our recent developed test-driven reuse approach. In section 5 we discuss a secure implementation for black box brokerage and test-driven reuse before we conclude our contribution in section 6.

2 Black Box Brokerage

The basic principle behind our approach is simple. Since testing is still ultimately the only means by which a software component can be judged to be "fit for purpose", the basic idea is to extend component search engines with the ability to test components. As well as delivering components that syntactically match users' queries, search engines enhanced in this way will also be able to determine whether components match semantically. In contrast with current testing approaches, however, a new form of "blind testing" is needed – that is, a form of testing in which the user is only provided with an indication of whether a test has been passed, not with the results returned by the component. Furthermore, it is also important that the expected results of a test are not disclosed to the component under test since they could be used to return spoofed correct results.

In effect, a search infrastructure enhanced in this way would also become a testing engine. As illustrated in Figure 1, its role would be to serve as a trusted broker between component providers and potential component consumers. Component providers need to trust the engine with the access keys that it needs to test the components on behalf of potential consumers, while consumers need to trust the infrastructure with their tests and have confidence that it will execute them correctly on their behalf. Since the overall effect is to allow potential users to test components with minimal knowledge about them (i.e. as black boxes) we refer to the overall model as black box brokerage (BBB) and an engine which realizes this model as a BBB system.

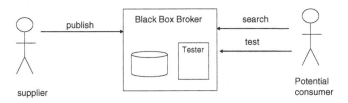

Fig. 1. Black-Box Brokerage Model

From the point of view of component or service providers, a black-box broker is little different from a standard component repository such as a UDDI repository [18]. The difference is that the component provider must deliver all information and content needed to execute the component. From the point of view of potential customers, the only difference between a black box broker and a normal component search engine is that once a component of interest has been identified (usually via a normal syntactic search) the user can supply one or more test cases which the broker will apply to the component on the user's behalf.

Although the idea is simple, there are some significant challenges to be overcome in its implementation. The first is to develop a test description approach which is sufficiently rich to allow all necessary information to be supplied in a platform independent manner and which shields the unit under test from direct access by the customer – something that is not guaranteed with normal xUnit (such as JUnit or NUnit) test cases. The second problem is dealing with the security issues involved in executing untrusted, third party components or test cases on the broker. Steps must be taken to ensure that rogue software cannot damage the broker itself or diminish the level of service delivered to users (e.g. by crashing the system or causing a denial of access problem by hogging resources). The third problem is dealing with the resource and scalability requirements of black box brokerage. Testing is a resource intensive activity, and a successful black box brokerage service can expect to handle many concurrent tests. The supporting architecture must therefore not only be robust, but also highly efficient and scalable.

3   BBB Testing with Test Sheets

Although programming-based testing approaches such as JUnit are very powerful and allow the full range of language features to be used to define test cases, they are platform-dependent and require extensive programming expertise. They are therefore not entirely suitable for black box brokerage. Fit [10], a table-based testing approach advocated in agile development [12], is much better in this regard since it allows developers to focus on the pure test logic (including test data) and results. However,

Fit is limited in handling complex parameter types and the description of arbitrary relations between input values and results. These limitations make Fit unsuitable for BBB in its basic form, but nevertheless it provides good inspiration. We therefore propose a new test definition approach which combines the power of programming approaches like JUnit with the readability and higher level of security (since it is not possible to execute arbitrary code) of table-based approaches like Fit by using a spreadsheet metaphor. We refer to tests developed in this approach as "test sheets".

3.1 Test Sheets

Test sheets are a first attempt to combine the advantages of both JUnit and Fit in an easy-to-use way. The simplicity and ease of use come through the spread sheet metaphor which is well-known from popular office suites. A spread sheet contains all the information needed to functionally test the component's interface and to check for possible misunderstandings in the contract between user and provider. An exemplary test sheet for a simple ShoppingCart component is shown in the following figure.

Table 1. A Fit-like test sheet for a shopping cart component

	ShoppingCartTest		A	B	C
1	ShoppingCart	create			
2	Product	create	"Pragmatic Unit Testing"	29.95	
3	Product	create	"Pragmatic Project Automation"	29.95	
4	C1	addItem	C2		
5	C1	addItem	C3		
6	C1	getBalance			B2 + B3
7	C1	getItemCount			2

Each row in the table represents an invocation of an operation of an object. The object is specified in the first column, the called operation in the second column and the actual parameters for the operation in columns A and B. The vertical double line between columns B and C is the so-called "invocation line". This serves to separate the input parameters (on the left hand side) from the output (i.e. result) parameters (on the right hand side). The mapping of input values to parameters is done according to the usual "order of appearance" mechanism used in most programming languages. In this example there are only two columns for input parameters, A and B, since no operation has more than two arguments.

Column C serves two purposes. First, it stores the output values generated by the execution of each operation that returns a value and, second, it can contain the expected return values specified by the test designer. Thus, each cell in column C that contains an explicit value (e.g. C6 and C7) plays the role of an assertEquals statement in JUnit. The values and expressions defined in cells C6 and C7 represent the expected values that are compared to the actual returned values to determine whether the test was passed. Although the example above shows only one column after the invocation line, C, it is possible to have more columns if there are more return (or output) values (e.g. a web service). The single column in this case results from the fact that Java methods only return one output value. In contrast with Fit, the state of a component is stored in our approach and is updated as the sequence of method invocations proceeds.

Table 1 shows a very simple case where the values in A2, B2, A3, and B3 as well as C7 are defined as literal values. However, because the rows and columns of the table can be addressed in a spreadsheet style, values can also be defined in terms of references to previous input or output values. For example, the expected value in C6 is not defined as a literal value but as an expression referring to the input values.

When this test sheet is executed in normal "open" mode, a new "output" test sheet is created which is the same as the original except that the output cells are colored red or green, depending on whether the expected value was returned. Also, in the former case, the "wrong" returned result is displayed in the cell alongside the expected value.

3.2 Blind Testing

In the blind testing mode, component consumers are also able to define the test cases they would like the software to satisfy and the results they would like returned (as usual). However, in this case, when running the tests the BBB system only returns information indicating whether or not failures have occurred. The actual results in the case of failure are not disclosed. For example, suppose a user were to create a test sheet with incorrect result values such as that in table 2, perhaps with the aim to exploit the ShoppingCart component without paying for it.

Table 2. Test sheet depicting a "blind test", which is hiding the actual test result

	ShoppingCartTest		A	B	C
1	ShoppingCart	create			
2	Product	create	"Pragmatic Unit Testing"	29.95	
3	Product	create	"Pragmatic Project Automation"	29.95	
4	C1	addItem	C2		
5	C1	addItem	C3		
6	C1	getBalance			59.00
7	C1	getItemCount			2

The table shows that, when applied to the software under test, the actual result (which is of course 59.90) of the invocation of the getBalance() operation (row 6) deviated from the value specified by the user, but the result of the invocation of the getItemCount() operation (row 7) was equal to the one expected. In the normal "open" testing scenario, a component consumer could surreptitiously "use" a component by disguising invocations as tests. Since the values calculated by the component are returned to the tester he/she has full visibility of the component's behavior. An unscrupulous consumer could therefore in principle create "fake" tests in which the required return values are artificial, but the input values represent real data for which the consumer needs results. However, with the blind versions of the tests this scenario is impossible. Because no results are ever returned to the tester, just an indication of whether the result matched the required value, no unscrupulous consumer can use the component surreptitiously. At the same time, genuine users who are searching for suitable components are still informed about whether a component is suitable for their needs (i.e. successfully returns the required values).

Besides blind testing, further testing approaches are imaginable to discover information about the behaviour (i.e. the semantics) of a component, all using the same basic interface metaphor. They differ according to two dichotomies – whether the component consumer or the component user defines the test data and whether or not the consumer is given visibility of the test results. This is depicted in the table below.

Table 3. Overview of test modes feasible with test sheets

	black box visibility	white box visibility	
consumer defined input	blind	open	definitive
		exploratory	
producer defined input		showcase	

Definitive Testing is a form of testing in which the consumer defines both the input values and the desired results. This implies that the user has a concrete idea of the behavior of the components he/she is searching for (hence the name definitive). There are two meaningful forms of definitive testing. Blind testing is the form of definitive testing in which the test results are black box (not visible to the user in the case of failure). Open testing is the forming of definitive testing in which the test results are white box (all returned values are visible to the user). This corresponds to the normal testing approach used in software engineering.

Exploratory Testing is also a form of testing in which the consumer defines the input values. However, in this case he/she defines no result. Instead, the tests are used by the consumer to explore and learn about the behavior of a component by stimulating it with values. In effect, the test sheet serves as a kind of "execution harness" that allows the consumer to test the component without the trouble of writing suitable invocation code. It provides a means for consumers to "try out" components through a simple and convenient interface.

Showcase Testing is a form of testing in which the producer, rather than the consumer, defines both the input parameter values and the results. In a sense, this is the opposite of definitive testing. The purpose of such a test is to demonstrate to potential consumers what the component can do. In other words, the producer uses test sheets to display the behavior that he/she believes best characterizes or "showcases" the component. This exploits the fact that tests sheets have a kinship with specification techniques (especially algebraic specification techniques).

4 Integration with Test-Driven Reuse

Instead of expecting the user to first perform a normal syntactic search and then to subsequently perform tests on the returned individual components, it would obviously makes more sense to let the user define the test sheets before a search is carried out in order to let the BBB system retrieve matching components automatically. In this case, the desired interface can be extracted directly from the test sheet and there is no need for the user to input a separate syntactic query. The result of such a test-driven search is simply a list of components which have passed the test. Test sheets can therefore also serve as query definitions as well as pure test definitions.

In previous work [14] [9] we have described a Java-based incarnation of a test-driven code search approach designed to support agile development methods such as Extreme Programming (XP). Due to its close relationship to XP, we refer to this approach as Extreme Harvesting. It provides a very natural complement to agile development [4] since the development of tests prior to the functional code is a core tenet of such approaches. Once a JUnit test case describing the desired behavior of a to-be-developed component has been defined, it can be used directly as the input for a test-driven search which may deliver prefabricated components with the required behaviour. This approach is perfectly suited for integration into a future BBB system since test sheets have to be translated into concrete testing code for execution anyway.

While the prototype presented in [9] was rather rudimentary, we have since then been able to improve the system and to seamlessly integrate a plugin for test-driven reuse into the well-known Eclipse IDE. In practice, the most notable feature to users is the automatic determination of the desired component's interface. Consider the above ShoppingCart example for a better understanding of this feature. The corresponding JUnit code would be similar to that shown in the upper part of the following screenshot from the Eclipse Java editor.

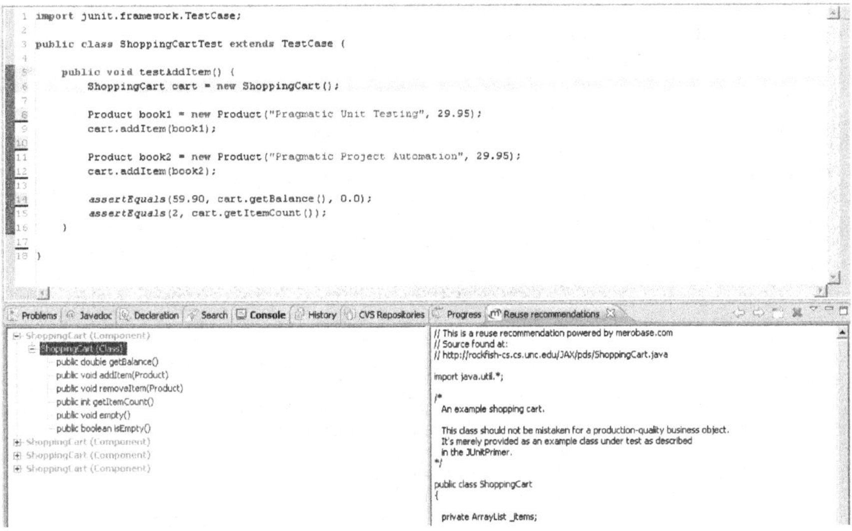

Fig. 2. Screenshot of test-driven reuse plugin in the Eclipse IDE

The lower part of the figure shows how our plugin has been able to extract the interface of the ShoppingCart from the code of the test case and to find appropriate candidates from a collection of about 4 million open source Java files [9] that match this interface syntactically. These were downloaded, compiled and tested in the secure environment of a virtual machine (see next section). The successfully tested candidates are printed in green in the figure. Our system was also able to recognize and retrieve the Product class that is referenced in the interface of the ShoppingCart.

If the test cases are well designed, this approach can deliver very high precision of typically 100% according to our experience so far. This is reinforced by experimental results in [19] where the sampling of functions with randomly created input values delivered 100% precision by the 12th sample at the latest. However, the recall can become rather low since a user has to anticipate the exact interface of a component. Thus, we recently implemented a broader search mode based on the well-known signature matching technique [14] that ignores all method and class names and tests all components having correct parameter signatures. However, this typically results in thousands of candidates and currently requires several hours to complete on a single server. In contrast, the above plugin delivers tested results typically within half a minute. Because of the lack of space we refer to [16] for more details on this topic.

5   Testing Infrastructure

As mentioned above, a major challenge in setting up a BBB service (as well as a test-driven reuse system) is the realization of a suitable testing infrastructure that is capable of testing software components on behalf of potential customers. Our way of dealing with this problem is motivated by the field of server hosting where multiple virtual servers can reside on one physical machine [5]. In our context we refer to them as Virtual Private Servers (VPS) for executing tests. Figure 3 shows our testing service architecture (simplified for illustration purposes).

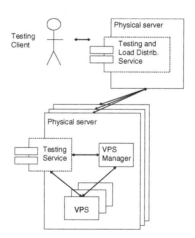

Fig. 3. Testing Service Architecture

Tests are sent to a Testing and Load Distribution Service that in turn distributes the tests to one of a "farm" of physical servers each hosting a number of virtual machines. The Testing and Load Distribution Service does not necessarily have to be on a dedicated physical server. From a software execution environment point of view, all VPSs are like independent servers. The key feature of such a server is that software executing within a given VPS can have no effect on any other VPS, since each can only use a predefined amount of shared physical resources such as CPU or memory. If a component under test causes any kind of damage, this damage will be limited to the VPS in which it is running.

The number of tests to be executed increases with the number of brokered components as well as with the number of users, thus both scalability and resource economy are required. As the dynamic creation of VPS instances is usually expensive in comparison to executing a test, a given VPS might execute more than one test concurrently. An important part of the system is thus the VPS manager. The main role of this manager is to monitor the state of VPS instances and to take appropriate action when a problem is detected. Examples of problems are deadlock and livelock or crashed components. The response to these situations is to restart the tests that were running after a suitable timeout has occurred or if necessary to restart the whole VPS instance.

The number of VPS instances must be optimized to provide the best balance between performance and robustness according to the following tradeoff. The higher the number of VPS instances, the greater the robustness (because a VPS crash will impact a smaller number of simultaneously running tests) but the lower the performance (because of the overhead associated with each VPS instance).

Another important job of the VPS manager is to keep a log of the progress of each of the tests carried out by each VPS. This is necessary in order to try to identify the components that lead to problems and to identify which tests need to be re-executed if a VPS fails due to the misbehavior of a component. Rogue components might be placed on a "black list" so that they are blocked from future tests and no longer block resources that could be used for other tests.

As Figure 3 illustrates, scalability can be realized on two levels. One level is the number of VPSs and the allocation of resources to each VPS on one physical test server. The creation of one VPS is usually much more expensive than the performance of a test, but it is still reasonably efficient to create VPSs dynamically if the number of tests per VPS increases and the physical test server still has free resources. The other level of scalability is the number of physical test servers, controlled by the Testing and Load Distribution Service.

6 Conclusion

The purpose of markets, in whatever domain, is to allow producers and consumers to come together and attempt to forge mutually beneficial trading relationships. This has always depended on producers being given the ability to showcase and advertise their "wares" and consumers being given the ability to fully evaluate these "wares" to assess their suitability. However, these basic mechanisms have never been fully supported in the context of third-party software reuse. The realization of these features in practical component repositories has to date been hampered by two main problems. The first is the lack of a simple testing interface that allows users to describe the functionality they need in a concise yet complete way and enables test results to be shielded from components when appropriate (so called blind testing). The second is the lack of a testing and search infrastructure with sufficient power, flexibility and robustness to provide the needed testing services to a large number of simultaneous users.

The solution to the first problem, presented in section 3, relies on a new testing metaphor, known as test sheets, that combines the power of program-oriented testing approaches such as JUnit, the simplicity of tabular testing approaches such as Fit, and the ubiquity of the spreadsheet metaphor exemplified by office applications such as Microsoft Excel. Using such a spreadsheet metaphor for designing tests not only lends itself to the definition of blind tests and semantic searches, it also supports the show-casing and exploratory discovery of component behaviour.

The solution to the second problem, presented in sections 4 and 5, is to use a large component collection combined with a test-driven reuse approach and a scalable architecture composed of multiple Virtual Private Servers (VPSs) that are controlled by a central test and load distribution service. Executing individual tests within the confines of a single VPS not only allows the testing load to be distributed evenly, even over multiple physical servers, but also limits the potential damage that can be caused by rogue component. It also allows the processing capacity of the infrastructure to be incrementally extended by adding new physical servers with a new suite of VPSs whenever new capacity is needed.

In combination, we believe that these capabilities change the economics of component reuse and shift the balance of the perennial "build or buy" dilemma towards the "buy" option. We therefore believe that this technology will enhance the chances of establishing viable component markets and thus boost industry's ability to deploy advanced software solutions in a rapid and cost effective way. In order to validate these claims we are currently building a prototype black box broker that supports the described technology. Our aim is to make the described facilities publicly available online and to establish user acceptance through controlled experiments and study groups.

References

1. McIlroy, D.: Mass-Produced Software Components. In: Software Engineering: Report of a Conference sponsored by the NATO Science Committee, Garmisch, Germany (1969)
2. Hummel, O., Atkinson, C.: Extreme Harvesting: Test Driven Discovery and Reuse of Software Components. In: Proceedings of the International Conference on Information Reuse and Integration (IEEE-IRI), Las Vegas, USA (2004)
3. Frakes, W.B., Fox, C.J.: Sixteen Questions about Software Reuse. Communications of the ACM 38(6) (1995)
4. Beck, K.: Extreme Programming Explained: Embrace Change. Addison-Wesley, Reading (1999)
5. SWSoft, Virtuozzo Server Virtualization (visited 09/2007), http://www.swsoft.com/en/products/virtuozzo/
6. Szyperski, C.: Component Software: Beyond Object-Oriented Programming, 2nd edn. Addison-Wesley, Reading (2002)
7. Mili, A., Mili, R., Mittermeir, R.: A Survey of Software Reuse Libraries. Annals of Software Engineering 5 (1998)
8. Ravichandran, T., Rothenberger, A.: Software reuse strategies and component markets. Communications of the ACM 46(8), 109–114 (2003)
9. Hummel, O., Atkinson, C.: Using the Web as a Reuse Repository. In: Proceedings of the International Conference on Software Reuse (ICSR-9), Torino, Italy (2006)
10. Mugridge, R., Cunningham, W.: Fit for Developing Software: Framework for Integrated Tests. Prentice-Hall, Englewood Cliffs (2005)

11. Tsai, W.T., Paul, R., Cao, Z., Yu, L., Saimi, A., Xiao, B.: Verification of Web Services Using an Enhanced UDDI Server. In: Proceedings of the International Workshop on Object-Oriented Real-Time Dependable Systems (2003)
12. Cockburn, A.: Agile Software Development. Addison-Wesley, Reading (2001)
13. Hummel, O., Atkinson, C.: Supporting Agile Reuse Through Extreme Harvesting. In: Concas, G., Damiani, E., Scotto, M., Succi, G. (eds.) XP 2007. LNCS, vol. 4536, Springer, Heidelberg (2007)
14. Zaremski, A.M., Wing, J.M.: Signature Matching: A Tool for Using Software Libraries. ACM Transact. on Software Engineering and Methodology 4(2) (1995)
15. Gamma, E., Helm, R., Johnson, R., Vlissides, J.: Design Patterns: Elements of Reusable Object-Oriented Software. Addison-Wesley, Reading (1995)
16. Hummel, O.: Semantic Component Retrieval in Software Engineering, PhD Dissertation, University of Mannheim, Germany (to appear, 2008)
17. Hummel, O., Bostan, P., Atkinson, C.: Towards the Automated Selling of Web Services over the Internet. In: Proceedings of the International Workshop for Technology, Economy, Social and Legal Aspects of Virtual Goods, Leeds, UK (2006)
18. Newcomer, E.: Understanding Web Services, XML, WSDL, SOAP and UDDI. Addison-Wesley, Reading (2002)
19. Podgurski, A., Pierce, L.: Retrieving Reusable Software by Sampling Behavior. ACM Transactions on Software Engineering and Methodology 2(3) (1993)

Recommending Typical Usage Examples for Component Retrieval in Reuse Repositories

Yan Li, Liangjie Zhang, Ge Li*, Bing Xie, and Jiasu Sun

Software Institution, School of Electronics Engineering and Computer Science,
Peking University, Beijing 100871, P.R. China
Key Laboratory of High Confidence Software Technologies, Ministry of Education,
Beijing 100871, P.R. China
{liyan,zhanglj06,lige,xiebing,sjs}@sei.pku.edu.cn

Abstract. Programmers tend to reuse existing components to reduce development cost as well as improve productivity. While retrieving components from the reuse repository, developers often need to know how the components are used in different ways in order to judge which one is more appropriate. An efficient way guiding developers to know how the components are utilized is by leveraging the example code. However, usually the examples provided in handbooks and online documents are not adequate enough. To address this problem, we propose an approach recommending typical usage examples to developers by leveraging source code acquired from the Internet. For each component developers want to utilize, our method first retrieves relevant code downloaded from the Internet as candidate examples. The candidate examples are then clustered and we choose a typical one from each cluster. Finally, the selected ones are ranked and returned to the developers. We implemented our method with a prototype system and conducted an experimental study to evaluate its effectiveness. The experimental results demonstrate that our approach can provide examples to help developers know different usages of the component and thus has the potential to assist developers in reuse.

1 Introduction

Reusing existing components can help developers create applications with less effort and improved quality. In order to achieve the benefits of reuse, developers need to find proper components from the reuse repository. In a reuse-based development process, developers first think out a reuse plan and then make queries for components according to the plan [1]. Queries submitted by the developers are matched against each component using the retrieval mechanism in the repository. The developers then browse the returned components to identify the appropriate ones according to the reuse plan. Finally, developers make adaptation on the components identified appropriate and integrate them together [1].

Identifying proper components from the retrieval results can be quite important for the success of software reuse [2]. Inappropriate components can waste developers a

---

* Corresponding author.

H. Mei (Ed.): ICSR 2008, LNCS 5030, pp. 76–87, 2008.

lot of time and efforts in the following adaptation and integration; and the situation may exacerbate when components are not cost-free. Currently, in many real-world reuse repositories, such as Source Forge [3] and Component Source [4]; developers identify whether a component is appropriate for the reuse plan by viewing its description text. However, sometimes the description text may not be clear and accurate enough to help the developers know which components are more appropriate in the following adaptation and integration. To assist developers in the identifying, reuse repositories should help them know how the components are used [5].

Using example code can be an efficient way guiding developers to know how a component is utilized. Therefore, reuse repositories can help developers by providing proper example code of the component. In the literature, researchers have already proposed several related work on providing example code to developers, which can be useful for reuse repositories. Holmes and Murphy proposed an approach to recommend developers with source code examples by using the structural context information [6]. Their work monitors the code that the developer is writing and locates relevant code in an example repository based on heuristically matching the code structure information. However, the examples provided by their work mainly concentrate on helping developers deal with problems in the software implementation phase. Further, at the moment of selecting components to start a reuse plan, it is common practice that developers do not have the exact structural context information yet, which limits the application of their method in reuse repositories.

Google is another way that can be employed by reuse repositories to get the example code for components. Currently, Google provides code search which can help users search publicly accessible source code hosted on the Internet [7]. However, Google's work mainly aims to help developers locate relevant code according to the text similarity. While employing Google to acquire typical usage examples for a component, it does not distinguish the usages of the component among examples and may bring developers a lot of redundant results.

To help developers save efforts in the adaptation and integration, reuse repositories should provide code examples to help developers know as many typical usages of a component as possible. If developers can know different usages of the components, they can pick the most appropriate components and carry out the reuse plan with a low operational cost. Therefore, the possibility of reuse success can be increased.

In this paper, we propose an approach to provide developers with examples that can help them know different usages of a component. To get the examples, our approach harvests source code from the Internet and then stores it in a code repository. For each component that the developers tend to reuse, our approach firstly finds relevant code acquired from the Internet as candidate examples. Then, our method clusters the candidates and selects typical ones from each cluster. Finally, the selected examples are ranked according to certain heuristic rules and presented to developers. We implemented a reuse assistant tool based on our method and evaluated its effectiveness in an experimental study. The results show that the example code acquired by our method can help developers know different usages of the components and thus hold the potential to promote software reuse.

The paper is organized as followings. In section 2, we will explain our method in detail. Section 3 gives the experimental study we carried out and makes an analysis on the results. Section 4 provides the related work. Discussion and future work are presented in section 5. In the last section, we conclude this paper.

2 Our Approach

Our method mainly takes three steps to provide code examples to help developers know different typical usages of a component, as shown in figure 1. Firstly, the code retriever selects candidates from the code downloaded from the Internet. Secondly, the code analyzer clusters the candidates and selects a typical one as example from each cluster. The clustering is based on the operation invocation frequency as well as the comment information. Thirdly, the result ranking mechanism ranks the examples and returns the result list.

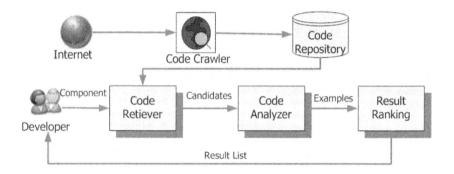

Fig. 1. The main process of our approach

2.1 Code Retriever

The first problem needed to deal with is how to get relevant code for the components. Despite examples are useful for developers, often the examples provided in the handbooks and online documents are not sufficient enough [8]. Meanwhile, with the development of Internet technology, more and more source code information is available on the web. Hummel and Atkinson investigated the number and categories of information resources on the Internet and found out a wealth of source code could be obtained [9].

In the vast amount of source code, we believe that many examples showing how to use the components in different ways have already been well developed. By leveraging these adequate source code resources on the Internet, we may acquire examples showing different usages for developers.

A benefit that can be achieved by leveraging source code on the Internet is that the process of getting relevant code can be highly automated with a relatively low operational cost. Another advantage of utilizing source code on the Internet lies in that we can acquire examples for components in all different application areas. Besides, by downloading code from the Internet periodically, examples can be up-to-date with the components.

We can acquire the code efficiently by using a crawler application. The crawler application mainly focuses on these open source projects which provide public access to their source code. The downloaded source code is stored in a code repository for further process.

Whenever the developer needs code examples for a particular component, our approach retrieves relevant source code in the code repository. In our approach, the retrieval is done at the class level. Any class that makes invocation on the component will be returned as candidates.

2.2 Code Analyzer

Due to the vast amount of source code downloaded, the number of candidates returned is usually quite large. Besides, many of them display duplicate usages of the component. To alleviate the developers' cognitive burden in understanding the examples, we need to select the typical examples from the candidates and remove the redundant ones. In order to achieve this goal, we cluster the candidates into different categories based on the usage of the component. By the clustering, we can remove code with duplicate usages and select the typical usage examples of the component.

To distinguish candidates with different usages of the component, we should find out which features can represent the usage. Then we can employ these features to calculate the similarity between any two candidates and cluster candidates into different categories. In our approach, the clustering is carried out according to the invocation frequency on different operations of the component as well as the comment information embedded in the source code of candidates.

Developers will make invocations on different operations of the component based on the reuse task. So, if two developers are carrying out the same task using the component, they are likely to invoke the same operation set. In the contrast, different usages of the component can often lead to distinct operation invocation frequencies. So, we believe that the invocation frequency on different operations can reflect the usage of the component to a certain extent.

Our approach makes a statistical analysis on the frequency of which operations are called in a candidate example. The operation invocation information for candidate j is represented in a vector $VO_j=<m_{1j}, m_{2j}, ..., m_{nj}>$. Here n is the total number of operations that the component holds. The element m_{ij} denotes the times that operation i is called by candidate example j.

To calculate the similarity between two candidates x and y on the operation invocation information $sim_{op}(x,y)$, we use the cosine value of the angle that the two vectors form. This value will fall in the range [-1, 1]. A cosine value of 1 denotes two vectors are identical whereas -1 indicates no similarity at all.

$$sim_{op}(x, y) = \cos(VO_x, VO_y)$$ (1)

The source code downloaded from the Internet often contains a certain amount of comment information. The comment information usually explains the purpose of the code. Thus, comment information can also be useful for distinguishing candidates with different usages.

Our approach parses the candidates and extracts the comment information embedded in the source code. Then we organize the comment information extracted using the vector space model after the process of stop words removing and stemming [10].

The comment information of candidate j is also represented in a vector $VC_j=<w_{1j}, w_{2j}, ..., w_{mj}>$, where m is the total number of distinct words in all comments. In the vector, element w_{ij} stands for the relative weight of the word i and is calculated as the frequency of word i appears in the comment of candidate j. Then, we figure out the similarity between two candidates from the comment information aspect. The computation is also carried out according to the cosine value of the two vectors formed by comment, as shown in formula 2.

$$sim_{co}(x, y) = \cos(VC_x, VC_y) \tag{2}$$

We then combine the two kinds of similarity together using a linear method which is easy to understand and implement. So, the overall similarity between two candidates x and y is carried out according to formula 3.

$$sim(x, y) = \alpha sim_{op}(x, y) + (1 - \alpha)sim_{co}(x, y) \tag{3}$$

Here the parameter α is assigned to a value between 0 and 1 to balance the weight between the two kinds of information resources. To one extreme, if we set α to 1, only the operation invocation frequency is applied. To another extreme, just the comment information is taken into consideration if α is assigned 0.

INPUT: The vectors of all candidates

OUTPUT: The clustering result

Step 1: Treat each candidate as an individual cluster;

Step 2: **REPEAT**

    Choose the two most similar clusters x and y;

      IF for any element m in x and any element n in y, $sim(m,n)$>threshold

        Merge x and y into one cluster;

    UNTIL the two most similar clusters can not be merged

Step 3: Return the remaining clusters;

Fig. 2. The algorithm for code clustering

Based on the criterion for calculating the similarity between two candidates, we can group the candidate examples into different categories by clustering. As the candidate examples involved can be many, the algorithm should be able to finish the clustering with high efficiency. We design a hierarchical clustering algorithm as depicted in figure 2. The key idea of this algorithm is to keep merging candidate examples similar enough until there are none.

After clustering, our approach chooses one example from each group. We consider that the candidate which has the maximum sum of similarity to others in the same group can represent this group better and should be selected as the example. We can explain the selection criterion in a more formal way here. Let G be a group formed by clustering, the candidate x is selected from G if it can satisfy the conditions list in formula 4.

$$x \in G \wedge \forall y \in G, \sum_{z \in G} sim(z, y) \le \sum_{z \in G} sim(z, x) \tag{4}$$

Since the example is selected to delegate the whole group, all other candidates in the group can be seen as duplicates and are eliminated in the result list.

2.3 Ranking Strategy

After clustering the candidates and selecting the typical ones from each cluster, we get examples with different usages, which can give developers hints about whether the component is suitable for the reuse plan. Still, we need to rank the examples selected from clusters properly because developers tend to view only the top part of the result list [11]. Furthermore, proper ranking can make developers know how the component is used with less effort. In our approach, we carry out the ranking by using the following criteria.

The first criterion defines that examples from larger clusters will get higher ranks. The rationale here lies in that if the cluster that the example belongs to owns a lot of candidates, the example can represent a usage of the component with high frequency. So the example can stand for a more typical usage of the component and is important for developers to know in reuse. Therefore, examples from larger clusters should be ranked higher.

The second criterion is that the more comments the example has, the higher rank should be given. This criterion is based on the observation that the comments contained in the example can give an introduction of the purpose of the source code. Developers can understand the examples with less effort if sufficient comments are given for explanation. So the examples with rich comment information are preferred in our ranking.

The third criterion is that the examples in small size will be rank higher. As stated previously, the developers need to understand the examples and then decide whether the component is appropriate. If the cognitive burden for understanding examples becomes too much, developers may tend to give up reuse. Smaller examples can be easier for developers to understand and thus has the potential to promote reuse. Consequently, we prefer examples with smaller size while ranking.

3 Experimental Study

3.1 Experimental Organization

To evaluate whether our method can help developers know different usages of a component, we implemented a prototype system and conducted an experimental study on the open source project Apache Lucene [12], which is a text search engine library written entirely in Java.

In our experiment, each class or interface in the Apache Lucene was viewed as a component. We selected 14 classes from the Apache Lucene and got example code by using our prototype. These 14 classes were chosen because they implemented basic functions of the Apache Lucene and were essential for developers to utilize it. In the experiment, the parameter α in formula 3 was set to 0.7 according to our observation of the data.

We compared our method with the Google code search [7]. To get example code from the Google code search, we used the class name with the keyword 'Lucene' as the query.

3.2 Experimental Results

We firstly compared the number of the results developers needed to browse by using the two methods if they got to know the same number of usages for a class. Since Google usually returned more results, our method was used as the base line in this comparison. For example, if the result list from our method contains 3 different usages of a class, we will calculate how many results the users have to view in Google's result list in order to know 3 different usages. If the method can help developers know various usages of the component more quickly, then the length of results needed to view is shorter.

The results are list in table 1. From the table, we can see that in most cases, to know the same number of usages, the number of results needed to view by using the Google code search is larger. The only exception happened on the class 'QueryParser' because there was only one usage for it. Based on these results, we can conclude that our method can distinguish examples with different usages better and help developers know how the component can be used in different ways within a shorter result list. So, our approach can increase the possibility of reuse success to a certain extent.

Table 1. The comparison on number of results needed to view

Class Name	Results needed to view		Class Name	Results needed to view	
	Ours	Google		Ours	Google
BooleanQuery	6	19	QueryParser	3	1
Document	9	29	Scorer	5	52
Field	4	35	Sort	2	6
Hits	5	72	SortField	7	16
IndexReader	10	51	StandardAnalyzer	24	29
IndexSearcher	9	10	Term	4	12
IndexWriter	4	8	TermQuery	2	9

In real-world scenarios, developers only have the time and patience to browse the top results. Therefore, we also compared the number of distinct usages appeared in the top results. Only the top ten examples for each result list were considered in this round of comparison if the size of result list exceeded 10.

Table 2 shows the experimental results. The last two columns show the number of usages for each class in the top 10 results. We also give the actual length of each result list for this comparison in the bracket. For instance, the 'BooleanQuery' class held total 6 results by using our approach and 3 different usages were involved. From table 2, we can find out that our method demonstrates more usages than the Google code search for 8 out of 14 classes. For the other 6 classes, our method displays as many usages as Google. However, by inspecting the length of the result list for these 6 classes, we notice that our method usually gets a list shorter than Google's, which means our method can make developers browse fewer results and reduce their cognitive efforts in identifying appropriate components.

Table 2. The comparison on number of distinct usages in top results

Class Name	Number of usages	
	Our method	Google
BooleanQuery	3(6)	2(10)
Document	3(9)	1(10)
Field	4(4)	3(10)
Hits	3(5)	2(10)
IndexReader	6(10)	3(10)
IndexSearcher	4(9)	4(10)
IndexWriter	3(4)	3(10)
QueryParser	1(3)	1(10)
Scorer	5(5)	4(10)
Sort	2(2)	2(10)
SortField	5(7)	4(10)
StandardAnalyzer	1(10)	1(10)
Term	3(4)	2(10)
TermQuery	2(2)	2(10)

Compared with the Google code search, our approach displays more usages in the top results and reduces the number of results needed to browse for most classes in the experimental study. So, we can conclude that our approach can better help developers know different usages of the components and thus facilitate the judgment about which component in the retrieval results is more appropriate.

4   Related Work

Helping developers acquire appropriate components is essential for successful software reuse. In the literature, researchers have proposed many different approaches to facilitate component retrieval [13][14], including 1) free-text based approaches [15], 2) facet based approaches [16], 3) signature based approaches [17] and 4) behavior based approaches [18]. Most research work only concentrates on improving the retrieval performance; whereas they do not pay attention to helping developers know which component returned in the result list is more appropriate by examples.

Suggesting relevant code examples is an efficient way to help developers know how a component is used. Strathcona is an Eclipse plugin developed by Holmes and Murphy which recommends developers relevant code from an example repository [6]. Strathcona monitors the code under development and locates relevant example code based on six structure-based heuristics. Hill and Rideout propose the automatic method completion technique which helps a developer to complete a method body by machine learning techniques [19]. The method to be completed is represented in a multi-dimensional vector then compared with vectors for the examples. The example with best matching is returned as result.

Different from their work which provides developers with examples under a specific context; in this paper our method focuses on presenting different typical usage examples of components in order to help developers identify which one is proper for reuse. Based on the example code we suggest, developers can select appropriate components and carry out their reuse plan easily. Further, both of the above two research efforts require developers to provide proper seed code to get useful results. However, developers often can not give such seed code at the moment of selecting components.

Mandelin et al. proposed an approach called Jungloid mining which can help developers synthesize code fragment they need [20]. Given the desired code in terms of an input type T_{in} and an output type T_{out}, their work synthesizes code snippets that takes an object of T_{in} and returns an object of T_{out}. The solution is generated based on the API signatures and a corpus of client programs.

XSnippet presented by Sahavechaphan and Claypool assists developers by providing code examples about the object instantiation task at hand [8]. XSnippet supports a range of queries and utilizes a graph-based code mining algorithm to get relevant code.

Both Jungloid mining and XSnippet focus on solving a particular kind of query about how to utilize a component. However, while trying to identify the appropriate components by code examples, developers may not have the ability to express his/her needs exactly in the form of query that can be accepted.

The RVM (Reuse View Matcher) can describe how an application makes use of a particular class in a framework from different views [21]. However, the RVM relies on hand-crafted examples developed by experts which can be time-consuming and may not have the ability to cover all the classes in the system.

There are also several pieces of work trying to promote reuse by making use of the information resources on the Internet. Seacord et al. designed a component search engine Agora [22]. Agora collects different categories of components from the Internet by using different agents and then indexes the components by an introspection process. Woogle is a web services search engine which acquires WSDL files from several service publication sites [23]. Woogle supports similarity search by clustering parameter names of operations into meaningful concepts. Google code search is a search engine specialized for source code [7]. Despite these research efforts also make use of information resources on the Internet, they do not pay attention to help developers identify proper components by providing typical usage examples.

5   Discussion and Future Work

5.1   Issues about Code Clustering

In our approach, we employ both the operation invocation frequency and the embedded comment to cluster the candidate examples. A parameter is used to balance the weight between the two kinds of information resources. In our experimental study, we set the parameter manually by inspecting the information available in the two kinds of information. In future, we will conduct more experiments in larger scale to discover rules about how to automatically determine the relative weight between the operation invocation frequency and the comment information.

In our approach, the order of operation invocation is not taken into consideration in the clustering. For instance, suppose the component holds two operations A and B, the operation invocation sequence 'A,B' and 'B,A' will be considered as the same usage in our approach. However, sometimes the information resided in the order of the invocation sequence can also be helpful for developers. Different invocation orders of operations may indicate distinct usages of the component. Thus, we will testify whether our approach can achieve better performance by taking the order of operation invocation into account. Further, we also try to find out other useful features for the example clustering.

5.2 The Inter-component Example

In our approach, we provide code examples about how a component is used in different ways to help developers. However, sometimes developers also need examples about how to cooperate several components together as to judge which component is more appropriate. For example, in a typical JDBC application, in order to execute a SQL statement in database, developers have to create an instance of 'java.sql.connection' class first which holds the database connection, and then use this object to create the instance of SQL statement to be executed. To address this kind of problems, we plan to extend our method to provide examples across component boundaries in the future.

5.3 Example Filtering Mechanism

In our approach, we provide developers with examples that display how a certain component is used in different ways. However, in certain scenarios, the reuse task at hand may have already formed several restrictions to the developers. Only examples that satisfy these restrictions can be helpful for developers. Hence, developers may have to filter code examples according to the task. Also, developers with different knowledge background may have distinct opinions about which examples are more helpful. We believe the personalized filtering and ranking service can enhance the effectiveness of our approach if provided. Therefore, setting up an efficient and convenient example filtering mechanism to facilitate developers is also required in our future work.

6 Conclusion

Learning by code examples is an efficient way for developers to know how components are used. While identifying proper components from the reuse repository, developers often need code examples to depict various typical usages of the components. However, the examples provided in the handbooks and online documents usually are not sufficient enough.

To address this problem, we propose an approach which recommends typical usage examples to developers by leveraging the source code from the Internet. To depict how a component is used in different ways, our approach firstly retrieves relevant code harvested from Internet as candidates, and then groups these candidates into different categories. In each category, a candidate is selected as an example. Finally, the examples are ranked according to several heuristic rules and returned to developers. We carried out an experimental study on the open source project Apache Lucene to evaluate our approach. Through the evaluation, our approach demonstrated the effectiveness in helping developers know different usages of the component.

Acknowledgement

We would like to thank Dr. Lu Zhang for his valuable contribution to this paper. This research was sponsored by the National Grand Fundamental Research 973 Program (SN: 2005CB321805), the State 863 High-Tech Program (SN: 2006AA01Z189), the National Key Technology R&D Program (No.2006BAH02A02) in China.

References

1. Mili, H., Mili, A., Yacoub, S., Addy, E.: Reuse-based software engineering: techniques, organization, and controls. Wiley-Interscience Press, Chichester (2001)
2. Mili, H., Mili, F., Mili, A.: Reusing software: issues and research directions. IEEE Transaction on Software Engineering 21(6), 528–562 (1995)
3. SourceForge (2007), http://sourceforge.net/
4. ComponentSource (2007), http://www.componentsource.com/
5. Ye, Y., Fischer, G.: Supporting reuse by delivering task-relevant and personalized information. In: Proceedings of the 24th International Conference on Software Engineering, pp. 513–523 (2002)
6. Holmes, R., Murphy, G.: Using structural context to recommend source code examples. In: Proceedings of the 27th International Conference on Software Engineering, pp. 117–125 (2005)
7. Google Code Search (2007), http://www.google.cn/codesearch/
8. Sahavechaphan, N., Claypool, K.: XSnippet: Mining for sample code. In: Proceedings of the 21st ACM SIGPLAN conference on Object-Oriented Programming Systems, Languages, and Applications (OOPSLA), pp. 413–430 (2006)
9. Hummel, O., Atkinson, C.: Using the web as a reuse repository. In: Proceedings of the 9th International Conference on Software Reuse, pp. 298–311 (2006)
10. Baeza-Yates, R., Ribeiro-Neto, B.: Modern information retrieval. Addison-Wesley/ACM Press (1999)
11. Drori, O.: Algorithm for documents ranking: Idea and simulation results. In: Proceedings of the 14th International Conference on Software Engineering and Knowledge Engineering, pp. 99–102 (2002)
12. Apache Lucene (2007), http://lucene.apache.org/java/docs/index.html
13. Mili, R., Mili, A., Mittermeir, R.T.: A survey of software storage and retrieval. Annual of Software Engineering 5(2), 349–414 (1998)
14. Frakes, W., Pole, T.: An empirical study of representation methods for reuseable software components. IEEE Transaction on Software Engineering 20(8), 617–630 (1994)
15. Maarek, Y., Berry, D., Kaiser, G.: An information retrieval approach for automatically constructing software libraries. IEEE Transactions on Software Engineering 17(8), 800–813 (1991)

16. Prieto-Diaz, R., Freeman, P.: Classifying software for reuse. IEEE Software 4(1), 6–16 (1987)
17. Zaremski, A., Wing, J.M.: Specification matching of software components. ACM Transactions on Software Engineering and Methodology 6(4), 333–369 (1997)
18. Podgurski, A., Pierce, L.: Retrieving reusable software by sampling behavior. ACM Transactions on Software Engineering and Methodology 2(3), 286–303 (1993)
19. Hill, R., Rideout, J.: Automatic method completion. In: Proceedings of the 19th International Conference on Automated Software Engineering, pp. 228–235 (2004)
20. Mandelin, D., Xu, L., Bodk, R., Kimelman, D.: Jungloid mining: helping to navigate the API jungle. In: Proceedings of the 2005 ACM Conference on Programming Language Design and Implementation (PLDI), pp. 48–61 (2005)
21. Rosson, M.B., Carroll, J.M.: The reuse of uses in Smalltalk programming. ACM Transactions on Computer-Human Interaction 3(3), 219–253 (1996)
22. Seacord, R., Hissam, S., Wallnau, K.: AGORA: A search engine for software components. IEEE Internet Computing 2(6), 62–70 (1998)
23. Dong, X., Halevy, A., Madhavan, J., Nemes, E., Zhang, J.: Similarity search for web services. In: Proceedings of the 30th Very Large Data Bases (VLDB) Conference, pp. 372–383 (2004)

A Reuse Repository System: From Specification to Deployment

Vanilson Arruda Burégio[1], Eduardo Santana de Almeida[1], Daniel Ludrédio[2], and Silvio Lemos Meira[1]

[1] Federal University of Pernambuco (CIn-UFPE and C.E.S.A.R.), Recife, Brazil
{vaab,esa2}@cin.ufpe.br, silvio@cesar.org.br
[2] University of São Paulo (ICMC-USP), São Paulo, Brazil
lucredio@icmc.usp.br

Abstract. A repository is a necessary prerequisite to support software engineers and other users in the process of developing software with and for reuse. In the literature, there are several works that explore reuse repositories, however their focus is mostly on reusable component search and retrieval issues, while important aspects of reuse repositories have not been properly explored. On the other hand, some questions raised by companies that desire to adopt or build a reuse repository remain unanswered. Such questions often include: What are the main roles and requirements of a reuse repository? What are the practical alternatives? How a reuse repository must be designed? Motivated by these questions, this paper presents a systematic approach with comparisons to existing tools and techniques for specifying, designing and implementing a reuse repository that was successfully constructed and deployed in real Brazilian software factories. Additionally, we describe the main design decisions, problems found, and future directions for research and development.

1 Introduction

Reuse is not just a simple development technique and the success of software reuse programs depends on an effective application of both technical and non-technical aspects [5]. The technical aspects comprise, among other things, the creation of a software reuse repository that supports software engineers and other users in the process of developing software for and with reuse.

However, in practice, repositories are used as mechanisms to store, search and retrieve artifacts, lacking important services, such as supporting enterprise reuse management and component certification process. As a consequence, some existing reuse repositories have failed to deliver its expectations [6]. At the same time, some questions raised by companies that desire to adopt a reuse repository remain unanswered. Such questions often include: What are the main requirements of a reuse repository? What kind of artifacts should be stored? What are the practical alternatives? How a reuse repository must be designed? Under such motivation, this paper extends a previous one [11] and presents the specification, design, implementation and deployment of a reuse repository system based on analysis of practical alternatives and solutions used in academy.

H. Mei (Ed.): ICSR 2008, LNCS 5030, pp. 88–99, 2008.

2 Background

There is an essential requirement of building a reuse repository not only as a component storage mechanism, but also as a tool to support the following roles in an enterprise context [10]: i) *a communication bus among stakeholders,* ii) *a management assistant,* iii) *a reuse promoter* and iv) *a quality assurer.* In practice, different kinds of tools are used by companies as an option to store reusable assets and make them available to software developers [2]. In general, we can divide the practical alternatives into two main types, i.e. general-usage and reuse-specific tools.

- **General-usage tools.** This class comprises general purpose tools and systems commonly used by companies in the development and management of applications. This category includes: *Configuration Management Systems (CMS), Metadata Repositories, Collaborative Systems* and *CASE tool repositories.*
- **Reuse-specific tools.** This type is formed by reuse-specific tools designed with the main goal of promoting software reuse. In this category we have the *code search tools* [4] and the *component asset managers.*

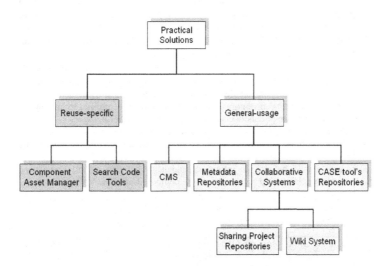

Fig. 1. This summarizes the taxonomy of solutions that can be used, in practice, as reuse repositories

3 Repository Specification

From the analysis of the roles that a repository should perform to support a reuse process and the solutions commonly used in industry and academy, we defined a set of requirements (Table 1) that should be considered when building a reuse repository.

The requirements listed in Table 1 do not represent a final or complete set of functionalities which must be fully present in all reuse-specific repositories, since they depend on the real necessities of each company. However, the identified requirements can serve as a basis for constructing a standard reuse repository to support a systematic reuse process. We have obtained good results in practical experiences involving the development of repositories that implements the set of defined requirements.

Table 1. List of requirements

Requirement	Description
1. Asset Description	The repository must define a generic element (asset) that can represent a reusable software unit of different types. An asset model should include two parts [4]: the asset contents (set of reusable artifacts) and the asset metadata.
2. Insertion	Producers need to make their assets available for consumption and then repositories should allow asset insertion operation.
3. Publish specification	In some cases users should be able to publish only the asset specification (without its implementation/content). This allows developers to register interest in implementing such assets, to be notified when new demands arrive at the repository.
4. Browsing	Each asset should be grouped in different categories and it must be possible for users to browse assets through such categories. According to [2], this function is adequate to find the desirable asset when the repository contains relatively few of them.
5. Search	Repositories with a large number of assets must provide search mechanisms that allow users to find assets that meet their needs [3]. These mechanisms can be a combination of the following search types: Free-text, Keyword, Facet-based classification and semantic.
6. Report generation	The repository should provide services to generate reports that allow, among other things, to get an overview of how the repository is being used.
7. User Notification	Users should be able to register interest in different events with the aim of receiving notification from the repository when, for instance, new assets are added.
8. Maintenance Services	The repository system should implement administrative services that allow the maintenance of the users' inventory and also other inventories utilized by the repository such as asset artifact types, asset classifiers and hierarchies of catalogues.
9. Version Management	The repository should be able to store different versions of its assets, so developers are able to retrieve previous version of an asset and maintain its alternative implementations.
10. Dependency management	Users should be able to inform dependencies between assets. These dependencies represent relationship such as "uses" or "composed-of" relations.
11. Feedback Services	Users should be able to provide feedback about the assets they are using. The feedback services permit the identification of well-evaluated assets and also tracking of assets usage
12. Advertisement of Services	With the aim of promoting the reuse culture across the organization, repositories should offer services that allow the maintenance of reuse-related news, such as reuse initiatives, best assets producers, most reused components and so on.
13. Multiple asset sources	It should be possible to store assets that point to artifacts (asset contents) stored in different kinds of asset sources that exist in the repository deploy context
14. Certification process	The repository should support a certification process which assures the quality of its available assets.
15. Metrics	Users should be able to define, capture and measure reuse-oriented metrics and ROI models. The metrics analysis can indicate a lot of useful things about reuse and can help managers to reduce costs and measure the business impact of reuse [9][12].
16. Access Control	The system should have mechanisms to limit user access to system services and repositories, if multiple repositories are supported. So, it should be possible to define different views among users.
17. Change Control	Users should be able to request and accept changes to assets. Such changes requests also include bug reports.

3.1 Existing Solutions vs. Requirements

The different existing solutions categories presented in Section 2 have different levels of support to the requirements defined in Table 1, as can be seen in Table 2. Such table was constructed based on a comprehensive analysis of 35 tools (5 per category). The meaning of a ●/*blank* is that the requirement is well or not supported by the majority (at least 3 of 5) of analyzed tools in a given category (see [8] for more details about this analysis).

Hence, from Table 2, we can conclude that most of the analyzed solutions do not support effectively all functions listed in Table 1. Under such motivation, we attempted to handle this gap by designing a skeleton for a reuse repository architecture that satisfies the set of requirements defined in Section 3. The next Section shows the details of this architecture.

Table 2. Solutions Analysis

# Require-ments	Reuse-specific		General-usage				
	Asset Managers	Code Search Tools	CMS	Metadata Reposito-ries	Collaborative Systems		CASE Tool's Reposito-ries
					Shared Projects Repositories	Wiki Systems	
1	●				●		
2	●		●	●		●	●
3							
4	●			●	●	●	●
5	●	●		●	●	●	
6	●			●			
7	●						
8	●			●	●		
9			●				
10			●				
11							
12						●	
13		●		●	●		●
14							
15							
16	●		●	●	●	●	●
17			●				

Legend: ● - typically supported; blank: not supported in a comprehensive way

4 Repository Design

A general definition of the reuse repository architecture is presented in this Section. The overall goal is to satisfy the set of requirements defined in Section 3 in a consistent way, providing a unified vision of what the repository looks like and how its internal elements are combined in order to provide users with a standard reuse repository that supports the *produce-manager-consumer process* explained in [1].

Figure 2 summarizes the architecture of the reuse repository decomposed into modules and sub-modules. The main modules of the reuse repository are: (1) *Infrastructure*, (2) *Production*, (3) *Management* and (4) *Consumption*. The following sections describe the details of each module and how its components work in conjunction to provide the necessary functionality.

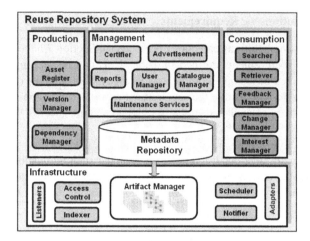

Fig. 2. Repository Architecture Overview

4.1 Infrastructure

This module groups a set of common services which are shared by the other modules. Figure 3 shows how the infrastructure module is internally organized. At the center of the infrastructure module is the *Asset Metadata Repository*. This is where all asset metadata are stored and managed. Another important element of the infrastructure module is the *Artifact Manager*. The *Artifact Manager* represents a repository of asset contents (set of reusable software artifacts). Artifacts can be stored in two ways – logically and physically. The latter means that the artifact is saved locally in the repository system. On the other hand, a logically stored artifact means that the artifact is stored in an external source, such as an internet site or any other reuse repository. In

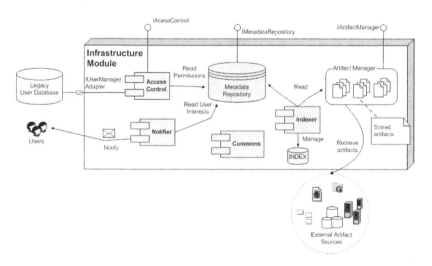

Fig. 3. Infrastructure Module

that case, a reference to an artifact, which allows its retrieval in the future, is saved. In both cases - logically and physically - metadata about the artifacts are stored in the metadata repository. Artifact metadata include things such as artifact description and artifact type (ex.: source code, test report, executable code, design model, user documentation). Once the asset content and its metadata has been updated or inserted, listeners automatically start the indexing phase. During this phase, performed by the Indexer component, the artifacts and metadata of the asset are read from the *Metadata Repository* and the *Artifact Manager*, and then such data is parsed, being actually indexed. The resultant index is used to search the assets in repository.

Another element in the infrastructure module is the *Notifier* component, which is responsible for automatic support to user notification triggered by some system events. Examples of such events are modifications on existing assets, inclusion of new versions, deletions and so on.

Finally the *Access Control* sub-module is responsible for determining and verifying user permissions. This sub-module contains the definition of a generic access control and can interact with an existent base of users. In this case, an implementation of a simple interface (*IUserManagerAdapter*) must be provided.

4.2 Production Module

This module is responsible for services commonly used by assets producers. Such services are provided by the *Asset Register* component. The *Asset Registry* is responsible for the insertion of assets. It treats two types of data: the asset metadata, which must be stored in the *Metadata Repository*; and the asset contents, which represent artifacts to be managed by the *Artifact Manager* component. Beyond that, the *Asset Registry* interacts with two other production elements: *Version* and *Dependency Manager*.

Version Manager: Includes the operations related to asset version management, i.e., create, update or delete a version. In addition, other operations must be supported, such as, view differences between two versions, list the previous and next versions of a specific asset;

Dependency Manager: This component should contain all functionalities that permit asset producers to manage relations among assets, which can be stored or not in the same reuse repository. It must have a flexible classification schema that allows defining different types of relations, such as "is part of", "is a", "use", "is composed of".

Figure 4 shows the production module in details. The dashed arrows represent planned operations that are not implemented in the initial version of the repository. Also, the *Asset Extractor* module, faded in the Figure 4, is not available in the initial set of functionalities. The *Asset Extractor* module accesses the source of information on the various existing legacy artifacts repositories, such as *CVS* and *Subversion*, as well as any other sources of information, such as file systems and databases, and making them available for the indexing and indexed contents retrieval phases. This is done so the actual source of information is decoupled from the reuse repository once its contents are retrieved, eliminating the dependency to the original source and possible communication failures during search execution or content retrieval from end users.

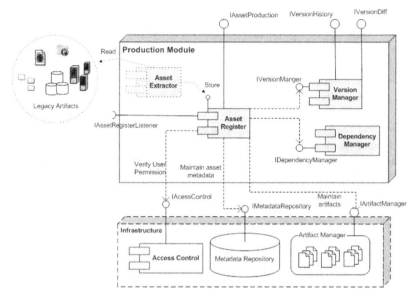

Fig. 4. Production Module

4.3 Management Module

This module is responsible for all services used by repository administrators and asset/component certifiers. Repository administrators represent users responsible for controlling and maintaining the reuse repository. Certifiers are the users responsible for assuring assets quality. The management module can be divided into five other sub-modules as showed in Figure 5:

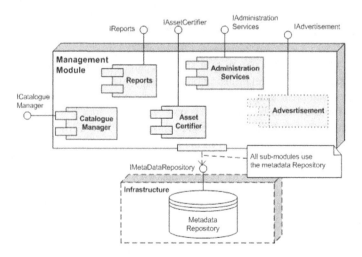

Fig. 5. Management Module

Asset Certifier: It is responsible for implementing the state machine related to the asset certification process used to certify the assets available in repository;

Advertisement: It includes the operations that allow management of public announcements and news;

Reports: Sub-module responsible for generation of all reports that can be used by project and organizational managers;

Administration services: It includes the operations related to maintenance of the general inventories utilized by the repository, such as asset artifact types, asset classifiers, hierarchies of catalogues, organizational groups and so on;

Catalogue Manager: It is responsible for maintaining the catalogue of assets. Such catalogues represent virtual repositories that are associated to a specific organizational group. The virtual repositories can form a hierarchical structure that represents the company's projects, teams or departments.

4.4 Consumption Module

This module is responsible for services used commonly by assets consumers. Such services are grouped into the sub-modules specified in Figure 6.

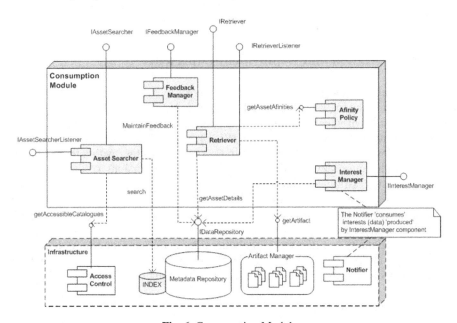

Fig. 6. Consumption Module

Asset Searcher: It is responsible for searching and browsing assets stored in the repository. The search service uses indexes provided by Indexer element - located in infrastructure module - and the browse service utilizes hierarchies of catalogues - maintained by the Catalogue Manager of the Management module. It is possible to configure what service (search, browsing or both) the repository should support. This flexibility is useful, because the repository can be adapted according to the quantity of stored assets (for example, browsing is adequate to repositories that contain relatively few assets [2]).

Feedback Manager: It includes the operations related to maintenance of consumers' impressions (feedbacks) about the assets used by them. The set of user feedbacks serves as an asset usage history, and can reveal the degree of acceptance and efficiency that an asset has achieved. Hence, each feedback should record author, creation date, context in which the asset has been used, the result of the usage and other things that provide information about the effort required to use the asset.

Retriever: This sub-module is responsible for implementing services that allow the asset retrieval, i.e., the retrieval of artifacts that compose asset content. With the aim of retrieving artifacts from multiple sources, this module interacts with the *Artifact Manager* component. During the retrieving phase the repository calculates a list of affinity assets thought the *Affinity Policy* component. Such list represents a suggestion of a set of assets related to the asset selected by the user;

Interest Manager: this sub-module allows users to configure their interests in receiving notifications from the repository. Such interests range from interest in a specific asset to more general interest in a domain of components.

5   Implementation and Deployment Experience

In order to validate and refine our proposed repository we developed a solution in conjunction with the industry. We have been engaged in two industrial reuse projects which focus on environments and tools to support a reuse process. These projects are part of the Reuse in Software Engineering (RiSE) project [5].

Our first developed product was a web-based asset repository with a three-tier client-server architecture developed in Java. Two released versions of the repository system were successfully implanted in a large Brazilian software factory and about 2.500 developers have direct access to the corporate repository. The first version of repository implementation contained 423 classes, divided into 83 packages, with 19.367 lines of code (not counting comments).

The next Sections describe the initially provided reuse repository search components and the integrations with existing development tools. Design decisions and the internal details of the components are presented in the remainder of this Section.

5.1   Outline Implementation

The main goal of the initial implementation was to provide a strong foundation with core components, where new components may be incrementally incorporated, improving the overall performance of the repository.

Search components. The basic search functionality of the solution is provided by two core components: (1) *Searcher* and (2) *Indexer*. The indexer and the searcher components use the *Lucene* [7] class library. The searcher component is responsible for formulating and executing queries. The search result ranking is performed on top of Lucene's default relevance function by the ranking element that reads data from an internal tracer component to prioritize more widely used assets. The proposed model also contemplates a search result filtering mechanism based on an access control policy.

Integrations. The reuse repository must integrate with existing development and general usage tools in order to transparently provide developers and managers with an integrated environment that maximizes the reuse activity throughout the organization. The core implementation provides an extensible framework that supports integrations with a small effort from the solution side. The actual effort depends on the tool being integrated. The initial integration includes an *Eclipse* plug-in that is provided to invoke the searcher component and present the search results in its editor window.

5.2 Design Decisions

This Section analyses the main issues and problems raised during the implementation and deployment of the first repository system versions. This analysis has the aim of clarifying some of our decisions and helping others who desire to construct a reuse repository. The main issues are grouped as follows:

Asset Model. The first question was to decide what asset model should be considered in the repository. Hence, we performed a comparative study between some component and content specification models, and then we decided to adopt a RAS (Reusable Asset Specification) compatible asset model , mainly because the RAS model is more focused on the content type (asset) which we desire to store in a reuse repository and has became the most accepted standard in industry.

Access Control. Our implemented repository has a role-based access control with four user roles: consumer, producer, administrator and certifier. Each of them is associated to a set of system functionalities which are filtered when a user logs on the system. However, this approach alone was not enough to support the security needs of the company where the repository was deployed. The company was a software factory which had the necessity to limit the scope of access to group of assets, because there are several development teams that should not be able to access some assets owned by other internal teams. Moreover, there is a necessity to interact with outsourced development teams, which should not have access to some private assets.

Such problem was resolved through the definition of virtual repositories associated to a specific organizational group. The virtual repositories can form a hierarchical structure that represents the company's projects, teams or departments. The virtual repository can assume one of the three related types:

- **Private** – repositories of this type are only accessible to restricted users (the permission is defined through the system) that pertain to the same organizational group associated to repository;
- **Private to organization** – repositories of this type are accessible to all users that pertain to the same organizational group associated to the virtual repository;
- **Public** – represents repositories that are accessible to any organizational group's users.

With this approach, each group can manage their own assets and users can have different permissions within different organizational groups.

Legacy systems and standards. Initially, we had some problems with deploying and adapting the repository to existent systems and standards used by the company. Such problems were resolved through the implementation of a set of adapters that represent repository system's extension points. Examples of such implemented adapters are:

- **Security policy adapter** – it allows the company to configure the repository system with its own security rules (ex.: user password policy) ; and
- **User base adapter** – it represents an abstraction of the existent company's user base infrastructure, such as, LDAP systems. This adapter allows validating users against existing LDAP systems, for improved access control for administrators and single sign-on for users.

6   Concluding Remarks and Future Works

Companies are always struggling to achieve cheaper, faster and better products. Appropriate reuse repositories can make these goals more easily achievable. However, the existing practical and academic solutions present gaps and lack of support to some desirable roles that a reuse repository should play.

In this paper, we present a work resulting from the application of a research made in conjunction with the industry, i.e. research and development together. Pragmatic considerations and practical solutions were taken into account in conjunction with state-of-the-art in order to specify, design and implement a reuse repository. Such work has been directly applied in Brazilian software factories with the aim of improving productivity, obtaining low costs and high quality through software reuse during the whole software development cycle.

As future work, we are developing a set plug-ins to be integrated in several user environments, such as *Eclipe* and *Microsoft Word*. Thus, the reuse repository solution will be less intrusive to companies that already use such environments. Additionally, we have some works for integrating active searches in the developed plug-ins. All of these works form the first step in defining a complete reuse environment product line which is also in development and can be seen in RiSE's website[1].

Acknowledgments

This work is sponsored by Brazilian Agency (CNPq process number:475743/2007-5).

References

1. Apperly, H.: Component-Based Software Engineering: Putting the Pieces Together, pp. 513–526. Addison Wesley, Reading (2001)
2. Ezran, M., Morisio, M., Tully, C.: Practical Software Reuse. Springer, Heidelberg (2002)

---

[1] http://www.rise.com.br/research/

3. Lucrédio, D., Prado, A.F., Almeida, E.S.: A Survey on Software Components Search and Retrieval. In: Proceedings of the 30th EUROMICRO Conference (2004)
4. Garcia, V.C., et al.: Specification, Design and Implementation of an Architecture for a Component Search Engine. In: The 5° Workshop de Desenvolvimento Baseado em Componentes (WDBC 2005) (2005)
5. Almeida, E.S., Alvaro, A., Lucrédio, D., Garcia, V.C., Meira, S.R.L.: RiSE Project: Towards a Robust Framework for Software Reuse. In: IEEE International Conference on Information Reuse and Integration (IRI), Las Vegas, USA, November 2004, pp. 48–53 (2004)
6. Frakes, W.B., Fox, C.J.: Sixteen Questions about Software Reuse. Communications of the ACM 38(06), 75–87 (1995)
7. Gospodnetic, O., Hatcher, E.: Lucene in Action. Manning Publications Co. (2004) ISBN 1-932394-28-1
8. Burégio, V.: Specification, Design and Implementation of a Reuse Repository, MSc dissertation, Federal University of Pernambuco, Brazil (2006)
9. Poulin, J.: Measuring Software Reuse. Addison-Wesley, Reading (1997)
10. Almeida, E.S., Alvaro, A., Garcia, V.C., Mascena, J.C.C.P., Burégio, V.A.A., Nascimento, L.M., Lucrédio, D., Meira, S.R.L.: C.R.U.I.S.E: Component Reuse in Software Engineering, C.E.S.A.R e-book, Brazil (2007)
11. Burégio, V., Almeida, E., Lucredio, D., Meira, S.: Specification, Design and Implementation of a Reuse Repository. In: The 31st IEEE Annual International Computer Software and Applications (COMPSAC) Conference, Short Paper, Beijing, China (2007)
12. Mascena, J., Almeida, E., Meira, S.: A Comparative Study on Software Reuse Metrics and Economic Models from a Traceability Perspective. In: IEEE Information Reuse and Integration, Las Vegas, USA (2005)

COTS Selection Best Practices
in Literature and in Industry

Rikard Land[1], Laurens Blankers[2,3], Michel Chaudron[3], and Ivica Crnković[1]

[1]Mälardalen University, School of Innovation, Design and Engineering, Västerås, Sweden
[2] Logica, The Netherlands
[3] Eindhoven University of Technology, Dept. of Mathematics and Computing Science,
The Netherlands
{rikard.land,ivica.crnkovic}@mdh.se,
laurens.blankers@logica.com, m.r.v.chaudron@TUE.nl

Abstract. This paper presents an extensive literature survey of the software COTS component selection methods published to date, followed by a meta-model consolidating the activities and practices of these methods. Together with data collected from practitioners and researchers in the embedded systems domain, we provide concrete recommendations which will enable organizations to identify suitable practices when designing a customized selection processes.

1 Introduction

As software development organizations build software using components developed by others (OTS = Off-The-Shelf; COTS = Commercial ditto), there is an increasing need to select the right components in a systematic, explicit, objective, and cost-efficient way. Many processes and methods for COTS selection have been published, many funded by, and applied in large well-reputed organizations in demanding domains (e.g. safety-critical systems, financial systems). The published processes thus build on a rich and hard-earned body of experience, but it is a major task to penetrate all relevant publications, compare them, and adopt and combine the most relevant parts for a particular organization's needs. For this purpose, we have performed an extensive literature survey and a questionnaire survey and provide recommendations which can be used as a checklist when defining the strategy and procedures in the COTS component selection process. (In the rest of this paper, the term "component" is used to mean "COTS component").

1.1 Related Work and Scope Limitation

In 1997 a workshop on COTS-based systems [1] was organized by the SEI (Software Engineering Institute) together with the industry where a number of issues were raised which seem to have found their way into the surveyed component selection methods. The few previous literature surveys that exist are more limited than ours in various ways: one brief overview was presented four years ago [2], however without any substantial comparison (and we include the more recent methods). In another study, three of the methods were compared with eight principles of agile software development [3].

H. Mei (Ed.): ICSR 2008, LNCS 5030, pp. 100–111, 2008.

The brief survey of three earlier methods in the presentation of the method CRE [4] focused only on requirements. The relation between the selection process and surrounding processes has been described briefly in e.g. [5].

This survey includes literature which presents itself as a complete method or process for component selection. The elements of these methods (e.g. comparison methods) could each be the starting point of a major literature survey.

Section 2 presents the research methods used in this study, followed by an overview of existing published component selection methods in section 3. Section 4 presents a meta-model which consolidates the best practices of these methods. Section 5 provides recommendations for the design of customized COTS selection methods, and section 6 concludes the paper.

2   Research Method

The first part of the research has been an exploratory, systematic literature review of published COTS selection methods. In order to identify similarities and differences, we listed preliminary dimensions of comparison, and defined, populated, rejected items, and thus grown this list iteratively until we arrived at the meta-model described in section 4. See more details in our report [6]. As a second part of this study, we conducted a qualitative survey with industrial practitioners and researchers in the embedded systems domain. We constructed a questionnaire with open and qualitative questions, which was then distributed to a targeted group of experts (typically software architects/designers) in different companies and projects with the goal of collecting as many and varying opinions as possible. This approach can be expected to give a good indication of the current state of practice. We received responses from eight industry practitioners (in eight different companies), with roles central to COTS selection (e.g. software architects), plus responses from five researchers in the field. Quotes from these responses are sometimes included (chosen with the purpose of illustrating issues mentioned by several of the respondents). As an additional validation measure, we used some interview data from earlier studies on related topics.

3   Brief Survey of Component Selection Methods

Table 1 provides a historical overview of the existing, published COTS selection methods and summarizes the main novelties introduced by each (if any). For space reasons we cannot here present the methods in more detail (for this, please refer to our report [6] or directly to the references for the methods); nor do the table intend to show how methods have adopted elements from earlier methods. When a method has not been given an explicit name by its authors, we have indicated this in italics and provide an acronym based on the title of the publication or main activities of the method. The main changes discernible over time, as new methods have been proposed are: first, the list of suggested attributes to evaluate has been extended; second, the issues of architectural compatibility have become a fundamental part through the evaluation of several complementary components simultaneously as single candidates. Another difference is that some methods assume component requirements have been defined beforehand, others that they are developed the selection process.

Table 1. Historical overview of published component selection methods

Year	Method	Main Novelty
1995	OTSO [7] (Off-The-Shelf Option)	Progressive filtering; evaluation criteria includes functionality, non-functional properties, strategic considerations and architecture compatibility; AHP suggested for comparison
1997	PRISM [8] (Portable, Reusable, Integrated, Software Modules)	Stand-alone test phase followed by integration evaluation and field test
1998	PORE [9,10] (Procurement-Oriented Requirements Engineering)	Closely intertwined selection of components and definition of system requirements
1999	STACE [11] (Socio-Technical Approach to COTS Evaluation)	Stresses importance of non-technical factors to evaluate
2000	COTS Score [12]	-
2001	RCPEP [13] (Requirements-driven COTS Product Evaluation Process)	Stresses evaluation objectivity
2002	CAP [14]	Large number of quality metrics (>100)
	i-MATE [15]	Reusable requirements for middleware selection
	PECA [16]	Flexible structure of activities
	RDR [17] (Requirements and Design Reviews)	Explicitly describes the relation between acquired components and system parts being built in-house
	CRE [4] (COTS-Based Requirements Engineering)	Requirements engineering process drives the selection; NFR framework is used to discuss non-functional attributes
	CSCC [18] (Combined Selection of COTS Components)	Considers the total cost for a system rather than specifying in advance the individual costs for different components
2003	CEP [19] (Comparative Evaluation Process)	-
2004	CARE [20] (COTS-Aware Requirements Engineering)	Intertwines system requirements engineering with component evaluation; later named CARE/SA [21] when giving software architecture a stronger focus
2005	*CCCS* [22] (Compatible COTS Component Selection)	Considers sets of complementary component as candidates, focusing on how well components will fit together; also emphasizes prototyping as a means to collect reliable information.
	CPF [23] (Commitment, Pre-filtering, Final filtering)	Strong focus on continuous improvement of the selection process itself
2006	*CSSP* [24] (COTS Software Selection Process)	-

4 Meta-model of Existing Component Selection Methods

The meta-model is in this section introduced briefly in a top-down manner; each element is then discussed in more detail in section 5.

The published methods can be described in terms of four processes (at the top of Fig. 1): there is a *preparation process*, an *evaluation process*, a *selection process* and

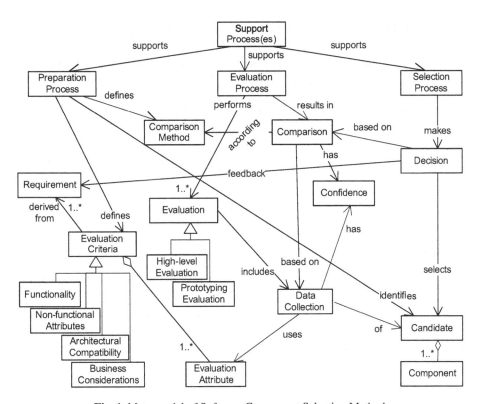

Fig. 1. Meta-model of Software Component Selection Methods

(only in some of the methods) *supporting process(es)*. In the *preparation process*, potential component *candidates* are identified, *evaluation criteria* are defined (which are related to system *requirements* and defined with *evaluation attributes* to use as metrics), as well as a *comparison method* which determines how to do the required multi-criteria selection. The evaluation criteria are of up to four types: *Funtionality*, *Non-functional Attributes*, *Architectural Compatibility*, and *Business Considerations*. A candidate could be either a single component or a set of complementary components that are evaluated together as a candidate solution. In the *evaluation process*, actual data is collected (*data collection*) that answers the evaluation criteria and are used to perform a *comparison* of the candidates. Two types of *evaluations* can be discerned: high-level evaluation (based only on easily collected information) and *prototyping evaluation* (where the candidate component itself is available). In the *selection process*, a decision is made based on this comparison. Both the data collected and the comparison is associated with a level of *confidence*, which may range from confidence in the statistical sense (for quantifiable metrics) to the "gut feeling" when collecting qualitative data (e.g. concerning vendor claims and when evaluating the future prospects for the vendor). Other activities found in the literature can be classified as *supporting process(es)* with activities such as team formation, documentation, planning and following up the selection process, and reflecting on the selection process as such and documenting experiences for future improvement.

5 How to Design a Customized Component Selection Method

This section discusses the elements of the meta-model. For each such element, we first describe the different approaches suggested by the surveyed component selection methods, and the results from our questionnaire and secondly suggest a number of recommendations. We have for convenience labelled these with letters, but this should not be taken as a suggestion for which order to consider them in. Some recommendations are inferred mainly from the methods survey, and should be generally applicable. By also considering the questionnaire responses, we provide recommendations directed mainly to the selection of COTS for embedded systems.

We expect that during the design of a customized component selection method in an organization, some additional issues need to be considered. It must therefore be ensured that all relevant stakeholders are involved in this process.

5.1 Structure of the Activities

Typically, a progressive filtering of components [1] is described in a process where candidates are evaluated, first using some easily measured but clearly discriminating criteria, and as components are discarded the level of evaluation detail and confidence in the results is increased. The concept of an increasingly detailed evaluation of a decreasing number of components is universal, but the overall structure of the activities suggested by the published methods differs:

- **Sequential with branches (and possibly a predefined number of loops).** Methods: (PRISM), *CCCS*, (*CSSP*).
- **Iterative, i.e. continues until some exit criteria is met**: PRISM, STACE, (PECA), CRE.
- **Situation-driven/opportunistic/flexible.** I.e., given the information gathered so far, what is the most reasonable to do next? Methods: PORE, PECA.
- **Concurrent and interrelated processes.** Methods: OTSO, CAP, (CRE), CPF.

Supporting processes are mentioned in only some of the methods. Combining the suggested activities, this would include setting up a team (*CSSP*), planning and management of the evaluation and acquisition process (*CSCC, RDR*), and reflecting and documenting the process itself for future improvements including the actual component data collected and evaluation attributes used and how costly and useful they were during the data collection (CAP, CEP, *CCCS*). Component selection methods developed together with organizations developing embedded, safety-critical systems tend to favour waterfall-like, plan-driven component selection method (RCPEP, *RDR, CSSP*). However, we believe the main reason for this is that these organizations are used to plan-driven processes in general. Generally, our comple-mentary data instead suggest that component assessment and selection should also for safety-critical and mission-critical systems be iterative, opportunistic and flexible rather than plan-driven. The COTS selection process can (with advantage) be seen as part of the requirements and design phases (which may however be part of a formalized plan-driven process). Two illustrative questionnaire responses:

- "It is inevitable that new criteria emerge".
- "...it is like when people make the decision. We always make up our mind with the information gathered so far and choose the most optimistic option."

This analysis results in the following three recommendations when selecting an overall layout:

Recommendation A: If your organization prefers some specific structure of activities (i.e. sequential, etc.), study the references to the presented methods in the bulleted list above in more detail.

Recommendation B: Strongly consider a requirements-driven and iterative or flexible selection process – even if you are developing highly critical software and are used to plan-driven processes.

Recommendation C: Since the supporting processes are mostly out of scope of the published methods, use combinations of available supporting processes (by following the references above), and when possible combine them with other sources of good practices (e.g. process guidelines already existing internally in the organization, or general process standards).

5.2 System Requirements

The methods differ in how they consider the relation between requirements engineering and component selection. A few selection methods describe themselves as driven by the requirements engineering process (CRE, CARE). In other methods the requirements are developed simultaneously with the component selection process (PORE, i-MATE). However, the majority of the methods assume system requirements exist (OTSO, PRISM, STACE, COTS Score, RCPEP, CAP, *CSCC*, PECA, *RDR*, CEP, *CCCS*, CPF, *CSSP*), but it is typically mentioned that the requirements can be renegotiated based on the component evaluation (most explicitly in PRISM, STACE, CAP, *CCCS*). PECA stresses that system requirements have to be translated into component evaluation requirements, which are not identical for all components under evaluation. CEP points out that evaluation criteria should be broad so as not to limit the search by too many constraints. The questionnaire respondents prefer loosely defined system requirements before components are searched for; example quotes:

- "detailed but on a high level of abstraction"
- "It depends on the product to be developed. It could be that the system requirements could be changed due to available software component."
- "Too detailed specification might make it unlikely that suitable components can be found"
- "Very often, clients only have a very vague idea about the functions the system should provide. Due to time constraint, the system requirements could be formulated and specified in parallel with the system development."

This discussion again leads to recommendation B in section 5.1.

5.3 Evaluation Criteria

The methods in combination suggest four types of evaluation criteria:

- **Functionality.** (Essentially all methods.)
- **Non-functional attributes.** (Essentially all methods.)
- **Architectural compatibility.** (OTSO, PRISM, CAP, PECA, *RDR*, CRE, CARE, *CCCS*, CPF, *CSSP*; we can also note that architectural compatibility is addressed when sets of components are evaluated together, see section 5.6.)
- **Business considerations.** This includes evaluation of the vendors (e.g. their reputation and financial stability; RCPEP, PECA, *RDR*, CARE, *CCCS*, *CSSP*), estimated cost and risk in both the short and long term (considering e.g. available support for the component, frequencies of updates, maintaining backward compatibility and going out of business; RCPEP, CAP, *RDR*, CRE, CARE, *CCCS*), and organization infrastructure (e.g. skills; *RDR*, CRE).

The methods generally do not specify some particular order of importance among these factors, and the general opinion among the questionnaire respondents is that "it depends" (on the domain, on the organization, on the particular system and component criticality, etc.). If anything, cost seems to be the least important, because "the proper solution will save money in the long run" (quote); however any per-deployment cost (e.g. in terms of licensing or hardware resources) is an important factor for products with large volumes. Several of the questionnaire respondents emphasize architectural compatibility. Thus, everything is important, and the non-fulfilment of a single individual evaluation criterion could exclude a component.

As said, some selection methods interleave system requirements with search for and evaluation of components (PORE, i-MATE, CRE, CARE). One reason is that it is not trivial to decompose system requirements into component requirements; one questionnaire respondent explained it as: "In addition to the component requirements, there will be additional requirements concerning several components and their interconnections (e.g., end-to-end deadlines)." Most component selection methods however assume that component requirements exist, to which the component features can be related. Concerning the level of detail to which component requirements should be specified, the questionnaire responses are inconclusive:

- "The first challenge is decomposition of the system requirements, and the initial system architecture. This architecture can then be used to loosely define the component functionalities and then their behaviour."
- "Until the system requirements are understood, it is hard to make a selection between similar choices."
- "a range of functionality is initially chosen"
- "Too much details may exclude components that could be appropriate."
- "component market within [domain] is non-existing to some extend. Component requirements could be specified in more detail, if the component market is larger."
- "[challenging to] define the responsibilities and interfaces (both syntax and semantics) ... at a stage that not everything about the architecture is known yet"

This analysis results in the following two recommendations:

Recommendation D: The following four types of attributes should all be considered: functionality, non-functional attributes, architectural compatibility, business considerations. Elaborate what they mean more specifically for your particular system and organization, and their relative importance.

Recommendation E: Consider what level of detail component evaluation criteria need to be specified in advance, since this depends on the system and organization.

5.4 Evaluation Attribute, Data Collection, and Confidence

It is possible to distinguish between two types of evaluations, based on how the actual data collection can be carried out (visible in most methods as well as in the questionnaire responses). We label these two phases *high-level evaluation* and *prototyping evaluation*. Some methods describe these as explicit phases (e.g. PRISM); in others they are implicit, as a consequence of iteration and refinement.

In the first type of evaluation, *high-level evaluation*, typically many components are briefly evaluated based on information about components and vendors, gathered e.g. from in-house sources, literature reviews and interviews with other customers, from the vendors in the form of marketing material, by request to the vendor, vendor appraisals, or by publicly available information about the financial stability of the vendor. Illustrative questionnaire quote: "Get opinions from different people, other departments, or even other companies (use network to gather experiences)". In the high-level evaluation, all four types of evaluation criteria should be considered (functionality, non-functional attributes, architectural compatibility, and business considerations). There are several things to bear in mind when planning this high-level evaluation: to increase confidence in the results several sources of information should be used (triangulation), focus should be on information that can discriminate between components (PECA), and criteria should be selected for which data are easy to find.

A limited number of candidates are then selected for the second type of evaluation, *prototyping evaluation*, where the actual components are used for prototypes, systematic tests and/or experiments. This is done to assess certain properties in the context of the envisioned system with a high degree of confidence, and also to learn and understand the component. Prototyping is explicit and important in some methods (PRISM, PORE, RCPEP, i-MATE, PECA, *CCCS*) and stressed by several questionnaire respondents (example: "involving the component prior to deployment and by using extensive simulation, monitoring, or testing of the composition").

The main distinction between the two evaluation phases is whether the component needs to be available during the evaluation or not. In prototyping, the acquisition of a component may come with a (high) cost and can introduce (substantial) effort into the evaluation process, and the evaluation itself requires learning the component and systematically setting up, executing, and documenting many tests thoroughly. This consequently limits the number of components that can practically be evaluated.

This analysis results in the following five recommendations:

Recommendation F: Use as discriminating evaluation attributes as possible, to ensure an efficient filtering process.

Recommendation G: Use evaluation attributes for which data is as easy to collect as possible, to ensure an efficient filtering process.

Recommendation H: Based on the (expected) number of existing component, the criticality of the components when used in the envisioned system, estimate how much time is acceptable and needed for high-level evaluation.

Recommendation I: Consider how many components are expected to be subject to prototyping evaluation and how detailed the evaluation needs to be (which is a consequence of the required confidence), and estimate the time and cost accordingly.

Recommendation J: If there is a conflict between project budget and the evaluation estimates, the issue need to be satisfactory resolved as early as possible; in general it can be expected that choosing an insufficient component will negatively affect the system development greatly.

5.5 Comparison Method, Comparison, and Decision

The comparison and ranking of components is naturally based on many criteria. The evaluation of the criteria could either be made subjectively, or could be based on or supported by a systematic comparison method. The comparison method most commonly proposed by the published component selection methods is AHP, Analytical Hierarchy Process (OTSO, PORE, STACE, COTS Score, CRE). Other methods are WSM (Weighted Scoring Method) and Weighted Average (RCPEP, CRE, CEP), and using COCOTS [25] for effort estimation (CRE, *CSSP*). Our questionnaire suggests that these are with a few exceptions not known to practitioners (i.e. there is an adoption cost associated with these methods). Others have argued that all of these evaluation methods ("decision-making techniques") have their drawbacks when applied to component selection [26]: the techniques may require disproportionate effort, requiring stakeholders to provide preferences and weights for many criteria and specify how to aggregate the criteria into a one-dimensional scale (i.e. ranking) in the absence of concrete products, which is difficult and inefficient. Instead, gap analysis is suggested [26], meaning that for each component, the gap between requirements and provided capabilities is analyzed, followed by an estimation of the costs of bridging the gap. Since a formal comparison runs the risk of not catching the intent of the comparison, some methods also suggest or mention discussions, reasoning, and argumentation techniques (CARE, PECA, PORE). The questionnaire responses suggest that although formalized techniques bring a necessary structure into decision-making, they are using subjective and incomplete input. They must therefore be complemented with informal discussions to ensure "the 'real' issues" are ultimately considered (quote from a questionnaire response). The complexity of the decision is illustrated by another quote: "The final selection is based on a combination of the technical evaluation, the related business case for the tool and vendor, and trying to optimize cost. The final selection is always a trade off."

The option of building a component in-house may in some cases be a realistic solution (especially if no suitable component is found), and a few methods discuss this (CAP, (CRE), *RDR*, *CCCS*). The build alternative can be treated as one alternative among others during gap analysis, with an associated effort, cost, risk etc.

This analysis results in the following recommendation:

Recommendation K: Combine a formalized comparison method with (structured) discussions. Consider gap analysis for the formalized comparison method.

5.6 Components and Candidates

It has been proposed that combinations of the available components should be evaluated together as a single candidate (*CSCC, CCCS*). There are two reasons for this: first, to minimize architectural mismatch, and secondly because the (hypothetical) choice of an initial component will help decomposing system requirements into component requirements (a "crystallizing seed"). This "puzzle assembly" was identified in the previously mentioned SEI workshop in 1997 [1] but has only become explicitly exploited in two of the recent selection methods. *CSCC* implements this approach by comparing the estimated total system cost using various component alternatives (rather than focusing on the cost of individual components), and *CCCS* by explicitly considering a "candidate" to be a set of components which are architecturally compatible. The questionnaire responses indicate this is the advantageous approach: "Integration can be difficult otherwise"; "Systems have to work together as a whole, and decisions cannot be made in isolation". Apart from the technical aspect of integration, business considerations are also addressed by this approach; for example, if already several risky components are used, a project might want to avoid including more (risky) components in a project. A related approach is to maintain a list of potential components for each "slot" in the architecture. If further downstream (also after development and deployment) a component is found to be insufficient (e.g. too low quality, or support is discontinued) the list will help identify a replacement component.

"Keystone identification" [1] means the selection of a central component, technology, or strategy that will have a great impact the selection of other components (e.g. "we will build on .NET", "we will use middleware from a certain vendor and then choose other products known to integrate well"). None of the surveyed methods implement this strategy explicitly. However, the questionnaire responses indicate that this commonly happens in practice:

- "Yes it is common. E.g. LINUX vs Windows."
- "For example, a central database may be the most important part of a system for functionality and performance. That choice needs to be optimized, and other choices must be made with respect to that decision."
- "If another platform is chosen (e.g. VxWorks in stead of Windows CE) this has a lot of impact on the available components."

This analysis results in the following two recommendations:

Recommendation L: Evaluate combinations of components together, in order to address architectural mismatch inherently in the process.

Recommendation M: Identify any keystone technologies, platforms, and strategies early in the process, since that will exclude many other components.

6 Summary and Conclusion

In this paper we have surveyed published software component selection methods, and provided a meta-model which provides a common terminology and comparison framework for selection methods. By bringing the collected best practices into the light, and with the additional data provided by a questionnaire distributed to software architects and researchers in the embedded systems domain, we have provided 13 recommendations which will help organizations to more rapidly design customized COTS selection processes. In brief summary, our recommendations are:

- Use four types of evaluation criteria: functionality, non-functional attributes, architectural compatibility, business considerations.
- Consider an iterative process intertwined with requirements engineering.
- Address architectural compatibility by evaluating combinations of components, and consider the cost of the total system rather than individual components.
- Consider the criticality of components, and what level of confidence is needed in the evaluation and selection decision, and allocate sufficient resources.

This work will be followed up by industrial case studies of component-based systems life-cycles and processes.

Acknowledgements

This work was partially supported by the Swedish Foundation for Strategic Research (SSF) via the strategic research centre PROGRESS. The authors would like to thank the questionnaire respondents, the people who have reviewed earlier versions of this paper, and those who in other ways been helpful in this study.

References

1. Oberndorf, P., Brownsword, L., Morris, E., Sledge, C.: Workshop on COTS-Based Systems, Special report CMU/SEI-97-SR-019, SEI (1997)
2. Ruhe, G.: Intelligent Support for Selection of COTS Products. In: Chaudhri, A.B., Jeckle, M., Rahm, E., Unland, R. (eds.) NODe-WS 2002. LNCS, vol. 2593. Springer, Heidelberg (2003)
3. Navarrete, F., Botella, P., Franch, X.: How Agile COTS Selection Methods are (and can be)? In: Proceedings of the 31st EUROMICRO Conference on Software Engineering and Advanced Applications, pp. 160–167. IEEE, Los Alamitos (2005)
4. Alves, C., Castro, J.: CRE: a systematic method for COTS components Selection. In: Proceedings of the XV Brazilian Symposium on Software Engineering (SBES), Rio de Janeiro (2001)
5. Crnkovic, I., Chaudron, M., Larsson, S.: Component-based Development Process and Component Lifecycle. Journal of Computing and Information Technology 13(4), 321–327 (2005)
6. Land, R., Blankers, L.: Classifying and Consolidating Software Component Selection Methods, MRTC report ISSN 1404-3041 ISRN MDH-MRTC-218/2007-1-SE, Mälardalen Real-Time Research Centre, Mälardalen University (November 2007)
7. Kontio, J.: OTSO: A Systematic Process for Reusable Software Component Selection, Univ. Maryland report CS-TR-3478, UMIACS-TR-95-63 (1995)

8. Lichota, R.W., Vesprini, R.L., Swanson, B.: PRISM Product Examination Process for component based development. In: Proceedings Fifth International Symposium on Assessment of Software Tools and Technologies. IEEE, Los Alamitos (1997)
9. Maiden, N.A., Ncube, C.: Acquiring COTS Software Selection Requirements. IEEE Software 15(2), 46–56 (1998)
10. Ncube, C., Maiden, N.A.: PORE: Procurement-Oriented Requirements Engineering Method for the Component-Based Systems Engineering Development Paradigm. In: Second International Workshop on Component-Based Software Engineering, Los Angeles (1999)
11. Kunda, D., Brooks, L.: Applying Social-Technical Approach For Cots Selection. In: Proceedings of the 4th UKAIS Conference. McGraw-Hill, New York (1999)
12. Morris, A.T.: COTS Score: an acceptance methodology for COTS software. In: Proceedings of the 19th Digital Avionics Systems Conferences (DASC), vol. 1, pp. 4B2/1–4B2/8 (2000)
13. Lawlis, P.K., Mark, K.E., Thomas, D.A., Courtheyn, T.: A Formal Process for Evaluating COTS Software Products. IEEE Computer 34(5) (2001)
14. Ochs, M., Pfahl, D., Chrobok-Diening, G., Nothhelfer-Kolb, B.: A COTS Acquisition Process: Definition and Application Experience, ISERN report 00-02, Fraunhofer Institute for Experimental Software Engineering (IESE) (2002)
15. Liu, A., Gorton, I.: Accelerating COTS Middleware Acquisition: The i-Mate Process. IEEE Software 20(2), 72–79 (2003)
16. Comella-Dorda, S., Dean, J., Morris, E., Oberndorf, P.: A Process for COTS Software Product Evaluation. In: Dean, J., Gravel, A. (eds.) ICCBSS 2002. LNCS, vol. 2255, pp. 86–96. Springer, Heidelberg (2002)
17. Morizio, M., Seaman, C.B., Basili, V.R., Parra, A.T., Kraft, S.E., Condon, S.E.: COTS-based software development: Processes and open issues. Journal of Systems and Software 61(3), 189–199 (2002)
18. Burgués, X., Estay, C., Franch, X., Pastor, J.A., Quer, C.: Combined Selection of COTS Components. In: Dean, J., Gravel, A. (eds.) ICCBSS 2002. LNCS, vol. 2255, pp. 54–64. Springer, Heidelberg (2002)
19. Phillips, B.C., Polen, S.M.: Add Decision Analysis to Your COTS Selection Process. Software Technology Support Center Crosstalk (April 2002)
20. Chung, L., Cooper, K.: Defining Goals in a COTS-Aware Requirements Engineering Approach. Systems Engineering 7(1), 61–83 (2004)
21. Chung, L., Cooper, K.: COTS-Aware Requirements Engineering and Software Architecting. In: Proceedings of the 4th International Workshop on System/Software Architectures (IWSSA) (2004)
22. Bhuta, J., Boehm, B.: A Method for Compatible COTS Component Selection. In: Franch, X., Port, D. (eds.) ICCBSS 2005. LNCS, vol. 3412. Springer, Heidelberg (2005)
23. Cechich, A., Piattini, M.: Filtering COTS Components Through an Improvement-Based Process. In: Franch, X., Port, D. (eds.) ICCBSS 2005. LNCS, vol. 3412. Springer, Heidelberg (2005)
24. Lin, H., Lai, A., Ullrich, R., Kuca, M., Shaffer-Gant, J., Pacheco, S., Dalton, K., McClelland, K., Watkins, W., Khajenoori, S.: COTS Software Selection Process, SANDIA REPORT SAND2006-0478, Sandia National Laboratories (May 2006)
25. Abts, C.: Extending the COCOMO II Software Cost Model to Estimate Effort and Schedule for Software Systems Using Commercial-Off-The-Shelf (COTS) Software Components: the COCOTS Model, Ph.D. Dissertation, University of Southern California (October 2001)
26. Ncube, C., Dean, J.C.: The Limitations of Current Decision-Making Techniques in the Procurement of COTS Software Components. In: Dean, J., Gravel, A. (eds.) ICCBSS 2002. LNCS, vol. 2255. Springer, Heidelberg (2002)

Mining Open Source Component Behavior for Reuse Evaluation*

Ji Wu, Chun Wang, Xiao-xia Jia, and Chao Liu

School of Computer Science and Engineering, BeiHang University, Beijing 100083, China
{wuji,liuchao}@buaa.edu.cn,
wangchun.think@gmail.com, sailgao76@hotmail.com

Abstract. Reusing Open Source Component (OSC) has become more and more popular in developing in-house applications. Before integrating an OSC into project, the component has to be evaluated according to the project. This paper proposes the usage and dependency model to help understand OSC from the interactions with its usage context. The usage and dependency model extends the traditional usage model with the context dependency and backward dependency, which are widely observed in open source project. Based on the usage model, this paper proposes three metrics to measure the interaction complexity. To construct the usage and dependency model, the invocation matrix and the mining algorithm are proposed. The framework component in open source project Junit 4.4 is selected to validate this research.

Keywords: Open source component, usage model, usage and dependency model.

1 Introduction

Before integrating an OSC, the component has to be evaluated according to the project requirements. There is several evaluation criteria (framework) proposed toward selecting proper components [1] [2]. How an OSC acts in its original project is always a concern, for example, the importance the component plays in its context and the ratio of the component interfaces used by the context are proposed as evaluation factors in [3]. OSC now is widely reused even in NASA, Norris presented the experiences to evaluate and reuse OSC in NASA Mars project [4].

When we evaluate an OSC under a project, the *component* and its usage *context* could be identified. The *component* provides services to the *context* and depends on the services provided by the *context* at the same time. How to define and evaluate the *component* **behavior** under the *context* arises as the research problem in this paper. This paper proposes the usage and dependency model focusing on the interdependencies between the *component* and its usage *context*. Three metrics are proposed to measure the complexity of the dependency between *component* and *context*. This paper is structured into 5 sections. Section 2 presents the usage and dependency model; the algorithm to mine the model is presented in section 3. Section 4 presents the case study to validate this research. Section 5 concludes this paper.

---

* This project is sponsored by National Science Foundation under the project No. 60603039.

H. Mei (Ed.): ICSR 2008, LNCS 5030, pp. 112–115, 2008.

2   Usage and Dependency Model

Usage model is widely used in reliability testing. We extend the traditional usage model with the dependencies of OSC on its usage context to model OSC behavior.

Definition 1: Usage and Dependency Model (UDM) is a directed graph $\{N, T, P\}$, $N=\{S, E\}\cup F\cup C$, $T=\{<S, x>|x\in F\}\cup\{<x, y>,<x, E>|x, y\in F\cup C\}$, $P:<x, y>\in T \rightarrow (l, p)$, $l\in Z$, $p\in[0, 1.0]$.

S is start node and E is end node. F is the set of component interface nodes, and C is the set of context nodes. T contains all the legal transitions among nodes. $P(<x, y>)$ is transition parameter in which l is the invocation length, i.e. the number of calls within the transition, and p is the transition probability. Any node $x\in N$, there is at least one path from S to E covers x. For any node $x\in$ N, $\sum_y P(< x, y >).p = 1.0$; for any node $y\in F$, $P(<S, y>).l=1$; and for any node $x\in F\cup C$, $P(<x, E>).l=0$.

3   UDM Mining and Measurement

The UDM could be built from method invocations. The dynamic invocation is mined from LBM [5], and the static one is mined from source code.

Definition 2: Invocation matrix M is an $n*m$ matrix that has n callers and m callees, $M(x, y) = (l, c)$ denotes the length and occurrence of invocations from x to y.

The algorithm extracts all the invocations from LBM and code and checks its qualification with UDM. Any invocation that happens outside of the *component* will be ignored. We do not track into the invocations that happen in *context* unless there is a back-call to the *component*. The method that is only invocated by the component itself is not real interface and need to be pruned from matrix. To prune any component method x, every predecessor of x will be connected to every successor of x.

The UDM structure can be directly generated from matrix. The transition parameter is computed by following equation, where m is the total number of callees.

$$\left(l_{ij}, p_{ij}\right) = (\frac{M_{ij}.l}{M_{ij}.c} , \frac{M_{ij}.c}{\sum_{k=1}^{m} M_{ik}.c}) \qquad (1)$$

Based on UDM, we propose the following three metrics to measure in what degree OSC is used, OSC depends on its context and the context can be substituted.

Metric 1: *Component Usage Strength (CUS) measures the extent to which the component is used.* Let an OSC have n interfaces (after pruning), the static and dynamic usage occurrences for these interfaces are $s_1,...,s_n$, and $a_1,...,a_n$, then

$$CUS = \sum_{i\leq n}\frac{a_i}{s_i} \qquad (2)$$

Metric 2: *Component Backward Dependency Strength (CBDS) measures the extent to which a component depends on its context in its usage.* Let there are n non-loop usage paths from S to E, and m of them having at least one C node, then

$$CBDS = \frac{m}{n} \qquad (3)$$

Metric 3: *Context Substitution Degree (CSD) measures the difficulty to substitute the context of an OSC with a different one.*

$$\text{CSD} = \sum_{t=<x\in F,y\in C>} \frac{t.l}{t.p} + \sum_{t=<x\in C,y\in F>} \frac{t.l}{t.p} \tag{4}$$

Transition length and probability contributes to CSD. The smaller probability means the bigger transition space, thus more difficulty to substitute.

4 Case Study

We select the *junit.framework* package, which provides the infrastructure to run test cases, in Junit 4.4 project to evaluate the models and metrics proposed. The package has three interface classes and seven normal classes to provide 82 public methods.

This paper assumes the Java package as the granularity of OSC. The framework component, core of Junit, is reused and extended in many open source projects. We use all the 129 tests in *junit.samples* package to run Junit. The corresponding LBM and traces are collected. The UDM is mined and drawn manually in figure 1.

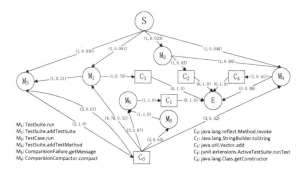

Fig. 1. The usage and dependency model for *junit.framework* component

From the model, we can find there are only 6 public methods are retained against the 82 ones. There are 5 context methods are depended by this component, and the C_0 backwardly depends on this component. This is in fact an evidence of tight coupling between the component and its context. The backward invocation of M_1 has the average length 4.79 (not an integer). It shows there are multiple paths to invoke M_1 in C_0. We can find several indirect self-dependencies of the component: M_1-M_3-C_0-M_5, M_3-C_0-M_4, etc. These indirect self-dependencies are very hard to test and to adapt to new context, because developer has to implement the new C_0 not only to provide correct service to M_3, but also request proper service from M_1, M_3, M_4, M_5 and M_6.

At the same time, we can find the backward transitions from C_0 are complicated by the evidence of transition length and probability. Takes C_0-M_5 and C_0-M_4 as example, their occurrence chances are 0.03 and 0.52. It means the conditions and the context to invoke M_4 and M_5 are quite different. Because transition probability of M_3-C_0 is 1.0 and the sum of the five backward transition probabilities is 1.0, C_0 must be invoked and then C_0 must invoke one of the five methods whenever M_3 is invoked.

The C_0 has complicated behaviors observed in the matrix. There are 10 context methods are involved in the backward transitions from C_0. There are two popular strategies to cluster the context nodes: (1) to group by the component interface being invoked; (2) to group by the root caller, i.e. C_0. These two strategies indicate the way to substitute the context. For the first one, developer would design context method according to component interface. This kind of context method design may be easier, but developer has to design five ones. For the second one, developer needs to design only one context method, but the method is quite complicated.

The *CUS* is (0.4+0.6+1+1)/4=0.75. The *CUS* shows that the test on the framework is not complete in the sense of call-coverage. There are 22 non-loop usage paths, and 16 of them has *C* node. Therefore the *CBDS* is 16/22 = 0.73. The *CSD* has two parts to take into account. The first part focuses on the dependency complexity of OSC on the context: 26.7; the second part focuses on the complexity of the backward dependency on OSC: 183. We can find the difficulty to substitute the context lies mainly on the complexity of the backward dependencies.

5 Conclusions

Reusing open source components has been popular in development now. The search and evaluation of open source component, however, is still trivial. This paper proposes the UDM (and mining algorithm) to model the component behavior and dependencies on its context. The UDM extends the traditional usage model with context dependency and backward dependency and thus gives a new vision on reusing component: to acquire high performance component, developers have to provide a high performance context. Moreover, this paper proposes three quantitative metrics to evaluate the complexity of a component interacts with its context. To validate the approach and model, we select one component from Junit 4.4. The results show that the model and metrics can provide quantitative results directly, which are not available in the existing approaches. In the future, we would select more components to evaluate and provide guideline on how to use the UDM and the metrics.

References

1. Briand, L.C.: COTS Evaluation and Selection. In: Proceedings of the International Conference on Software Maintenance, pp. 222–223 (1998)
2. Michel, R., et al.: Information System for Evaluation of COTS. In: Third ACIS International Conference on Software Engineering Research, Management and Applications, pp. 64–69 (2005)
3. Norris, J.S.: Mission critical software development with open source software: lessons learned. IEEE Software, 42–49 (January/February 2004)
4. Wohlin, C., et al.: Certification of Software Components. IEEE Transactions on Software Engineering 20(06), 494–499 (1994)
5. Ji, W., et al.: Java object behavior modeling and visualization. In: International Conference on Software Engineering Advances, ICSEA 2006, pp. 60–65 (2006)

Combining Different Product Line Models to Balance Needs of Product Differentiation and Reuse

Juha Savolainen[1], Juha Kuusela[2], Mike Mannion[3], and Tuomo Vehkomäki[1]

[1] Nokia Research Center
{Juha.Savolainen,Tuomo.Vehkomaki}@nokia.com
[2] Nokia Devices
Juha.ha.Kuusela@nokia.com
[3] Glasgow Caledonian University
M.A.G.Mannion@gcal.ac.uk

Abstract. Software reuse is a key enabler for producing successful software intensive consumer products. Initially, just adopting reuse was enough to achieve competitive advantage; today an efficiently running product line is almost expected for any organization producing widely varying, software intensive consumer products. The major source for competitive advantage has shifted to product line management, and especially an organization's ability to optimize the alignment of its product line development approach with its competitive strategy. In this paper, we explore ways to match product line development for an organization pursuing differentiation strategy. In this context, the success of the product line is determined by the success of the resulting products, their ability to gain differentiation against the competition as well as within the product portfolio. If all products appear too similar to each other, market segmentation fails. In this paper, we first discuss the problems hounding real industrial product lines. All the experiences are based on experiences gathered being closely involved with more than ten operating product lines and observing multiple failures in being able to realize true benefits of reuse. Then we show how a product line organization can be tuned so that the benefits of reuse are attainable while supporting significantly varying set of products. Finally, we give examples of product lines that have evolved into the direction suggested by us.

1 Introduction

Reuse is a prominent method for achieving faster time to market, higher quality and lower costs in the production of complex software intensive systems [1, 2]. In reuse process, a *reusable asset* is applied in a new context to create a product. Almost any work products can become a reusable asset [3]. The sharing of reusable assets may happen with or without a defined process, established infrastructure, or dedicated organization. In practice, different approaches range from informal reuse to product

H. Mei (Ed.): ICSR 2008, LNCS 5030, pp. 116–129, 2008.
© Springer-Verlag Berlin Heidelberg 2008

line development [4].   Typically, when product line development methods are adopted, the overall quality of the reusable assets improves, a more stable software architecture is produced and it becomes possible to reach market niches that cannot alone support product development costs.

There are many reasons why, when and how an organization decides on its approach to product line development.   These are aligned to the organization's business strategy.   Porter [5] identified 4 primary generic competitive strategies across two axes cost and market scope (Figure 1).

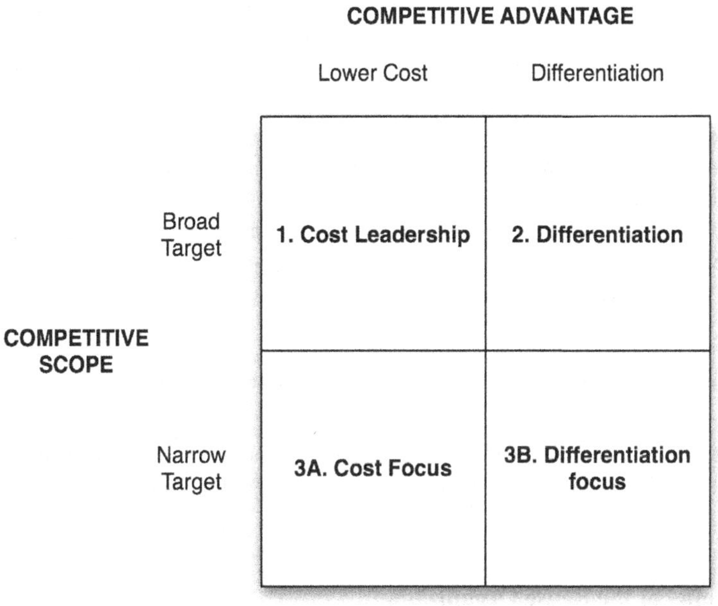

COMPETITIVE ADVANTAGE

	Lower Cost	Differentiation
Broad Target	1. Cost Leadership	2. Differentiation
Narrow Target	3A. Cost Focus	3B. Differentiation focus

COMPETITIVE SCOPE

Fig. 1. Competitive business strategies

In most industries, market leadership is held by organizations that maximize customer appeal by reconciling effective differentiation with low cost.   This presents difficult technical challenges for product line development teams.   A core motivation for reuse adoption is to exploit the benefits of shared reusable assets.   When the primary generic competitive strategy is Cost Leadership or Cost Focus the emphasis for the product development team is on maximizing the reuse of common assets more than permitting variation.   However when the primary generic competitive strategy is Broad or Focused Differentiation the emphasis is more on permitting variation than maximizing reuse.

This conflict is made more complex by the level of variation required in the Differentiation strategy. Within this strategy there is a spectrum of approaches. At one end an organization may simply generate a large number of product variants that are actually very similar but overwhelm the market, and rely more on the brand of the organization for sales and less on understanding the differences across the product set. At the other end is mass-customization where the goal is to create customized product variants and taken to extreme, each customer receives a personalized copy of the product.

This paper explores the implications for product line development for maintaining market leadership. The question that this paper intends to answer is: how can we optimize the structure of the product line so that an organization achieves the benefits of reuse by reducing the time to market, reducing the unit cost of a single product variant and the benefits of significant differentiation for the products.

In the section two we discuss forces that prevent organizations for achieving a balance between the reuse and differentiation. Section three introduces our approach for product line development and explains why it solves the issues discussed. Section four gives some industrial examples of this approach. Related work is discussed in the section five and the relationship with our approach is considered. Finally, we conclude and propose future work in the section six.

2   Problems in Complex Industrial Product Lines

Achieving the benefits of product lines in complex consumer products is not easy. There are a number of different forces that prevent organizations achieving the appropriate balance between reuse and differentiation.

2.1   Tyranny of the Reuse Organization

In reuse driven organizations there is a tendency to try to always maximize reuse. Emphasis is placed on ensuring all products use every reusable component, common user interface guidelines, standard interfaces, and ever increasing number of common components to give a common structure and behavior to all products. A real problem in only focusing on reuse is that the differentiation between the products will be reduced.

Tyranny of reuse occurs when an organization prioritizes reuse maximization in conflict with the business needs. Common development practice characteristics of reuse tyranny that have a detrimental effect on product line development road mapping include

   1.   gold plating existing features and extending their reach for all the products in
        the product family

2. introducing only those features that are seen as important by all products - this may lead in to a situation where it is hard to get a new feature in for a particular product regardless of its added value for that product (and having been disregarded for one product that feature's perceived value for other products is also reduced)

3. de-valuing and de-emphasizing features that are distinguishing and not common for all products

4. delaying the introduction of new distinctive features by insisting that they are designed and implemented so that they can be used by all products in the product line.

The consequences of this tyranny over time are either that new products are introduced slower than competitors' or the portfolio of products is insufficiently diverse. In each case the organization's market share declines. When this happens a knee-jerk reaction is to add new features to existing products without the discipline of product line development which in turn leads to a reduction in the percentage of products that are supported directly by the reusable components. A project centric approach then emerges and quickly diminishes any competitive advantage gained by reuse. Options thereafter typically are reduced to constructing a highly configurable platform with only optional components or adopting compositional approach where the individual products are responsible for the integrating reusable components. It is even possible to revert back to "Altmeister"–model, where project groups trust only code inherited from their own earlier efforts and go for clone-and-own reuse.

2.2 Local Product Optimization

Within a very broad product line e.g. a mobile phone there are often sub-product lines of particular products, each with its own product manager. Naturally each product manager wants to have a successful product where success is often measured by the number of products sold. Even though this seems to be a sensible metric, its sole use can lead to a poorly optimized product portfolio. In search of success a product manager wants to make their product line appealing to as large market segment as possible. Several different tactics can be adopted.

First, the feature set of the product line is broadened to reach beyond the initial planned market segment. Second, product managers will lobby hard to keep new features unique to their sub-product line as these are likely to be the key selling points and distinguish their product from the pack. Third, price increases for new features are often kept to a minimum for fear of losing market share. In principle, if a target price has been set for a product, increasing the number of features should be reflected in the price of the product. However, product managers work around this and typically only features requiring extra hardware cause a target price increase. Software features are often "given away for free" for several reasons: they were already in the code base but had not been enabled, or because a feature has to be included as part another feature and it can be harder to exclude it than to include it, or because it takes little effort to implement one or more features.

2.3   Too Narrow View for Product Line Portfolio Management

Product line management has a tendency to increase the number of features that can be supported across the entire product line. With product line technology it is possible to roll out a new feature for all products thus upgrading the entire product portfolio in a very short time. A good example is the rapid roll-out of color displays across the entire Nokia mobile phone product line or the introduction of video capture for all Nokia camera phones. In many cases this can lead to tangible advantage as it rapidly raises consumer expectations and can make the competing product lines look old fashioned.

Taking this approach to extremes can lead to a very technical approach to portfolio management where only common features can find their way into the product portfolio. The principle argument is that it is better to have a set of similar products with only small variations which are packaged so that they are distinctive and easy to use rather than a more complex product line, in which some products are tailored only to a small group of customers. Similarity supports brand recognition and customers can easily move from one product to another. However, the role of market segmentation and identification of unique consumer needs is often lost.

2.4   Problems in Applying a Single Product Line Development Method

The most simple product line development method is to use a product platform. The platform includes all the common software for the product line variants. The platform is then provided as an integrated software "product". This approach works well when the commonality between the product line variants is high. However, many product lines are plagued by the near commonality problem [6] i.e. as a product line expands and the number of product line variants increases, the number of assets common to all or even many products decreases, thus reducing the benefits of reuse and making the development of a common product line architecture harder. To address this problem, a common solution is to include optional assets in the platform, thus allowing the reuse of partially common assets. However, since the platform is always reused as one element many products end up getting features they do not need. This may make using this variant of the platform approach not commercially viable.

In an architecture-centric, asset-based reuse, assets are reused when needed by the products. Being able to choose the required assets allows products to have an optimal feature set that matches their requirements. To create an efficient product line architecture the ways in which current and future products will vary must be known. This will become difficult when product line scope is continuously expanding [7]. Lack of mandatory domain assumptions makes creating a high quality reuse infrastructure a difficult task. When near commonality increases, products are based on widely different sets of components, affecting the ability to optimize feature dependency structures [8].

A compositional product line development has been proposed as a solution for managing product lines with extending scope. In this approach, a product line architecture only guarantees that the components can be connected together. This does not require centralized variability management and each product is responsible for creating its own configuration of components. In our experience, the compositional development works great for certain types of software, notably when a developer of a reusable component can correctly estimate customer requirements and architect the component to match these requirements. However, in general this is very hard and based on our experience not all types of software are suitable for this approach. Creating components for e.g. user interface software with constantly changing, varying customer requirements is often very difficult, whereas making e.g. a WLAN component with standardized interfaces is relatively easy.

3 An Approach for Organizing Product Line Development

There is an ongoing conflict between the objectives of a product line development organization and those of the product organizations. The goal of product line development is to maximize the use of common assets. The product organization aims to optimize a product's characteristics in terms of differentiation in its particular market segment. Balancing these objectives is crucial for all the steps in the product line development lifecycle.

We have identified two different aspects of product differentiation [9]:

1. **Differentiation against the competition:** Each product should be competitive against its competitors regardless how competitors' products are manufactured. In our model this is managed by the product value proposition, created for each differentiated feature.
2. **Differentiation within the product portfolio:** Each product within a product line should be different from each other in ways that are meaningful to the customers in each relevant market segment.

There is a difference between the importance of a feature and whether it is a differentiating feature. A feature is not differentiating if it is considered by the customers as something that they expect from all that type of product or all the products that belong to a particular market segment. For all mobile phones "**an ability to make a phone call**" is certainly an important feature, but it will not differentiate any mobile phone in the product portfolio. A related feature "**an ability to use head phones to make a phone call**" used to be differentiating. Now it is common and in most markets does not differentiate.

Similarly, in a market segment of mobile phones for active people, a feature for "**tolerance for vibrations and humidity**" is an expected feature for mobiles phone belonging into this category. However, a "**GPS assisted navigating**" is still a differentiating feature in this market segment. A clear value proposition can be made for a product containing this feature.

We propose a new way to balance reuse and differentiation. In our approach, products can only propose new features if those features are truly differentiating for them. For each differentiating feature a clear value proposition must be made. These value propositions are later validated to verify that non-differentiating features are not added to a product by disguising them as differentiating features. This will help us to prevent local product optimization. The intent is to limit the number of new differentiating features for each product. The only exception is a new group of features that support each other to define a new product category. Such a group has much more value than the sum of these features independently. Our approach proposes using three different product line development methods to create products. These three different methods are applied to their own layers of a product line architecture Fig 2 shows that differentiated products in the product differentiation layer are constructed by a combination of organized reuse in the product line infrastructure layer and opportunistic reuse in the product reuse layer. Different methods are applied to each layer:

- the product differentiation layer uses independent product development as the way to create new features
- the product reuse layer uses centralized variability management to create reusable components using traditional product line techniques
- the product line infrastructure layer uses a compositional approach to scale up to product lines that have a wide scope.

Table 1 summarises the different methods used at the different layers.

Products are responsible for identifying and implementing their own differentiating features. The product line infrastructure is not involved in this development unless new supporting functionality is required from the reusable components. The product development process allows the realization of features using any technique available. This development is not guided by reuse but by product priorities. If a product's time to market needs require, the differentiating functionality can be developed in a "dirty" way – even as throw away code. However, a small part of the project incentives should be tied to the reuse of the product specific code base. If the developed code becomes a part of the product reuse layer or a part of the product line infrastructure the project and its developers should be rewarded.

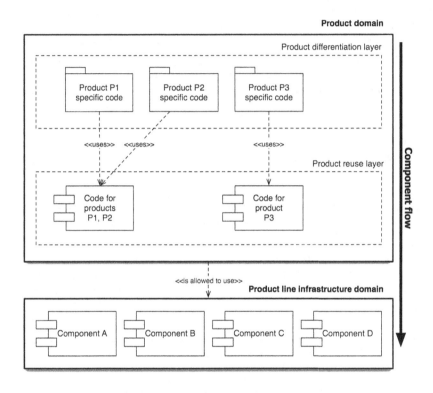

Fig. 2. Product line development for complex product lines

In this paper, we use the term "layer" loosely. The separation of the product domain and the product line infrastructure domain represents a true layering. The product domain is allowed to use the infrastructure domain, but dependencies are not allowed in the other direction. This is not true between the product differentiation layer and the product reuse layer. The usage relationships are still allowed upwards if absolutely needed for the product purposes. However, strict usage use layering is encouraged, since it will help reuse this functionality in the later phases.

Product line infrastructure management can make new reusable assets when they, either by their own judgment see it as important, or it is seen as an important feature common for many products. However, this feature cannot be differentiating to any product. Existing components, especially from the product reuse layer, can be migrated to the product line infrastructure domain. This migration reflects the fact that this functionality has become common. This is a typical evolution in most product lines. A previously differentiating feature may become non-differentiating because one or more competitors has added or intends to add the same feature to majority of their products.

The component flow from differentiating product features to reusable product functionality and finally to the reuse infrastructure layer creates new reusable components. However, the product line infrastructure is not allowed to create new reusable components unless it has realized all feature requests from the products to the existing components. In real product lines, a lot of work is generated by changes to the reusable components to allow vertical integration of new product functionality.

The abstraction level of the reusable components may rise over time. This happens when the value in software moves upwards in the whole software stack. This may make creating the lower levels of the software stack uneconomical even using compositional reuse. In response an organization may substitute some internal development by using open source software or subcontracting. We recommend that all products are allowed to use open source equivalent in place of internally developed infrastructure components. Organizations developing internal components have very little competition and this brings some. If many products prefer an external component in place of an in-house one, then the in-house development for that component should be discontinued.

This division of responsibilities has clear implications on which product line development technique is applied in each layer and what are the key architectural goals that should be achieved. The product differentiation layer has no limitations how the software is created. The main goal is to achieve extremely fast time to market and guarantee great user experience for the particular market segment.

In the product reuse layer, traditional methods for controlled variability management apply. Since each reusable component is developed for a limited set of products, the near commonality does not become a problem. Here traditional variability modeling works well. The main architectural goals are to separate the reusable and the product parts, creating components that are easy to integrate, and enforcing the rules of variability for configurability.

For a product line infrastructure team things are different. They support potentially thousands or tens of thousands of product variants. The near commonality problem will make using traditional product line management techniques very difficult. This also means that there are no definite variability constraints that architects can use for their work. The different products may use infrastructure components in very different configurations. This implies that a key criterion for the architecture is to maximize flexibility and make the components such that it is easy for the products to integrate their required set of components. These goals are similar to ones proposed by the composition based product line development. The only difference is that the infrastructure team supports only a limited set of product line features.

Table 1. Summary of the development appraoches

Layer	PL development	Architectural goal
Product differentiation	Product development	Time to market Complete product functionality
Product reuse for each set of similar products	Controlled variability management Product domain reference architecture	Reuse in the domain Strong rules on variability Flexible architecture Time to market
Product line infrastructure, common for all products	Component oriented Composition based	Maximum flexibility in components Composability Simple interfaces Ability of products to choose only a part of the components in the layer Common component framework

4 Industrial Evidence and Related Work

The continuously extending scope of current products lines complicates developing products using rigid, centralized variability management. There is also a growing amount of evidence that compositional product line development is possible in many domains [10, 11]. However, not all software is naturally aligned for compositional software development.

The battle ground between reference architecture based reuse and product specific functionality is most visible in attempts to reuse application functionality. The Nokia S60 platform has systematically expanded its reference architecture to include abstract interfaces to access functionality provided by application [12]. Applications often contain functionality that could be used also for other purposes. For example all navigation applications include map management functionality. A public interface defined on the level of a reference architecture can bring this functionality to other applications assuming that navigation applications are willing to support it.

Unfortunately applications are not well defined components and their development is not necessarily controlled by the reuse organization. Applications are large and their invocation model does not necessarily support multiple parallel invocations. Public common interfaces end up being compromises between different interface requirements and applications. Their development is slow and applications can conform to them when they consider appropriate. Pair wise negotiations for application specific interfaces could fulfill the need much faster and more precisely.

Many existing architectures can be easily mapped to our model. Many banking systems have a natural three-layered approach. On the top, a presentation layer contains various web applications, bank staff PC applications, and interfaces to other institutions. These applications are often specific for the particular user group. The middle layer is typically composed of different banking solutions. These solutions are intended to be reused as much as possible in the different development projects. Finally, the data layer provides information centric services to the upper layers in a very reusable way. In practice, developing reusable data services is an extensive, but realizable task. Encapsulating data behind well-defined, stable interfaces is possible. In fact, this is also the basis of most service oriented architecture (SOA) solutions. By having stateless data services allows large-scale reuse in multiple contexts.

For very large-scale systems, achieving a balance between reuse and differentiation is hard especially for systems requiring vertical integration thought many abstraction levels; using just one product line development model, is difficult. Furthermore, trying to change the whole development model of such system to align with one methodology is extremely risky. Our experience in many domains indicates that for systems involving software from user specific applications to hardware related software is better served by applying multiple product line development models.

Product line research has proposed many different models for organizing reuse [13]. We separate most methods into three different approaches as shown in the Table 3. Product platforms separate the reusable part from the application parts. Our approach can be viewed as a variation of the platform approach. However, in the platform model the reuse organization is typically in charge of integration and provides only one unified interface to its clients. We employ the compositional approach for the product line infrastructure, allowing widely varying number of components to be reused by the products.

In our work we have taken a technical viewpoint on differentiation. We see differentiation based on the needs of the customers that is then converted into the characteristics of the products. However, it is possible to differentiate even if there is no real difference between the products. Impressions of difference, marketing, branding and many other factors can equally provide differentiation and thus competitive advantage [18]. We acknowledge the need for marketing techniques to enhance differentiation. Our approach is complementary to non-technical means to achieve differentiation.

Table 2. Related work and potential problems in complex product lines

Research topic	Studies	Problems in complex product lines
Platform development	DX200[14]	Near commonality leading to very fat or very thin platform Stability of the platform interface Integration effort Long implementation cycle
Centralized variability management	FODA [15] FORM [16] PULSE [17] ...	Near commonality High complexity for large product lines Stress of dependency management
Compositional	Product populations [10]	Not suitable for the whole software stack Very difficult for component developers

5 Conclusions

In this paper, we have proposed a practical approach for balancing needs for differentiation and reuse in complex product lines. It is based on practical knowledge and experience obtained when being involved in the development of many software product lines. We see our method as a combination of previously proposed approaches. We apply these techniques for real products lines, in a way, that allows them to incrementally move towards a better balance between the reuse and differentiation. Our intent is to help practitioners manage their product lines and identify important industrial considerations for researchers. Our approach is not about changing the basis of product line development nor does it really require huge changes to the traditional product line development models. We suggest using multiple product line development methods when creating a single product line. Products should focus on product requirements, but for each new feature a clear value proposition must be made. A reuse organization's first priority is to serve the needs of the products, but with some time allocated to identifying sets of common products and create new reusable components for these. The product line infrastructure team should focus on creating a set of well-defined high reusable components.

References

[1] McLure, C.: Software Reuse Techniques - Adding Reuse to the Systems Development Process. Prentice Hall, New Jersey (1997)

[2] Lim, W.C.: Managing Software Reuse - A Comprehensive Guide to Strategically Reengineering the Organization for Reusable Components. Prentice-Hall, New Jersey (1998)

[3] OMG, Reusable Asset Specification, 05-11-02, Version 2.2 (2005)

[4] Jacobson, I., Griss, M., Jonsson, P.: Software Reuse - Architecture, Process and Organization for Business Success. Addison-Wesley, Reading (1997)

[5] Porter, M.: Competitive Advantage: Creating and Sustaining Superior Performance. First Free Press Export Edition ed., Free Press, New York (2004)

[6] Lutz, R.R.: Toward Safe Reuse of Product Family Specifications. In: Proceedings of the 1999 Symposium on Software Reusability (SSR 1999), pp. 17–26. ACM Press, New York (1999)

[7] Bosch, J.: The challenges of broadening the scope of software product families. Communications of the ACM 49(12), 41–44 (2006)

[8] Savolainen, J., Oliver, I., Myllärniemi, V., Männistö, T.: Analyzing and Re-structuring Product Line Dependencies. In: Computer Software & Applications Conference, pp. 569–572. IEEE, Los Alamitos (2007)

[9] Savolainen, J., Kauppinen, M., Männistö, T.: Identifying Key Requirements for a New Product Line. In: 14th Asia-Pacific Software Engineering Conference, pp. 478–485. IEEE, Los Alamitos (2007)

[10] van Ommering, R.: Software Reuse in Product Populations. IEEE Transactions on Software Engineering 31(7), 537–550 (2005)

[11] van Ommering, R., Bosch, J.: Widening the scope of software product lines - from variation to composition. In: Software Product Line Conference, pp. 328–347. Springer, Heidelberg (2002)

[12] Bosch, J.: Software Product Families in Nokia. In: Software Product Lines Conference (SPLC 2005), pp. 2–6. Springer, Heidelberg (2005)

[13] Bosch, J.: Software product lines: organizational alternatives. In: 23rd International Conference on Software Engineering, pp. 91–100 (2001)

[14] Ylä-Rotiala, A.: How to convince the management. In: Workshop on Software Reuse, WISR7

[15] Kang, K.C., Cohen, S.G., Hess, J.A., Novak, W.E., Peterson, A.S.: Feature-Oriented Domain Analysis (FODA) Feasibility Study, Software Engineering Institute, Carnegie Mellon University, Pittsburgh, Pennsylvania, USA, Technical Report CMU/SEI-90-TR-21 (1990)

[16] Kang, K.C., Lee, J., Donohoe, P.: Feature-oriented product line engineering. Software, IEEE 19(4), 58–65 (2002)

[17] Atkinson, C., Bayer, J., Bunse, C., Kamsties, E., Laitenberger, O., Laqua, R., Muthig, D., Paech, B., Wust, J., Zettel, J.: Component-based Product Line Engineering with UML. Addison-Wesley, London (2002)

[18] Trout, J.: Differentiate or Die - Survival in Our Era of Killer Competition. Wiley, New York (2000)

Integrating Component and Product Lines Technologies

Elder Cirilo[1], Uirá Kulesza[2,3], Roberta Coelho[1],
Carlos J.P. de Lucena[1], and Arndt von Staa[1]

[1] PUC-Rio, Computer Science Department, Rio de Janeiro, Brazil
{ecirilo,roberta,lucena,arndt}@inf.puc-rio.br
[2] Recife Center for Advanced Studies and Systems – C.E.S.A.R., Recife, Brazil
uira@cesar.org.br
[3] CITI/DI/FCT, New University of Lisbon, Lisboa, Portugal

Abstract. In this paper, we explore the integration of product line and component technologies in the context of the product derivation process. In particular, we propose new extensions to our existing model-based product derivation tool, called GenArch, in order to address the new abstractions and mechanisms provided by the Spring and OSGi component models. The GenArch extensions enable the automatic instantiation of product lines and applications - implemented using these component technologies. Moreover, it also enables different levels of customization, from fine-grained configuration of component properties to the automatic selection of components that will compose the final product.

1 Introduction

A software product line (SPL) [5] can be seen as a system family that addresses a specific market segment. A system family [10] is a set of programs that shares common functionalities and maintain specific functionalities that vary according to specific systems being considered. Software product lines and system families are typically specified, modeled and implemented in terms of common and variable features. A feature [13] is a system property or functionality that is relevant to some stakeholder and is used to capture commonalities or discriminate among systems in SPLs.

Many approaches for SPL development [21,5,6,10] propose the definition of an architecture which comprises their common and variable features. This architecture is typically defined in a process called *domain engineering*. Different technologies can be adopted to implement the code artifacts of SPLs architectures, for instance: object-oriented frameworks and design patterns [8,3,9], aspect-oriented programming [1,15], feature-oriented programming [18], conditional compilation [1] and code generation [6]. Each one of them brings benefits and drawbacks to the modularization of common and variable features (*variabilities*) of SPL. Therefore, it is common to combine two or more of these technologies to implement different code assets of typical SPL architectures.

In the *application engineering* stage of SPL development [6], the core assets produced during the *domain engineering* stage [6] are composed and integrated to generate an instance (product) of the SPL architecture. This process is also known as *product derivation* [7]. Recent proposed approaches, such as Generative Programming [6] and

H. Mei (Ed.): ICSR 2008, LNCS 5030, pp. 130–141, 2008.

Software Factories [10] motivate the definition of mechanisms to support automatic product derivations. Such mechanisms can improve the productivity and quality of the derivation process. Domain-specific languages (DSLs) and code generators are the main technologies adopted by them. Several product derivation tools based on the feature model [13] or DSLs [6] have already been used in industry.

Over the last years, new component infrastructure technologies have been proposed. The main goal of them is to offer a unified model to allow the adequate management (i.e., assembling, adapting and connecting) of components and their configuration. Two important examples of such technologies based on Java platform are Spring and OSGi. The Spring framework [19] is a widely adopted Java/J2EE application framework. It offers a model to build applications as a collection of simple components (called beans) which can be connected or customized using dependency injection and aspect-oriented technologies. The OSGi [16] technology provides an infrastructure to manage the life-cycle of application components. The OSGi applications are structured as a set of *bundles* [16] - a *bundle* represents an application component that provides services to the end-user or other components. In the context of SPL development, these component infrastructure technologies can be combined with the programming techniques mentioned above to allow a better management of the SPL features.

This paper explores the integration of product line and component technologies in the context of the *product derivation process*. In particular, we propose new extensions to our existing model-based product derivation tool, called GenArch [4], in order to address the abstractions and mechanisms provided by the Spring and OSGi component models. The proposed extensions enable the automatic instantiation of product lines and applications implemented using these mainstream component technologies. Moreover, the GenArch extensions also provide different levels of customization from fine-grained configuration of component properties to the automatic selection of components that will compose the final product generated.

The remainder of this paper is structured as follows. Section 2 briefly describes GenArch tool in the context of an illustrative *product derivation* scenario - each subsection (Sections 2.1 to 2.3) presents one step in the generative approach supported by the tool. Section 3 details the GenArch extensions that integrate Spring (Section 3.1) and OSGi (Section 3.2) technologies to support automatic *product derivation*. Section 4 presents discussions and lessons learned while extending the tool and using it on *product derivation* scenarios. Finally, Section 5 presents our conclusions and directions for future work.

2 GenArch – A Model-Based Derivation Tool

GenArch [4] is a model-based tool which enables the mainstream software developer community to use the concepts and foundations of the SPL approach in the product derivation process [7] without the need to understand complex concepts or models from existing product derivation tools. This section presents an overview of the GenArch through an illustrative example of a *product derivation* scenario in JUnit framework.

2.1 Annotating Java Code with Annotations

The first step of the *domain engineering* consists in the creation of a domain model which defines which features exist in a specific domain and which of them are mandatory, optional and alternative features. Our approach starts at the end of the domain engineering stage, when the engineers annotates the existing code (classes, interfaces and aspects) of SPL architectures using GenArch specific annotations. These annotations map product line *features* and *variabilities*, defined in the domain model, to implementation elements of the SPL architecture. Two kinds of annotations are supported by our approach:

(i) @Feature - this annotation is used to indicate that a particular implementation element addresses a specific feature. It also allows to specify the kind of feature (mandatory, alternative, optional) being implemented and its respective feature parent if exists; and

(ii) @Variability - it indicates that the annotated element represents an extension point (e.g. a hotspot framework class) in the SPL architecture.

Figure 1 shows an example of the use of the GenArch annotations in the context of JUnit framework. The TestCase class is a framework hotspot in JUnit that needs to be extended in order to create specific test cases. Thus, according to our approach, the TestCase class was annotated with two GenArch annotations (see Figure 1). The @Feature annotation indicates that this class implements the **Test Case** feature, which is mandatory. This means that every instance of the JUnit framework requires the implementation of this class. The @Variability annotation specifies that the **Test Case** is an extension point of the JUnit framework. It represents a hotspot that needs to be specialized when creating instances of the framework. Although the **Test Case** is a variation point, it is also as a mandatory feature since all JUnit instances must have at least one instance of TestCase class.

```
@Feature(name="Test Case",parent="Test Suite",
                                 type=FeatureType.mandatory)
@Variability(type=VariabilityType.hotSpot,feature="Test Case")
public abstract class TestCase extends Assert implements Test {
        private String fName;
        [...]
}
```

Fig. 1. TestSuite Class Annotated

Next subsection shows how GenArch annotations are processed to generate the initial version of the derivation models.

2.2 Generating and Refining the Approach Models

The GenArch approach encompasses three models: (i) the *product line implementation model*; (ii) the *feature model*; and (iii) the *configuration model*. These models must be specified in our approach to enable the automatic derivation of SPL members. The *product line implementation* model defines a visual representation of the

SPL implementation elements (i.e., classes, aspects, templates, configuration and extra files) in order to relate them to feature models. *Feature models* [6,13] are used in our approach to represent the variabilities of SPL architectures. The configuration model is responsible for defining the mapping between features and implementation elements.

After the developer annotates the source code, the GenArch tool processes these annotations and generates initial versions of the models. The models are automatically derived by parsing the directory that contains the implementation elements. In this parsing step, each @Feature annotation demands the creation of a new feature in the feature model, and the creation of a mapping relationship between the created feature and the respective annotated implementation element in the configuration model. The GenArch tool also generates code templates based on the @Variability annotation. After the generation of the initial versions of GenArch models, the domain engineer can refine them - including, modifying or removing any feature, implementation element or mapping relationship.

The JUnit product line implementation model contains all JUnit implementation elements and templates. The configuration model specifies the mapping relationships between JUnit implementation elements and features from the JUnit feature model. Some mapping relationships can be created automatically based on GenArch annotations, such as: (i) the mapping between `TestCase` class and **Test Case** feature can be created based on the @Feature annotation from the `TestCase` class (Figure 1); and (ii) the mapping between `TestCaseTemplate` and **Test Case** feature can be created based on the @Variability annotation from the `TestCase` class (Figure 1). On the other hand, the mappings between some components need to be created manually. For instance, the mapping between the runner components (awtui, swingui and txtui) and runner features (**TXT**, **AWT** and **Swing**). The runner components are responsible to starting and tracking the execution of test cases and suites. JUnit provides three alternative implementations of test runners: command-line based user interface; an AWT based interface; and a Swing based interface. These mapping was not created automatically because it is not possible to annotate Java libraries.

2.3 Product Derivation Process in GenArch

The derivation process supported by GenArch, demands the specification of a feature model instance (also called a configuration) in which product variabilities are chosen and configured. The GenArch tool supports the SPL architecture customization by deciding which implementation elements need to be instantiated to constitute the final application requested and by customizing classes, aspects or configuration files. Each element that must be customized is represented by a template. The customization of each template is accomplished by GenArch tool using information collected by the *feature* and *product line implementation models.*

The last step of the derivation process in GenArch is characterized by the selection of existing implementation elements and the template-based code generation. The implementation elements that were selected and generated are then included in a source folder of a specific Eclipse Java project. The complete algorithm used by GenArch tool can be found in [4, 14].

3 Extending GenArch with Component-Based Technologies

In this section, we present the GenArch extensions that enable the automatic instantiation of product lines (and applications) implemented using Spring and OSGi component technologies. We use a web application to illustrate the proposed extensions. The web application is a simple shopping store that allows the management of customers' orders. Its main features are: (i) registering customers' orders; (ii) presenting administration reports - such as the number of orders by customer, orders that contain expensive products and list of expensive products; and (iii) logging of application's operations, database queries, and exceptions thrown inside the application. In this application, we assume that the reports generation and the logging are optional features. Additionally, the logging feature also offers two alternative ways of persistence: database and xml files, respectively. Figure 2 shows the feature model of this web application.

The shopping store application is structured according to the Layer pattern [9], following the traditional web architecture of three layers [22]: web (front-end), business and data access. It is organized in terms of six main components: (i) web – it specifies the Java classes responsible to process the user web requests; (ii) service – defines the base business services offered by the application; (iii) data – defines the classes that implement the database access; (iv) reports – aggregates the business classes the implement the application reports; (v) logging – provides different implementations of the logging crosscutting feature (**Query, Exception** and **Operation**); and (vi) util – it is composed of the utility classes.

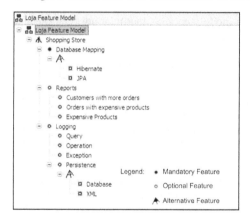

Fig. 2. Shopping Store Feature Model

Next subsections illustrate how this web application and its variabilities can be automatically instantiated using the GenArch extensions provided to support the Spring and OSGi component models.

3.1 Spring Framework

Spring [19] is an open-source framework created to address the complexity of Java enterprise application development. Spring enables the development through use of components, called POJOs (*Plain Old Java Objects*) [19]. Each POJO contains only *business logic*. The Spring framework is responsible for addressing additional features (e.g., transaction, security, logging), which increment the base functionality provided by POJOs with characteristics required to build enterprise applications.

Spring makes it possible to use Java Beans component model to address the design of Java based enterprise applications in a flexible way, as opposed to complex component models like Enterprise Java Beans [15]. However, the usefulness of Spring is not limited to server-side development. Any Java application can benefit from Spring in terms of simplicity, testability, and loose coupling. The simplicity and loose coupling is reached by the inversion of control principle [12] (IoC), also called dependency injection [12], and the aspect-oriented container provided by the Spring framework. In the IoC technique, the objects are passively given their dependencies instead of creating or looking for dependent objects for themselves. A component expresses its dependency on other components by exposing setter methods or through constructor arguments. Due to this approach, Spring components are simpler to write and maintain. The Spring AOP (Aspect-Oriented Programming) framework provides a flexible solution for addressing crosscutting enterprise concerns, such as transaction management, logging and security. Spring container uses a XML configuration file to specify the dependency injection on application components. This file contains one or more bean definitions which typically specify: (i) the class that implements the bean, (ii) the bean properties and (iii) the respective bean dependencies. Additionally, this configuration file also defines which aspects will be applied to each bean (component) of the application.

In this work, we developed an extension to GenArch tool that enables the use of Spring technology in the implementation of SPL architectures. It allows the automatic instantiation of applications during product derivation by helping the decision of which Spring components (beans) will integrate the final product. In our implementation, we extend the GenArch product line implementation model to incorporate the Spring Bean abstraction. In this new model version, each Java class (a POJO in Spring terminology) can be associated with a bean abstraction, which can be related with other beans. Based on this description, GenArch can choose which beans will compose the final application and automatically generate a specific Spring configuration file for this final application.

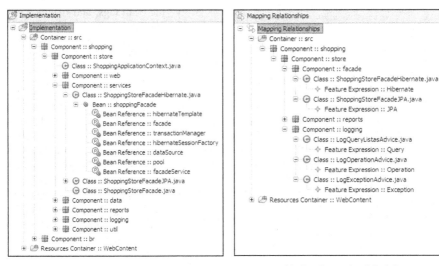

(a) Product Line Implementation Model   (b) Configuration Model

Fig. 3. Shopping Store GenArch Models

Figure 3(a) shows the product line implementation model of the shopping store web application with some associated Spring beans. The `ShoppingStoreFacadeHibernate` class that implements the Facade design pattern (see Figure 3(a)), is associated with the `shoppingFacade` bean. It means that this class implements a Spring Bean, called `shoppingFacade`. This bean depends on different beans, marked with the `Reference` abstractions in the GenArch implementation model, such as: `hibernateTemplate`, `facade`, `hibernateSessionFactory`, `pool` and `facadeService`, `transaction-Manager`, `dataSource`. The Spring beans definitions can be created manually or automatically in the product line implementation model. The automatic creation is based on the Spring configuration file defined by domain engineers during the SPL implementation. The GenArch tool also parses the configuration files while processing the annotations and automatically generate the derivation models (Section 2.1).

The configuration model that incorporates the Spring extension, keeps the same characteristics of the GenArch original version (Section 2). The domain engineers must create mapping relationships between the features and the implementation elements in the configuration model (Figure 3(b)). If a specific Java class, which is also a Spring bean, is marked with a @Feature annotation, the mapping relationship between that class and the feature specified in the annotation is automatically created in the configuration model.

Each Spring application configuration file is defined as an XPand template [17] in our extension. These templates are processed by GenArch tool in two steps: (i) customization of the bean tags; and (ii) choice of the beans tags that will compose the final application configuration file. Figure 4 shows the template used to generate Spring configuration file of the shopping store application. During the product derivation process, this template is processed to customize its respective variabilities. For example, the property called `interceptorNames` need to be configured in agreement with selected logging policies. In this template (lines 26-32), the Spring AOP Proxy Interface, which are responsible to intercept methods and weave advises, only weave the `Exception-Advise` if the feature with id **exception** (line 26) was

```
01.«IMPORT br::pucrio::inf::
02.    les::genarch::models::feature»
03.«EXTENSION br::pucrio::inf
04.    ::les::genarch::models::Model»
05.«DEFINE Main FOR Model»
06. [...]
07. <beans>
08.<bean id="shoppingFacade"
09.    class=" shopping.store.data
10.    .ShoppingStoreFacadeHibernate">
11.
12.    <property name="template">
13.    <ref bean="hibernateTemplate" />
14.    </property>
15. </bean>
16. [...]
17. <bean id="facadeService"
18.    class="org.springframework.
19.    aop.framework.ProxyFactoryBean">
20. <property name="proxyInterfaces">
21.    <value>shopping.store.
22.    services.ShoppingStoreFacade</value>
23. </property>
24. <property name="interceptorNames">
25.    <list>
26.    «LET feature("exception",
27.    featureElements) AS e»
28.    «IF e.isSelected »
29.    <value>ExceptionAdvise</value>
30.    «ENDIF»
32.    «ENDLET»
33.    [...]
34.    </list>
36. </property>
37. [...]
38. </bean>
39. [...]
28. </beans>
```

Fig. 4. Spring Configuration File Template

selected (line 28). After the previous configuration, the GenArch chooses, based in the feature model instance and the mappings on the configuration model, which Spring beans will compose the final application.

At the end of the derivation process, the Java classes (representing beans) and the customized configuration file are then loaded in a specific source folder of an Eclipse Java project that represents the product.

3.2 OSGi Technology

The Open Services Gateway Initiative (OSGi) [16] is a consortium of approximately eighty companies from around the world that collaborate to create a platform and infrastructure to enable the deployment of services from wide area networks to local networks and devices. The OSGi specifies an open, common architecture to develop, deploy and manage services in a coordinated fashion. According to the OSGi specification, Java applications are structured into a set of bundles. Each bundle represents an application component that provides services to the end-user or other components. A bundle is defined as the only entity responsible for deploying Java applications. It is typically deployed as a Java .jar archive file that contains, besides other implementation resources (e.g., classes, aspects, pictures), the manifest file which comprises information about the bundle. This information includes the location of a class, called the activator, that is called when the installed bundle is started or stopped. The manifest also contains other interesting information, such as package dependencies, used and provided services and additional general information about the bundle.

In the present study, we developed a GenArch extension that enables the customization and configurable deployment of OSGi bundles through a feature model. Our extension enables the customization in two levels: (i) the definition of resources (classes, files, etc) that compose the bundles; and (ii) the definition of bundles that will be part of the final application.

Figure 5 shows the product line implementation model of our shopping store case study using the OSGi extension developed to GenArch tool. Figure 5(a) shows the implementation elements in the traditional view of the product line implementation model. This view was already supported in the base version of GenArch (Section 3). Figure 5(b) shows the deployment OSGi view of GenArch considering the shopping store case study. It specifies the bundles that implement the application or product line. The `shopping.store.service` bundle implements the application facade component. It requires two other bundles: (i) `shopping.store.data` – that implements the database access; and (ii) `shopping.store.logging` – that implements the logging crosscutting feature. The `shopping.store.web` bundle implements the application web interface. It requires the services implemented by the `shopping.store.service` and `shopping.store.reports` bundles.

The OSGi technology requires the definition of a manifest file (MANIFEST.MF) for each bundle of an application. The main information about bundles is described in the following properties: `Bundle-Name`, `Require-Bundle`, and `Export-Package`. In our OSGi extension, GenArch is responsible for customizing this file during *product derivation* in order to include the specification of bundles as part of the final generated application. More specifically, these three properties are customized based on information provided by the derivation models (feature, configuration and implementation).

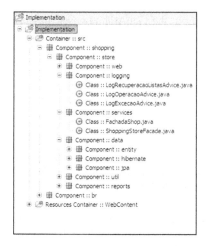

(a) Implementation Elements

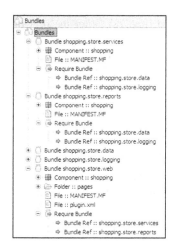

(b) Bundles

Fig. 5. OSGi Product Line Implementation Model

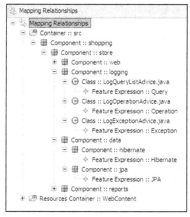

(a) Mapping Relationships

(b) Bundles Relationships

Fig. 6. OSGi Configuration Model

Two levels of configuration are supported by our GenArch OSGi extension. Figure 6 illustrates these levels by showing the different views of the configuration model for an OSGi based product line. In the first level, the domain engineer can define fine-grained configurations by creating mapping relationships of specific implementation elements to any feature. Figure 6(a) shows, for example, that each aspect of the logging component depends on a specific logging optional feature from the feature model. The `LogQueryListAdvice` aspect, for example, depends on the `Query` feature. The definition of such mapping relationships (in the configuration model) enables our tool to decide which elements will compose the final bundles of a specific product.

In the second level, the domain engineer can define mapping relationships between bundles and any feature. Figure 6(b) illustrates a new view provided by the GenArch OSGi extension to the configuration model. It allows the definition of specific bundles of a product line, according to the features selected to be included in the product (during *application engineering*). The shop-ping.store.logging bundle, for example, depends on the occurrence of the **Logging** feature.

The information provided by the OSGi configuration model enables the GenArch tool to decide which bundles will compose the final product, based on the feature selection. During the product derivation, our tool proceeds in the following way to generate each bundle of the final product: (i) it creates an Eclipse plug-in project; (ii) it loads the selected implementation elements and template generated elements in this project; and, finally, (iii) it customizes the `Bundle-Name`, `Require-Bundle` and `Export-Package` fields in the OSGi manifest file. The fields of the OSGi manifest file are customized based on the information available in the product line implementation model and feature model instance. These models work as DSLs that provide custom information for the template processing. Differently from previous versions of GenArch, which demands the derivation of only one Eclipse Java project, the OSGi extension generates one Eclipse project for each bundle, because the OSGi implementation requires the definition of one project per bundle.

4 Discussions and Lessons Learned

Integrating Spring and OSGi. Some recent works [20] have emphasized the combined adoption of Spring and OSGi as complementary component technologies. While the Spring framework offers a flexible and effective component model to manage static and more fine-grained component dependencies of both crosscutting and non-crosscutting services, the OSGi provides a dynamic runtime infrastructure that allows the management of components in runtime. The GenArch extensions presented in this work already take into consideration the possibilities and benefits for integration of both technologies. The developers can create and manipulate a series of Spring beans in the product line implementation model, and after that they can assign to a specific OSGi bundle the Java classes that implement the Spring beans. Although our tool already addresses these scenarios, it has not considered the implementation of the Spring OSGi module [20], which is currently under development. This module is responsible for providing a smooth integration between Spring and OSGi frameworks by allowing an OSGi application to import and export Spring packages and services. We are currently investigating this new Spring support to OSGi in order to provide support to it in our product derivation tool.

Runtime Customization of Product Lines. Many of the component infrastructure technologies developed over the last years have emphasized the need to provide support to dynamic customization of applications. J2EE technology, for example, enables the dynamic deployment of enterprise beans components. The deployment of new components or the management (e.g, update or removal) of existing ones is supported by means of mechanisms provided by the application servers, such as, JBoss. OSGi technology also allows flexible dynamic management of components. However, it has not been much explored in the context of Java server-side applications. The Spring OSGi [20] module is an initiative in this way. The Spring and OSGi extensions to the GenArch tool proposed in this work already represent an advance in the use of these technologies to implement product lines architectures. They can enable the dynamic customization of product lines. However, this customization is accomplished mainly based on the product line components. One interesting direction to investigate is to explore the dynamic customization of product lines based on the feature model. In this kind of approach, feature based tools would drive the customizations based on the selection of features. The feature selection performed by the application engineer would demand the automatic deployment (e.g., removal or updating) of several components associated to the selected features.

5 Conclusions and Future Work

In this paper, we presented two extensions to a product derivation tool which address the integration of Spring and OSGi mainstream component-based technologies. Our extensions consider the use of these technologies in the implementation of SPL architectures by incorporating their abstractions and mechanisms to the derivation models adopted by GenArch tool [4]. Automatic mechanisms are used to generate partial version of these models based on the specific artifacts (configuration and manifest files) and abstractions (beans, aspects, bundles, dependencies, etc) of Spring and OSGi technologies. During the product derivation process, the GenArch tool enables the automatic instantiation of product lines (or applications implemented using the mechanisms available in Spring and OSGi) by selecting and customizing components based on a set of selected features.

As a future work, we intend: (i) to apply and evaluate the proposed extensions in the context of complex component based product lines; (ii) to address the support to the under development Spring OSGi module; (iii) to investigate the use of feature models in the dynamic customization of product lines.

Acknowledgments. The authors are supported by LatinAOSD/Prosul Project - CNPq/Brazil. Uirá is also partially supported by European Commission Grant IST-33710: Aspect-Oriented, Model-Driven Product Line Engineering (AMPLE).

References

[1] Alves, V., Matos, P., Cole, L., Borba, P., Ramalho, G.: Extracting and Evolving Mobile Games Product Lines. In: Obbink, H., Pohl, K. (eds.) SPLC 2005. LNCS, vol. 3714, pp. 70–81. Springer, Heidelberg (2005)

[2] Anastasopoulos, M., Muthig, D.: An Evaluation of Aspect-Oriented Programming as a Product Line Implementation Technology. In: Bosch, J., Krueger, C. (eds.) ICOIN 2004 and ICSR 2004. LNCS, vol. 3107, pp. 141–156. Springer, Heidelberg (2004)

[3] Buschmann, F., Meunier, R., Rohnert, H., Sommerlad, P., Stal, M.: Pattern-Oriented Software Architecture, A System of Patterns, vol. 1. Wiley, Chichester (1996)

[4] Cirilo, E., Kulesza, U., Lucena, C.: GenArch: A Model-Based Product Derivation Tool. In: Proceedings of Brazilian Symposium on Software Components, Architectures and Reuse (SBCARS 2007), Campinas - Brazil (August 2007)

[5] Clements, P., Northrop, L.: Software Product Lines: Practices and Patterns. Addison-Wesley Professional, Reading (2001)

[6] Czarnecki, K., Eisenecker, U.: Generative Programming: Methods, Tools, and Applications. Addison-Wesley, Reading (2000)

[7] Deelstra, S., Sinnema, M., Bosch, J.: Product Derivation in Software Product Families: a Case Study. Journal of Systems and Software 74(2), 173–194 (2005)

[8] Fayad, M., Schmidt, D., Johnson, R.: Building Application Frameworks: Object-Oriented Foundations of Framework Design. John Wiley & Sons, Chichester (1999)

[9] Gamma, E., Helm, R., Johnson, R., Vlissides, J.: Design Patterns: Elements of Reusable Object-Oriented Software, vol. 395. Addison-Wesley Longman Publishing Co., Inc., Amsterdam (1995)

[10] Greenfield, J., Short, K.: Software Factories: Assembling Applications with Patterns, Frameworks, Models and Tools. John Wiley and Sons, Chichester (2005)

[11] Harold, E., Means, W.: XML in a Nutshell. O'Reilly, Sebastopol (2004)

[12] Johnson, R.: Expert One-on-One J2EE Design and Development. Worx (2002)

[13] Kang, K., et al.: Feature-oriented domain analysis (FODA) feasibility study. Technical Report CMU/SEI-90-TR-021, SEI, Pittsburgh, PA (November 1990)

[14] Kulesza, U.: An Aspect-Oriented Approach to Framework Development, PhD Thesis, Computer Science Department (in Portuguese), PUC-Rio, Brazil (April 2007)

[15] Monson-Haefel, R.: Enterprise JavaBeans. O'Reilly, Sebastopol (2001)

[16] OSGi, http://www.osgi.org

[17] openArchitectureWare, http://www.eclipse.org/gmt/oaw/

[18] Smaragdakis, Y., Batory, D.: Mixin Layers: An Object-Oriented Implementation Technique for Refinements and Collaboration-Based Designs. ACM TOSEM 11(2), 215–255 (2002)

[19] Spring Framework, http://www.springframework.org

[20] Spring OSGi, http://www.springframework.org/osgi

[21] Weiss, D., Lai, C.: Software Product-Line Engineering: A Family-Based Software Development Process. Addison-Wesley Professional, Reading (1999)

[22] Fowler, M.: Patterns of Enterprise Application Architecture. Addison-Wesley, Reading (2002)

Feature Implementation Modeling Based Product Derivation in Software Product Line

Xin Peng, Liwei Shen, and Wenyun Zhao

Computer Science and Engineering Department, Fudan University, Shanghai 200433, China
{pengxin,061021062,wyzhao}@fudan.edu.cn

Abstract. Although there has been significant research spent on feature modeling and application-oriented customization and some effective methods have been proposed, product derivation in SPL (Software Product Line) development is still a time- and effort-consuming activity due to the complicated mapping between feature model and program implementation. In this paper, we propose a feature implementation modeling based method for product derivation. In the method, feature implementation model is introduced as the intermediate level between feature model and program implementation. The feature implementation model captures feature interactions (including cross-cutting interactions) in the finer role level, and help to clarify the complex mapping between feature and program implementation. So, feature-driven program-level customization and configuration can be enabled by the model and role instantiation. AOP (Aspect-Oriented Programming) is adopted as the implementation technology for product derivation on the program level. Then program-level composition can be implemented by aspect weaving to finally achieve the feature-driven product derivation.

1 Introduction

A fundamental reason for investing in SPL is to minimize the costs of product derivation [1]. The ideal mode of product derivation is constructing the final product by configuring and tailoring of core assets, following a prescribed process, and complemented by application-specific implementation of some parts. Feature-oriented domain requirements modeling points out a possible way to implement the customization-based requirement reuse [2]. So, most methods on feature modeling support application-oriented customization with constraint dependencies (e.g. [2][3]). However, the big gap between problem domain and solution domain make it difficult to map customization and tailoring on feature model to implementation program level.

The relation between problem and solution space is a many-to-many relation ([2][4][5]). Some intermediate mechanisms between features and components are proposed to improve feature-based architecture design and product derivation, e.g. responsibilities in [2] and component role in [4]. On the other hand, AOP (Aspect-Oriented Programming) as SPL implementation technology has attracted much attention (e.g. [6][7]) due to its enhancement on crosscutting features, adaptability and configurability. These concepts can help understand the reality of feature based design and implementation and provide guidance in practice. However, we still need

H. Mei (Ed.): ICSR 2008, LNCS 5030, pp. 142–153, 2008.

systematic and practical methods for feature oriented product derivation, which should provide some automatic mechanism and tool support.

In this paper, we propose a feature implementation modeling based product derivation method for SPL development. Feature implementation model, an intermediate level between feature and program implementation, is introduced to link feature variability and program variability. In the model, each feature is logically implemented by some roles and interactions between roles are also modeled. Roles are instantiated by elements in the base programs or variability-related programs. AOP is adopted to implement the program-level composition for role interactions.

The remainder of this paper is organized as follows. Section 2 analyzes the problem of product derivation in SPL development. Feature implementation model and product derivation are introduced in section 3 and 4 respectively. Then a case study and tool support for the method are presented in section 5. Related works are discussed in section 6. Finally, we draw our conclusions with discussion in section 7.

2 Problem of Product Derivation in Software Product Line

In this section, we will analyze problems in product derivation with a simplified example of library management domain. The feature model is showed in figure 1 according to the ontology-based meta-model proposed in our previous work [3], in which decomposition relations are presented and lines with hollow circle represent optional elements. In the system, *BookAdd*, *Search&Browse*, *BorrowBook* and *ReturnBook* are basic functions. *BookPicShow* (show the book picture when browsing), *BorrowControl* (control book borrowing by prescribed policy) and *BookLog* (log when a book is added, borrowed or returned) are optional functions. Even if all the features are implemented, we will still find it hard to derive customized products from these core assets. Usually we will implement some business classes and several visual forms for book adding, browsing, borrowing and returning. Then we can see the bound of *BookPicShow* usually needs both an image container and a code segment of image data fetching to be added. Furthermore, there is interaction between *Search&Browse* and *BookPicShow*: *BookPicShow* should be activated when a book is searched and showed in the browsing form.

The interaction can be more complicated. The optional *BorrowControl* can even change the execution of base programs: if *BorrowControl* is bound, it will interrupt the execution of *BorrowBook* if it doesn't meet prescribed policy. Furthermore, feature interaction can even affects multiple features, e.g. *BookLog* affects *BookAdd*, *BorrowBook* and *ReturnBook*. Besides feature-level variability, there is also variability on design and program level, e.g. fetching image data from database or file system if *BookPicShow* is bound. This kind of variability is not visible on the feature level, but it will affect the product derivation also.

From this case, we can see problems in product derivation include: feature implementation scatters and bound of a feature may need adaptations on multiple program units; complex interactions between features and even crosscutting feature interactions; variability on multiple levels (requirement, design, etc). The root of the problem is the complicated mapping between feature and program implementation. In our method, role based feature implementation model is introduced to improve the situation by clarifying the mapping and feature interactions.

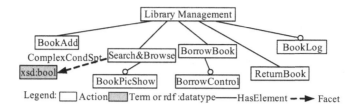

Fig. 1. Feature model of simplified library management domain

3   Feature Implementation Model

Feature implementation model is the logical design model for the implementation of features. It specifies all the necessary implementation roles for each feature and instantiates roles to program elements (i.e. class, method, etc), so as to map feature-level customization to program-level implementation. An SPL consists of a base implementation (mandatory features) and a number of variability-related features, and a product can be derived by selecting an arbitrary number of these features and combining with the base implementation [4]. In our feature implementation model, there are also base roles and variability-related roles. The latter are to be selected and configured to implement bound variability-related features, while the former provide linking points for variability-related programs to be composed into the product.

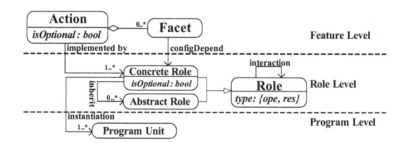

Fig. 2. Meta-model of the feature implementation model

3.1   Feature Implementation Meta-model

Meta-model of the feature implementation model is presented in figure 2, which is extended from our previous ontology-based feature model [3]. In the feature model, *Action*, representing business operations, is the basic element. *Facet* is introduced to provide more business details for actions, which can be construed as perspectives, viewpoints, or dimensions of precise description for Action [3]. Each action is implemented by one or more roles. A role is a logical unit, a responsibility which should be taken by program fragment for feature implementation. The concept of role here is similar to the responsibility in [2] and the role in [4]. Two kinds of roles are distinguished, one is operational role (*type=ope*), the other is resource role (*type=res*). An operational role is a functional segment, e.g. fetching image data for show. Resource role represents specific internal or external entity necessary for the implementation of a feature, e.g. an image container to show picture. Resource role in our method is similar to resource container proposed in [2], which can passively accept features' requests for resource storing, querying, and retrieving, and play the role of a medium of interaction between features.

A series of roles can interact with each other to implement a feature (mostly *Action* in our model) together. For example, from figure 3 we can see *BookPicShow* can be implemented by three roles. *ImageContainer* is an image container for picture show, *ImageFetch* is to fetch image data from database or file system, and *PicShowControl* takes the responsibility of controlling image fetching and showing. There are also interactions between roles from different features, e.g. *PicShowControl* is activated by role from *Search&Browse* to fetch and show the picture. Then the feature *BookPicShow* can be implemented by role interactions within it and across the role boundary. Role interaction clarifies how a user-visible feature is implemented by several logical sides and guides the program-level customization and composition. In our method, five kinds of interactions are identified as in table 1, in which interaction point denotes a role activates another role before or after execution of itself.

Table 1. Interactions between roles

Interaction	Description	Interaction Point
Involve	An operational role activates another operational role in a synchronous mode and makes it a part of the host operation.	**Before** or **After**
Inform	An operational role informs another operational role to activate in an asynchronous mode.	**Before** or **After**
Determine	Execution result of an operational role can determine the execution of another operational role, including whether execute or not and choosing a variant from several choices.	**N/A**
Access	An operational role reads or writes a resource role, or both, to fulfill its responsibility in specific feature implementation.	**N/A**
Introduce	A resource role is introduced into implementation unit of another operational role to be a sub-element.	**N/A**

Among the five kinds of interactions, the first three are between two operational roles, the last two between an operational role and a resource role. All these five kinds of interactions are embodied in figure 3. For example, *ImageFetch* is involved in *PicShowControl*, *BookChange* will inform *BookLog* to activate, *BorrowControl* (if bound) will determine the execution of *BorrowBook*, *PicShowControl* will access *ImageContainer* to show the image, and *ImageContainer* (if bound) will be introduced as an element of *BookSearch*. Interactions can occur between roles from different features, e.g. the interaction between *BookSearch* and *PicShowControl* in figure 3. Inter-feature role interactions are the embodiment of feature interactions and clarify the interactions in a finer granularity. It should be emphasized that not all the modeled role interactions will appear in a final product, since some roles reside in optional or variable features, e.g. *Determine* relation between *BorrowControl* and *BorrowBook* will not take effect if the feature *BorrowControl* is not bound. However, this interaction can help to compose the behaviors of *BorrowControl* and *BorrowBook* in the right way once *BorrowControl* is bound.

In some cases, role interactions will occur between a role and a set of roles with common characteristics. These interactions usually crosscut multiple parts of a system. For example, *BookLog* will be informed to activate by all the changes on books, e.g. *BorrowBook*, *ReturnBook*, etc. So, abstract role is introduced to denote a class of roles and provide expressions for crosscutting interactions. Abstract role does not reside in any feature and will be inherited by other concrete roles. For example, in figure 3, if the optional *BookLog* is bound, it will be attached to both *BorrowBook* and *ReturnBook*. An abstract role also has its role type (operational role or resource role), and role inheritance can only occur between roles with the same role type.

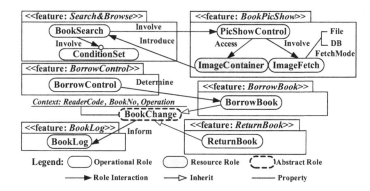

Fig. 3. Segment of feature implementation model for the library management domain

3.2   Variability in Feature Implementation Model

Role-level implementation for optional features is plain: roles for an optional feature are involved in the system or not according to whether the feature is bound. Similarly, as for specialization, each variant feature has its own role design and related roles are involved or not according to whether the variant is bound. In these cases, no additional variability should be considered. Our feature model provides the mechanism of partial variability for features, i.e. variable facet-value in our feature model, e.g. the facet *ComplexCondSpt* defined on the feature *Search&Browse* in figure 1. In this case, role-level variability should be modeled to support it. On the other hand, feature implementation model can also introduce new design-level variations for different implementation choices. For example, *ImageFetch* contains a design-level variation of fetching mode, i.e. read the image data from DB or file system. In our method, role-level variability is supported by optional roles and role properties. Optional roles should be further evaluated to be bound or removed even if the feature it resides in is bound. Role properties provide a kind of partial variability for roles, e.g. the property *FetchMode*. Different property-values mean different implementation modes in program level, e.g. different instantiations or parameters.

As mentioned above, some role-level variations are related to feature-level, others are completely design-level considerations. Example of the former is the optional role *ConditionSet*, which is designed to support the variable facet *ComplexCondSpt*. So, there exist configuration dependencies between feature variations and role variations. The dependency is denoted by the relation *configDepend* between action facets and roles in our method (see figure 2). It is similar to configuration dependency on *Facet-Value* in our feature model [3], and the difference is that dependency here is between feature and role. An atomic feature-role dependency can be expressed as:

$$(action, facet=term) \rightarrow (role, [property=value]),$$

in which "*facet=term*" means a facet value assumption for *action*, optional "*property=value*" is a property value assumption for *role* (absence means configuration depending on bound of the role). Then the feature-driven configuration dependency on *ConditionSet* can be expressed as (*Search&Browse, ComplexCondSpt=true*) → (*ConditionSet*).

3.3   Design Consideration in Feature Implementation Model

Different designers can have different implementation model designs for the same feature model. However, there still some guidance. Role interaction is to provide direct guidance for program-level customization and composition. Intuitively, if different parts of a role are involved in interactions with different roles, usually they should be separated as several roles to enable program-level composition. Role granularity should also be carefully designed to maximize commonalities and localize variations. For example, the role design for the feature *BookPicShow* separates variable role *ImageFetch* from *PicShowControl* to localize the variability. If *ImageFetch* has no variability, it can be merged with *PicShowControl* for simplicity.

3.4   Role Instantiation and Role Context

From figure 2, we can see each concrete role is instantiated by a program unit. Program unit here can be a class or method in an object-oriented language. These program units correspond to roles with different types (*ope* or *res*), different interactions and different variability (mandatory, optional or variable). Operational roles are instantiated by methods, in which variability-related roles are implemented by separated method segments to be composed into the base program. Instantiation of determining role can determine the execution of other methods, so return value and the policy (specifying what return value corresponds to what decision) are also needed. Resource roles are instantiated by classes, e.g. *ImageContainer* in figure 3 can be instantiated by a Java Canvas class. As for resource roles introduced by other roles, additional initialization code is also needed to initialize it in the host class, e.g. create a Canvas object, and set its size and position, etc.

In program-level composition, necessary mechanisms of data sharing and transfer should also be established between interacting program units. In our method, role context is introduced to model inter-role interaction information. Role context is runtime information about the role, which can be accessed by other roles in interactions. For example, *ReaderCode*, *BookNo* and *Operation* are identified as the context of *BookChange*, representing code of the current reader, book number and the current operation in an execution of *BookChange*. In this example, *BorrowBook* and *ReturenBook* will inherit the context, since they are specialized roles of *BookChange*. In role instantiation, each role context should be instantiated to enable runtime context access. On the other hand, role property should also be instantiated to make the role-level customization implemented on the program-level.

The entire schema of role instantiation is presented in figure 4. We can see a role can have multiple instantiations, e.g. Role 4, and a property-value of it can determine which implementation is bound in product derivation. Other properties can be mapped to parameters of the implementation method, and then role-level customization can be embodied by program-level parameters. Role context is instantiated by constants or runtime expressions. Constant context is applicable for several roles inheriting the same abstract role. For example, the context *Operation* of *BookChange* provides description for the current operation to be recorded in the operation log, and can be instantiated as constant strings "borrow book" and "return book" in the specialized roles *BorrowBook* and *ReturenBook* respectively. Runtime expression can provide runtime context for other interacting roles, e.g. *ReaderCode* and *BookNo*. It can be any legal expressions in the runtime context of the method, e.g. "getCurrentBookNo()" (get the book number by a method call) or "bookNo" (get the book number by an object property). These expressions can be used in the glue code to share the context with interacting program units.

There are also roles with application-specific implementation, e.g. role *BorrowControl* may be different in each product. These roles can be instantiated by method or class declaration, which can be implemented by application engineers. It should be emphasized that role property and context are different mechanisms for product derivation. Role property is determined in role-level customization and affects the implementation of the same role, while role context is declared for references of other interacting roles and the value is usually determined at runtime.

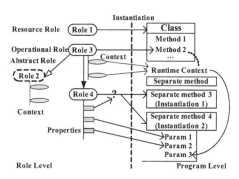

Fig. 4. Role instantiation schema

3.5 Role-Level Customization

Product derivation is first driven by application requirement, i.e. feature-level customization in SPL development. Feature customization is guided and verified by feature constraints, which is well discussed in works on feature modeling (e.g. [2][3]).

After feature customization, role-level customization can be considered for those roles residing in bound features. Feature-role dependency introduced in 3.2 will help to achieve the feature-driven role customization. Each feature-role dependency like "*(action, facet=term)* → *(role, [property=value])*" will be applied to determine the property-value of a role or bound of an optional role. If no inconsistency emerges, role-level refinement ends. Then other pending role variations, which are additional variability introduced in logical design, will be considered. For example, *FetchModel* defined in figure 3 will be determined to be *File* or *DB* completely from the design consideration (whether to use database or not).

4 Program-Level Customization and Composition

After role-level customization, variability-related program units can be selected and configured according to the role instantiation. If a role corresponds to more than one program unit, its property values are used to determine which instantiation is chosen. Program configuration is to map customized property values to program parameters, which will be transferred to the program unit by the glue code. After that, variability-related program units will be composed with each other and base programs by aspect weaving. In our implementation, AspectJ [8] is adopted to implement the program composition, so related concepts such as advice, join point are used.

Table 2. Composition rules for various role interactions

Interaction	Advice	Glue Code
Involve	**before** or **after execution**	Context acquisition, parameter preparation and transfer
Inform	**before** or **after execution**	Context acquisition, parameter preparation and transfer; Startup a new thread to execute the informed program
Determine	**around call**	Context acquisition, parameter preparation and transfer; Determine whether proceed the method or not by return value of the determining method
Access	N/A	Prepare the resource reference expression and transfer to the call to the accessing method
Introduce	resource: **Introduce** initialization: **after execution**	Embodied in the initialization code

4.1 Composition with Base Programs

Composition rules for various interaction types are listed in table 2. In each case, variability-related program unit is woven into base program. **Involve** interaction weaves the involved program by a **before** or **after execution** advice according to the interaction point. Automatically generated glue code included in the advice will acquire the context, prepare the parameters and transfer them to the involved method. **Inform** interaction is similarly treated, but a new thread will be started up to execute the informed program in an asynchronous mode. Both **Involve and Inform** interactions are implemented on the **execution** level. **Determine** interaction is implemented by **around call** advice. It is implemented on the **call** level, so that it can control other woven programs. Implementation of **Introduce** interaction includes two parts: introduce the resource object as a property of the host class; weave the initialization code into the constructor of the host class. Interaction with abstract role is cross-cutting, e.g. each role inherited from *BookChange* should inform *BookLog* and provide context information (*Reader-Code*, *BookNo* and *Operation*) for logging if it is bound. In this case, weaving and glue code will be generated for program units corresponding to all the concrete roles, each with different context information.

4.2 Composition between Variability-Related Programs

Composition between variability-related programs implements feature-dimension composition. That is program units corresponding to roles of the same feature are composed together to implement the feature, even if they are woven into different base classes. Generally, interactions between variability-related roles fall into two categories. One is the **Access** interaction between an operational role and a resource role, e.g. interaction between *PicShowControl* and *ImageContainer* in figure 3. In this case, the resource role may have another **Introduce** interaction with a base role. Programs for the two roles may be woven into different base classes, so a reference chain between them should be established to enable implementation of the **Access** interaction. It can be achieved by navigation between objects of the two classes, since the resource object can be accessed from its host by a get method added in the weaving (see table 2). So when instantiations of two roles with **Access** interaction are woven into two different classes, a navigation expression from the runtime context of the operational role will be requested from the developer, e.g. "currentBook.getAuthor()". The implementation method of accessing role can declare the resource object as a parameter. Then, in composition, the resource reference expression can be generated with the navigation expression and transferred to calls to the accessing method (see table 2).

The other category is interaction between two operational roles, e.g. interaction between *PicShowControl* and *ImageFetch* in figure 3. In this case, at most one of them may have interaction with base roles, so interaction between their instantiation can be fixed in the program. For example, invocation to *ImageFetch* can be included in the *PicShowControl* implementation, but the implementation version for *ImageFetch* may be different since it has more than one instantiation (with the same method signature) due to the role variability of *FetchMode*.

4.3 Class-Dimension Coordination

In program composition, instantiations of multiple variability-related roles may be woven into the same base method. These advices should be well coordinated to eliminate possible conflicts. In our method, two kinds of coordination are provided. One is for multiple determinations, e.g. *BorrowBook* may be determined by a new role *ReaderCheck* (check the account status) besides *BorrowControl*. In this case, multiple determinations are imposed on the same base method, so these determination rules can combined in a conjunctive mode. The other is coordination for determination and other interactions. In this case, determination is on the domination position, which can determine not only the base method, but also other interaction advices. This domination is implemented by different weaving policies: **Determine** is woven on the **call** level, while **Involve** and **Inform** are on the **execution** level.

5 Tool Support and Case Study

The method proposed in this paper has been implemented in our prototype of feature-driven product derivation tool. It is integrated with OntoFeature, the feature modeling tool developed in our previous work [3], by importing and capturing the feature list and dependencies. The tool provides editing space for each feature, supports the role customization and program-level composition by invoking the AspectJ Compiler.

Now we will demonstrate a case study of the *BookPicShow* implementation of the library management showed in figure 3. We can see the resource role *ImageContainer* has an **introduce** interaction with a base role, so it is instantiated by both an implementation class and a code segment of initialization. In this example, *ImageContainer* is instantiated by the *Canvas* class and the initialization code is to set the size and listener. Then, when *BookPicShow* is bound in the product derivation, the role *ImageContainer* can be composed by an automatically generated aspect, which declares a *Canvas* object as the inter-type of *BookForm* (the class which instantiation method of *BookSearch* resides in) and adds the initialization code after the execution of the constructor of *BookForm* (see the left part of figure 5).

```
//introduce the 'canvas' resource and its initialization method
//do the initialization after the create method in bookform
private org.eclipse.swt.widgets.Canvas BookForm.canvas;

public org.eclipse.swt.widgets.Canvas BookForm.getImageContainer() {
    return this.canvas;
}

pointcut addCanvas(BookForm form) :
    (execution(* create*(..))) && this(form);

after(BookForm form) returning :
addCanvas(form) {
    form.addBookCoverFrame();
}

public void BookForm.addBookCoverFrame() {
    this.setSize(500, 294);
    this.canvas = new Canvas(this, SWT.BORDER);
    this.canvas.addPaintListener(new PaintListener() {
        public void paintControl(final PaintEvent event) {
            Image image = (Image) canvas.getData();
            if (image != null) {
                event.gc.drawImage(image, 10, 10);
            }
        }
    });
    this.canvas.setBounds(350, 10, 140, 200);
    this.canvas.setData(null);
    this.canvas.redraw();
}
```

```
//after searching a book in bookform
//get the context (bookname,imagecontainer)
//and invoke the picShowControl function
pointcut showPic(BookForm form) :
    (execution(* searchBook(..))) && this(form);

after(BookForm form) returning :
showPic(form) {
    ExtraOperation.picShowControl(
        form.getCurrentBook().getBookname()
        form.getImageContainer());
}
//get picture through bookname by
//invoking getImage function
//then set the picture into container
public static void picShowControl
                (String bookname,Canvas container) {
    Image image = null;
    try {
        image = ExtraOperation.getImage(bookname);
    } catch (Exception e) {
    }
    if (image!=null) {
        container.setData(image);
        container.redraw();
    }
}
//get picture from database or file system
public static Image getImage(String bookname) {
    ......
}
```

Fig. 5. Aspect glue code generated

On the other hand, there is an **Access** interaction between *PicShowControl* and *ImageContainer*, so a navigation expression should be given to enable the interaction. In this example, both of them are woven into the same class *BookForm*, since instantiation method of *BookSearch* also resides in it. So, the navigation expression is an empty string, because they are in the context of the same class. In our example, *PicShowControl* is composed after *searchBook* (instantiation method for *BookSearch*) by an aspect which fetches picture of searched book and set it into *ImageContainer* (see the right part of figure 5).

After feature- and role-level customization, aspects for all the bound variability-related roles can be automatically generated. Then they can be compiled together with all the base programs and variability-related instantiation programs by invoking AspectJ compiler (by *ajc* command) and a product is derived. Figure 6 shows the snapshots of the book borrow form before and after the binding of *PicShowControl*.

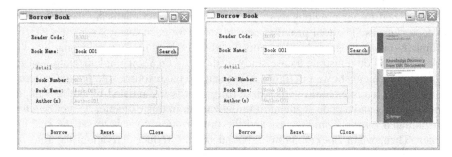

Fig. 6. Book borrow form before and after the binding of *PicShowControl*

6 Related Works

In SPL researches, there has been significant effort spent on the early steps, including scope definition, domain and feature modeling and architectural design, but less attention has been paid to the implementation level [6]. Deelstra et al. [1] analyze the problems during product derivation and point out that complexity of the SPL in terms of the number of variation points and variants and implicit properties (e.g., dependencies) of variation points and variants are the two core issues. Deursen et al. [5] propose a source-level packages based method for product derivation. In the method, product is derived by packaging source-code components according to feature selections. This source code based method has no explicit model for feature interaction and feature-driven customization.

Jansen et al. [4] propose a feature based method for product derivation. Their method also introduces role model to help relate features with components, and then products can be derived by selecting a number of base components and features based on their composition algorithm. In the method, role interactions are not explicitly modeled and the composition is implemented by inheritance in object-oriented language (both base component and role are implanted by classes). Our method provides comprehensive support for role interaction modeling and implementation (by property, context, etc), and adopts a lightweight and flexible mechanism for product composition by aspect weaving.

Some researchers have noticed the potential of AOP as a SPL implementation technology. Anastasopoulos et al. [6] performed a case study to evaluate AOP as a SPL implementation technology, and drew the conclusion that AOP is especially suitable for variability across several components and whether AOP is suitable for other variability still need further study. Lee et al. [7] propose to combine feature analysis and AOP to enhance reusability, adaptability, and configurability of product line assets. They provide some good guidelines for AOP based SPL assets development by considering commonality and variability, dependency and binding time. However, the method lacks an intermediate level to clarify the connection between feature and program implementation, so can not support feature-driven program customization and composition.

7   Conclusion and Discussion

In this paper, we propose a product derivation method in which feature-driven program-level customization and composition are supported by feature implementation modeling, instantiation and aspect weaving in AOP. The main contribution of this paper is enabling feature-driven program-level customization and composition for product derivation by introducing an intermediate feature implementation model between feature model and program implementation along with corresponding customization and instantiation. However, our method doses not cover the issue of feature-driven DSSA (Domain Specific Software Architecture) design. In fact, domain-level design and implementation are assumed to have been done. Our method provides a mechanism of feature implementation design and instantiation to map feature-level customization to program-level configuration and composition. It is an implementation technology for product derivation in SPL. In the future research, we will focus on more systematic and comprehensive support for feature-driven implementation design and SPL evolution management.

Acknowledgments. This work is supported by National Natural Science Foundation of China under Grant No. 60703092, and National High Technology Development 863 Program of China under Grant No. 2006AA01Z189 and 2007AA01Z125.

References

1. Deelstra, S., Sinnema, M., Bosch, J.: Experiences in Software Product Families: Problems and Issues During Product Derivation. In: Nord, R.L. (ed.) SPLC 2004. LNCS, vol. 3154. Springer, Heidelberg (2004)
2. Zhang, W., Mei, H., Zhao, H.: Feature-driven requirement dependency analysis and high-level software design. Requirements Eng. 11, 205–220 (2006)
3. Peng, X., Zhao, W., Xue, Y., Wu, Y.: Ontology-Based Feature Modeling and Application-Oriented Tailoring. In: Morisio, M. (ed.) ICSR 2006. LNCS, vol. 4039. Springer, Heidelberg (2006)
4. Jansen, A.G.J., Smedinga, R., van Gurp, J., Bosch, J.: First class feature abstractions for product derivation. IEE Proc.-Softw. 151(4) (2004)
5. van Deursen, A., de Jonge, M., Kuipers, T.: Feature-Based Product Line Instantiation Using Source-Level Packages. In: Chastek, G.J. (ed.) SPLC 2002. LNCS, vol. 2379. Springer, Heidelberg (2002)
6. Anastasopoulos, M., Muthig, D.: An Evaluation of Aspect-Oriented Programming as a Product Line Implementation Technology. In: Bosch, J., Krueger, C. (eds.) ICOIN 2004 and ICSR 2004. LNCS, vol. 3107. Springer, Heidelberg (2004)
7. Lee, K., Kang, K.C., Kim, M., Park, S.: Combining Feature-Oriented Analysis and Aspect-Oriented Programming for Product Line Asset Development. In: SPLC 2006. IEEE Computer Society, Los Alamitos (2006)
8. AspectJ Team. AspectJ Project, http://www.eclipse.org/aspectj/

Feature-Oriented Analysis and Specification of Dynamic Product Reconfiguration

Jaejoon Lee[1,*] and Dirk Muthig[2]

[1] Computing Department, Lancaster University,
InfoLab21, Lancaster, LA14WA, United Kingdom
j.lee@comp.lancs.ac.uk
[2] Fraunhofer Institute for Experimental Software Engineering (IESE),
Fraunhofer Platz 1, 67663 Kaiserslautern, Germany
dirk.muthig@iese.fraunhofer.de

Abstract. In many application domains, scenarios have been developed that benefit from the idea of ambience; Systems will not necessarily be activated by people anymore, but will react on their own to situations they recognize. It, thereby, must dynamically adapt itself to changes in the technical environment or user context. In addition, such dynamically reconfigurable products must be customized to the individual needs of particular users. Product line engineering can be applied to create these variants efficiently; however, means for handling adaptation capabilities at a generic level are required. This paper introduces the front-end of such a means by describing an approach for analysis and specification of features that vary as a part of reconfigurations at runtime.

1 Introduction

In the near future, systems will not necessarily be activated by people anymore, but will react on their own to situations they recognize. "Ambient Applications" is the name for such applications, which are characterized by situation-caused, proactive reactions and dynamic system configuration.

During the past few years, scenarios were developed in many application domains that benefit from the idea of "ambience." For example, diverse pieces of end user equipments interact on their own in a "virtual office" domain - either because certain persons are identified, messages are received from other equipments, or based on status of higher-level business workflows. Additionally, office equipment will provide services to its potentially mobile users that are useful in their current context (i.e., their role and responsibilities, the active workflows, and the available technical infrastructure).

Hence systems must change at all levels: business logic, user interface, and system services. This implies that dynamically reconfigurable products are required, which are able to continuously:

- monitor their current situation (i.e., their operational context),
- validate and execute reconfiguration requests with consideration of change impacts and available resources, and
- maintain system integrity and running services even during reconfigurations.

---

* This work is done while Jaejoon Lee was with Fraunhofer IESE.

H. Mei (Ed.): ICSR 2008, LNCS 5030, pp. 154–165, 2008.

In addition, products must be individually customized to their particular users, that is, different users in a virtual office organization use different variants of office equipment.

We apply product line engineering to efficiently construct these variants. Thereby, product line engineering is an approach that systematically exploits common characteristics and predicted variations of product families [1][2]. It constructs, on the one hand, a generic reuse infrastructure, which is, on the other hand, systematically instantiated and reused while developing particular products. Clearly, variants of dynamically reconfigurable products also differ in aspects relevant to the adaptation and thus to reconfiguration capabilities of these products. Hence, approaches for engineering families of dynamically reconfigurable products must provide means for handling generic adaptation capabilities.

In this paper, we address the front-end part of this problem: the proposed approach focuses on the analysis and specification of features that vary as a part of reconfigurations at runtime.

1.1 Related Work

The approach is related to two areas of work: dynamic product reconfiguration and product line engineering. Dynamic product reconfiguration, on the one hand, has been studied in various research areas such as self-healing systems [3][4][5], context-aware computing [6][7], software component deployment [8][9][10], and ubiquitous computing [11][12]. Dynamic addition, deletion, or modification of product features, or dynamic changes of architectural structures [13][14] are some examples of dynamic reconfiguration. When a change in the operational context is detected, it may trigger product reconfiguration to provide context-relevant services or to meet quality requirements (e.g., performance).

Dynamic reconfiguration approaches in the literature, however, have focused on *reconfiguration of single products*, not on families of products. That is, accommodation of product-specific dynamic reconfiguration needs that may differ from one product to another has not been considered in engineering software assets. On the other hand, most efforts in product line engineering have focused on the development of reusable assets with variation points for *static configuration* of products: identification and specification of variation points, consistency management among them, and techniques for product code generation [1][2][15].

Recently, Reconfigurable Product Line UML Based SE Environment (RPLUSEE) [13] is proposed and its specialty is the provision of software dynamic reconfiguration patterns. Depending on the location of dynamic reconfiguration information, these patterns are classified into master-slave, centralized, client-server, and decentralized. This method also provides Statecharts and transaction models for specifying the dynamic reconfigurations. This approach focuses on high-level specifications of dynamic reconfigurable units; however, it does not describe techniques and guidelines for identifying reconfigurable units and specifying reconfiguration strategies in detail. In this paper, we focus on providing a formal base that can be used as a basis for adding other new definitions and consistency rules easily.

1.2 Approach

To develop dynamically reconfigurable and reusable core assets, we should be able to answer the following questions:

- What are the units for dynamic changes in a product and how are they related to variations of a product line?
- What is a common operational context and what is a product specific one?
- How can we support various reconfiguration strategies such as continuous provision or suspension of a service during reconfiguration, etc. that may vary among products?
- How can we identify change impacts of dynamic reconfiguration in a current product configuration?

The feature-oriented approach to analyzing and specifying dynamic product reconfiguration proposed in this paper first analyzes a product line in terms of features. Then, it specifies dynamic product reconfiguration by using the analysis results as a key driver. The specification is developed with consideration of three concerns: reconfiguration situations (when to reconfigure), reconfiguration strategies (how to reconfigure), and consistency rules between specifications.

As a case study, a virtual office of the future (VOF) product line, which controls and manages a collection of devices to provide a any-time any-where office environment, is used [16]. The rest of this paper is organized as follows. Section 2 describes feature analysis activities and Section 3 explains how the feature analysis results are used to specify dynamic product reconfiguration. Section 4 discusses the proposed approach and concludes this paper with some future work.

2 Feature Analysis

Feature modeling is the activity of identifying externally visible characteristics of products in a product line and organizing them into a model called feature model [2]. Fig. 1 shows, for instance, a part of the feature model for the VOF product line. The primary goal of feature modeling is to identify commonalities and differences of products in a product line and represent them in an exploitable form, i.e., a feature model.

Common features among different products in a product line are modeled as mandatory features (e.g., *Resource Manager* and *Smart Fax*), while different features among them may be optional (e.g., *Follow Me* and *Auto Log-on*) or alternative (e.g., *User Positioning Method*). Optional features represent selectable features for products of a given product line, and alternative features indicate that no more than one feature can be selected for a product. Details of feature analysis and guidelines can be found in [17].

Once we have a feature model, it is further analyzed through feature binding analysis [18]. Feature binding analysis consists of two activities: feature binding unit (FBU in short) identification and feature binding time determination. FBU identification starts with identification of service features. A service feature represents a major functionality of a system and may be added or removed as a service unit. In VOF, *FM*, *RM*, and *SF* features are examples of service features.

A set of features that should be included in an FBU are identified by traversing the feature model along feature relationships. For example, *Follow Me*, *User Authentication*, *Manual Log-on*, *Auto Log-on*, *User Positioning Method*, *Access Point based Method*, and *RFID based Method* belong to the *FOLLOW ME (FM)* FBU. Note that the optional *AUTO LOG-ON* FBU and the alternative *USER POSITIONING METHOD*

FBU are identified as separate FBUs, because they may have different binding time from their parent FBUs. For an alternative FBU, its alternative variants are listed in parenthesis (e.g., *AP* or *RFID* for *USER POSITIONING METHOD* in Fig. 1.

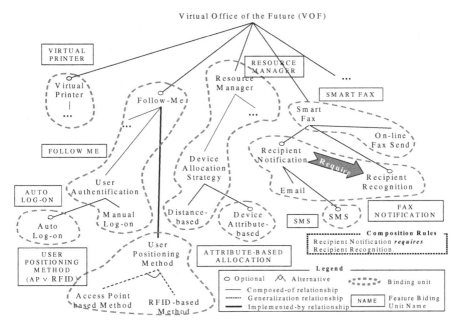

Fig. 1. A Feature Model and Binding Units of VOF (Adapted from [19])

Next, we need to identify and specify explicitly what feature should be bound into a product at runtime[1]. For that purpose, we adopted the graph theory [20] by taking binding units as vertexes and binding relations as edges. In the following, we introduce some definitions for the specification. First, we define features, FBUs, and a feature binding graph.

Definition 1 (feature)
A feature is defined as a 2-tuple *<FName, C>*, where

– *FName*: the name of a feature.
– *C*: the commonality of a feature, which is one of mandatory, optional, or alternative.

Definition 2 (feature binding unit)
An FBU is defined as a 3-tuple *<FBUName, C, CF>*, where

– *FBUName*: the name of a feature binding unit.
– *C*: the commonality of a feature binding unit, which is one of mandatory, optional, or alternative.
– *CF*: a set of features that constitute a feature binding unit.

---

[1] The feature binding at earlier phase of lifecycle (e.g., product development time, installation time) is discussed in [18]. In this paper, we focus on feature binding at runtime.

Definition 3 (feature binding graph)
A feature binding graph *G* is defined as a labeled digraph without cycles, where:

– Each vertex is a feature binding unit and V(*G*) is the vertex set.
– *G* has a unique root vertex r, which represents a system.
– The vertex types *m*, *o*, and *a* represent mandatory, optional, and alternative feature binding units, respectively.
– Each label of a vertex is the name of a feature binding unit.
– Each edge indicates a binding relation of two feature binding units and the binding relation is either static or dynamic binding. E(*G*) is the edge set.
– Two vertices cannot have multiple relations.

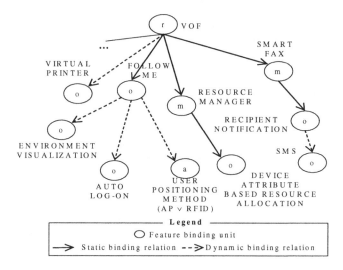

Fig. 2. A Feature Binding Graph of VOF

Fig. 2 shows a feature binding graph of VOF based on the definitions. The root vertex (*VOF*) represents a VOF system and its descendent vertices are binding units that constitute the VOF system. The binding graph in Fig. 2 has five dynamic binding relations (e.g., the binding relation between *VOF* and *VIRTUAL PRINTER (VP)*) and those binding will be made at runtime. Decision on the binding relation type (i.e., static or dynamic) is made with considerations of operational context. For example, the binding of *USER POSITIONING METHOD* (i.e., AP based or RFID based) can be only made at runtime based on available positioning devices nearby a user.

In this section, ways to analyze and specify FBUs were introduced. In the next section, a graph based dynamic reconfiguration specification is introduced. Also, consistency rules to check for the specifications are explained.

3 Dynamic Reconfiguration Specifications

In our approach, the dynamic reconfiguration is specified through three sub-activities: reconfiguration context analysis and specification, reconfiguration strategy specification, and confirmation of consistency rules between specifications. Each of these activities is explained with examples in the following.

3.1 Context Analysis and Specification

The context analysis starts with identifying *contextual parameters* of a product line. A contextual parameter is defined as an environmental element that has a piece of information about a system's context (e.g., current location of a user, battery remaining time, etc.). Once contextual parameters are identified, we refine them by defining attributes of each parameter. The attributes may include data type, sampling rates, and validity conditions. (See Table 1 for a part of dynamic parameter definitions for *VOF*.) In the *Type* column, the types of contextual parameter values are defined. The *Sampling Rate* defines how often the contextual parameters should be checked. A contextual parameter may be valid only if its value is within a pre-defined range or a set of values: such conditions are defined in the *Validity* column. The validity conditions of each contextual parameter should be satisfied before a contextual parameter is used to detect contextual changes.

Table 1. Contextual parameter definition

Attributes Contextual Parameters	Type	Sampling Rate	Validity (a valid range of value or a set of valid values)	Commonality (dependent FBU)
Privilege Level (P)	String	Log-in time	P = "Director" ∨ "D-Head" ∨ "Manager" ∨ "Scientist" ∨ "Visitor" ∨ "Administrator"	Mandatory (–)
Locations (L)	String	30 seconds	L = "Entry" ∨ "D-office" ∨ "Meeting Room 1" ∨ "Meeting Room 2"	Optional (FM)
User in Move (UM)	Boolean	60 seconds	UM == True if L ≠ L' UM == False if L = L'	Optional (FM)

Then, reconfiguration situations are specified as a logical expression of dynamic parameters. A reconfiguration situation is an event that triggers a dynamic reconfiguration. For instance, a *Director in Move* situation is true when *Privilege Level (P)* is *Director* and the *User in Move (UM)* is true. For this situation, the *AUTO LOG-ON* FBU is bound and activated.

Note that the commonality and variability of contextual parameters and their attributes' value should also be considered. For example, *Privilege Level* is common for the *VOF* product line, while *Locations* and *User in Move* are optional and their availabilities depend on the selection of the *FM* FBU. (See the *Commonality* column of Table 1.) Therefore, when a product does not include *FM*, these two contextual parameters are not applicable for the context recognition of the product.

Next, a reconfiguration strategy specification for each reconfiguration situation is explained.

3.2 Specification of Reconfiguration Strategy

A dynamic reconfiguration strategy is about "how" to perform dynamic reconfiguration and is specified for each reconfiguration situation with considerations of binding dependencies (i.e., require and exclude), change impact to other binding units, and required resources (e.g., components). Therefore, the action specification should include information on:

– Pre/post-conditions for reconfiguration (e.g., required binding units or hardware resources),
– Identification of FBUs that are involved in reconfiguration (e.g., binding units to be added, removed, or substituted), and
– Ways to handle currently active services (e.g., stop, suspend, or keep providing current active services).

For the specification of first two items, we adopt a graph transformation [20], which is explained in the following.

Definition 4 (graph transformation) [20]
A graph transformation is defined as a production $p: L \rightarrow R$, where,

– Feature binding graphs L and R are called the left- and the right-hand side, respectively.
– p is a schematic description of direct derivations.
– A production p defines a partial correspondence between the elements of L and R, determining which vertices and edges of L should be preserved, deleted, and created at R by an application of p.

In this paper, L_u is a *pre-image graph* for binding of an FBU u and R_u is *a resulting graph* after the binding of u. The pre-image graph L_u of u is specified with the consideration of "require" and "exclude" dependencies of u. For the formal definition of a pre-image graph, the following sets are used.

Definition 5 (dangling vertex)
The degree d of a vertex v is the number of edges connected to v. If $d(v) = 0$, the vertex v is called a dangling vertex.

Definition 6 (require set for feature binding of u)
– Require(u): A set of feature binding units that must be present in a current configuration for the binding of an FBU u.

Definition 7 (exclude set for feature binding of u)
– Exclude(u): A set of feature binding units that must not be present in a current configuration for the binding of u.

Definition 8 (pre-image graph of u)
A pre-image graph L_u of an FBU u is a feature binding graph, where

– A root vertex $r \in$ Require(u)
– $\forall bu \in$ Require(u) • there exists a path from the root vertex r to bu
– $\forall bu \in$ Exclude(u) • $d(bu) = 0$
– Require(u) $\cap$ Exclude(u) = $\varnothing$
– $\forall bu \in$ V(L_u) • $bu \in$ Require(u) $\vee$ $bu \in$ Exclude(u)

As the definition 8 shows, L_u has the *require* vertices of u as a connected graph from r and has the *exclude* vertex of u as a dangling vertex. For example, *VOF*, *FM*, and *USER POSITIONING METHOD (RFID)* (*UPM(RFID)* in short) are the *require* vertices to bind *AUTO LON-ON*, and the *exclude* vertex is the dangling vertex *UMP(AP)*. This means that *AUTO LON-ON* requires its parent FBU bound in a current configuration and the user position method should be *RFID based*, not *AP based*. Like this, we can explicitly specify pre-conditions for the binding of FBUs.

A pre-image graph is specified for each FBU and used to determine whether or not a binding request is acceptable under a current configuration of a product. To check the acceptability, the following rules are used.

Rule 1 (inclusion of require binding units)
Let C be a feature binding graph that presents a current configuration of a product at runtime. Let L_u be a pre-image graph of an FBU u. For binding of u, C must include the binding units in Require (u). This rule is formally defined as

- $\forall\, bu \in \text{Require}(u) \bullet bu \in V(C)$

Rule 2 (absence of exclude binding units)
Let C be a feature binding graph that presents a current configuration of a product at runtime. Let L_u be a pre-image graph of a binding unit u. For the binding of u, C must not include the binding units in Exclude (u). This rule is formally defined as

- $\forall\, bu \in \text{Exclude}(u) \bullet bu \notin V(C)$

These two rules are checked as a pre-condition for binding of a binding unit. In addition, the following rule is checked as a post-condition.

Rule 3 (inclusion of a resulting binding graph)
Let H be a feature binding graph that presents a current configuration after a reconfiguration at runtime. Let R_u be a resulting graph of a binding unit u. After binding of u, H must include the binding graph R_u as its sub-graph. This rule is formally defined as

- $\forall\, bu \in V(R_u) \bullet bu \in V(H)$
- $\forall\, e \in E(R_u) \bullet e \in E(H)$

Next, six phases of reconfiguration is specified with the consideration of feature binding units to be reconfigured and impacts to other binding units. (See Fig. 3.) The six phases are 1) check pre-condition, 2) suspend active binding units that are involved in reconfiguration, 3) remove or parameterize binding units that have to be deleted or have to change their behaviors, 4) instantiate and bind binding units that are newly added, 5) check post-conditions, and 6) activate new or suspended binding units. By "active" we mean that the state of a binding unit is in the normal operational state.

The first and fifth phases, which check pre/post-conditions of a reconfiguration, are performed based on the rules 1), 2), and 3). At the second phase, we determine whether an involved FBU should be suspended or should provide services continuously during reconfiguration. For example, the *FM* FBU at *Phase 2* in Fig. 3 is suspended for reconfiguration. This means that *FM* finishes its current service and prepares reconfiguration. However, *VOF* coordinates other services (e.g., *SF*, *VP*) continuously during reconfiguration: *VOF* is notified that *FM* is being reconfigured and should not request a service to *FM* during reconfiguration.

At the third phase, FBUs that are no longer needed in the product configuration are removed. If an FBU's behavior can be changed through parameterization instead of removing and newly instantiating the FBU, relevant parameters for a new configuration are sent to the FBU. For example, the behavior of *FM* is changed from the one that does not include *AUTO LOG-ON* to the one with *AUTO LOG-ON*. At the fourth phase, binding units to be newly added to a current configuration are instantiated and bound to a product. Finally, FBUs are activated, after checking the post-condition of the reconfiguration.

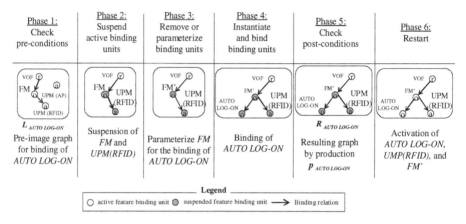

Fig. 3. Six Phases for Dynamic Reconfiguration

In the following section, consistency rules for dynamic reconfiguration specification are introduced.

3.3 Confirmation of Consistency Rules

In this section, two categories of consistency rules are introduced: consistency between FBUs and consistency between reconfiguration strategy specification and behavior specification of FBUs. When more than two FBUs are reconfigured, we have to check the dependency between pre/post-conditions of binding units. They are sequential and parallel dependencies, and their definitions are as follows:

Definition 9 (Sequential Dependency)
– Given two reconfigurations p_1 and p_2 such that $G \overset{p_1}{\Rightarrow} H_1 \overset{p_2}{\Rightarrow} H_2$, p_2 is sequentially dependent on p_1, if and only if at least one of "require" vertices (say v_r) of p_2 such that $v_r \notin G$ is added to the graph G by p_1 and H_1 satisfies the pre-condition of p_2.

This dependency means that the reconfiguration p_2 can only be performed after the reconfiguration p_1. For example, *AUTO LOG-ON* can be bound only when its parent binding unit *FM* is bound beforehand.

Definition 10 (Parallel Dependency)

– Two alternative reconfigurations p_1 and p_2 such that $H_1^{p_1} \Leftarrow G \Rightarrow^{p_2} H_2$ are parallel dependent, if and only if at least one of "exclude" vertices (say v_{e2}) of p_2 such that $v_{e2} \notin G$ is added to the graph G by p_1, and at least one of "exclude" vertices (say v_{e1}) of p_1 such that $v_{e1} \notin G$ is added to the graph G by p_2.

This dependency means that only one of the reconfigurations p_1 and p_2 can be performed. Suppose, for example, that *AUTO LOG-ON* and *VP* may require two distinct variants of the *USER MONITORING METHOD* FBU (i.e., *AP- based* or *RFID-based*). Then, only one of *AUTO LOG-ON* and *VP* can be bound to a product configuration at the same time.

Next, we should consider the consistency between reconfiguration strategy specification and behavior specification of FBUs. During reconfiguration, some events (e.g., *Suspend*, *Terminate*, or *Resume* events) are sent to FBUs to control their behavior for reconfiguration. To maintain system integrity, we have to be sure that these events are processed correctly at each FBU. That is, the behavior specification of each FBU should be able to handle the received events and to generate corresponding responses (e.g., an acknowledging message for a successful process of the *Suspend* event) so that the phases of reconfiguration strategy can be proceeded. The consistency between the two specifications can be checked by tracing events and state transitions.

In this section, activities to analyze and specify dynamic reconfiguration strategy are explained. The next section discusses and evaluates our approach.

4   Conclusions

From our experience in applying product line engineering methods for many industry collaborations, we know the number of product features increases quickly. Hence, the management of features and their variations becomes a big burden to product line asset developers in practice.

While applying these technologies in analyzing and specifying product lines of dynamically reconfigurable products in the domain of robots or virtual office applications, we experienced that these burden gets even bigger. The presented approach alleviates this difficulty through the grouping of features into FBUs that have the same binding time, as well as by taking feature binding units as a key driver for specifying dynamic product reconfiguration.

The practical applications of the feature-oriented analysis and specification so far have improved manageability of product variations and visibility of change impacts of a reconfiguration by:

– Supporting the identification of units of product configuration at the right level of granularity: A binding unit contains a set of features that need to be bound together into a product to provide a service correctly and share a same binding time. Therefore, a product can be considered as a composition of feature binding units. This grouping helps engineers to see a product in an abstract way and, thus, increases visibility and manageability of product configuration.

– Enabling an intuitive and visual description of dynamically changing product configuration: One of the challenges for dynamic product reconfiguration is the tracking of current product configuration and the decision making whether or not to accept a reconfiguration request to the current configuration. Our approach alleviates this difficulty by adopting the graph and graph transformation based specifications. It specifies pre/post-condition and change impacts of a dynamic reconfiguration request in an explicit and graphical way.

– Improving management of variation point dependencies: A feature binding unit presents a unit of a variation and, therefore, feature binding unit based mapping to variation points of the artifacts could help managing consistency between variation points. That is, binding time dependency between variation points can be identified and managed efficiently with the mapping to feature binding units, as well as with the consistency rules between reconfiguration specifications and binding behavior specification of each binding unit.

The presented, feature-oriented approach for analyzing and specifying dynamically reconfigurable products has been applied successfully in different projects. It has proven to clearly ease the development of product lines of reconfigurable systems. In this paper, we focused on providing a formal base that can be used as a basis for adding other new definitions and consistency rules easily. Our approach, however, needs to be extended to address other issues for dynamic reconfiguration such as exception handling strategies during dynamic reconfiguration, a formal base for analyzing consistency between various specifications (e.g., behavior specifications and various reconfiguration strategies), and a support for evolutionary changes.

References

[1] Clements, P., Northrop, L.: Software Product Lines: Practices and Pattern. Addison-Wesley, Upper Saddle River (2002)

[2] Kang, K., Lee, J., Donohoe, P.: Feature-Oriented Product Line Engineering. IEEE Software 19(4), 58–65 (2002)

[3] Garlan, D., Schmerl, B.: Model-based Adaptation for Self-Healing Systems. In: Proceeding of the Workshop on Self-Healing Systems (WOSS 2002), November 18-19, 2002, pp. 27–32 (2002)

[4] Ganek, A.G., Corbi, T.A.: The drawing of the autonomic computing era. IBM Systems Journal 42(1), 5–18 (2003)

[5] Oreizy, P., et al.: An Architecture-Based Approach to Self-Adaptive Software. IEEE Intelligent Systems, 54–62 (May/June 1999)

[6] Yau, S.S., Karim, F., Wang, Y., Wang, B., Gupta, S.K.S.: Reconfigurable Context-Sensitive Middleware for Pervasive Computing. Pervasive Computing, 33–40 (July/September 2002)

[7] Schilit, B., Adams, N., Want, R.: Context-Aware Computing Applications. In: Proceedings of IEEE Workshop Mobile Computing Systems and Applications, pp. 85–90. IEEE CS Press, Los Alamitos, Calf. (1994)

[8] Mikic-Rakic, M., Medvidovic, N.: Architecture-Level Support for Software Component Deployment in Resource Constrained Environments. In: Proceedings of First International IFIP/ACM Working Conference on Component Deployment, Berlin, Germany, pp. 31–50 (2002)

[9] van der Hoek, A., Wolf, A.L.: Software release management for component-based software. Software-Practice and Experience 33, 77–98 (2003)

[10] Hall, R.S., Heimbigner, D.M., Wolf, A.L.: A cooperative approach to support software deployment using the software dock. In: Proceedings of the 1999 International Conference on Software Engineering, pp. 174–183. ACM Press, New York (1999)

[11] Sousa, J.P., Garlan, D.: Aura: An Architectural Framework for User Mobility in Ubiquitous Computing Environments. In: Proceeding of the 3rd Working IEEE/IFIP Conference on Software Architecture, pp. 294–317. Kluwer Academic Publishers, Dordrecht (2002)

[12] Banavar, G., Bernstein, A.: Software infrastructure and design challenges for ubiquitous computing applications. Communications of ACM 45(12), 92–96 (2002)

[13] Gomaa, H., Hussein, M.: Dynamic Software Reconfiguration in Software Product Families. In: van der Linden, F.J. (ed.) PFE 2003. LNCS, vol. 3014, pp. 435–444. Springer, Heidelberg (2004)

[14] Kramer, J., Magee, J.: The Evolving Philosophers Problem: Dynamic Change Management. Transaction on Software Engineering 16(11), 1293–1306 (1990)

[15] Bosch, J., Florijn, G., Greefhorst, D., Kuusela, J., Obbink, J.H., Pohl, K.: Variability Issues in Software Product Lines. In: van der Linden, F.J. (ed.) PFE 2002. LNCS, vol. 2290, pp. 13–21. Springer, Heidelberg (2002)

[16] Competence Center for Virtual Office of the Future, http://www.ricoh.rlp-labs.de/index.html

[17] Lee, K., Kang, K., Lee, J.: Concepts and Guidelines of Feature Modeling for Product Line Software Engineering. In: Gacek, C. (ed.) ICSR 2002. LNCS, vol. 2319, pp. 62–77. Springer, Heidelberg (2002)

[18] Lee, J., Kang, K.: Feature Binding Analysis for Product Line Component Development. In: van der Linden, F.J. (ed.) PFE 2003. LNCS, vol. 3014, pp. 266–276. Springer, Heidelberg (2004)

[19] Lee, J., Muthig, D.: Feature-Oriented Variability Management in Product Line Engineering. Communications of ACM (December 2006)

[20] Corradini, A., et al.: Algebraic Approaches to Graph Transformation, Part I: Basic Concepts and Double Pushout Approach. Technical Report TR-96-17, Pisa, Italy, Universita Di Pisa (March 1996)

Managing Large Scale Reuse Across Multiple Software Product Lines*

N. Ilker Altintas[1] and Semih Cetin[1,2]

[1] Cybersoft Information Technologies,
Ata Plaza 3/3, Kat:3, 34758, Istanbul, Turkey
{ilker.altintas,semih.cetin}@cs.com.tr
[2] Department of Computer Engineering
Middle East Technical University, Ankara, Turkey

Abstract. For large scale applications in today's competitive business environment, partial reuse at class, library, component or module level is still inadequate. Software product lines provide systematic reuse only within a product family. Better gains in productivity and high confidentiality can be achieved by large scale reuse across multiple product lines. This paper puts a methodical way, articulated as "Software Factory Automation", which can manage reusable assets across distinct software product lines based on "domain specific kits" and "software asset meta model". The approach is validated by analyzing the software asset reuse in two different product lines implemented in banking domain and practically used in real life. The results show that high level of reuse within and across multiple product lines can be achieved with the charted roadmap.

1 Introduction

Large scale software systems underlie the core of competitive business environments today, which requires strict high confidentiality in terms of efficiency, reliability, security, safety, fault-tolerance, and trustworthiness. The term "large scale" mainly identifies the following attributes in a software system: dynamic business requirements, complex business rules and workflows, mission criticality, distributed architectures, integration with diverse information sources, hundreds of end users, etc. Hence, achieving high confidentiality in large scale software systems is not straightforward. It requires new analysis techniques for requirements, resolution of crosscutting concerns, modeling of mission critical architectures, effective composition of components, and validation procedures [13].

That is why constructing and maintaining large scale software systems require extreme levels of time, dedication and budget. Similar to other industries, systematic reuse is the cure for cost-effective achievement of high confident large scale software systems. Reuse has always been a major goal in software engineering, since it promises large gains in productivity, quality and time to market

* This research has been partially supported by Technology and Innovation Funding Programs Directorate (TEYDEB) of The Scientific and Technological Research Council of Turkey (TUBITAK) (ProjectNo/Date: 3060543 and 01.09.2006).

H. Mei (Ed.): ICSR 2008, LNCS 5030, pp. 166–177, 2008.

reduction. Practical experience has shown that substantial reuse has only successfully happened in two cases: libraries, where many generic and small components can be found; and product lines, where domain specific components can be assembled in different ways to produce variations of a given product [8].

Throughout the years, several proposals have been on the stage for improving the reuse. Recent approaches like Model Driven Development [9,20], Asset-Based Development [16], Feature-Based Approaches [11,14], Software Product Lines (SPL) [7,18], and Software Factories [10,15] are all aiming to improve systematic reuse with different perspectives.

In a recent analysis of reuse strategies, Rothenberger et al. [19] have investigated the practical reuse strategy alternatives and their effectiveness for a successful reuse program. This study concludes that the success of reuse is independent from the choice of technology; rather it is mainly dependent on how an organization is effective in all dimensions to reuse assets across the design and development of different products. Similarly, Buhne et al. [4] state that the reuse of requirement artifacts for different products leads to an additional dimension of product lines, so called multiple product lines.

This paper puts a methodical way, articulated as "Software Factory Automation", which can manage reusable assets across distinct software product lines based on "Domain Specific Kits" and "Software Asset Meta Model". The paper validates the approach by analyzing the software asset reuse in two different product lines, i.e. Investment Banking and Financial Gateways, implemented in banking domain and practically used in real-life. The reuse results obtained with the charted roadmap across multiple product lines are also discussed.

2   The Approach: Software Factory Automation

Software Factory Automation (SFA) is inspired by the way other industries have been realizing factory automation for decades. Industrial Factory Automation utilizes the concept of "Programmable Logic Controllers (PLCs)" to facilitate the production of domain specific artifacts in isolated units. PLCs may also take place in moving assembly lines to unify the production process.

PLCs improve the reusability of domain specific artifacts with a consistent design in mind: PLC has a Programmable Processor (PP) to be programmed with a Computer Language (CL) through a Development Environment (DE).

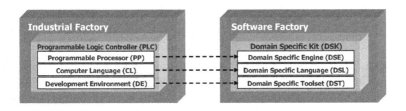

Fig. 1. Software Factory Automation and PLC analogy

So does DSK abstraction of SFA model: the DSK has a Domain Specific Engine corresponding to PP, a Domain Specific Language corresponding to CL, and a Domain Specific Toolset corresponding to DE of PLC concept (See Figure 1).

As the way PLCs are used for abstracting a wide range of functionalities like basic relay control or motion control, DSKs in SFA approach can be designed specifically to abstract certain things such as screen/report rendering or business rule execution. We proceed with presenting Domain Specific Kits in Section 2.1, and later discuss the overview of SFA approach in Section 2.2.

2.1 Domain Specific Kits as the Main Building Block

Domain Specific Kits (DSKs) have been devised to isolate diverse concerns in solution space and specify reusable Domain Specific Artifacts to abstract them. They let the modeling and development of artifacts in isolation and enable their composition via a choreography model. The concept of DSK has been shaped with the following constituents, and Figure 2 depicts the interrelation among them:

– *Domain Specific Language (DSL):* A language dedicated to a particular domain or problem with appropriate built-in abstractions and notations.
– *Domain Specific Engine (DSE):* An engine particularly designed and tailored to execute a specific DSL.
– *Domain Specific Toolset (DST):* An environment to design, develop, and manage software artifacts of a specific DSL.
– *Domain Specific Kit (DSK):* A composite of a Domain Specific Language (DSL), Engine (DSE) and a Toolset (DST).
– *Domain Specific Artifact (DSA):* An artifact that is expressed, developed, and executed by a DSL, DST, DSE, respectively.
– *Domain Specific Artifact Type (DSAT):* An artifact type that a certain DSK can express, execute and facilitate the development. There might be multiple types associated with a DSK.

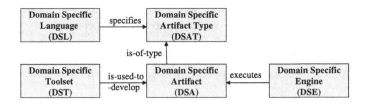

Fig. 2. Conceptual model of DSK

The term "Domain Specific Kits" was first used by Griss and Wentzel within the context of "flexible software factories" [12]. The DSK concept in SFA model diverges from the Griss's definition and attributes a new content to the old term. DSKs in SFA are lightweight and loosely coupled with each other; so their artifacts can be designed to be composed with others. The artifacts are defined and composed by declarative approaches. DSKs are not particular to a product family, they can be reused across different product lines.

In order to exemplify the DSK concept, a Business Rules Management System (BRMS) has been discussed here briefly. A BRMS enables the segregation of business rules from the application where they crosscut almost every tier from content to service. RUMBA [6] provides a clear separation of a crosscutting concern, and enables dynamic integration of business rules with other business processes or business services. RuleML[1] is a domain specific language to define business rules as independent artifacts. *Rule* and *Composite-rule* are the artifact types. RUMBA has a RuleEditor (a domain specific toolset), and a corresponding runtime engine for rule execution, which takes part in business choreography.

Domain Specific Kit abstraction plays a key role for the separation of concerns during domain design. Upon selecting DSKs, corresponding domain specific engines are plugged onto the product line reference architecture. Reference architecture employs a choreography-based composition model for the composition of domain specific artifacts. Modeling environment utilizes corresponding domain specific toolsets and constraints of the architecture in providing an integrated environment for specifying artifacts and their compositions using DSLs and a choreography language, respectively.

2.2 Product Line Setup with SFA

By placing DSKs at the center, *Software Factory Automation (SFA)* proposes a methodical approach to set up software product lines for development of family of products [2,1]. The main strategy is to separate family design concerns properly by isolating them in discrete building blocks, and later to compose them by means of a choreography model. It prescribes three modeling activities that constitute the domain engineering in software product line approach: *Feature-Oriented Requirements Engineering*, *Reference Architecture Modeling* [5], and *Software Asset Modeling* [2]. An overview of major modeling activities that

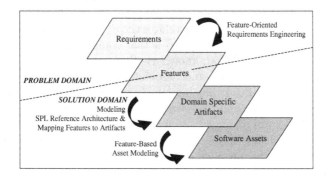

Fig. 3. Overview of Software Factory Automation

---

[1] Rule Markup Initiative. http://www.ruleml.org/

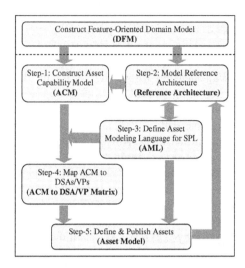

Fig. 4. Overview of asset modeling approach

paves the way from requirements to reusable assets has been presented in Figure 3.

Similar to Turner et al. [21], we treat features as life cycle entities to bridge the problem and solution domains and they are meant to be logically modularizing the requirements. *Feature-Oriented Requirements Engineering* yields the feature models and their descriptions which provide the functional and non-functional features of a product family. The domain requirements are modeled as *Domain Feature Model (DFM)* in compliant with the Mei et al.'s terminology [17]. The content of DFM is a combination of FORM [14] and FODM [17]. A DFM includes feature diagrams, composition rules, feature dictionary, list of requirements (functional and non-functional), quality attributes of the domain, other issues and decisions. DFM is fed into reference architecture modeling and software asset modeling activities (See Figure 4).

Reference Architecture Modeling correlates the architectural aspects and quality attributes of the problem domain to actual components and connectors of the solution domain. This method, known as "Symmetric Alignment" [5], assists the identification of components and associated connectors in structuring the SPL Reference Architecture. It has later been extended in [1] to identify DSEs to be employed in product line reference architecture. The communication and coordination of DSEs are managed through a choreography engine.

Software Asset Modeling uses a feature-based approach to construct the software assets that are coarse-grained collections of domain specific artifacts with variability points. A five-step feature-based asset modeling roadmap has been charted as shown in Figure 4. It yields the definition of product line and its assets in terms of domain specific kits, artifacts, their compositions, their dependencies, and the global contextual information.

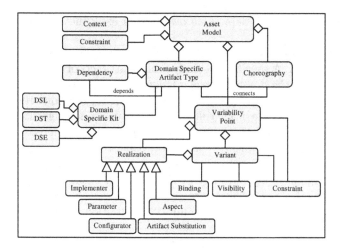

Fig. 5. Software Asset Meta Model (AMM)

The first step is determining asset capabilities in terms of feature diagrams exposing the structural, functional and behavioral properties, and their constraints. The reference architecture modeling yields the SPL reference architecture at Step 2. The reference architecture identifies the set of DSEs and associated DSLs. At Step 3, a modeling language compliant with reference architecture has been derived from a common meta model. (See below for the details of meta model and modeling language). Once the modeling language has been defined at Step 3, asset features are mapped to artifacts and variability points at Step 4. Mapping determines how those features will be realized, and it is governed by asset modeling language. Finally, Step 5 defines and publishes the software assets. A published asset model describes the artifacts, variability points, public artifacts (accessible from the outer world) and external artifacts.

This approach encapsulates correlated features within more cohesive asset models and manages them as higher-level abstractions. As these coarse-grained software assets include a set of variability points which can be managed declaratively, they are easily reusable within a product family. Furthermore, they can also be reused in other product lines even if they are not specifically designed for that domain.

Software Asset Meta Model (AMM). The structure of Asset Meta Model (AMM) and its relationship with Asset Modeling Language (AML) is crucial for the understanding of the model. Asset meta model is used to define a asset modeling language tailored precisely for a product family. AML determines the artifacts types, choreography rules, dependencies, context information, variability types and their realization mechanisms within a product family. Deriving asset modeling languages for different domains from the same meta model enables the design and cross-utilization of reusable software assets across multiple product lines as long as they are using the same DSK set and compliant contextual information. Figure 5 depicts an overview of asset meta model and a brief explanation follows.

Domain Specific Artifact Type (DSAT) identifies the type of artifacts that can be built by using a DSK. A specific asset may contain artifacts of these types. *Domain Specific Kit* defines the domain specific language, engine and the toolset associated with a DSAT. *Dependency* indicates the dependency relation between artifact types, which elucidates the usage rules of artifact types and their interrelation.

Choreography defines the terms and conditions for interactions of artifacts. A choreography definition indicates that two artifacts may communicate subject to the property definitions such as link type, communication model, etc. *Context* includes all variables to be shared by DSEs through a global namespace, which is the outcome of reference architecture and asset modeling activities. *Constraint* defines the product family level constraint type definitions that will be applicable to all assets.

Variability Point definition plays a key role for the assembly of products by reusing predefined and adjustable artifacts. The built-in support to define variability in SFA approach has been adapted from the Orthogonal Variability Model [18]. A variability point definition identifies its name, associated artifact type (or artifact), variants, constraints, binding time, visibility and type of realization. Supported realization mechanisms are *Artifact substitution, Implementers (Plugins), Parameters, Configurators*, and *Aspects*. An asset has to be equipped with implementations of variability points with suitable mechanisms to support its optional and alternative features.

3   Case Study

In order to present the reuse achievements, we introduce two product families: Investment Banking (INV) and Financial Gateways (FGW). Then we present a consolidated table of assets for two product families and analyze the reuse ratio and scope as the outcome of this case study.

The Scopes of Product Lines. The scopes of INV and FGW product lines have been defined by enumerating the members of the families and determining the common and variable features of the products. The scope definition here has been kept concise just to provide an overview to the reader.

Investment Banking (INV) product family has six products: *Fixed Income Securities (FIS), Mutual Funds (FND), Equities (EQT)* and *Derivatives Exchange (DEX)* products support all order management, buy/sell, clearing, custody, stock management, transfer operations of financial instruments such as fixed income securities, mutual funds, equities, and derivatives, respectively. *Fund Management (FDM)* supports the life cycle of mutual funds from the viewpoint of fund managers. *Portfolio Management (PRT)* is similar to the *FDM*; but operations are executed on behalf of the investor as a private banking service.

Financial Gateways (FGW) product family has three products: *EFT Gateway (EFT)* is a gateway to Central Bank of Turkey for electronic fund transfer.

CRA Gateway (CRA) is a gateway to Central Registry Agency of Turkey for electronic registration of securities. *Credit Bureau Gateway (CRB)* is a gateway to Credit Bureau of Turkey for accessing the credit history of consumers for credit application processing. Integration with value-added services such as blacklists and scoring, effective logging and alerting are crucial for all products.

The Domain Specific Kits Employed in Reference Architectures. Product line reference architectures of INV and FGW product families have been constructed with the roadmap presented in [5]. Domain Specific Kits that are used in this case study have been presented in Table 1.

The Asset Models. Following the roadmap given in Section 2.2, Table 2 presents a consolidated list of modeled assets, which is structured as follows: the first column is the name of the asset, the second column shows the scope of asset utilization, the next group of columns indicate whether an asset has been used in that product. The columns under these groups are marked with the product codes given in previous section. The cell is marked with ($\sqrt{}$) if the asset is being used by that product.

The asset utilization column in Table 2 indicates the reuse scope of assets with the following symbols: "$\star$" indicates that an asset is being used in two product families, "•" indicates that an asset is being used in at least two products of a family, whereas "○" indicates that an asset is being used only in a single product.

Table 1. Domain Specific Kits used in case study

Name of the Kit: Description/Purpose *(Artifact types)*
RIA Presentation Kit: Business domain independent XML-based technology used for power screen design in Internet applications [3]. *(Page, Region,* and *Popup)*
Reporting Kit: Business domain independent XML-based technology used for report content generation, rendering and presentation in Internet applications (based on JasperReports[a]). *(Report)*
Business Services Kit: A lightweight kit for development, publishing, administration of business services with a registry, repository, meta-model and policy management services [3]. *(Service)*
RUMBA Business Rules Kit: Business domain independent kit for business rules segregation where all aspects, facts, rules and rule-sets can be defined and managed dynamically by means of a GUI console [6]. *(Rule* and *Composite-Rule)*
BPM Kit: A jBPM[b]-based kit for business process management (BPM) providing design, development and execution of business processes. *(Process)*
Persistence (POM) Kit: An XML-based Object-to-Relational (O2R) mapping kit for defining, deploying and executing SQL queries by mapping to Plain Old Java Objects (POJOs) [3]. *(POM (Persistent Object Model))*
Batch Processing Kit: A special purpose kit for defining, scheduling and execution of batch jobs with enterprise-class features (based on Quartz[c]). *(Job)*

[a] JasperReports, http://jasperforge.org/sf/projects/jasperreports
[b] JBoss jBPM, http://www.jboss.com/products/jbpm,
[c] Quartz, http://www.opensymphony.com/quartz/

Table 2. Asset utilization within and cross product families

Assets		INV Products						FGW Products		
		FIS	FND	EQT	DEX	FDM	PRT	EFT	CRA	CRB
Customer Core	★					√	√	√	√	√
Customer Advanced	●	√	√	√	√					
Blacklist Manager	★	√		√				√	√	
Document Manager	★	√	√	√	√	√	√	√		
Account Manager	★	√	√	√	√	√	√	√	√	
Deduction	★	√	√	√	√	√	√	√		
Accounting Gateway	★	√	√	√	√			√		
Accounting	●					√	√			
Administration	★	√	√	√	√	√	√	√	√	√
Ext. System Data Transfer	★	√		√		√	√		√	√
Alert and Notification Man.	★	√	√	√	√	√	√	√	√	
Repo	○	√								
Fixed Income Common	○	√								
Fixed Income Trade	○	√								
BPP	○	√								
Asset Delivery	○	√								
Auction	●	√					√			
Asset Lending	○	√								
DEX Operations	○				√					
Equity Common Operations	○			√						
Order Management	○			√						
Credit	○			√						
Capital Increase	○			√						
Public Offering	○			√						
Mutual Fund Buy/Sell Ops.	○		√							
Fund Transfer	●		√			√				
Fund Man. Backend	○					√				
Portfolio Man. Backend	○						√			
Asset/Stock Invest Core	●	√	√	√	√	√	√			
Cash Invest Core	●	√	√				√			
Asset Transfer	●	√	√							
FGW Core	★					√	√	√	√	√
FGW Communication	●								√	√
EFT Messaging (HLP)	○							√		
EFT Operations	★					√	√	√		
KKB KRS	○									√
KKB LKS	○									√
CRA Electronic Registry	★		√	√		√	√		√	
CRA Core Operations	○								√	

4   Results and Discussions

The success of reuse can be measured by primarily two factors [8]: *Reuse Scope* for a reusable component indicates how wide a component is reusable, and *Reuse Ratio* in the target application indicates the percentage of reusable components used in the application. Satisfying these two measures at the same time is not trivial [8]. Large reuse scope is achieved by those reusable components that provide relatively low level of functionality (e.g. libraries). Improving the level of functionality decreases the reuse scope, but at the same time increases the reuse ratio of the final product. The latter case is common for the product line approaches (with coarse-grained assets) but only in the limited scope of product family. Therefore, increasing the reuse scope beyond the boundaries of a single product family while keeping the reuse ratio high is critical.

There are 39 assets used to build INV and FGW product lines. The distribution of assets according to reuse scope is as follows: there are 12 assets used in two product families (31%), 8 assets used within at least two products in a family (20%), and 19 assets used only in a single product of a family (49%). These results show that half of the assets are reused in at least two products and large reuse scope beyond the product lines has been achieved.

On the other hand, the reuse ratio for each product can be calculated as follows (call this Product as P): A_r/A_P where

A_r: the number of assets used in P and in at least one more product, and
A_P: the total number of assets used in building the product P.

For example, 19 assets have been used in building the FIS product (A_P is 19), 13 of 19 assets that are used in FIS and in at least one more product (A_r is 13), the reuse ratio for FIS is $13/19 = 68\%$.

The reuse ratio for all products varies between 68% and 92%. The reuse ratio for individual products decreases if product families are considered independently. For instance, EFT product uses many assets that are also reused in INV product line, therefore the reuse ratio of EFT is 81% if both product families are taken into consideration. However, the value is 55% if it is calculated only in the context of FGW product line. In any case, the ratio is above 50%.

There are several other factors that have to be noted for the right interpretation of these results: Those products that share a large number of common business functionality, such as DEX, FND, FDM, have better reuse ratios since they only differ in their core business flows and functionality. The domain knowledge has been collected and modeled by senior business analysts with many years of experience in banking. Some of the domain assets are the end products of banking projects, which have been carried out for several years, and they have been redesigned from scratch within the scope of these product lines.

Software assets contain large number of domain specific artifacts, and not all of them have been reused in those products that have been built using that asset. Our analysis here considers software assets as the main reusable unit which is compliant with general SPL approach. However, specific to our approach, it will be meaningful to make a further analysis of reuse results considering the number of artifacts contained in assets and their reusability in different products.

If multiple product lines share many common features and variations, developing and maintaining the common artifacts become a critical requirement [4]. Since asset modeling languages are derived from the same meta model and they depend on a common DSK set, the model enables reuse of software assets across multiple product lines. Furthermore, keeping a single copy of capability features and maintaining the variations within these assets eliminate the redundancies and possibility of inconsistencies when assets are used in multiple product lines independently.

5 Conclusions and Future Work

Implementing high confidence large scale software systems is still a challenge and systematic reuse is a cure for the cost effective achievement of such systems. This paper explains a methodical way, i.e. Software Factory Automation, for managing large scale reuse across multiple software product lines based on "Domain Specific Kit" abstraction and "Software Asset Meta Model" concordance. Having coherent abstractions in DSKs and loosely coupled integrations through a choreography model improved the reuse of software assets not only within a single product family but also across different software product lines. The achievements in high level of reuse with the charted roadmap have been given from real life cases and discussed in the paper.

As an extension to this study, we have been defining a "software process automation" model based on a Software Processes Hyperframe, which will help automating the development and integration processes of reusable software assets and, hence, bridge the domain engineering and application engineering activities. Another future work might be researching the improvement in software reuse by developing business related Domain Specific Kits and incorporating them to the production environment.

References

1. Altintas, N.I.: Feature-Based Software Asset Modeling with Domain Specific Kits. PhD thesis, Middle East Technical University, Department of Computer Engineering (2007)
2. Altintas, N.I., Cetin, S., Dogru, A.H.: Industrializing software development: The "Factory Automation" way. In: Draheim, D., Weber, G. (eds.) TEAA 2006. LNCS, vol. 4473, pp. 54–68. Springer, Heidelberg (2007)
3. Altintas, N.I., Surav, M., Keskin, O., Cetin, S.: Aurora software product line. In: Turkish Software Architecture Workshop, Ankara (2005)
4. Bühne, S., Lauenroth, K., Pohl, K.: Why is it not sufficient to model requiements variability with feature models? In: AURE 2004, Japan, pp. 5–12 (2004)
5. Cetin, S., Altintas, N.I., Sener, C.: An architectural modeling approach with symmetric alignment of multiple concern spaces. In: ICSEA 2006. Proceedings of the International Conference on Software Engineering Advances, p. 48. IEEE Computer Society, Los Alamitos (2006)
6. Cetin, S., Altintas, N.I., Solmaz, R.: Business rules segregation for dynamic process management with an aspect-oriented framework. In: Eder, J., Dustdar, S. (eds.) BPM Workshops 2006. LNCS, vol. 4103, pp. 193–204. Springer, Heidelberg (2006)
7. Clements, P., Northrop, L.: Software Product Lines: Practices and Patterns. Addison-Wesley Longman Publishing Co., Inc., Boston (2001)
8. Estublier, J., Vega, G.: Reuse and variability in large software applications. In: ESEC/FSE-13: Proceedings of the 10th European Software Engineering Conference held jointly with 13th ACM SIGSOFT International Symposium on Foundations of Software Engineering, pp. 316–325. ACM Press, New York (2005)
9. Gitzel, R., Korthaus, A.: The role of metamodeling in model-driven development. In: Proceedings of the 8th World Multi-Conference on Systemics, Cybernetics and Informatics (SCI 2004), Orlando, USA, July 19-21 (2004)
10. Greenfield, J., Short, K., Cook, S., Kent, S.: Software Factories: Assembling Applications with Patterns, Models, Frameworks, and Tools. Wiley, Chichester (2004)
11. Griss, M.L., Favaro, J., d' Alessandro, M.: Integrating feature modeling with the RSEB. In: ICSR 1998. Proceedings of the 5th International Conference on Software Reuse, p. 76. IEEE Computer Society, Los Alamitos (1998)

12. Griss, M.L., Wentzel, K.: Hybrid domain specific kits for a flexible software factory. In: Proceedings of the Ann. ACM Symp. Applied Computing, pp. 47–52 (1994)
13. High Confidence Software and Systems Coordinating Group. High confidence software and systems research needs, White House National Science and Technology Council (2001)
14. Kang, K.C., Kim, S., Lee, J., Kim, K., Shin, E., Huh, M.: FORM: A feature-oriented reuse method with domain-specific reference architectures. Ann. Softw. Eng. 5, 143–168 (1998)
15. Langlois, B., Exertier, D.: MDSoFa: a Model-Driven Software Factory. In: Proceedings of the International Workshop on MDSD at OOPSLA 2004, October 25 (2004)
16. Larsen, G.: Model-driven development: Assets and reuse. IBM Systems Journal 45(3), 541–553 (2006)
17. Mei, H., Zhang, W., Gu, F.: A feature oriented approach to modeling and reusing requirements of software product lines. In: Proceedings of the 27th Annual International Computer Software and Applications Conference (COMPSAC 2003). IEEE Computer Society, Los Alamitos (2003)
18. Pohl, K., Böckle, G., van der Linden, F.J.: Software Product Line Engineering: Foundations, Principles and Techniques. Springer, Heidelberg (2005)
19. Rothenberger, M.A., Dooley, K.J., Kulkarni, U.R., Nada, N.: Strategies for software reuse: A principal component analysis of reuse practices. IEEE Transactions on Software Engineering 29(9), 825–837 (2003)
20. Rothenberger, M.A., Hershauer, J.C.: A software reuse measure: monitoring an enterprise-level model driven development process. Information and Management 35(5), 283–293 (1999)
21. Turner, C.R., Fuggetta, A., Lavazza, L., Wolf, A.L.: A conceptual basis for feature engineering. J. Syst. Softw. 49(1), 3–15 (1999)

Quality Assessment in Software Product Lines*

Leire Etxeberria and Goiuria Sagardui

Computer Science Department, University of Mondragon,
Loramendi 4, 20500, Mondragon, Spain
letxeberria@eps.mondragon.edu, gsagardui@eps.mondragon.edu

Abstract. In a software product line, quality assessment is especially important because an error or an inadequate design decision can be spread into a lot of products. Moreover, in a product line, different members of the line may require different quality attributes. In this paper, a method for quality aware software product line engineering that takes into account the variability of quality aspects and facilitates quality assessment is presented.

1 Introduction

Quality assessment in a reuse context (software product line…) becomes essential because an error or mismatch in a reusable asset can be propagated to a lot of products. It also posses some challenges that are not present in single-systems evaluation due to the inherent variability of a software product line. In a software product line, traditionally the focus has been on functional variability and the evaluation of *product-line quality attributes* such as extensibility, modifiability, etc.: whether the line covers all the functionality of the envisioned products in the scope. However, checking whether all the products meet the required levels of *Domain-relevant quality attributes* has been neglected, especially when those attributes have variability. In a software product line, different members of the line may require different levels of a quality attribute. One product may require a very high reliability whereas in another reliability is not important. In this context, one of the possible strategies for evaluation is to assess all the products. However, this strategy may not be worthwhile due to the high cost. The method proposed in this paper deals with capturing and managing *domain-relevant quality attributes* variability to facilitate quality assessment in software product lines in a cost-effective way.

2 Quality Aware Software Product Line Engineering

An extended feature model is proposed to gather the variability at different abstraction levels (requirements, design and implementation); including functional and quality attribute variability and the relationship among functional variability and quality aspects. The model is completed with a process that facilitates quality aware analysis, design and implementation, quality validation and quality aware product derivation.

---

* This work was partially funded by the Basque Government (a doctoral grant) and the Spanish Ministry of Science and Education under grant TIN2007-61779 (OPTIMA).

H. Mei (Ed.): ICSR 2008, LNCS 5030, pp. 178–181, 2008.

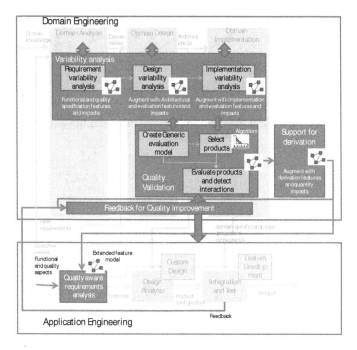

Fig. 1. Quality aware Software Product Line development method

The Fig 1 illustrates the process in a traditional product line lifecycle. The proposed method is performed in concurrence with traditional activities of product line development. The phases of the method are the following ones:

Variability analysis: The FeatuRSEB's feature model [4] has been extended with an extension of the Quality attribute utility tree of ATAM (Architecture Trade-off Analysis Method) [2] for characterizing quality attributes and with impacts for specifying indirect variation (functional variability that causes variation on quality attributes). Variability (functional and quality) and impacts from functional features to quality features are modelled at different abstraction levels: requirements, design and implementation.

Quality validation: This phase tests if the line supports the key quality aspects of the products. The evaluation to be cost-effective, a generic evaluation model (with variability, to evaluate any of the products) is defined or/and representative products are selected to be able to extrapolate the evaluation results to all the line. An algorithm that helps to select the minimum number of products to quantify impacts taking into account possible feature interactions is used.

Once single products or designs have been selected, it is possible to use validation methods for single systems which is a quite a mature field where a lot of techniques and methods have been developed. The validation can be performed at different stages: at early stages such as design (software architecture evaluation methods) or after implementation (quality measurement methods). After validation, the results will be analyzed to see if the desired quality requirements are met and whether a redesign is necessary.

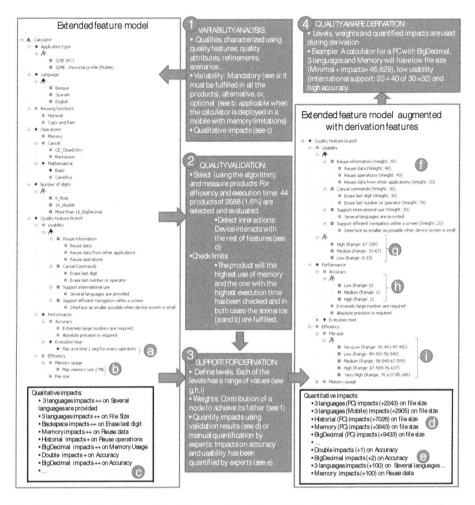

Fig. 2. Extended feature model of the example at two different stages and the phases of the process

Support for derivation: In this phase the extended feature model is augmented with information for facilitating the derivation. This new information consists on *quantitative impacts* (derived from the validation results and the previous existing qualitative impacts) and groups of quality *levels* (alternative features associated with a range of quality values) to make quality something that can be selected or that it is explicit and observable during product derivation.

Quality improvement: The extended feature model resultant of the previous phase can be also very useful as a base for detection and analysis of quality improvement opportunities. For instance, design and implementation decisions that affect negatively to quality can be detected and analyzed.

Quality aware derivation (requirement analysis): Product derivation changes because information is available for selecting the required quality levels or observing the quality attribute values when selecting functional features.

The method has been applied in a calculator software product line (see Fig 2) developed using AHEAD [1] (products generation is automatic). In this case, quality validation has been applied via execution using measurement techniques. The product line includes products for different devices (PC and Mobile) and with different functionalities (memory operators, scientific operations, languages, etc.) and quality levels: usability, performance and efficiency attributes.

3   Conclusions and Future Work

The method helps to identify and specify the variability that impacts on quality. This favors quality aware product line engineering: quality aware design and implementation, cost effective evaluation of the line and quality aware derivation. It specially provides approaches for reducing evaluation cost and effort.

As future work, we are developing tools to provide support for the process. In the example, quality validation has been applied after implementation using measurement techniques. However, we have also applied the method at design time using software architecture evaluation methods [3].

References

[1] Batory, D.S., Sarvela, J.N., Rauschmayer, A.: Scaling step-wise refinement. IEEE Trans. Software Eng. 30(6), 355–371 (2004)
[2] Clements, P., Kazman, R., Klein, M.: Evaluating Software Architectures: Methods and Case Studies. Addison-Wesley Professional, Reading (2002)
[3] Etxeberria, L., Sagardui, G.: Evaluation of quality attribute variability in software product families. In: 15th ECBS (2008) (accepted for publication)
[4] Griss, M., Favaro, J., d'Alessandro, M.: Integrating feature modeling with the rseb. In: 5th International Conference on Software Reuse, ICSR 1998, pp. 76–85 (1998)

Managing Variability in Reusable Requirement Models for Software Product Lines

Hassan Gomaa and Erika Mir Olimpiew

Department of Computer Science
George Mason University, Fairfax, VA
{hgomaa,eolimpie}@gmu.edu

Abstract. This paper describes a feature-oriented approach for managing variability in reusable requirement models for software product lines. The functional requirements of a SPL are described with reusable use case models, reusable activity models and reusable test models. A feature model provides a central point for analyzing the commonality and variability in these functional models, and for managing variability across these models.

Keywords: Reuse, requirements, software product lines, feature model, use case model, activity diagrams, variability mechanism, test specifications.

1 Introduction

Managing features is an essential part of software product line (SPL) development. Using a feature-oriented approach in a model-based SPL development method can facilitate the representation and analysis of variability in the functional requirements models of a SPL. This paper describes how a feature-oriented approach is used to relate features to variability in reusable functional requirement models of a SPL, and to distinguish between coarse-grained and fine-grained functional variability in these models. The reusable requirement models described in this paper are reusable feature models, reusable use case models, reusable activity models, and reusable test models.

2 Model-Based Requirements Models for Software Product Lines

SPL development consists of SPL engineering and application engineering (Figure 1). Model-based SPL engineering consists of the development of requirements, analysis and design models for a family of systems that comprise the application domain. During application engineering, an application configuration is derived from the SPL, which includes all the common features and selected optional and alternative features. The requirements, analysis, and design models, as well as component implementations, are also customized based on the features selected for that application. Any unsatisfied requirements, errors and adaptations are addressed iteratively in SPL engineering.

Product Line UML-Based Software Engineering (PLUS) is a feature-oriented UML-based design method. In the Requirements phase, PLUS uses feature modeling

H. Mei (Ed.): ICSR 2008, LNCS 5030, pp. 182–185, 2008.
© Springer-Verlag Berlin Heidelberg 2008

to model variability and use case modeling to describe the SPL functional requirements [2]. The relationship between features and use case is explicitly modeled by means of a feature/use case dependency table.

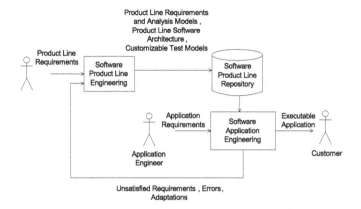

Fig. 1. SPL development process used with PLUS

3   Reusable Feature Models

Feature modeling is an important aspect of SPL engineering [4]. Features are analyzed and categorized as common features (must be supported in all SPL members), optional features (only required in some SPL members), alternative features (a choice of feature is available) and prerequisite features (dependent upon other features). There may also be dependencies among features, such as mutually exclusive features. The emphasis in feature modeling is capturing the SPL variability, as given by optional and alternative features, since these features differentiate one member of the family from the others.

With PLUS, features can be incorporated into UML using the meta-class concept, in which features are modeled using the UML static modeling notation and given stereotypes to differentiate between «common feature», «optional feature» and «alternative feature» [2]. Furthermore, feature groups, which place a constraint on how certain features can be selected for a SPL member, such as mutually exclusive features, are also modeled using meta-classes and given stereotypes, e.g., «zero-or-one-of feature group» or «exactly-one-of feature group» [2].

4   Reusable Use Case Models

In single applications, use cases describe the functional requirements of a system; they can also serve this purpose in SPLs. The goal of the use case analysis is to get a good understanding of the functional requirements whereas the goal of feature analysis is to enable reuse [5]. Use cases and features complement each other. Thus optional and alternative use cases are mapped to optional and alternative features respectively, while use cases variation points are also mapped to features [2].

In a SPL, kernel use cases are required by all members of the SPL. Other use cases are optional, in that they are required by some but not all members of the SPL. Some use cases may be alternative, that is different versions of the use case are required by different members of the SPL. In addition, variation points specify locations in the use case where variability can be introduced [2].

5   Reusable Activity Models

Functional models, such as activity diagrams, can be used to make the sequencing of activities in a use case description more precise for analysis and testing. An activity diagram is created from each use case description in the use case model, and then activities in the activity diagrams are associated with the features in the feature model. An engineer uses the feature to use case relationship table of PLUS [2] to analyze the impact of common, optional, and alternative features on the activity diagrams. Activity nodes are categorized as kernel, optional, variant, or adaptable. Feature conditions [2] are added to associate the variability in the control flow of an activity diagram with a feature in a feature model. The values of a feature condition represent possible feature selections.

6   Reusable Test Models

Use-case based testing methods for SPLs extend use cases, or functional models developed from these use cases, to be configurable for an application derived from a

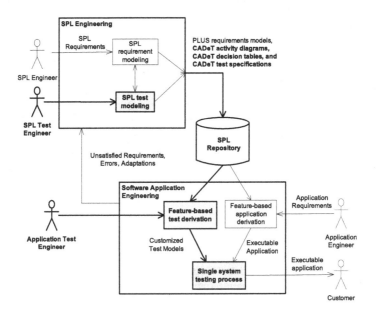

Fig. 2. Extending PLUS with CADeT

SPL [1, 6] while feature-based testing approaches for SPLs use feature models to select representative configurations to test. Customizable Activity Diagrams, Decision Tables and Test Specifications (CADeT) is a functional testing method that creates test specifications from the use case and feature models of a SPL.

CADeT extends PLUS to create functional models that can be used to generate functional system test specifications. Figure 2 shows how CADeT (shaded in gray) impacts the PLUS method [2]. A SPL engineer develops the SPL requirement models, analysis models, and software architecture using PLUS. Then, a test engineer uses CADeT to develop customizable activity diagrams, decision tables, and test specifications from the feature and use case requirements models. An application engineer applies feature-based application derivation to derive one or more applications from the SPL, while a test engineer uses CADeT to apply feature-based test derivation to select and customize the test specifications for these applications.

7 Conclusions

This paper has described a feature-oriented approach for modeling and managing variability in reusable functional requirement models of a SPL, in particular reusable feature models, reusable use case models, reusable activity models, and reusable test models. It is important to understand how the modeling elements in the different models relate to each other; meta-modeling can be used for this purpose [3].

References

1. Bertolino, A., Gnesi, S.: PLUTO: A Test Methodology for Product Families. In: Software Product-Family Engineering: 5th Int'l. Workshop, Siena, Italy (2003)
2. Gomaa, H.: Designing Software Product Lines with UML: From Use Cases to Pattern-based Software Architectures. Addison-Wesley, Reading (2005)
3. Gomaa, H., Shin, M.E.: A Multiple-View Meta-modeling Approach for Variability Management in Software Product Lines. In: Bosch, J., Krueger, C. (eds.) Int'l. Conf. on Software Reuse, pp. 274–285. Springer, Heidelberg (2004)
4. Kang, K.: Feature Oriented Domain Analysis. Software Engineering Institute, Pittsburg, PA (1990)
5. Griss, M.L., Favaro, J., Alessandro, M.d.: Integrating Feature Modeling with the RSEB. In: International Conference on Software Reuse. IEEE Computer Society, Victoria, Canada (1998)
6. Reuys, A., Kamsties, E., Pohl, K., Reis, S.: Model-based Testing of Software Product Families. In: Pastor, Ó., Falcão e Cunha, J. (eds.) CAiSE 2005. LNCS, vol. 3520, pp. 519–534. Springer, Heidelberg (2005)

A BDD-Based Approach to Verifying Clone-Enabled Feature Models' Constraints and Customization

Wei Zhang[1,2], Hua Yan[1,2], Haiyan Zhao[1,2], and Zhi Jin[3]

[1] Key Laboratory of High Confidence Software Technology,
Ministry of Education of China
[2] Insitute of Software, School of Electronics Engineering and Computer Science,
Peking University, Beijing, 100871, China
[3] Chinese Academy of Sciences, Beijing, China
`{zhangw,yanhua07,zhhy}@sei.pku.edu.cn, zhijin@amss.ac.cn`

Abstract. In this paper, we present a kind of semantics for constraints in clone-enabled feature models, which resolves the problem of what kinds of constraint should be added to a feature model after some features are cloned. The semantics is composed of two patterns: the *generating* pattern and the *adapting* pattern, to address the two problems of what kind of constraints should be imposed on a clonable feature and its clones, and how an existing constraint should be transformed in the context that features involved in the constraint are cloned, respectively. After that, we propose a BDD-based approach to verifying clone-enabled feature models, an approach that makes efficient use of the BDD (*binary decision diagram*) data structures, by considering the specific characteristics of feature models' verification. Experiments show that this BDD-based approach is more efficient and can verify more complex feature models than our previous method.

Keywords: Feature models, Clonable features, Constraints, Customization, Verification.

1 Introduction

Feature models have been recognized as an important technique to capture and organize the reusable requirements in a specific software domain [7,8,5,2,1,9,13]. One important purpose of feature models is to facilitate the reusing of these reusable requirements, and this purpose is usually achieved by using a customizing-based approach. That is, when developing a new application in a software domain, you do not need to elicit and analyze the application's requirements from scratch, but can just customize the domain's feature model (selecting a subset of features from it), and use the customizing result as a starting point for the application's requirements engineering activity.

One problem in a feature model's customization is the verification problem [9]. This problem is caused by the fact that not any subset of features from a feature model is a valid customizing result. Usually, there are constraints among features, and a valid customizing result must satisfy all these constraints. For this reason, when a customizing

H. Mei (Ed.): ICSR 2008, LNCS 5030, pp. 186–199, 2008.

decision[1] is made on a feature model, we need to verify that those constraints among features are not violated by the decision (namely, *the verification of feature models' customization*). Otherwise, the inappropriate decision will be propagated implicitly to latter customizing activities, and thus decrease the efficiency of customization. In addition, before customization, we should first ensure the correctness of constraints among features (namely, *the verification of feature models' constraints*).

The difficulty of the verification problem is caused by its *NP-hard* nature. In essence, the verification of feature models is a constraint satisfaction problem (CSP), and researchers have recognized that the CSP is an *NP-hard* problem in general [11]. In our experience, when a feature model contains a large number of features with a complex set of constraints among them, the verification using a third-party's model checker usually consumes an intolerable period of time, or even runs into a live-lock state. The *NP-hard* nature makes it difficult to find an efficient way to solve the verification problem of feature models.

Another problem relating to the verification of a feature model's customization is caused by the introduction of clonable features into the feature model[2]. In customization, the tree structure containing a clonable feature and all its offspring features can be cloned into many copies, and each copy can be customized individually. The problem caused by clonable features is that some constraints among features will lose their original semantics after a feature is cloned [3]. As a result, we will lose the capability of verifying whether a customizing result is a valid one based on the constraints among features.

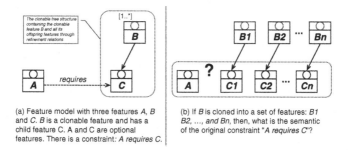

(a) Feature model with three features A, B and C. B is a clonable feature and has a child feature C. A and C are optional features. There is a constraint: *A requires C*.

(b) If B is cloned into a set of features: B1 B2, ..., and Bn, then, what is the semantic of the original constraint "*A requires C*"?

Fig. 1. The semantic-losing problems caused by clonable features: an example

An example of the problem is depicted in Fig. 1 (see Table 1 for the exact meaning of the symbols). The constraint "*A requires C*" means that if A is bound (i.e. selected) in a customizing result, then C should also be bound in it. In customization, if C is cloned into a set of clones: Ci ($i = 1, 2, ..., n$), how should the constraint "*A requires C*" be adapted to these clones? Should the binding of A require or be independent of the binding of these clones.

According to the two problems above, the main contributions of this paper are two-fold. For the semantic-losing problem, we present a kind of semantics for constraints

---

[1] A customizing decision on a feature model means deciding whether to make a feature remaining in the customizing result (*binding a feature*) or to remove the feature from the result (*removing a feature*).

[2] In this paper, a feature model with clonable features is called a clone-enabled feature model.

in clone-enabled feature models. For the verification problem, we propose a BDD-based approach to verifying both feature models' constraints and customization, an approach that makes efficient use of the BDD (*binary decision diagram*) data structures based on the specific characteristics of feature models' verification.

The rest of this paper is organized as following. Section 2 introduces some preliminary knowledge. Section 3 presents the semantics for constraints in clone-enabled feature models. Section 4 proposes the BDD-based approach to verifying feature models. Related work is discussed in Section 5. Finally, Section 6 concludes this paper with a short summary.

2 Preliminary

In this section, we first introduce a notation for clone-enabled feature models, and a propositional logic based definitions of constraints among features. After that, we clarify a fact about clonable features, that is, there is actually a clonable structure related to each clonable feature.

2.1 A Notation for Feature Models

Table 1. Symbols in the notation for feature models

Symbol	Name	Explanation
X	A *mandatory feature* with the name "*X*".	A mandatory feature must be selected in a customizing result, if its parent feature is selected. If its parent is removed, it must also be removed. If it hasn't a parent feature, then it must be selected in any customizing result.
Y	An *optional feature* with the name "*Y*".	An optional feature can either be selected in or be removed from a customizing result, if its parent feature is selected or it hasn't a parent. If its parent is removed, it must also be removed.
Z	A feature that can be either mandatory or optional.	In our presentation, we use this symbol to denote a feature that can be replaced by either a mandatory feature or an optional feature.
Z	A *feature reference*.	A reference to a feature that has the name Z.
[*a..b*]	A symbol for *clonable* features.	When the symbol is placed at the top of a feature, it means that the feature is clonable. In the symbol, a and b are two integers satisfying the property: $0 < a \le b$, and the meanings is that the number of the clonable feature' clones should not less than a and not greater than b.
╲	A *refinement* relation between two features.	A refinement relation connects two features. The feature connecting to the non-arrow end is called the *parent* of the feature connecting to the arrow end. A feature can only have one parent feature at most.
⤫	A *refinement path*	In our presentation, we use this symbol to denote a path containing one or more refinement relations, and zero or more features. Each feature connects to two different refinement relations' arrow and non-arrow ends, respectively.

Table 1. (*continued*)

	A *requires* constraint between two features.	A *requires* constraint connects two features. The feature connecting to the non-arrow end is called the *requirer*, and the other the *requiree*. This constraint means that if the *requirer* is bound in a customizing result, the *requiree* also be bound.
	An *excludes* constraint between two features.	An *excludes* constraint connects two features. This constraint means that the two features should not be both bound in a same customizing result.
	A *binding predicate* among a set of features and binding predicates	The left end connects to a *composite* constraint or to one of the right ends of a binding predicate. The right ends connect to a set of features and binding predicates, respectively. We define three *types* of binding predicate: *and* (denoted by ∧); *or* (denoted by ∨); *xor* (denoted by *1*). See **Table 2** for the formal definition of binding predicates.
	A *composite* constraint between two binding predicate	We define two *types* of composite constraint: *requires* (denoted by →); *excludes* (denoted by ✶). See **Table 3** for their formal definition.

Table 2. The formal definition of binding predicates. In this table, A and B denotes features, and p and q denotes binding predicates. For a feature F, bind(F) is a predicate; it is true if F is bound, and false if removed. In our notation, we only use binding predicates as constituent parts of the composite constraints, but not use them to represent individual constraints.

	$or(A, ..., B, ..., p, ..., q)$	$and(A, ..., B, ..., p, ..., q)$	$xor(A, ..., B, ..., p, ..., q)$
Binding Predicate			
Formal Definition	$bind(A)\lor...\lor\neg bind(B)$ $\lor...\lor p\lor...\lor\neg q$	$bind(A)\land... \land\neg bind(B)$ $\land...\land p\land...\land\neg q$	$bind(A)\otimes... \otimes\neg bind(B)$ $\otimes...\otimes p\otimes...\otimes\neg q$

Table 3. The formal definition of composite constraints. In this table, p and q denotes binding predicates. In the situation that p and q only contains one feature, the two types composite constraints becomes the *requires* and the *excludes* constraints between two features.

	$requires(p, q)$	$excludes(p, q)$
Composite Constraint		
Formal Definition	$p \rightarrow q$	$p \rightarrow \neg q$

2.2 The Clonable Structure Related to a Clonable Feature

A clonable feature does not mean that only the feature itself can be cloned into many copies. Usually, it means that a structure related to the clonable feature can be cloned into many copies. The structure is formed from three kinds of element: the clonable feature, all its offspring features, and all the refinement relations between these features.

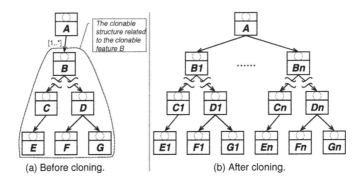

(a) Before cloning.   (b) After cloning.

Fig. 2. The clonable structure related to a clonable feature: an example

Such a structure is exemplified in Fig. 2 (a), in which, feature B is clonable, and the dashed shape shows the clonable structure related to B. In customization, the cloning of B actually leads to the cloning of the related structure, and after cloning, each clone of B becomes a child feature of B's parent feature A (see Fig. 2 (b)). For any feature in a clonable structure, the property whether it is mandatory or optional is not changed after cloning. In the rest of this paper, we use *the cloning of a clonable feature* to denote the meaning of *the cloning of the clonable structure related to the clonable feature*. For a clonable feature F, we use $cs(F)$ to denote the set that contains all the elements in the clonable structure related to F.

3   Semantics for Constraints in Clone-Enabled Feature Models

In this section, we present a kind of semantics for constraints in clone-enabled feature models. The semantics is composed of two patterns: the *generating* pattern, and the *adapting* pattern. The former handles the problem of what kind of constraints should be imposed on a clonable feature and its clones. The latter deals with the problem of how an existing constraint should be adapted in the context that some features involved in the constraint are cloned. Before giving more details about the semantics, we first introduce a description structure for the two patterns' definitions.

3.1   A Description Structure for the *Generating* and the *Adapting* Patterns

Table 4 shows the components contained in the description structure and the descriptions of these components.

3.2   The *Generating* Pattern

One question related to a clonable feature is whether we should impose any constraint on the feature and its clones. In this paper, we adopt a positive answer to this question. We treat the relation between a feature and its clones as the *type-instance* relation. One understanding of a type is that it is a set consisting of all the type's instances. Based on this understanding, we can derive that, if a type is removed, any of its instances should also be removed. However, this understanding does not tell us how many instances should be bound if the type is bound.

Table 4. Components in the description structure

Components		Description
Pattern Name		*A meaningful name for a pattern.*
Context	Clonable Feature	*A clonable feature.*
	Cloned Features	*All the clones of the clonable feature.*
	Source Constraint	*An existing constraint that will be transformed by the pattern.*
Trigger Condition		*A condition satisfied by components in the context. If the trigger condition is true, the pattern must be applied, that is, transforming the source constraint into the target constraints.*
Target Constraints		*Constraints transformed from the source constraint.*

Table 5. Definition of the *generating* pattern

Pattern Name		*Generating*		
Context	Clonable Feature	F		
	Cloned Features	$Fi, (i = 1, 2, ..., n)$		
	Source Constraint	*<Empty>*		
Trigger Condition		*true*		
Target Constraints		*Case 1: single- binding*	*Case 2: multi-binding*	*Case 3: all-binding*

Based on the analysis above, we developed the *generating* pattern (see Table 5), to address the problem of what kind of constraints should be imposed on a clonable feature and its clones. The name *"generating"* means that some constraints are generated after the cloning of a clonable feature. The *generating* pattern defines three cases of generated constraints. For a clonable feature F, if it is bound, the *single-binding* will require that exactly one of its clones should be bound, the *multi-binding* will require that one or more clones should be bound, and the *all-binding* will require that all it clones should be bound. If F is not bound, all the three cases will require that none of its clones can be bound.

Since there are three kinds of target constraints in the pattern, a related question is which kind should be selected when applying the pattern. We think that the question should be answered according to more specific semantics related to each clonable feature. A special situation is that: when a clonable feature is mandatory, only the *all-binding* target constraints are suitable. Otherwise, the mandatory feature may need to be changed into optional.

3.3 The *Adapting* Pattern

In a clone-enabled feature models, a problem related to a constraint is that how the constraint should be adapted in the context that one or more features involved in the constraint belong to a clonable structure and that the structure is cloned.

Table 6. Definition of the *adapting* pattern

Pattern Name		*Adapting*
Context	Clonable Feature	F
	Cloned Features	$Fi, (i = 1, 2, ..., n)$.
	Source Constraint	$const(A, B, ..., C, D, ..., E)$: a constraint among a set of features.
Trigger Condition		$\{A, B, ..., C, D, ..., E\} \cap cs(F) = \{A, B, ..., C\} \neq \varnothing$
Target Constraints		$const(A, B, ..., C, D, ..., E) \wedge$ $(\wedge_{i=(1,2,...n)} (bind(Fi) \rightarrow const(Ai, Bi, ..., Ci, D, E, ..., F)))$

For this problem, we introduce the *generating* pattern (see Table 6). The name "*adapting*" means that some existing constraints should be adapted after the cloning of a clonable feature F. The target constraints defined in the *adapting* pattern contains two parts. The first part contains exactly the source constraint, which means the source constraint is still maintained after the cloning of F (this is an important characteristic of the *generating* pattern). The second part contains a set of constraints for each of the clones of F, respectively. For each clone Fi, the constraint requires that if Fi is bound, then the original constraint should also be satisfied by replacing each feature X in the constraint that belongs to $cs(F)$ with its clone Xi.

4   BDD-Based Verification of Feature Models

As we can see in Section 3, after a sequence of clone transformations, even simple binary constraints (i.e. *requires* and *excludes*) could be transformed into complex *composite* constraints. This further increases the difficulty of feature models' verification.

In this section, we present a BDD-based approach to verifying feature models. First, we introduce three verification criteria, which are proposed in our previous work [13], and have been proven to be effective in detecting deficiencies in feature models [14]. Base on the three criteria, we proposed a BDD-based algorithm that can check the three criteria's satisfiability by only traversing once to the nodes in a BDD (*binary decision diagram*). We also provide two strategies to improve the efficiency of creating a feature model's BDD. Experiments show that this approach is more efficient and can verify more complex feature models than our previous method.

4.1   Three Criteria for Feature Models' Verification

From the viewpoint of feature models' verification, a feature model can be abstracted into a set of features and a set of constraints among features [13]. According to a feature's binding state, features in a feature models can be partitioned into three sets. The *bound* set contains exactly all the features having been bound, the *removed* set contains exactly all the features having been removed, and the *undecided* set contains all the other features which will be bound or removed in later customizing activities. A customizing decision to an undecided feature either binds the feature or removes it.

Given a feature model, if any of the following three criteria is not satisfied, there must be errors or deficiencies either in the constraints among features or in the customizing decisions to features [13].

Criterion 1: There exists at least a set of customizing decisions to all features in the *undecided* set that will not violate any constraints among features.

Criterion 2: Each feature in the *undecided* set has a chance to be bound, without violating any constraints among features.

Criterion 3: Each feature in the *undecided* set has a chance to be removed, without violating any constraints among features.

Von der Maßen and Lichter [15] have created a deficiency framework for feature models. Our previous investigation [14] shows that the three criteria can detect most kinds of anomaly and inconsistency among constraints at an early stage (i.e. before customization). Further details about the three criteria and the deficiency framework can be found in [13,14,15].

Although the three criteria are very effective, the checking of them is not easy. *Criterion 1* is a binary *CSP*, and the time complexity of its checking is $O(2^n)$, where n is the number of features in the undecided set. For each undecided feature, *Criterion 2 and 3* can also be easily transformed into two binary CSPs with the time complexity of $O(2^n)$, respectively. That is to say, the three criteria's checking could be transformed into the checking of $2n+1$ binary CSPs, and the total time complexity would be $O(2^n+2n \cdot 2^n)$, which equals to $O((2n+1) \cdot 2^n)$.

4.2 BDD-Based Checking Algorithm for the Three Criteria

Although the three criteria's checking could to be transformed into the checking of $2n+1$ CSPs, there is a shortcoming in such an approach, that is, it treats the $2n+1$ CSPs as independent problems, without considering the connections between these problems. In fact, we could find that the $2n+1$ CSPs are very similar; the only difference between them is that a different undecided feature's binding state is assigned to *bound* or *removed*. If the similarity could be fully explored, the time complexity would be further decreased.

Based on this observation, we investigate the BDD technique and find an algorithm that can check the three criteria's satifiability by only traversing once to the nodes in a BDD. Before giving more details about the algorithm, we first give a short introduction to BDDs.

In general, a BDD is a compact data structure for representing a Boolean function [6]. Fig. 3 shows an example of BDDs. We can see that a BDD is composed of multiple layers, each layer contains a set of nodes related to a propositional variable, and each node connects to right layers' nodes through a *true* branch or a *false* branch, which means that the node is assigned the value of *true* or *false*, respectively. The rightmost layer contains two nodes of *true* and *false*, which denotes the Boolean function's two possible value. A path from the leftmost node to the *true* node means that the function's value is *true* in the value assignment indicated by the path, and a path to the *false* node means the function's value is *false*.

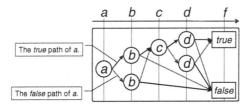

Fig. 3. The BDD representation of Boolean functions: an example. This show a BDD of the Boolean function: $f = (a \leftrightarrow b) \wedge (c \leftrightarrow b)$, where, a, b, c, and d are four propositional variables. The path "a *true*, b *true*, c *false*, d *false*, *true*" means that, in the following value assignment: $a=true$, $b=true$, $c=false$, and $d=false$, the function f's value is *true*. Similarly, the path "a *false*, b *true*, *false*" means that f's value is *false* in the value assignment indicated by the path.

Now, we explain how to check the three criteria's satisfiability efficiently, in the context that the set of constraints among features are transformed into a BDD[3]. For *Criterion 1*, the checking method is simple; if there is a node whose *true* path or *false* path connects to the *true* node, then this criterion is satisfied. For *Criterion 2* and *3*, we use the idea illustrated in Fig. 4 to check their satisfiability.

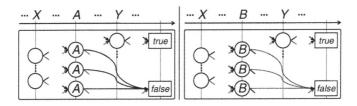

Fig. 4. The idea to check the satisfiability of *Criterion 2* and *3*. For a feature *A*, in order to check whether it has a chance to be bound, we only need to examine whether all the *true* paths of A's nodes connect to the *false* node (see the left part). The answer *yes* means that *A* has no chance to be bound, and the answer *no* means *A* still has the chance. Following the same idea, we can check whether a feature has a chance to be removed. The only difference is to examine whether all the *false* paths of the feature's nodes connect to the *false* node (see the right part).

To realize the idea above into an algorithm, we have to consider the situation that a BDD contains crossing paths. A crossing path eliminates some nodes from a BDD in order to maintain the BDD's compactness. We need to recover those eliminated nodes, before applying the idea above. Fig. 5 shows an example of this situation.

Based on the general idea and the special situation, we develop the following algorithm to check the satisfiability of *Criterion 2* and *3*, an algorithm that take a breadth-first traversal to a BDD's nodes.

---

[3] See section 4.3 for how to transform a set of constraints among features into to a BDD.

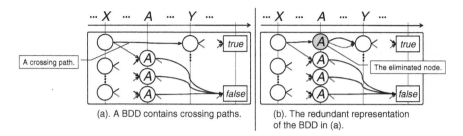

(a). A BDD contains crossing paths.   (b). The redundant representation
                                                of the BDD in (a).

Fig. 5. A BDD containing crossing paths and its redundant representation. In (a), although all the *true* paths of A's nodes connect to the *false* node, A still has a chance to be bound. This is caused by the crossing path that eliminates a node of A. If recovering the eliminated node, we can get a redundant representation of the BDD. In the redundant BDD, there is a node of A, whose *true* path does not connect to the *false* node, and thus A still could be bound.

A BDD-based algorithm for *Criterion 2* and *3*. Where, *get_true_branch(Node e)* returns *e*'s child node through the *true* path, *get_false_branch(Node e)* returns *e*'s child node through the *false* path, and *isNonCrossedLayer(Layer layer)* returns whether the *layer* is crossed by any crossing paths. The three functions are created in a BDD's construction.

```
Input: The root of BDD
Output: A set that contains all the features violating Crite-
rion 2 or 3.

Verify(root){
    Set violatedFeatures := Ø;
    for (layer = getLayer(root) to getLayer(0)){
        If (isNonCrossedLayer(layer)=true){
            isCriterion1Violated := true;
            isCriterion2Violated := true;
            for each node e of layer{
                if (get_true_branch(e)!=false_node)
                    isCriterion1Violated := false;
                if (get_false_branch(e)!=false_node)
                    isCriterion2Violated := false;
            }
            if (isCriterion1Violated = true ||
                isCriterion2Violated = true    ){
                featureName = getFeatureName(layer)
                    violatedFeatures.add(featureName);
            }
        }
    }
    return violatedFeatures;
}
```

4.3   Constructing a BDD for a Feature Models

Constructing a BDD for a feature model is to transform the conjunction of constraints in the feature model into a BDD. There are two issues to be considered:

1. How to get a BDD with a smaller size?
2. How to ensure that the constructing process consume less memory space?

We adopt two strategies to deal with the two issues.

Strategy 1: Use the order of the depth-first traversal to feature trees as the variable order of BDD.

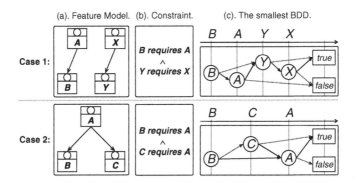

Fig. 6. The smallest BDDs in two basic cases. In case 1 with two feature trees, a smallest BDD has a variable order, in that, any child feature precedes its parent or the inverse, and variables belonging to different feature trees do not mix. In case 2 with a parent feature and its two children, a smallest BDD has a variable order, in that, the parent is the last or the first variable. A depth-first order to feature trees (whether in pre-order or post-order) can satisfy both of the two cases. The analysis above can also apply to feature models with multiple feature trees, in each of which, there may be multi-levels of features, and a feature may have three or more children.

This strategy is concluded from two basic cases in feature models (see Fig. 6). In the two cases, we only consider the feature trees (formed by features and refinement relations between them) in feature models. As recognized in our previous research [13], for a refinement between two features, there is a constraint: *child requires parent*. Based on these constraints, we find that it leads to a smallest BDD by using the variable order generated from the depth-first traversal to feature trees.

Strategy 2: Construct BDDs for each of the feature trees and for each of the constraints in a feature model, then combine these BDDs into the final BDD.

The purpose of this strategy is trying to decrease the possibility that the intermediate results in BDDs' construction consume huge memory space. The idea behind this strategy is to avoid considering too many constraints at one time. For the words limitation, we will not give further details about this strategy.

4.4 Experiments

To examine the approach's efficiency and capability, we apply it to verify two sets of designed feature models. One set contains 20 feature models only with binary constraints, and the number of features in them varies from 10, 20 to 90, and then from 100, 200, to 1000. The other set contains 20 feature models with both binary and composite constraints, and the number of features also varies from 10 to 1000. We also use the same two sets of feature models to examine the effect of our previous SMV-based method for feature models' verification [13], a method which transforms feature models' verification into *2n+1* independent CSPs, and uses the model checker SMV [10] to verify these CSPs. The environment for our experiments is a notebook with a 2.0G HZ CPU, 512 MB memory, and a Windows XP OS.

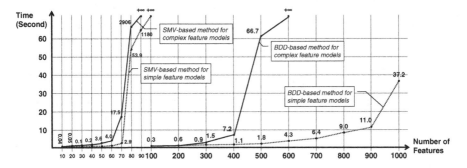

Fig. 7. The result of experiments

Fig. 7 shows the result of our experiments. We can see that, the SMV-based approach can not handle feature models with more than 100 features, while for feature models with 100 features, the BDD-based approach only needs a time less than one second. Furthermore, the BDD-based approach can verify complex feature models with 500 features using 66.7 seconds, and verify simple feature models with 1000 features using 37.2 seconds. The experiments show that the BDD-based approach is more efficient and can verify more complex feature models than the SMV-based approach.

5   Related Work

Feature models are first proposed by Kang et al. [7] in the feature-oriented domain analysis (FODA) method, and then developed by many researchers in the field of software reuse [8,5,2,9]. In these researchers, Czarnecki et al. introduced feature models into the generative software reuse [2] and proposed the concepts of clonable features [4]. Czarnecki et al. also recognized the semantic-losing problem caused by clonable features [3], but they did not give a systematic method to resolve this problem. As far as our knowledge, we do not find any researchers who have given solutions to this problem.

Mannion [9] proposed a verifying method of feature models, in which, constraints among features are formalized using the propositional logic. Based on his research, we classified constraints in feature models into several types. For each of them, we gave its formal definition, and a graphic representation of it, which is used for feature modelers to create constraints in an easy way. We also proposed the three criteria to verify feature models [13], and have examined their effectiveness according to the deficiency framework created by Von der Maßen and Lichter [15]. However, for the checking problem of the three criteria, we transformed it into *2n+1* independent binary CSPs, without considering the connections between them.

Our research on BDD-based verification is inspired by Czarnecki's research [3], in which, Czarnecki used a commercial BDD package to verifying properties of feature models. However, it seems that Czarnecki only considered simple binary constraints between features (i.e. *requires*, and *excludes*) and those local composite constraints between a feature and its children. In addition, Czarnecki did not give details about how to decide the BDD's variable order for a feature model, and how to use a BDD in efficient ways.

Batory [1] proposed a LTMS-based approach to detect deficiencies in constraints or customization. As we have pointed out [14], this algorithm can check most of the deficiencies that our criteria can check, but in a later stage (i.e. after certain customizing decisions have been made). In addition, this approach's time complexity is same with our approach, namely, $O(2^{n+1})$. Where, n is the number of features in a feature model. In this approach, the transformation from constraints to a CNF (*conjunctive normal form*) needs a $O(2^n)$ time, and the checking of deficiencies also needs a $O(2^n)$ time, since it have to traverse all the disjunction clauses in the CNF. In our approach, a BDD's construction needs a $O(2^n)$ time, and the traversal of a BDD also needs a $O(2^n)$ time.

In addition, based on our previous work, we develop a graphical notation for constraints in clonable-enabled feature models in this paper. We do not notice that there are other researchers who have proposed such kind of graphical notations.

6   Conclusions

In this paper, we provided a kind of semantics for constraints in clone-enabled feature models. The semantics resolved two problems related to clone-enabled feature models. One is the problem of what kind of constraints should be imposed on a clonable feature and its clones, and the other is the problem of how an existing constraint should be transformed after some features in the constraint are cloned. To verify feature models with complex constraints, we proposed a BDD-based approach, which makes efficient use of the BDD data structures by considering the characteristics of the three verification criteria for feature models. Experiments showed that the BDD-based approach proposed in this paper is more efficient and can handle more complex feature models than our previous approach.

Acknowledgments. This work is supported by the National Grand Fundamental Research 973 Program of China under Grant No. 2005CB321805, the Hi-Tech Research and Development Program of China under Grant No. 2006AA01Z156 and 2006AA01Z189, and the Natural Science Foundation of China under Grant No. 90612011, 60528006 and 60703065.

References

1. Batory, D.: Feature Models, Grammars, and Propositional Formulas. In: Obbink, H., Pohl, K. (eds.) SPLC 2005. LNCS, vol. 3714. Springer, Heidelberg (2005)
2. Czarnecki, K., Eisenecker, U.: Generative Programming: Methods, Tools, and Applications. Addison-Wesley, Reading (2000)

3. Czarnecki, K., Kim, C.H.P.: Cardinality-Based Feature Modeling and Constraints: A Progress Report. In: OOPSLA 2005 International Workshop on Software Factories (online proceedings) (2005)
4. Czarnecki, K., Helsen, S., Eisenecker, U.: Formalizing Cardinality-based Feature Models and their Specialization. Software Process Improvement and Practice, special issue of best papers from SPLC 2004 10(1), 7–29 (2005)
5. Griss, M.L., Favaro, J., d'Alessandro, M.: Integrating Feature Modeling with the RSEB. In: Proceedings of Fifth International Conference on Software Reuse, pp. 76–85. IEEE Computer Society, Canada (1998)
6. Hu, A.J.: Techniques for Efficient Formal Verification using Binary Decision Diagram. PhD thesis, Stanford University (1995)
7. Kang, K.C., Cohen, S.G., Hess, J.A., Novak, W.E., Peterson, A.S.: Feature-Oriented Domain Analysis Feasibility Study. Technical reports, Software Engineering Institute, Carnegie Mellon University (1990)
8. Kang, K.C., Kim, S., Lee, J., Kim, K., Shin, E., Huh, M.: FORM: A Feature-Oriented Reuse Method with Domain-Specific Reference Architectures. Annals of Software Engineering 5, 143–168 (2004)
9. Mannion, M.: Using First-Order Logic for Product Line Model Validation. In: Chastek, G.J. (ed.) SPLC 2002. LNCS, vol. 2379, pp. 176–187. Springer, Heidelberg (2002)
10. The SMV System. Carnegie Mellon University,
    http://www.cs.cmu.edu/~modelcheck/smv.html
11. Tsang, E.: Foundations of Constraint Satisfaction. Academic Press, London (1993)
12. Yang, B.: Optimizing Model Checking Based on BDD Characterization, PhD thesis, CMU (1999)
13. Zhang, W., Zhao, H., Mei, H.: A Propositional Logic-Based Method for Verification of Feature Models. In: Davies, J., Schulte, W., Barnett, M. (eds.) ICFEM 2004. LNCS, vol. 3308, pp. 115–130. Springer, Heidelberg (2004)
14. Zhang, W., Mei, H., Zhao, H.: Feature-Driven Requirements Dependency Analysis and High-Level Software Design. Requirements Engineering, vol. 11(3), pp. 205–220. Springer, London (2006)
15. von der Maßen, T., Lichter, H.: Deficiencies in feature models. In: Workshop on Software Variability Management for Product Derivation, in Conjunction with the 3rd Software Product Line Conference (2004)

Performing Domain Analysis for Model-Driven Software Reuse

Daniel Lucrédio[1], Renata P. de M. Fortes[1], Eduardo S. de Almeida[2],
and Silvio Lemos Meira[2]

[1] Institute of Mathematical and Computer Science - Universidade de São Paulo
Av. Trab. São-carlense, 400 - Centro - CEP 13560-970 - São Carlos - SP, Brazil
{lucredio,renata}@icmc.usp.br
[2] C.E.S.A.R. - Recife Center for Advanced Studies and Systems and RiSE
Rua Bione, 220 - Bairro do Recife - CEP 50030-390 - Recife - PE, Brazil
esa@rise.com.br, silvio@cesar.org.br

Abstract. This paper presents a domain analysis approach for model-driven domain engineering projects. The objective is to address the problem of identifying which parts of a domain can be automated using model-driven development techniques. We argue that this task should be performed together with domain analysis. In this sense, the paper presents the main activities, guidelines, inputs and outputs of this task. It concludes by presenting the iterative life cycle approach for dealing with complex domains.

Keywords: Software reuse, model-driven development, domain analysis, domain engineering.

1 Introduction

Domain engineering is the process of building reusable assets in a domain, so that applications can be more easily built reusing those parts. In this context, domain analysis involves identifying the main concepts and elements from a domain, and determining its scope, i.e. what will be included and what will be excluded from the domain. One approach of doing this is feature-based domain analysis [1,2].

Another way to promote reuse is Model-Driven Development (MDD). MDD is the combination of generative programming, domain-specific languages and software transformations, which were already being explored back in 1980 [3,4]. Its goal is to reduce the semantic gap between the problem domain and the implementation/solution domain, by using high-level models that shield software developers from the complexities of the underlying implementation platform [5]. In MDD, models are used to more effectively express concepts, while transformations are used to automatically generate implementation assets that reflect the solution expressed in the models [6].

One of the main challenges in designing/implementing a domain is how to map the features to the design and code, considering all the relationships and constraints involving the features. This is where MDD techniques can be used

H. Mei (Ed.): ICSR 2008, LNCS 5030, pp. 200–211, 2008.
© Springer-Verlag Berlin Heidelberg 2008

to increase software reuse in domain engineering. Instead of leaving this task to be handcrafted by the product developer, the knowledge of how to implement these constraints is encapsulated in MDD transformations and domain-specific modelers [7]. In an ideal scenario, all the product developer needs to do is to choose which features will be present, specify some product-specific parameters, and automatically generate the design and code for that product.

Of course, this scenario is still far from reality, since not every piece of code can be automatically generated. However, there are some parts of the domain where this is not only possible, but can lead to gains in productivity, by increasing the reuse level. But how to identify which parts of a domain can be automated?

We argue in that this activity should be part of domain analysis. While analyzing the features of a domain, there should be means to identify the potential for automation in some sub-domains, already preparing for the subsequent developments of transformations and/or domain specific languages. Next section presents how domain analysis is inserted into the domain engineering approach.

2   Context: Model-Driven Domain Engineering Approach

The domain analysis approach described in this paper is part of a larger approach, for developing reusable MDD-based domains [8]. Figure 1 summarizes the approach, which is divided into three cycles:

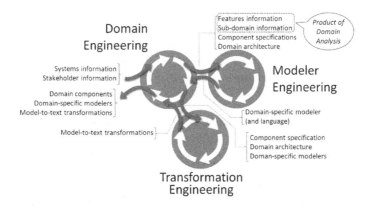

Fig. 1. Basic cycles for developing model-driven reusable software

The basic cycle is **domain engineering**, which aims at developing reusable assets based on information about the domain. The input for this cycle includes *Systems information*, i.e. all kinds of informations related to applications from the domain (existing, future and potential applications), and *Stakeholder information*, which includes the knowledge from the domain expert, the project manager, market experts, software architects, developers, and other stakeholders. The output of this cycle is a set of reusable domain assets, which can be used to develop applications for the domain. This includes *domain components*, but also *domain-specific modelers*, which can be used to create models for that domain, and *model-to-text transformations* (also known as platform-specific model (PSM) to code transformations [9]), used to generate code for these models.

The development of domain-specific modelers and transformations is a complex task, and therefore there are two auxiliary cycles:

The **modeler engineering** cycle is responsible for producing domain specific modelers for the parts of the domain (sub-domains) where automation is possible. It is also responsible for developing a domain-specific language, if it does not exist. The input for this cycle comes from the domain engineering cycle: *features information*, containing the features of the domain, including the variability and commonality information, *sub-domain information*, including the related features and variability inside the sub-domain, *component specifications*, including their interfaces and other design specifications, and *domain architecture*, which represents the design decisions that reflect the variability and commonality inside the domain. The output of this cycle is a *domain-specific modeler*, and in some cases a newly developed *domain-specific language*, if necessary.

The second auxiliary cycle is **transformation engineering**, responsible for developing model-to-text transformations. Its input includes the *component specifications* and *domain architecture*, and also the **domain-specific modelers** developed in the modeler engineering cycle. The output are the *model-to-text transformations*, which are created using a design by-example approach [10].

The domain analysis activity, subject of this paper, is part of the domain engineering cycle, and is responsible for gathering information for subsequent design and implementation phases. It delivers two necessary inputs for developing modelers and transformations: the **domain features**, which represent the variability and commonality inside the domain, and the **sub-domains where automation is possible**. Both are indicated in Figure 1.

3   Activities of the Domain Analysis Approach

The domain analysis approach is based on a previous work [11], which does not have the focus on Model-Driven Development. This paper focuses on the main differences, emphasizing the aspects related to model-driven development. The approach has activities for identifying the features [1,2] of the domain, followed by activities that determine how these features can be implemented using MDD.

3.1   Domain Planning

The first step of the approach is a preparation phase. It involves gathering all domain information (preparation) and mapping all applications for the domain (domain scoping [12,13]). It also involves the determination of whether it makes sense to invest in building a reuse infrastructure in a given domain or not. This activity is carried out by the domain analyst, with the help from the domain experts and market specialists[11].

3.2   Domain Modeling

This activity is responsible for creating expressive models describing the features
and their relationships [1], with focus on the variability and commonality within
the domain. While the previous activity was concerned with *scoping*, here the
concern is on the structure of the domain, and the inclusion of more details of
its elements. A set of guidelines can also be useful in this task, which is carried
out by the domain analyst with the help from domain experts [11,14]. The result
is a set of models describing the features of the domain and their relationships.

3.3   Sub-domains Identification

This activity, which was not present in the original work [11], deals with the
identification of sub-domains that can be automated through MDD techniques,
with focus on increasing the reusability of the domain assets.

There is not much information regarding domain decomposition for Model-
Driven Development available in the literature. Also, we were unable to determine fixed ways or precise metrics and algorithms that can be used to do this
sub-domain identification. Due to this uncertainty, this activity is dependent
on two principles: successive iterations and guidelines. The rationale behind the
iterative process is presented later, in section 4. The guidelines, which were identified from similar problems regarding software reuse in the literature, and from
our experience with MDD projects, are presented next:

- *Focus on automation*: although most authors do not present a clear criteria
  when performing domain decomposition, in MDD this is very clear: the identified sub-domains must be automated using modelers and transformations.
- *The domain expert holds the key*: several authors agree that the knowledge
  from the domain expert is extremely valuable [15,16,17]. In this sense, the
  sub-domain identification should always be guided by this professional.
- *Atomic domains*: the identified sub-domain should be *atomic*, which means
  that it cannot be decomposed without altering its primary property [16].
  This is important to keep the sub-domain simple, thus easier to automate.
- *Features relationships*: Closely related features are normally good candidates
  to pertain to a same sub-domain. Looking for features that appear to be
  separated from the others are also a good hint for finding sub-domains.
- *Repetition*: If some piece of design or code repeatedly appears inside a product, even if not exactly, it is likely that a machine can do some parameterized
  copying and pasting, and it is worthy to try to find a sub-domain here. Another technique is to search for implementation or design patterns [18].

With these guidelines in mind, the following steps are carried out:

Candidate Sub-domains Selection. In this first step, the domain analyst
tries to identify possibly automatable sub-domains within the domain. Although
the knowledge from the domain expert is the main source of information, the
features model can be useful. By looking at the features model, starting at the

top features and going down, the domain analyst can identify keywords that may represent a sub-domain. As pointed out by [17], the natural categorization of the domain is the best indication of whether to find a sub-domain.

For each sub-domain candidate, the corresponding features need to be identified. This can be performed in a matrix, relating each feature to its correspondent sub-domain, with an optional graphical representation.

Modeling Languages Identification. Once the sub-domain candidates are identified, the domain analyst tries to determine if there are modeling languages for them, consulting the domain expert and existent documentation and source code. It is important to stress that models are not always a graphical representation using known languages, such as UML. Other languages, including domain-specific languages and textual models should be considered.

This is performed by searching inside existent applications and documentation for files that contain models. The features model can also offer tips of what to look for. Keywords present in the features model, such as feature names, are likely to appear inside documents and samples, and could be used by an automated search mechanism to find these files.

Finally, the domain analyst lists the identified modeling languages, associating them with their correspondent sub-domains.

Tools Identification. If a sub-domain is well known, there is a chance that there may already be a tool for creating models for it, or even generating code. Here, the domain analyst and the domain experts try to identify such tools.

Again, the knowledge from the domain expert is essential, but manuals and deployment documents should also be consulted, since they may have references to third-party tools used to create models or to generate parts of the application. Source code can also be inspected in search for indication that it was generated.

The identified tools are then listed and described, including a description of their functionalities, generated assets, and references to external sources.

Confidence Level Attribution. Identified sub-domains can not always be automated using MDD techniques. Even for those that can, the cost of developing modelers and transformations can be too high. Determining this cost is a complex task. The development of modelers and transformations may lead to changes and refinements in the features model, which will have great impact on the development. Also, depending on which sub-domain is implemented first, other related or overlapping sub-domains may need to be reconsidered.

We are unaware of a study that investigates a way to determine the cost of the development of these assets in this scenario. For this reason, the approach takes a different direction. All identified sub-domains are treated as mere candidates until they are fully realized. And this is why there must be a certain level of confidence that some sub-domain will render its expected results when realized as MDD assets, before actually proceeding to design and implementation.

The level of confidence measurement serves as a risk management tool, helping to ensure that critical changes in the architecture and the analysis models will lead to the desired results. Although not as precise as a cost-based technique, we believe this approach serves as a decision-making support mechanism in this complex scenario, and can be used to coordinate the efforts during the iterative process of the domain engineering approach.

The determination of a level of confidence in a sub-domain is highly subjective and dependent on the knowledge of the domain expert. However, the following aspects have impact on the decision, and should be considered:

- Is there a modeling language for the sub-domain?
- If the answer for the previous question is positive, what is the maturity of this language: Is it a well-known language, known and used by domain experts in several organizations? Does it exists only inside the organization? Was it developed only for this project?
- Was the modeling language validated through case studies for this project?
- Is there a tool available for the sub-domain?
- If the answer for the previous question is positive, what is the maturity of this tool: Is it a well-known tool, known and used by domain experts in several organizations? Does it exists only inside the organization? Was it developed only for this project?
- Has the tool been validated, through case studies, for this project?
- How does the tool fit in the project? Does it generate executable code? If not, can it be adapted to generate code? How much effort is needed to use the tool output in the project?
- Has a pilot project been conducted for this sub-domain, using a modeling language and a tool for generating code?

In order to more systematically determine the confidence level, the domain analyst can develop a measurement involving these and other questions that may arise. A simple way to do that is to develop a questionnaire with these questions, assigning a weighted value for each answer. The sum of all values is the level of confidence. If this value is greater than a predefined minimum, the sub-domain should be considered for implementation.

The domain analyst must consult all stakeholders when defining this measurement. There are multiple factors that must be considered, and different situations may require different values. For example, for safety-critical systems, it is reasonable to use only well-known languages and tools, and therefore higher weight values are attributed to these questions. In projects with little time-to-market, this may also be the only option. However, in projects with more time available, the values can be adjusted to include more potential sub-domains, since there is more time to develop tools and modeling languages. This is also the case where the goal is to build larger domains for reuse.

Candidate Sub-domains Documentation. In this step, the domain analyst creates a document for each identified sub-domain, including all information gathered in the previous steps: the involved features, modeling languages and tools, and the level of confidence.

Here the domain analyst also describes the interaction between the sub-domain candidate and the remainder of the domain. At this point, this description should focus on high-level cooperation between the features, aiming to help in the decision of whether it is worthy to invest in the automation of this sub-domain. In later stages, if it is decided that this sub-domain will be automated, this interaction will be refined, including detailed definition of the interface between the generated assets for this sub-domain and the other assets.

3.4 Domain Validation and Documentation

Most of the documentation was already produced in the previous activities, such as domain models, and documents describing the features. However, before the domain is ready to be used, it is necessary to validate and package all information in a more organized structure, designed to facilitate reuse.

The validation involves checking for inconsistencies and missing information. First, the features are documented according to a template [19], including their semantic description, rationale, exemplar applications, constraints, among other information [11]. Then, the domain analyst checks for homonyms and synonyms, in order to reduce the ambiguity in the documentation of the features. Next, the domain is validated against the stakeholder information and the initial requirements. The domain analyst checks the documented features and related documents, validating the accuracy and completeness of the domain. Finally, the domain documentation is finalized, including its description, the scoping criteria used for including/excluding its elements, exemplar systems, domain genealogy, the features and the documented sub-domains.

3.5 Decision Upon Sub-domain Inclusion/Exclusion

In this activity, which was also not present in the original work [11], the domain analyst, together with the stakeholders and the domain experts, analyzes the identified sub-domains, in order to determine if they will be included in the subsequent design and implementation phases.

According to the level of confidence of the sub-domain candidates, their interrelationship with the remaining domain elements, and other external factors, including the business goals, market conditions, among others, each sub-domain will be selected for inclusion or exclusion.

However, the process is iterative, and some sub-domains may be more mature, while others may need further development. In this sense, instead of merely including or excluding a sub-domain, there are different levels of decisions (D) that can be taken:

D_1. **Immediate exclusion.** This means that the sub-domain candidate is not suitable for automation, and should be discarded immediately. Typically, this sub-domain candidate has a low level of confidence, and no modeling language nor tool to create models for it.

D_2. **Keep for later evaluation.** This means that this sub-domain has a chance of being automated, but there are no concrete evidence that it could be used someday. Typically, it has a low level of confidence, no modeling language, no tool, but the domain experts knowledge or the experience in the development indicate that it may become useful after some development. However, there are no ways of estimating effort for turning it into a concrete sub-domain, i.e. it is too risky to start any development on it. Therefore no action is taken in this iteration. However, if the stakeholders decide to take the risk, the same sub-domain can fall into the next decision level (D_3).

D_3. **Start investigation.** If a sub-domain has a chance of being automated, but the tools for doing it are not available, it can be subject of further investigation, involving the development of prototypes of modeling languages and/or modeling/transformation tools. Typically, in order to start an investigation, there should be a way to estimate the effort necessary, in order to reduce the risks. Also, although this decision involves effort and resources, these may be limited, since there is no impact on the other domain elements. Therefore, it is always possible to stop the investigation at any time.

D_4. **Start the development of production assets.** This is the point of no return for a sub-domain. By making this decision, the organization makes a commitment that this sub-domain will be included in the development process, differently from D_3, where there is a possibility that the sub-domain is discarded. A sub-domain in this level should have a high level of confidence, but may not have the necessary tools for being automated yet. This is a critical decision, since it means spending more serious efforts and resources in automating the sub-domain and managing its impacts on the domain.

D_5. **Start a pilot project.** After the sub-domain is implemented, but before it is included in the actual product development, it may be a good practice to run a pilot project, in order to reduce the risks of introducing the new technologies in the development, and reduce the barriers to the technology transfer. It can also serve as a way to verify the real benefits of the new technology and plan the best way of applying it to real projects.

D_6. **Immediate inclusion.** This means that the sub-domain is mature enough, has a tool and one or more modeling languages that are stable and validated. The level of confidence is high, and the sub-domain may be included in the subsequent design and implementation, meaning that the development of domain assets should be driven by the existing languages and tools for this sub-domain. While most sub-domains will only reach this level after passing through levels 2,3 and 4, some well-known domains may start directly on level 5. Some may even start on level 6, if the organization has already some previous experience with them.

In order to take this decision, the domain analyst should consider all information that is available, and the decision should be agreed by all stakeholders.

4   The Basic Cycle of Domain Analysis for MDD

As discussed earlier, the domain analysis approach is iterative. While the first iteration is where most of the effort is performed, in subsequent iterations the developed assets are refined according to the development of transformers and modelers for the sub-domains. This section describes the basic cycle of the domain analysis approach (Figure 2), focusing on what happens at each iteration.

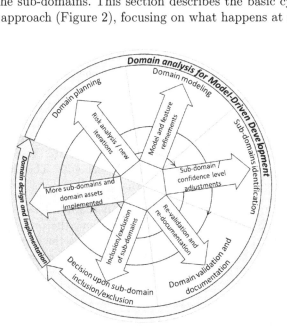

Fig. 2. Basic cycle of the domain analysis approach for MDD. The outer arrows show the boundaries between the analysis, design and implementation phases. The names in the slices represent the activities. The names inside the arrows indicate what happens at each iteration, for each activity.

Starting from the center, the process iterates, passing through the activities described in Section 3: *Domain planning, Domain modeling, Sub-domains identification, Domain validation and documentation,* and *Decision upon sub-domain inclusion/exclusion.* After each iteration, domain design and implementation takes place, including the sub-domains that were identified, analyzed and selected for inclusion in the previous activities.

Each iteration may lead to refinements and adjustments in the assets developed in the previous iterations. Each activity introduces refinements in different assets, as shown in the large arrows in the center of Figure 2.

The *Domain planning* activity, at the beginning of each new iteration, revisits the initial plan, including new considerations. It is also where a risk analysis is performed, in order to determine if new iterations are needed.

In the *Domain modeling* activity, the domain analyst refines the features model to consider the newly developed assets and the included sub-domains. This refinement can also be made in parallel with domain design and implementation, updating the features as domain assets are developed.

The *Sub-domain identification* activity revisits the list of sub-domains after the implementation and investigation performed on the previous iterations. New confidence levels may be attributed to the identified sub-domains, leading them to new decisions later. Also, new sub-domain candidates may be identified.

In the *Domain validation and documentation* activity, the existent documents are updated to reflect the changes. Change management and version control should be used to organize these documents.

During *Decision upon sub-domain inclusion/exclusion*, the information about sub-domain candidates is reviewed and new decisions are made for them.

The result of these successive iterations is a continuous growth in the number of domain assets and, mainly, in the level of confidence of the sub-domains that are supported by automation. Also, more sub-domains are discarded, as experience proves them difficult or impossible to automate.

5   Related Work

Knodel et al. [18] present an approach for using Model-Driven Development in software product lines, called Pulse-MDD. This approach has many similarities with our approach, also being iterative, but specially in the sense that the development of transformations and modelers is tailored to the architecture of the product line, and not on general concepts of the implementation technologies. The results are therefore closer to an organization's needs. However, in Pulse-MDD this concern starts in the domain design phase, while in our approach we argue that this should be considered earlier, during analysis, since we believe that features models should be adapted to reflect the existence of MDD assets.

Czarnecki et al. [20] describe two techniques to support model-driven product lines: features modeling and templates, to represent variability and commonality. These techniques are complementary to our approach, and could be used to describe domains and sub-domains for model-driven development.

Deelstra et al. [21] describe an approach for model-driven product lines development. They argue that MDD can have several benefits to product lines. However, they do not present details on how to systematically create transformations that lead from domain models to concrete software artifacts.

6   Conclusion

This paper describes a domain analysis approach that extends a previous work [11] with activities for dealing with Model-Driven Development. The thesis behind this work is that MDD can leverage reuse in domain engineering projects to a different level, when compared to conventional code-based development.

The main contributions of this paper are the systematic activities and guidelines for identifying sub-domains for automation. It also presents a basic cycle for carrying out these activities in a controlled and gradual way, helping to reduce risks and maintaining the development manageable.

Two case studies were developed to help in the definition of the approach: one for the *web navigation domain*, involving modeling the user navigation [22,23] in web applications and generating the corresponding web pages and controller code in Java/JSP/Servlets; and another one for the *data administration domain*, including the modeling of data structures and generation of data access and interface code for basic CRUD operations (Create, Retrieve, Update, Delete), also in Java technology. The implementation of modelers and transformations was performed using GMF (Graphical Modeling Framework) and JET (Java Emitter Templates) technologies[1].

As future work, the related activities of the domain design and implementation phases are being developed, as well as the activities of the other two cycles.

Acknowledgments. This work was developed with the financial support from CAPES and CNPq (process number: 475743/2007-5). The authors would also like to thank the people who contributed with insights to this work with discussions in worldofreuse.blogspot.com.

References

1. Kang, K., Cohen, S., Hess, J., Novak, W., Peterson, A.: Feature-Oriented Domain Analysis (FODA) Feasibility Study. Technical report cmu/sei-90-tr-21, Software Engineering Institute, Carnegie Mellon University (1990)
2. Kang, K., Lee, J., Donohoe, P.: Feature-Oriented Product Line Engineering. IEEE Software 19(04), 58–65 (2002)
3. Neighbors, J.M.: Software Construction Using Components. Ph.d. thesis, University of California at Irvine (1980)
4. Lucrédio, D., Fortes, R.P.d.M., Almeida, E.S.d., Meira, S.R.d.L.: The Draco Approach Revisited: Model-Driven Software Reuse. In: VI WDBC - Workshop de Desenvolvimento Baseado em Componentes, Recife - PE - Brazil (2006)
5. France, R., Rumpe, B.: Model-driven Development of Complex Software: A Research Roadmap. In: 29th International Conference on Software Engineering 2007 - Future of Software Engineering, Minneapolis, MN, USA, pp. 37–54. IEEE Computer Society, Los Alamitos (2007)
6. Schmidt, D.C.: Guest Editor's Introduction: Model-Driven Engineering. IEEE Computer 39(2), 25–31 (2006)
7. Ledeczi, A., Bakay, A., Maroti, M., Volgyesi, P., Nordstrom, G., Sprinkle, J., Karsai, G.: Composing Domain-Specific Design Environments. IEEE Computer 34(11), 44–51 (2001)
8. Lucrédio, D., Fortes, R.P.d.M., Alvaro, A., Almeida, E.S.d., Meira, S.R.d.L.: Towards a Model-Driven Reuse Process. In: 31st IEEE EUROMICRO Conference on Software Engineering and Advanced Applications (SEAA), Work in Progress Session, Porto, Portugal. IEEE Computer Society, Los Alamitos (2005)
9. Bézivin, J., Barbero, M., Jouault, F.: On the Applicability Scope of Model Driven Engineering. In: Fourth International Workshop on Model-Based Methodologies for Pervasive and Embedded Software (MOMPES 2007), Braga, Portugal, pp. 3–7. IEEE, Los Alamitos (2007)
10. Wimmer, M., Strommer, M., Kargl, H., Kramler, G.: Towards Model Transformation Generation By-Example. In: 40th Hawaii International Conference on System Sciences (HICSS 2007), Hawaii (2007)

---

[1] http://www.eclipse.org/gmf/ and http://www.eclipse.org/emft/projects/jet/

11. Almeida, E.S.d., Mascena, J.C.C.P., Cavalcanti, A.P.C., Alvaro, A., Garcia, V.C., Lucrédio, D., Meira, S.R.d.L.: The Domain Analysis Concept Revisited: A Practical Approach. In: 9th International Conference on Software Reuse (ICSR), Torino, Italy. Springer, Heidelberg (2006)

12. Griss, M., Favaro, J., d'Alessandro, M.: Integrating Feature Modeling with the RSEB. In: The Fifty International Conference on Software Reuse (ICSR), Victoria, Canada, pp. 76–85. IEEE/CS Press, Los Alamitos (1998)

13. Bayer, J., Flege, O., Knauber, P., Laqua, R., Muthig, D., Schmid, K., Widen, T., DeBaud, J.: PuLSE: A Methodology to Develop Software Product Lines. In: Symposium on Software Reusability (SSR), Los Angeles, USA, pp. 122–131. ACM Press, New York (1999)

14. Lee, K., Kang, K.C., Lee, J.: Concepts and Guidelines of Feature Modeling for Product Line Software Engineering. In: 7th International Conference on Software Reuse (ICSR): Methods, Techniques, and Tools, Austin, Texas, pp. 62–77 (2002)

15. Jarzabek, S.: Modeling multiple domains in software reuse. In: The 1997 Symposium on Software Reusability, Boston, Massachusetts, United States, pp. 65–74. ACM Press, New York (1997)

16. Haddad, H., Tesser, H.: Reusable Subsystems: Domain-Based Approach. In: 2002 ACM Symposium on Applied Computing (SAC 2002), pp. 971–975. ACM, New York (2003)

17. Maiden, N., Sutcliffe, A.: A computational mechanism for parallel problem decomposition during requirements engineering. In: 8th International Workshop on Software Specification and Design, Germany, pp. 159–163 (1996)

18. Knodel, J., Anastasopolous, M., Forster, T., Muthig, D.: An Efficient Migration to Model-driven Development (MDD). Electronic Notes in Theoretical Computer Science 137(3), 17–27 (2005)

19. Czarnecki, K., Eisenecker, U.W.: Generative Programming: Methods, Tools, and Applications. Addison-Wesley, Reading (2000)

20. Czarnecki, K., Antkiewicz, M., Kim, C.H.P., Lau, S., Pietroszek, K.: Model-driven software product lines. In: 20th Annual ACM SIGPLAN Conference on Object-Oriented Programming, Systems, Languages, and Applications (OOPSLA 2005), San Diego, CA, USA, pp. 126–127. ACM, New York (2005)

21. Deelstra, M., Sinnema, M., Van Gurp, J., Bosch, J.: Model Driven Architecture as Approach to Manage Variability in Software Product Families. In: Aßmann, U., Aksit, M., Rensink, A. (eds.) MDAFA 2003. LNCS, vol. 3599, pp. 109–114. Springer, Heidelberg (2005)

22. Newman, M.W., Landay, J.A.: Sitemaps, storyboards, and specifications: a sketch of Web site design practice. In: DIS 2000. Proceedings of the conference on Designing interactive systems, New York City, New York, United States, pp. 263–274. ACM Press, New York (2000)

23. Gitzel, R., Korthaus, A., Schader, M.: Using established Web Engineering knowledge in model-driven approaches. Science of Computer Programming 66, 105–124 (2007)

Exploiting COTS-Based RE Methods: An Experience Report

Nan Niu and Steve Easterbrook

Department of Computer Science, University of Toronto
Toronto, Ontario, Canada M5S 3G4
{nn,sme}@cs.toronto.edu

Abstract. This paper reports on an exploratory study of a key hypothesis of enterprise resource planning (ERP) requirements engineering (RE) adoption, namely that framing applications to the packaged RE model leads to integral practices and economic development. We analyzed two interrelated pilot projects developed for a business division of a large IT company, using Oracle's commercial off-the-shelf (COTS) application implementation method (AIM). The study showed that AIM RE improved team collaboration and project management experience, but needed to make hidden assumptions explicit to support data visibility and integrity. Our study can help practitioners generate more effective and mature processes when exploiting COTS-based RE methods.

1 Introduction

Developing software with commercial off-the-shelf (COTS) components support saves an organization from reinventing the wheel. The effective use of COTS software requires a systematic method that facilitates the exploitation of the benefits of COTS components while guarding against their technical and business pitfalls, and we can better understand and optimize the COTS software if the method is applied during requirements engineering (RE) activities [1].

The underlying philosophy of building an application on top of COTS components is illustrated in Fig. 1. Two parties are involved: the COTS vendor and the application developer, and their perspectives are labeled outside and inside the parentheses in Fig. 1. The real world picture is a lot messier than Fig. 1. The interplays between the modules present many risks for RE to assess. These include mismatches between customer's needs and COTS features, interferences arising from unused components, and inconsistencies during integration of newly built portions. Therefore, the reuse benefits claimed for COTS-based development have to be weighed against the cost of mitigating the risks. From Fig. 1, it is clear that the fitness of COTS-based RE is concerned with reconciling the COTS system and the customer requirements. This fitness coin has two sides:

1. Choose what's fit: procuring the COTS system that maximizes the reuse to unused ratio [4]; and
2. Fit what's chosen: tailoring the application development so that customization and extension are achieved.

H. Mei (Ed.): ICSR 2008, LNCS 5030, pp. 212–216, 2008.
© Springer-Verlag Berlin Heidelberg 2008

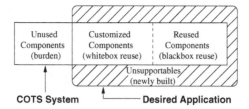

Fig. 1. Exploiting COTS software in application development

The literature in COTS-based reuse has focused mainly on the first aspect, and some fundamental issues of procuring software package requirements were outlined in [3,7]. In contrast, the literature has paid little attention to the second fitness criterion listed above, i.e., how to leverage the selected COTS package to construct high quality applications. In practices like building enterprise resource planning (ERP) systems, COTS candidates are relatively easy to identify among market leaders, such as SAP AG, Oracle Corporation, and PeopleSoft Inc. Selection tends to be a less pronounced bottleneck as experience is accumulated and reported. The success of ERP projects then strongly hinges on how well they align the business requirements and application components to the selected COTS system. One solution is to take advantage of the RE guidelines defined in the chosen ERP package. However, we are aware of no empirical studies that investigate this COTS-based reuse tenet, nor the scope of its applicability. The discipline remains under-explored. To address this gap, we conducted an evaluation of underpinning hypotheses of COTS-based RE methods.

2   Study Context and Design

A generic RE model helps conceptualize corporate-wide integrated solutions in that it offers defined processes, suggests process stakeholders, specifies steps to accomplish tasks, indicates task dependencies, and provides standard tool support for ERP RE [1]. Once the project decision is made, the initial resources are allocated, and COTS package is selected, there is little room for retreat. Among 42 Australian-based ERP implementations surveyed in [6], only one abandoned the project. Most companies felt impelled to continue once committed. In another word, after an ERP product is chosen, people live and die with their choice. Given that RE is any ERP project's most expensive stage [1], the RE knowledge is not only needed but also vital to the field. Our study investigates the issues arising when an organization makes the ERP RE model a live process.

The organization in our study is one of the largest PC manufacturers in the Asia-Pacific region. Its headquarter is located in Beijing, PR China, and it has approximately 10,000 employees as of 2006. To honor confidentiality agreements, we will call it ZT. ZT's ERP implementations began in the late 1990s. Among the motivations for ZT to adopt ERP were the need for a common IT platform and the desire for process improvement. ZT took an incremental and evolutionary

Table 1. Characteristics of ERP projects developed by AIM (release 3.0.0)

	PMIS	CRM
project duration	Dec. 2000 – Apr. 2001	Jan. 2002 – Aug. 2002
project scope	intra-division	inter-division & intra-corporation
development environment	JSP, Perl-CGI, IIS	J2EE, Apache
team formation breakdowns	1 project manager, 1 Oracle consultant, and 5 developers	1 project manager, 1 Oracle consultant, 7 developers, and 1 business analyst

ERP adoption strategy [6] to reduce risk. In particular, pilot ERP projects were launched in one of ZT's business divisions, allowing a trial-and-error inquiry to collect experience and assess feasibility.

ZT selected Oracle's application implementation method (AIM) [5] to implement its pilot ERP projects. Of particular interest to our RE study are the BP (business process architecture), RD (business requirements definition), and BR (business requirements mapping) processes of AIM [5]. We selected ZT's pilot ERP projects as an ideal case [2] to explore COTS-based RE methods for a number of reasons. First, ERP development is a critical case in testing COTS software adoption. ERP projects demand considerable resources and commitment, and are key to enduring business success. Second, AIM is representative in ERP packages. This indicates that the lessons learned from our case are informative about the experiences of the typical situation. Third, ZT's ERP development represent both a revelatory and a longitudinal case, in that pilot ERP studies were seldom investigated and two sequentially-linked ZT projects were included as units of analysis in our study design. Finally, ZT's business division under study was highly cooperative and generous with regards to our research, so we anticipated a high degree of access to key stakeholders and projects' data.

We derived several hypotheses from the philosophy of COTS software adoption to guide our study design. Our central hypothesis was that: *"Framing ERP projects to the AIM RE model leads to integral RE practices and economic application development."* This hypothesis reinforces the underpinning COTS-based development philosophy: if the chosen ERP RE were not fully exploited, the application development would remain separated and costly. Auxiliary hypotheses were that AIM RE could improve team collaboration experience, project management experience, data visibility and integrity, the ability to map application-specific requirements, and the flexibility of building customized applications.

To investigate the hypotheses, we chose two ERP projects from ZT's pilot repository: product management information system (PMIS) and customer relationship management system (CRM). Table 1 summarizes some characteristics of these projects, As was mentioned, ZT launched these projects as pilot trials of an incremental ERP adoption process. These projects were sequentially-linked, and it was ZT's intention to assign similar management and development personnel to consolidate experience from the interrelated projects. Both developments were Java-based, so the effects of technical environment were overshadowed by business processes. Notably, a business analyst with good interpersonal skills joined the CRM project. This was key to facilitating team collaborations.

3   Results and Concluding Remarks

Our data collection was based on semi-structured survey and artifact analysis [2]. The surveys involved project leaders, developers, AIM consultants, and the formats ranged from structured to open-ended questionnaires. Artifacts in our analysis included business baselines, specifications, meeting minutes, etc. Due to geographic constraints, most data collection was done via asynchronous communication such as e-mails and Web forms. A few teleconferences and on-site visits were held during our study. We took the actual project duration into account because some experience or answers were only obvious in hindsight.

In the two projects we studied, we found that the most critical success-enabler was the strong commitment of upper management to the ERP projects, viewing them as business change initiatives rather than self-possessed software projects. Leveraging AIM's documentation templates for project management is not trivial. There are more than 150 templates defined in AIM 3.0.0, so making use of each of them was clearly an overkill. One of ZT's solutions was to adopt generic documents and ignore detailed Oracle configurations. AIM 3.0.0 did not require conceptual data models as mandatory project deliverables, partly because having them was implicitly assumed in AIM. As a result, both ZT's ERP projects slowed down due to insufficient data specification and modeling in the RE stage. The lesson learned was to make the hidden assumption explicit. Identifying and resolving gaps between application requirements and ERP functionality were defined in AIM's BR process, which ZT found useful. The resolving methods included documenting workarounds, creating alternative possibilities, using application extensions, and changing the underlying business process [5]. The ERP functionality reuse rate [4] was estimated to be slightly over 50% in each of ZT's pilot projects. In ZT's trials, the biggest gain was probably developing two different kinds of ERP applications, PMIS and CRM, using AIM. On one hand, standard ERP functionality and process were bound early in the package to guide blackbox reuse. On the other hand, AIM allowed late binding (customization) through just-in-time requirements determination [3].

In summary, some auxiliary hypotheses were confirmed while others were under-explored. We considered having two sequentially-linked units of analysis was important because ZT was able to learn from its own mistakes. In terms of our central hypothesis, we felt that the study supported the claim. We suggest that, when possible, stick with the ERP vendor's architecture approach to better manage complexity and support requirements reuse. The application team could use the ERP framework to develop the first blueprint version, which reflects basic requirements and is unlikely to be met with disagreement. More sophisticated requirements could be gradually incorporated and controversial issues could be systematically addressed in the incremental adoption process. Finally, it is crucial to keep the requirements baseline evolving along with the stakeholders' changing desires and needs.

References

1. Daneva, M.: ERP RE practice: lessons learned. IEEE Softw. 21(2), 26–33 (2004)
2. Easterbrook, S., et al.: Selecting empirical methods for software engineering research. In: Guide to Advanced Empirical Software Engineering. Springer, Heidelberg (2007)
3. Finkelstein, A., Spanoudakis, G., Ryan, M.: Software package requirements & procurement. In: Wkshp. on Softw. Spec. and Design, pp. 141–145 (1996)
4. Frakes, W.B., Terry, C.: Software reuse: metrics and models. ACM Computing Surveys 28(2), 415–435 (1996)
5. Oracle application implementation method (release 3.0.0). Oracle Corp. (1999)
6. Parr, A.N., Shanks, G.: A taxonomy of ERP implementation approaches. In: Hawaii Intl. Conf. on System Sciences, p. 7018 (2000)
7. Rolland, C., Prakash, N.: Matching ERP system functionality to customer requirements. In: Intl. Symp. on RE, pp. 66–75 (2001)

Towards Reusable Automation System Components

Thomas Aschauer, Gerd Dauenhauer, and Wolfgang Pree

C. Doppler Laboratory *Embedded Software Systems*, University of Salzburg
Jakob-Haringer-Str. 2, 5020 Salzburg, Austria
`firstname.lastname@cs.uni-salzburg.at`

Abstract. In this paper we present a domain specific language for describing an automation system, that is, its hardware and software components. These domain components form the basis of large-scale reuse so that specific automation systems can be configured efficiently.

Keywords: Component reuse, domain specific modeling language.

1 Context and Motivation

Our research group cooperates with an industry partner that is a dominant player in the area of so-called engine test bed systems that are used, for example, in the automotive industry for developing and optimizing combustion engines. Engine test bed systems are specific automation systems. Typical functions of an engine test bed system are the parameterization and visualization of its real-world components, such as the engine under test, and the sensors, as well as the measured values. The corresponding software has evolved over the last two decades and comprises about 1.5 million lines of code, mainly written in C++ and C. Originally, one of the main goals was to improve the current system's usability. A major hurdle for the users of the current system is the fact that the domain entities they have in mind (such as engines, dynamometers, measurement and conditioning devices) do not match well with the entities in its user interface. For example, a person who configures a test bed would like to deal with a graphical representation of the test bed entities, with the parameters and measured values associated with the physical components. In a typical setup there are about 10,000 parameters with about 120,000 values to be set correctly. In other words, the domain components should also be the entities the user deals with. The domain components should be reusable assets that allow an efficient configuration of a specific engine test bed system. For that purpose we defined the *Domain Component Description Language* (DCDL) sketched in the next section.

2 Domain Component Description Language (DCDL)

DCDL is a domain specific language for describing the components of a test bed automation system, either as text or in an equivalent visual form. For the sake of brevity we use the textual representation below.

The primary entities of DCDL are components which describe the structure and the behavior of automation system components such as the engine under test or

H. Mei (Ed.): ICSR 2008, LNCS 5030, pp. 217–220, 2008.

measurement devices, but also the relevant properties of an automation system's software components. The electric current is an example of a physical component property. The explicit description of hardware and software properties is required to check the validity of compositions and thus to ensure the consistency of the DCDL model.

Consider, for example, a temperature sensor and a measurement device. The sensor's DCDL description comprises its plug's shape and its emitted electrical signal. The measurement device's description also comprises its plug's shape and its accepted electrical signal. If the sensor and the measurement device are connected in the test bed description, a validity check is performed that only allows the sensor to be plugged into the measurement device if both the plug shape and the electrical signals match.

Viewing Different Component Aspects. The various aspects of a DCDL component can be grouped and component editors typically show them in separate views:

- *Physical View*: Represents physical and if applicable electrical aspects such as plugs and wires (see figure 1).
- *Functional View*: Represents functional aspects, such as PID controllers and limit monitors. This view is similar to dataflow modeling languages such as Simulink [1].
- *Parameter View*: Represents variability aspects in terms of name/value pairs, e.g. plug shape descriptions or PID controller values.
- *Operation View*: Visualizes a component during the operation of the test bed automation system, for example, by showing relevant measurement values and changing their color in case they are not within predefined limits.

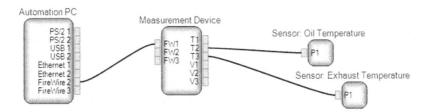

Fig. 1. Sample physical view of a test bed

DCDL Component Definition by Example. We use a table format to illustrate the definition of DCDL components (see figure 2). The table shows two simplified *Engines*, E_1 and E_2. Possible properties of engine components are specified in columns. It is not mandatory to define values for each property. E_2, for example, does not specify the property *Ignition*.

Category: Engine			
Component	*Cylinders*	*Inertia*	*Ignition*
E_1	8	1.06 kgm^2	Plug 15
E_2	6	1.04 kgm^2	

Fig. 2. Two sample DCDL components

DCDL offers mechanisms to reuse component definitions. Interviews with domain experts showed that for them copying and pasting a component definition is a natural way of reuseing it. Therefore DCDL supports what is called prototypical inheritance in the object-orientated programming paradigm [2]. Figure 3 shows an engine E_3, which is defined by copying the definition of engine E_1. The properties *Cylinders* and *Ignition* are inherited and their values are unchanged, the property *Inertia* is inherited but its value was changed, and a new property N_{max} is added.

Category: Engine				
Component	*Cylinders*	*Inertia*	N_{max}	*Ignition*
E_1	8	1.06 kgm^2		Plug 15
$E_3 \leftarrow E_1$	8	1.05 kgm^2	12,000 rpm	Plug 15

Fig. 3. Component extension via prototypical inheritance

DCDL-Based Composition. DCDL was designed so that the compatibility of automation system components can be checked. When components are reused to assemble a specific test bed system, the DCDL type system ensures that users can define only valid compositions. The following concepts form the backbone of the type compatibility check:

- Components are assigned to user defined categories. The type system treats components of different categories as incompatible. Since all components in figures 2 and 3 are classified as *Engine*, they are of the same category and are, for example, not compatible to any component of another category such as *Measurement Device*.
- Every view defines a separate type system. The physical view, for example, defines compatibility between plugs in terms of plug shape. The parameter view's type system is analogous to that of imperative programming languages with strong type checking such as Java.

Abstract DCDL Components. DCDL offers the possibility to define types and values of properties as *unspecified*. Components with at least one unspecified property are *abstract components*. A valid DCDL model must not contain abstract components. Abstracting from concrete components should further support the reuse of component definitions. The properties of abstract components are listed, but not yet typed. The following example shows how an abstract engine *AbstractEngine* could be modeled.

```
COMPONENT AbstractEngine CATEGORY 'Engine'
  Nmax : UNSPECIFIED := UNSPECIFIED
END
```

Hierarchical Composition. DCDL components can be hierarchically composed of other components. The dynamometer example shows how a dynamometer D and an abstract test bed *AbstractTestBed* are defined. *AbstractTestBed* is composed of D and *AbstractEngine*. Since *AbstractEngine* is an abstract component, *AbstractTestBed* is also abstract. The property *Nmax* of engine *AbstractEngine* is used to express the constraint that only engines with a lower maximum rotation speed than the dynamometer may be mounted. Although unspecified properties may be used to express constraints, these constraints can not be enforced until all referenced properties are fully specified in components that are based on abstract components.

```
COMPONENT D CATEGORY 'Dynamometer'
  Nmax : REAL := 20000[rpm]
END

COMPONENT AbstractTestBed CATEGORY 'Test bed'
  Engine : AbstractEngine
  Dyno : D
  Dyno.Nmax >= Engine.Nmax
END
```

From Abstract to Concrete Components. Finally we illustrate the transformation of an abstract component to a specific one. First, an engine *E1* is defined whose properties have the same names as the ones of *AbstractEngine*. Second, *SampleTestBed* is created as a clone of *AbstractTestBed*. *SampleTestBed* redefines the property *Engine* by replacing the component *AbstractEngine* with *E1*. *SampleTestBed* is a concrete component, since it neither contains abstract components nor does it contain unspecified properties itself.

In the context of *SampleTestBed*, *AbstractEngine* is substitutable by *E1* since a) both components are of category *Engine*, b) both components have a property *Nmax* and c) *D.Nmax* has the same data type and unit as *E1.Nmax*. All parameters are specified and thus the constraint inherited from *AbstractTestBed* can be enforced.

```
COMPONENT E1 CATEGORY 'Engine'
  Nmax : REAL := 12000[rpm]
END

COMPONENT SampleTestBed LIKE AbstractTestBed
  Engine : E1
END
```

3 Related Work

There is a trend in the embedded industry to explicitly describe the overall computing infrastructure, the static hardware and software setup as well as the interactions between the components. One example is AUTOSAR [3], an initiative by the automotive industry. As automation systems differ from automotive computing platforms, the description differs, though the vision is similar. Modeling languages such as UML and SysML [4] could be harnessed for the visual representation of CDCL.

References

1. The MathWorks Simulink, http://www.mathworks.com/products/simulink
2. Abadi, M., Cardelli, L.: A Theory of Objects, 2nd edn. Monographs in Computer Science. Springer, New York (1998)
3. AUTOSAR (an acronym abbreviating AUTOmotive open System ARchitecture), http://www.autosar.org
4. Object Management Group: OMG Systems Modeling Language (OMG SysML™), Unified Modeling Language (UML), http://www.omg.org

An Approach to Domain-Specific Reuse in Service-Oriented Environments

Jianwu Wang[1,2], Jian Yu[1], Paolo Falcarin[1], Yanbo Han[3], and Maurizio Morisio[1]

[1] Software Engineering Research Group, Dept. of Control and Computer Engineering,
Politecnico di Torino, 10129, Torino, Italy
[2] San Diego Supercomputer Center, University of California, San Diego, 92093, USA
[3] Research Centre for Grid and Service Computing, Institute of Computing Technology,
Chinese Academy of Sciences, 100080, Beijing, China
wangjianwu@gmail.com,
{jian.yu,paolo.falcarin,maurizio.morisio}@polito.it,
yhan@ict.ac.cn

Abstract. Domain engineering is successful in promoting reuse. An approach to domain-specific reuse in service-oriented environments is proposed to facilitate service requesters to reuse Web services. In the approach, we present a conceptual model of domain-specific services (called *domain service*). Domain services in a certain business domain are modeled by semantic and feature modeling techniques, and bound to Web services with diverse capabilities through a variability-supported matching mechanism. By reusing pre-modeled domain services, service requesters can describe their requests easily through a service customization mechanism. Web service selection based on customized results can also be optimized by reusing the pre-matching results between domain services and Web services. Feasibility of the whole approach is demonstrated on an example.

Keywords: Domain-Specific Reuse, Domain Service Model, Service Capability Diversity, Variability-Supported Service Matching, Service Customization.

1 Introduction

Service orientation is becoming a dominant paradigm in distributed computing. There are a large amount of available Web services on the Internet, and there will be more. In the bioinformatics domain, for instance, the number of Web services has added up to over 3000 [1]. On the one hand, the abundance of Web services facilitates on-demand application construction; on the other hand, since Web services are implemented and maintained independently, slight differences among them bring difficulties for their (re)use.

We will use a simplified example from the weather service domain throughout the paper (see Fig. 1). There are over 15 real Web services (including 179 independent operations)[1] providing weather forecast on the Internet. When the number of Web

---

[1] An incomplete list can be found at
http://wangjianwu.googlepages.com/webservicelistforweatherforecast

H. Mei (Ed.): ICSR 2008, LNCS 5030, pp. 221–232, 2008.

services with similar functionality is huge, it is very difficult for service requesters to directly select proper services and reuse them.

We can then split the problem into two parts:

1) *Similarity and diversity of service requests*[2]: As shown in Fig.1, *Req1* and *Req2* are two similar yet different service requests. For instance, wind speed information is mandatory in *Req1* but not in *Req2*; the target location areas and the preferred ways to describe locations are also different. A key problem at the service request level is how to facilitate service requesters to describe their service requests in a certain business domain where service requests are similar yet diverse.

2) *Similarity and diversity of Web services*: Also as shown in Fig.1, *WS1* and *WS2* are two similar yet different Web services. For instance, *WS1* can only forecast weather in the U.S., while *WS2* can forecast weather worldwide; their input parameters for location are also different; moreover, *WS2* has an additional output: wind speed. A key problem at the Web service level is how to optimize on demand selection of executable Web services in a service-oriented environment where Web services are abundant yet diverse in capability (namely Input, Output and QoS).

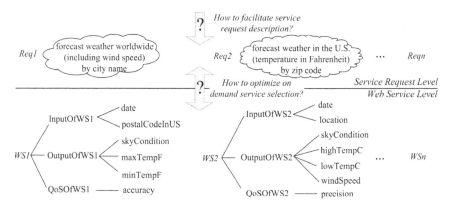

Fig. 1. Two levels of service usage in service-oriented environments

To tackle the above problems, we propose an approach to domain-specific reuse in service-oriented environments based on our previous work [2, 3]. The core of this approach is a conceptual model of domain-specific services (called *domain service*), which acts as a broker between service requesters and Web services. The following advantages can be obtained:

1) *Simplifying service request description by reusing pre-modeled domain services*: Feature modeling techniques [4, 5] are used in domain services to model the commonalities and variabilities of similar service capabilities. So instead of describing service requests from scratch, particular service requests can easily be described by reusing pre-modeled domain services.

---

[2] Service requests in this paper are restricted to single services. Complex service requests can be met through service composition, which is beyond the scope of this paper.

2) *Accelerating service request satisfaction by reusing pre-matching results between domain services and Web services*: With pre-modeled domain services, Web services can also be matched to proper domain services in advance. Then the matching between particular service requests and Web services can be optimized by reusing the pre-matching results between domain services and Web services.

The rest of this paper is organized as follows. Firstly, we discuss related work in Section 2. Then an overview of the approach is given in Section 3. Two parts of our approach, namely domain engineering process and application engineering process, are explored in detail in the following two sections. Finally, we conclude the paper in Section 6.

2   Related Work

Our approach can be seen as a kind of domain modeling applied to service-oriented environments in order to facilitate service request description and service matching.

Recently, some traditional approaches in requirement engineering researches have been applied on service request modeling, such as goal oriented [6] and value based [7]. Yet they do not tackle how to reuse service requests. There are also some researches addressing the importance of combining top-down requirement refinement and bottom-up existing service resource reuse [8, 9]. Our work also follows this way, and our work emphasizes the variability modeling of similar services which is omitted in the above work.

Feature modeling in domain engineering approaches has been proved to be successful in representing reusable and configurable requirements for its good capacity to express commonalities and variabilities [4, 5]. Recently, some effort has been put into importing feature modeling to model some aspects of commonalities and variabilities in service-oriented environments. In [10], each feature represents a service operation, which can support operation variabilities in similar systems. Feature modeling is also used to express non-functional properties [11, 12] and implementation techniques [13] of services. But none of the above proposals deal with service capability variability, which is a main difficulty for service requesters to directly select Web services.

There has been much research on service matching [14, 15, 16], however they usually assume that there is a given service request and an available service set, and emphasize on matching degree and theory foundation. How to reuse pre-matching results to facilitate future service matching is still an open challenge.

There are also some works on service virtualization [17, 18], which focus on how to abstract similar services for better (re)use. However, the abstraction mechanisms are rather rigid. For example, *WS1* and *WS2* in Fig. 1 can not be abstracted into one abstract weather forecast service for the capability differences between them. In a service-oriented environment where there are abundant Web services with diverse capabilities, these mechanisms can only bring limited promotion in reuse.

3   Overview of the Approach

Referring to the software development process in traditional domain engineering approaches [5], our approach also consists of a domain engineering process and an application engineering process (shown in Fig. 2). Activities (rectangles in Fig. 2) and deliverables (italics in Fig.2) in this approach will be outlined in this section and explained in detail in the following two sections.

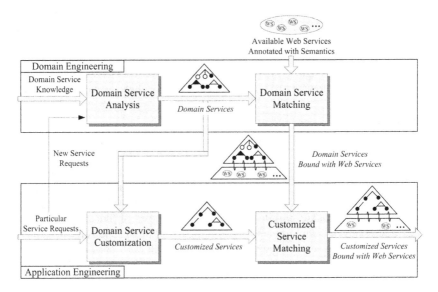

Fig. 2. Overview of the approach to domain-specific reuse in service-oriented environments

Domain Engineering Process: This process is to define domain services and bind them with Web services for future reuse. Firstly, domain services are modeled by domain experts through domain service analysis. Secondly, Web services are bound to proper domain services through service capability matching.

Application Engineering Process: This process is to reuse the deliverables generated in the domain engineering process in order to improve the satisfaction of particular service requests. Particular service requests are firstly described by customizing proper domain services, which can be made easier through reusing pre-modeled domain services. Secondly, suitable Web services are bound to customized services by customized service matching, which can be optimized through reusing pre-matching results between domain services and Web services. Then each Web service bound to customized services can be executed to perform the corresponding service requests.

For the applicable domains, our practice shows that the approach is suitable for the business (sub)domains, such as bioinformatics and travel information domain, which have the following characteristics: 1) Service requesters want to describe their personal-ized requests; 2) It is easy to define domain scope, and model domain on-tologies and services; 3) There are a large amount of available Web services provided by different organizations.

4   Domain Engineering Process

To discuss our domain engineering process, this section is divided into two subsections by its main activities.

4.1 Domain Service Analysis

Referring to traditional domain analysis activities, the domain service analysis also involves two main sub activities: domain service identification and domain service modeling. The first sub activity can refer to existing approaches, such as [8], and is omitted here. In the second sub activity, capability information of identified domain services is modeled for the matching with that of Web services. Here, the commonalities and variabilities of domain service capabilities are modeled by features to facilitate future service request description, and parameter semantics of domain services are annotated by domain ontology concepts for automatic and exact service matching. Besides, since domain ontologies express shared concepts in the domain, it is easy for service requesters to understand domain services.

To discuss our domain services in more detail, related formal definitions are given below, and the corresponding schemas in XML can easily be obtained from the definitions:

Def. 1 (Feature): *feature = < FeatureNode, FeatureEdge >, FeatureNode = {supernode} ∪ SubFeatureNode, SubFeatureNode ∈ {subnode$_1$, ... , subnode$_n$}, FeatureEdge = { <sn, sfn, ft> | sn=supernode, sfn∈ SubFeatureNode, ft∈ {Man, Opt, XOR, OR}}.* subnode$_i$ and the corresponding feature edges start from *subnode$_i$* also form a feature (called *sub feature*). Then a feature with all its descendent features forms a feature tree.

Def. 2 (Domain Service): *domainservice = < inputFeature, outputFeature, qosFeature >.* Hereinto, *inputFeature*, *outputFeature* and *qosFeature* are all features. And all the elements of *SubFeatureNode* of *inputFeature/outputFeature/qosFeature* are annotated with proper domain ontology concepts.

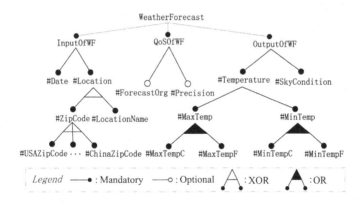

Fig. 3. A domain service example with capability variability

For the example of weather forecast, a simplified domain service in weather service domain, *WeatherForecast*, is modeled (shown in Fig. 3). For instance, typical location of *WeatherForecast* is expressed as *ZipCode* or *LocationName*, but not both. They are thus modeled as two sub features of *Location*, and the feature type is XOR. The partial formal definition of *WeatherForecast* is as follows:

> *WeatherForecast = <inputFeatureOfWF, outputFeatureOfWF, qosFeatureOfWF>*
> *inputFeatureOfWF = < { InputOfWF, Date, Location }, { <InputOfWF, Date,*
>   *Man>, <InputOfWF, Location, Man > } >*
> *locationFeature = < { Location, ZipCode, LocationName }, { <Location, ZipCode,*
>   *XOR>, <Location, LocationName, XOR> } >*
> ...

4.2 Domain Service Matching

Instead of separate domain implementations according to domain models in traditional domain engineering approaches, we think it is better to keep an eye on available Web services as well, which is also addressed in [8, 9]. So we employ a service matching mechanism to carry out domain implementation in service-oriented environments, which matches and binds domain services with proper executable Web services for future reuse. This way also realizes the seamless integration between the outputs from domain analysis and the inputs needed for domain implementation.

To enable automatic and exact service matching with domain services, techniques of semantic Web services [14, 19] are used. Parameters of Web services are all annotated with domain ontology concepts. Our definition on semantic Web service is given below and Fig.4 shows the corresponding semantic Web services of *WS1* and *WS2*. Note that, to be more precise, it should be semantic Web service operation. We use semantic Web service just for short.

Def. 3 (Semantic Web Service): *sws = <invokeUrl, InputPara, OutputPara, QoSPara>.* Hereinto, *invokeUrl* is the URL for service invocation; *InputPara/OutputPara/QoSPara* is the set of Input/Output/QoS parameters which are all annotated with proper domain ontology concepts.

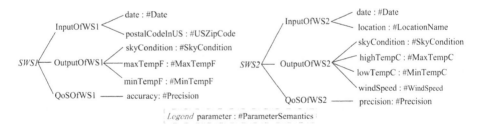

Fig. 4. Examples of semantic Web services

To adapt to the capability diversity of similar Web services, we employ a variability-supported service matching mechanism. Each domain service is shown as a feature tree. And a feature tree can be seen as a kind of AND/OR tree [20] extended with optional and XOR nodes. Then the solvability policy of feature trees can be obtained by extending that of AND/OR trees. Hence the principle of our matching is to firstly semantically match the parameters of Web services with those of domain services, and then to estimate the solvability of domain service feature trees. If a domain service feature tree is solvable on the condition of a certain Web service's capability, it means that the Web service's capability belongs to the capability variability (namely possible capability set) of the domain service, then we say the Web service matches the domain service.

The following formal definitions will be firstly given for detailed discussion.

Def. 4 (Concept Matching): Suppose *concept1* and *concept2* are two ontology concepts. If *concept1* is equal to or subclass of *concept2*, then *concept1* matches *concept2*, which is written as *cm(concept1, concept2) = TRUE*.

Def. 5 (Concept Set Matching): Suppose *Concept1* and *Concept2* are two ontology concept sets. If an injective function exists: $\{<x, y>|\ x \in Concept1,\ y \in Concept2$, *cm(x, y)* = *TRUE*$\}$, then *Concept1* matches *Concept2*, which is written as *csm(Concept1, Concept2) = TRUE*.

Def. 6 (Feature Tree Solvability Policy): If the feature type between one feature *feature* and its sub features is mandatory or optional, then *feature* is solvable if and only if all its mandatory sub features are solvable; if the feature type is OR, then *feature* is solvable if and only if one or more of its sub features are solvable; if the feature type is XOR, then *feature* is solvable if and only if one of its sub features is solvable. A feature tree is solvable if and only if its root feature is solvable.

Def. 7 (Feature Solvability): Suppose *feature* is a feature and *Feature* is a feature set. Given all the elements of *Feature* are solvable, if *feature* is solvable according to Def. 6, then *feature* is solvable on the condition of *Feature*, which is written as *fs(Feature, feature) = TRUE*.

Def. 8 (Semantic Solvability of Feature): Suppose *feature* is a feature, *Concept* is a concept set. If there exists a feature set *Feature* (its annotated concept set is written as *FeatureConcept*) such that *(csm(Concept, FeatureConcept)* $\wedge$ *fs(Feature, feature))* = *TRUE*, then *feature* is semantically solvable on the condition of *Concept*, which is written as *ss(Concept, feature) = TRUE*.

From the above definitions, we can get the following function to estimate the solvability of a feature y on the condition of a concept set x. It is a recursive function that the solvability of a feature depends on its semantic matching or the solvability of its sub features.

$$ss(x,y) = \begin{cases} m(x,y) & y \in LF \\ m(x,y) \vee (ss(x, sub_{11}(y)) \wedge ss(x, sub_{12}(y)) \wedge ... \wedge ss(x, sub_{1n}(y))) & y \notin LF \wedge (ft(y, Sub_1(y)) = Man) \\ \qquad\qquad\qquad\qquad\qquad\qquad\qquad\qquad \wedge (ft(y, Sub(y) - Sub_1(y)) = Opt) \\ m(x,y) \vee (ss(x, sub_1(y)) \wedge \neg ss(x, sub_2(y)) \wedge ... \wedge \neg ss(x, sub_n(y))) \\ \quad \vee (\neg ss(x, sub_1(y)) \wedge ss(x, sub_2(y)) \wedge ... \wedge \neg ss(x, sub_n(y))) \vee \\ \quad ... \vee (\neg ss(x, sub_1(y)) \wedge \neg ss(x, sub_2(y)) \wedge ... \wedge ss(x, sub_n(y))) & y \notin LF \wedge (ft(y, Sub(y)) = XOR) \\ m(x,y) \vee ss(x, sub_1(y)) \vee ss(x, sub_2(y)) \vee ... \vee ss(x, sub_n(y)) & y \notin LF \wedge (ft(y, Sub(y)) = OR) \end{cases}$$

Hereinto, *LF* is the leaf feature set whose elements do not have sub features; $Sub(y)$ is the sub feature set of y whose elements are $sub_1, ..., sub_n$; $Sub_1(y)$ is a sub set of $Sub(y)$ whose elements are $sub_{11}, ..., sub_{1n}$; $ft(y, Sub(y))$ is the feature type between feature y and its sub features.

Def. 9 (Service Matching): Suppose *sws* is a semantic Web service, and *ds* is a domain service. The annotated concept set of *sws*'s Input/Output/QoS parameters is written as *sws.InputConcept/OutputConcept/QoSConcept*. If *(ss(sws.InputConcept, ds.inputFeature)* $\wedge$ *ss(sws.OutputConcept, ds.outputFeature)* $\wedge$ *ss(sws.QoSConcept, ds.qosFeature))* = *TRUE*, then *sws* matches *ds*, which is written as *sm(sws, ds)* = *TRUE*.

The concrete service matching algorithm can easily be obtained from the above definitions and is then omitted for the space limitation.

Besides semantic and variability-supported, another property of the matching mechanism can also be obtained from the definitions, called *Additional Parameter Allowed*. Based on the above definitions, if *csm(Concept1, Concept2)* = *TRUE*, and *Concept1* $\subseteq$ *Concept1'*, then *csm(Concept1', Concept2)* = *TRUE*. So domain services can match Web services with additional parameters. This property fits the characteristic that independent Web services may have additional parameters compared to pre-modeled domain services.

For the above weather forecast example, both *SWS1* and *SWS2* matches domain service *WeatherForecast*. Let's take the input matching between *WeatherForecast* and *SWS1* for instance (Fig. 5), the annotated concept set of input parameters of *SWS1* matches feature set:{#Date, #USZipCode} (based on Def. 4), and the input feature of *WeatherForecast* is semantically solvable on the condition of {#Date, #USZipCode} according to Def. 8. So *ss(SWS1.InputConcept, WeatherForecast.inputFeatureOfWF)* = *TRUE*.

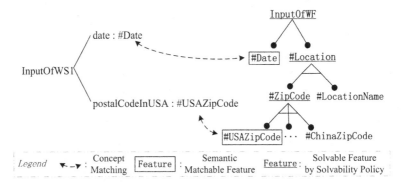

Fig. 5. Example of service matching between domain services and semantic Web services

5   Application Engineering Process

To reuse the deliverables generated in the above domain engineering process to facilitate the satisfaction of particular service requests, a corresponding application engineering process is discussed in this section. We will discuss it through two subsections according to its main activities.

5.1   Domain Service Customization

With reusable domain services, service requesters need not describe their requests from scratch. Yet there still may be a few differences between particular service requests and domain services. So we employ a domain service customization mechanism to enable service requesters to describe their requests by reusing domain services.

Based on existing works on feature configuration [21], service customization operations are defined, which can be classified into three categories: Add (e.g. add one mandatory sub feature), Delete (e.g. delete one optional sub feature) and Configure (e.g. select one sub feature from a XOR feature). All operations can be listed and formally defined following the way of the example below.

$$Feature \times SubFeatureNode \xrightarrow{selectXORFeature} Feature \; : \; \{ \; <x, \; y, \; z> \; |$$
$$x \in Feature, \; y \in x.SubFeatureNode, \; z \in Feature, \; z.FeatureNode \; = \; \{ \; y \; \} \cup \{$$
$$x.supernode \}, z.FeatureEdge = \{ \; <x.supernode, y, Man> \} \}$$

For *Req1* in the example of weather forecast, the service requester can customize *WeatherForecast* by adding wind speed as a sub feature of its output and selecting the sub feature LocationName of the Location feature. The customized result is shown in Fig.6. For the features she does not customize (such as Centigrade or Fahrenheit), it means they do not concern her, so each possibility of their variabilities is suitable to her.

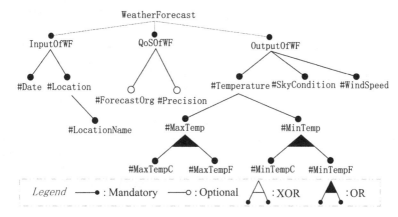

Fig. 6. An example of customized WeatherForecast domain service

5.2 Customized Service Matching

To perform particular service requests, not like product configuration on a separately implemented software in traditional domain engineering approaches, a mechanism to match and select Web services according to the customized service is employed, which can reuse the available Web services.

The service matching algorithm in Section 4 can also be applied in the customized service matching, and we find that pre-matching results of domain services is reusable for some customization operations which can then optimize the service selection.

Theorem 1: Suppose *ds* is a domain service, *op* is a customization operation on *ds*, and *SWS* is a semantic Web service set. The customization result of *ds* by *op* is written as *op(ds)*. For $SWS_1 = \{x \mid x \in SWS, \; sm(x,ds) = TRUE\}$ and $SWS_2 = \{x \mid x \in SWS, \; sm(x,op(ds)) = TRUE\}$, if the following proposition is true, then $SWS_2 \subseteq SWS_1$:

$$(\forall x)(\mathit{fs}(x, op(ds).inputFeature)) \Rightarrow (\mathit{fs}(x, ds.inputFeature))$$
$$\wedge (\forall x)(\mathit{fs}(x, op(ds).outputFeature)) \Rightarrow (\mathit{fs}(x, ds.outputFeature))$$
$$\wedge (\forall x)(\mathit{fs}(x, op(ds).qosFeature)) \Rightarrow (\mathit{fs}(x, ds.qosFeature))$$

Proof: For each element of SWS_2: sws, $ss(sws.InputConcept, op(ds).inputFeature)=$ *TRUE*, which is based on Def. 9. Then, there exists a feature set (written as *Feature*) and a corresponding annotated concept set (written as *FeatureConcept*), such that *(csm(sws.InputConcept, FeatureConcept)* $\wedge$ *fs(Feature, op(ds).inputFeature))* = *TRUE*. If the above proposition is true, then the following proposition is also true: (*fs(Feature, op(ds).inputFeature))* $\Rightarrow$ (*fs(Feature, ds.inputFeature))* . So *(csm(sws.InputConcept, FeatureConcept)* $\wedge$ *fs(Feature, ds.inputFeature))* = *TRUE*. Then *ss(sws.InputConcept, ds.inputFeature)* = *TRUE*, which is according to Def. 8. In similar ways, we can know that *ss(sws.OutputConcept, ds.outputFeature)* = *TRUE* and *ss(sws.QoSConcept, ds.qosFeature)* = *TRUE*. So *sm(sws, ds)* = *TRUE*, namely $sws \in SWS_1$.

For each customization operation, we can formally know whether it makes the proposition of Theorem 1 true. So, if a domain service is customized by the operations making the proposition true, the service selection for the customized service can be optimized. Not all the available Web services, but only Web services bound to the corresponding domain service need to be tested whether they match the customized service. Moreover, Web services can be matched automatically and executed instantly, then particular service requests can be performed on-the-fly.

For *Req1* in the example of weather forecast, both of the needed customization operations (namely *addNewFeature* and *selectXORFeature*) meet the proposition of Theorem 1, so only the Web services bound to *WeatherForecast* need to be tested again using the matching algorithm in sub section 4.2. Of *SWS1* and *SWS2*, only *SWS2* matches the customization result. So it can be executed to perform *Req1*.

6 Conclusions

To promote service reuse from a domain oriented perspective, an approach to domain-specific reuse in service-oriented environments is proposed. Hereinto, domain services in a certain business domain are modeled and matched to proper Web services for reuse in the domain engineering process. Then, new service requests in the same domain can be easily satisfied by reusing pre-modeled domain services and pre-matching results in the application engineering process. Feasibility of the whole approach has been primarily validated through running some sample services in a browser/server architecture-based prototype.

For future work, since the diversity of real service requests and Web services is very complicated, our approach needs to be extended to have more expressive power. We are supporting more complex feature models, such as feature constraints, and more complex service capability description, such as service precondition and effect. Moreover, a more robust and friendly tool, and more and in-depth empirical experiments will be implemented to obtain evidence, which can testify the advantages of our approach.

Acknowledgement

This research is partially funded by the National Natural Science Foundation of China (NSFC) under grand No. 60573117.

References

1. Hull, D., Zolin, E., et al.: Deciding Semantic Matching of Stateless Services. In: 21st National Conference on Artificial Intelligence and 18th Innovative Applications of Artificial Intelligence Conference (AAAI 2006), pp. 1319–1324 (2006)
2. Han, Y., Geng, H., et al.: VINCA - A Visual and Personalized Business-level Composition Language for Chaining Web-based Services. In: Orlowska, M.E., Weerawarana, S., Papazoglou, M.P., Yang, J. (eds.) ICSOC 2003. LNCS, vol. 2910, pp. 165–177. Springer, Heidelberg (2003)
3. Wang, J., Yu, J., et al.: A Service Modeling Approach with Business-Level Reusability and Extensibility. In: 1st IEEE Int. Workshop on Service-Oriented System Engineering, pp. 23–28 (2005)
4. Kang, K.C., Cohen, S.G., et al.: Feature-Oriented Domain Analysis Feasibility Study. Technical Report: SEI-90-TR-21. Pittsburgh, Software Engineering Institute, Carnegie Mellon University (1990)
5. Czarnecki, K., Eisenecker, U.W.: Generative Programming: Methods, Tools and Applications. Addison-Wesley, New York (2000)
6. Lo, A., Yu, E.: From Business Models to Service-Oriented Design: A Reference Catalog Approach. In: Parent, C., Schewe, K.-D., Storey, V.C., Thalheim, B. (eds.) ER 2007. LNCS, vol. 4801, pp. 87–101. Springer, Heidelberg (2007)
7. Gordijn, J., Yu, E., et al.: E-service design using i* and e3 value modeling. IEEE Software 23(3), 26–33 (2006)
8. Arsanjani, A.: Service-Oriented Modeling and Architecture (2004), http://www.ibm.com/developerworks/library/ws-soa-design1/
9. Maiden, N.: Servicing Your Requirements. IEEE Software 23(5), 14–16 (2006)
10. Chen, F., Li, S., et al.: Feature Analysis for Service-Oriented Reengineering. In: 12th Asia-Pacific Software Engineering Conference (APSEC 2005), pp. 201–208 (2005)
11. Wada, H., Suzuki, J., et al.: A Feature Modeling Support for Non-Functional Constraints in Service Oriented Architecture. In: 2007 IEEE Int. Conf. on Services Computing (SCC 2007), pp. 187–195 (2007)
12. Fantinato, M., Gimenes, I., et al.: Supporting QoS Negotiation with Feature Modeling. In: Krämer, B.J., Lin, K.-J., Narasimhan, P. (eds.) ICSOC 2007. LNCS, vol. 4749, pp. 429–434. Springer, Heidelberg (2007)
13. Robak, S., Franczyk, B.: Modeling Web Services Variability with Feature Diagrams. In: Chaudhri, A.B., Jeckle, M., Rahm, E., Unland, R. (eds.) NODe-WS 2002. LNCS, vol. 2593, pp. 120–128. Springer, Heidelberg (2003)
14. Martin, D., Paolucci, M., et al.: Bringing Semantics to Web Services: The OWL-S Approach. In: Cardoso, J., Sheth, A.P. (eds.) SWSWPC 2004. LNCS, vol. 3387, pp. 26–42. Springer, Heidelberg (2005)
15. Li., L., Horrocks, I.: A Software Framework for Matchmaking Based on Semantic Web Technology. In: 12th Int. World Wide Web Conference (WWW 2003), pp. 331–339 (2003)

16. Paolucci, M., Kawamura, T., et al.: Semantic Matching of Web Services Capabilities. In: Horrocks, I., Hendler, J. (eds.) ISWC 2002. LNCS, vol. 2342, pp. 333–347. Springer, Heidelberg (2002)
17. Tan, Y., Vellanki, V., et al.: Service Domains. IBM Systems Journal 43(4), 734–755 (2004)
18. Benatallah, B., Sheng, Q., et al.: The Self-Serv Environment for Web Services Composition. IEEE Internet Computing 7(1), 40–48 (2003)
19. McIlraith, S., Son, T., et al.: Semantic Web Services. IEEE Intelligent Systems 16(2), 46–53 (2001)
20. Luger, G.: Artificial Intelligence: Structures and Strategies for Complex Problem Solving, 5th edn. Pearson Addison Wesley, London (2004)
21. Czarnecki, K., Helsen, S., et al.: Staged Configuration through Specialization and Multi-Level Configuration of Feature Models. Software Process: Improvement and Practice 10(2), 143–169 (2005)

View-Based Reverse Engineering Approach for Enhancing Model Interoperability and Reusability in Process-Driven SOAs

Huy Tran, Uwe Zdun, and Schahram Dustdar

Distributed Systems Group, Information Systems Institute
Vienna University of Technology, Austria
{htran,zdun,dustdar}@infosys.tuwien.ac.at

Abstract. In many companies, process-driven SOAs are introduced using technical process languages, such as BPEL, to orchestrate services. The process models developed using this approach are often too complex and hard to reuse because all process-related concerns are tangled in only one type of model. To make the models more understandable for non-technical stakeholders, many companies additionally introduce high-level process descriptions, e.g., specified in BPMN or EPCs, to offer a non-technical view of the processes. This divergence of process languages often leads to inconsistencies after a few evolution steps. We propose a novel approach based on architectural views that not only offers models tailored to the various stakeholders' concerns but also provides an automated integration of models at different abstraction levels. In particular, we propose an extensible reverse-engineering tool-chain to automatically populate various view models with information from existing process descriptions and generate executable code from these view models.

1 Introduction

In a process-driven, service-oriented architecture (SOA), business functionality is accomplished by executing business processes invoking various services. A typical business process includes a number of activities and a control flow. Each activity corresponds to a communication task (e.g., it invokes other services or processes) or a data processing task. The control flow describes how these activities are orchestrated. A process is typically represented either in an executable language, such as BPEL [7] or XPDL [24], or in a high-level modeling language such as BPMN [15], EPC [10], or UML Activity Diagrams [14].

Nowadays, business process developers have to deal with increasing needs for change, for instance, concerning business requirement changes or IT technology changes. Therefore, the process models should enable a quicker reaction on business changes in the IT by manipulating business process models instead of code. Unfortunately, most of the existing business processes are developed and maintained by technical experts (aka the IT experts) in low-level, executable languages. It is difficult for the business analysts to get involved in process development and maintenance because for these tasks an understanding of many

H. Mei (Ed.): ICSR 2008, LNCS 5030, pp. 233–244, 2008.

technical details is required. Hence, technical experts are required for many task in managing, developing, and maintaining the process models. At the same time, the process models become too complex and the various process concerns are hard to reuse. In addition, there is a lack of adaptation of process models to suit the needs of particular stakeholders, e.g. business analysts or technical experts.

As a solution to these problems, some companies introduce high-level process descriptions, for instance, specified in BPMN or EPCs, to offer a non-technical view of the processes. This practice leads to yet another problem, namely, the divergence of process representations. That is, various more or less abstract descriptions of each business process are created, which might quickly become inconsistent as changes occur. As a consequence, neither the information in the high-level models is reused for defining the technical models, nor vice versa.

The aforementioned challenges have not been resolved in the context of process-driven SOAs yet. We present in this paper a novel view-based reverse engineering approach for addressing these challenges. Our approach harnesses the *concept of architectural views* and the *partial interpreter* pattern [25] to adapt process models to suit the requirements of particular stakeholders. Using the partial interpreter pattern, we devise a number of interpreters to extract more and less abstract views from process descriptions. The relationships between these views are maintained via our view-based modeling framework (VbMF) [20]. Using extension and view integration mechanisms, the views can be manipulated to produce more appropriate representations according to the stakeholders' requirements, and code in executable languages can be (re-)generated. VbMF not only supports the reuse of information in process models at different abstraction levels and in different process concerns, but also the reuse of information in existing process models, e.g. written in BPEL.

In this paper, first we give a short introduction to VbMF in Section 2. Section 3 describes the view-based reverse engineering approach. In Section 4 we present the details of using view-based interpreters to analyze existing business processes and extract various architectural views from the processes. Finally, in Section 5 we discuss related work and conclude in Section 6.

2   The View-Based Modeling Framework

2.1   Overview of the View-Based Modeling Framework

The view-based modeling framework [20] is based on the concept of architectural views. An architectural view is a representation of a system from the perspective of a related set of concerns [8]. Each particular concern is (semi-)formalized by a respective meta-model. VbMF defines a number of meta-models (see Figure 1(a)), one for each architectural view. A meta-model at a lower abstraction level is defined as an extension of the meta-models at higher levels. VbMF's meta-models are either directly or indirectly derived a Core meta-model (see Figure 1(b)). The relationships between meta-models are used to bridge the gaps between meta-models at different abstraction levels and to propagate changes.

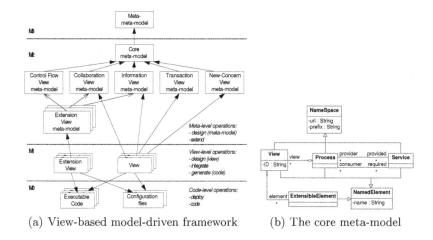

(a) View-based model-driven framework   (b) The core meta-model

Fig. 1. The VbMF modeling framework and the *Core* meta-model

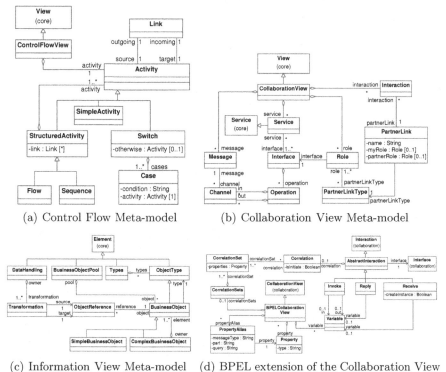

(a) Control Flow Meta-model   (b) Collaboration View Meta-model

(c) Information View Meta-model   (d) BPEL extension of the Collaboration View

Fig. 2. Three basic concern meta-models and a BPEL extension meta-model example

Example meta-models that we have derived from the Core meta-model are: Control Flow, Collaboration and Information View (see Figures 2(a), 2(b) and 2(c)). For particular technologies, e.g. BPEL/WSDL, the extension mechanisms can be used to enrich the abstract meta-models with the specifics of those technologies. To illustrate the extension mechanisms, we present a BPEL-specific collaboration view meta-model in Figure 2(d), which is defined by extending the elements from Figures 1(b) and 2(b). We use the distinction of the Core meta-model, generic view meta-models, and extension meta-models to represent different abstraction levels, such as business level and technical level.

In our implementation of these concepts, we exploit the model-driven software development (MDSD) paradigm [22] to separate the platform-neutral views from the platform-specific views. Code can be generated from the views by using model-to-code transformations. We have realized VbMF in openArchitectureWare (oAW) [16], a model-driven software development tool, and all meta-models are defined using the Eclipse Modeling Framework [5]. To demonstrate our approach, we have exemplified it using BPEL and WSDL, which are likely the most popular process/service modeling descriptions used by numerous companies today. Nevertheless, in general, the same approach can be taken for any other process-driven SOA technologies by defining respective meta-models.

2.2   View-Based Reverse Engineering Tool-Chain

VbMF mainly consists of a forward engineering tool-chain (see Figure 3) in which the stakeholders can develop process-driven view models, can generate process code from these views, or can extend the modeling framework with other process concerns by adding new meta-models or by enhancing existing meta-models.

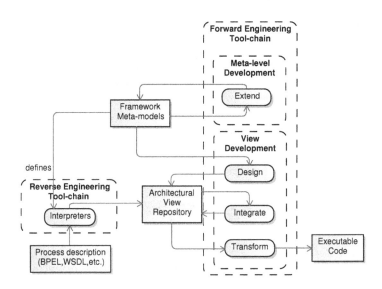

Fig. 3. The extended VbMF including the view-based reverse-engineering

Companies today have built up a vast amount of legacy process representations, either high-level or low-level, but there is no proper integration of these process descriptions, and no appropriate adaptation of process models to the stakeholders' needs and focus. Typically off-the-shelf process modeling tools, such as BPEL or BPMN tools, are used, and hence it is required to integrate them into VbMF. For these reasons, we extended VbMF with a reverse-engineering tool-chain for adapting process models and integrating various modeling representations. The outcome are tailored views that can be put into a common repository, and then be re-used in other processes or manipulated to re-generate new executable code, which corresponds to changes in the corresponding views (see Figure 3).

3   View-Based Reverse Engineering Approach

In the context of process-driven SOAs, many existing systems have built up an enormous repository of existing process code in executable languages, such as BPEL and WSDL. There are two important issues that have not been solved yet. Firstly, such process code integrates many tangled concerns such as message exchanges, data processing, service invocations, fault handling, transactions, and so forth. Secondly, these languages are rather technology-specific and therefore the abstract representations are not explicitly available at the code level. As a result, the process models become too complex for stakeholders to understand and maintain, to integrate, to cooperate with other processes, or to re-use process models from existing modeling tools.

Our view-based approach can potentially resolve these issues. However, for budgetary reasons, developing the view models, required in our approach, from scratch is a costly option. The alternative is an (automated) re-engineering approach comprising two activities: *reverse-engineering* for building more appropriate and relevant representations of the legacy code; *forward-engineering* for manipulating the process models and for re-generating certain parts of the process code. During the reverse engineering process, high-level, abstract and low-level, technology-specific views on the process models are recovered from the existing code. This way, the reverse engineering approach helps stakeholders to get involved in process re-development and maintenance at different abstraction levels. Reverse engineering of business processes should not only help to adapt process models to stakeholder needs but also offer the ability to integrate various process models to enhance the interoperability of process models. The view-based reverse engineering approach we propose in this paper aims at achieving these goals.

3.1   The Reverse Engineering Tool-Chain

The reverse engineering tool-chain (see Figure 4) consists of a number of view-based interpreters, such as *control flow interpreter, collaboration view interpreter*, and so forth. Each interpreter is used for interpreting and extracting the corresponding view from the process descriptions. An interpreter of a certain view must be defined based on the meta-model which that view conforms

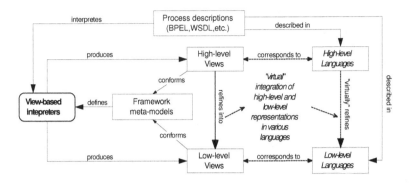

Fig. 4. The view-based reverse engineering tool-chain

to. For instance, the *control flow view* consists of elements such as *Activity*, *Flow*, *Sequence*, *Switch*, *Case* according to the *control flow view meta-model* (see Figure 2(a)). In order to extract the control flow view from process descriptions, the interpreter walks through the input descriptions to pick the above-mentioned elements. Other elements are ignored.

3.2   General Approach for View Extraction

The process descriptions comprise the specification of business functionality in a modeling language, for instance, as we exemplify in this paper, BPEL [7]. Moreover, the process functionality also exposes service interfaces, for instance, expressed in WSDL [23]. To demonstrate the extraction of appropriate views from process descriptions, we developed a number of interpreters such as *control flow interpreter*, *collaboration view interpreter*, as well as a *BPEL-specific extension view interpreter*.

Our general approach to define view interpreters is based on the Partial Interpreter pattern [25]. This pattern is typically applied when the relevant information to be interpreted from a language is only a (small) sub-set of the source document's language, and thus, the complexity of the whole language should be avoided in the subsequent interpretation. The approach based on Partial Interpreter enables us to define modular, pluggable interpreters, and the framework to be easily extensible with new views and view extraction interpreters. The solution is to provide a Partial Interpreter for view extraction, which only understands the specific language elements required for one view. There is a generic parser that is responsible for parsing the process descriptions. The parsing events generated by this generic parser are interpreted by the Partial Interpreters, which only interprets the language elements relevant for a particular view.

The Partial Interpreter's mapping specification and view-specific interpretation specification are both defined generically on basis of the meta-models. Hence, they can be reused for many concrete view models. In the subsequent sections, we present the details of the realization of the mapping specifications for basic process concerns, i.e., control flow interpreter, information view interpreter and collaboration view interpreter to illustrate our general approach. Other view interpreters can be implemented following the same approach.

4 Details of the View-Based Reverse Engineering Approach: Three Empirical Analyses

In this section, we empirically analyze the capabilities of the view-based reverse engineering approach, such as the adaptation of process models to stakeholders' needs and the integration of models at different levels of abstraction, by investigating three typical cases in which the view-based reverse engineering approach can get applied. In doing so, we also introduce the details of our approach for applying it to BPEL/WSDL as an exemplary process-driven SOA technology.

These empirical analyses have been carried out on an industrial case study, namely, customer care, billing and provisioning systems of an Austrian Internet Service Provider (see [6] for more details). In the following, we use the Billing Renewal process as an example. The billing platform includes a wide variety of services provided by various partners such as financial services, domain services, physical hosting services, retail/wholesale services, and so on. These services are exposed in WSDL interfaces and integrated by using BPEL processes.

4.1 Extracting Relevant Views

The basic analysis, we performed, was to deal with the extraction of the control flow view from BPEL code. The control flow interpreter walks through the process description in BPEL and collects necessary information of atomic and structured activities. Then, it creates the elements in the Control Flow View and assigns their attributes with relevant values as specified by the Control Flow View meta-model (see Figure 2(a)). We demonstrate the mapping of Billing Renewal specification in BPEL onto the Control Flow View in Figure 5.

4.2 Extracting Views at Different Abstraction Levels

To illustrate the ability of adapting views at different levels of abstraction, we devise two interpreters to extract the Collaboration View and the BPEL-specific extension of the Collaboration view. These interpreters are realized using the same approach as used for the control flow interpreter. However, these views comprise not only elements from the BPEL descriptions but also elements of the process interfaces specified in WSDL files. That is, the interpreters firstly collect information from WSDL descriptions, then walk through the BPEL specifications to the extract relevant elements, and finally create relevant elements on the views according to the Collaboration View meta-model in Figure 2(b). Figures 5 and 6 illustrate the extraction of the Collaboration View from BPEL descriptions of the Billing Renewal process.

The Collaboration View is a high-level representation compared to the BPEL extension of the Collaboration View, which is at a lower level of abstraction.

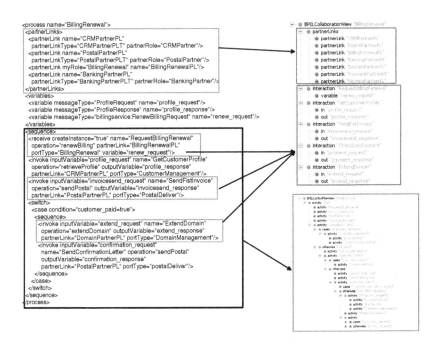

Fig. 5. Mapping the Billing Renewal process (left-hand side) onto the VbMF's views including the Collaboration View (top-right) and the Control Flow View (bottom-right)

Therefore, the BPEL extension view consists of additional elements and some of these elements have extra properties compared to those of the Collaboration View. This way, other process-driven modeling languages, either high-level or low-level, can be handled and integrated by using the view-based reverse engineering tool-chain and VbMF.

4.3   Enhancing the Adaptability of the Process Models

The adaptability of process models to the requirements of a certain stakeholder can be enhanced using two methods developed in VbMF: extension mechanisms and view integration. View extension mechanisms [20] allow us to enrich existing meta-models with additional elements and/or extra attributes for the existing elements of the original meta-models. This way, the abstract views can be gradually refined into less abstract views by increasing their granularity with added technology-specific features until the resulting views are well suited for a particular stakeholder's needs. Next, we define respective interpreters for these views and use the interpreters to extract the corresponding views from the existing process code. An example of view extension is the BPEL-specific extension of the Collaboration View shown in the previous analysis.

View integration [20] is another method to produce new richer views by merging existing views. For instance, in [20], we have developed a simple name-based

```
<definitions>
  <types>
    <portType name="BillingRenewal">
      <operation name="renewBilling">
        <input message="RenewBillingRequest" />
        <output message="RenewBillingResponse" />
      </operation>
    </portType>
    <partnerLinkType name="CRMPartnerPLT">
      <role name="CRMPartner">
        <portType name="crm:CustomerManagement"/>
      </role>
    </partnerLinkType>
    <partnerLinkType name="PostalPartnerPLT">
      <role name="PostalPartner">
        <portType name="PostalDeliver"/>
      </role>
    </partnerLinkType>
    <partnerLinkType name="BillingRenewalPLT">
      <role name="BillingRenewal">
        <portType name="BillingRenewal"/>
      </role>
    </partnerLinkType>
    <partnerLinkType name="BankingPartnerPLT">
      <role name="BankingPartner">
        <portType name="CreditCardManagement"/>
      </role>
    </partnerLinkType>
</definitions>
```

Fig. 6. Mapping the Billing Renewal process (left-hand side) onto the Collaboration View (right-hand side)

matching algorithm and presented an example of integrating the control flow view and the collaboration view. The matching algorithm searches the input views for integration points, which are, in this case, the conformable elements with the same name. Afterward, the two views are merged together at these integration points. The resulting view inherits the control flow that defines the execution order of activities. In addition, the activities in the resulting view that are responsible for invoking services inherit a number of additional attributes from the corresponding activities defined in the collaboration view.

5   Related Work

Our work presented in this paper is a *reverse engineering approach* [3] based on the concept of architectural views [8]. The whole VbMF tool-chain provides support for *reengineering* [17] as well. That is, in addition to the reverse engineering parts of the tool chain, means for re-structuring, modification, and forward engineering are provided to yield new system structures and functionality.

In the context of reverse engineering, view-based approaches are an emerging area of interest. For instance, the approaches reported in [2, 4, 19] focus on inter-organizational processes (in term of cross-organizational workflows) and use views to separate the abstract process representations (aka public processes) from the internal processes (aka private processes). Bobrik et al. [1] present an approach to process visualization using personalized views and a number of operations to customize the views. Zou et al. [27] propose an approach for extracting business logic, also in terms of workflows, from existing e-commerce applications. All these approaches aim at providing perspectives on business processes at a high level of abstraction and maintaining the relationships among different abstraction levels to quickly re-act to changes in business requirements. These approaches have in common that only the control flow of process activities (aka the workflows) is considered. Other process concerns, such as service/process interaction, data processing, etc. have only been partially exploited or not targeted. In addition, these approaches do not support enhancing process views or propagating changes as supported in our approach, for instance, through view integration, view extension and code generation.

Kazman et al. [9] describe the Dali workbench, an approach for understanding and analysis the system architecture. The extraction process begins with extracting views from source code using lexical analyzers, parsers or profilers. Next, the relationships among views are established by view fusion to improve the quality and the correctness of views. However, because of the complexity of typical process models, this approach is hardly applicable to capture the whole process description in a unique view.

In the context of process-driven modeling, there are a number of standard languages in which some provide high-level descriptions, for instance, BPMN [15], EPC [21, 10] and Abstract BPEL in WS-BPEL 2.0 [13]. There is no explicit link between these languages and the executable languages. This has led to a number of recent research approaches. For instance, Mendling et al. [12] discuss the transformation of BPEL to EPCs. Ziemann et al. [26] present an approach to model BPEL processes using EPC-based models. Recker et al. [18] translate between BPMN and BPEL. Mendling et al. [11] report on efforts in X-to-BPEL and BPEL-to-Y transformations. These transformation-based approaches mostly focus on one concern of the process models, namely, the control flow, which describes the execution order of process activities. They offer no support for extension of process models or integrating other concerns of process models, such as service interactions, data processing, transaction handling, etc. Hence, during the transformation from process code to abstract representations, necessary information required to re-generate executable code gets lost.

WS-BPEL 2.0, the newly revised standard, provides the concept of an Abstract BPEL process, which is represented by the same structures as an Executable BPEL process. Developers can explicitly hide some syntactic constructs in an Abstract BPEL process using predefined opaque tokens as explicit placeholders for the omitted details. An abstract process is often associated with a profile which specifies the semantics of the opaque tokens. Hence, one could use an approach akin to our approach where the high-level view is the abstract process profile, and low-level representations are respective profiles. Then our reverse engineering tool-chain could be used to extract the relevant views.

All the above-mentioned approaches and standards have difficulties in handling the complexity of process models: Because the business process integrates numerous concerns, the complexity of process model increases as the number of process elements, such as message exchanges, service invocations, data processing tasks, etc. grows. Hence, these approaches are less efficient than our approach in dealing with pretty huge existing process repositories, developed in other languages or dialects, or integrating arbitrary process modeling tools.

6   Conclusion

The view-based reverse engineering approach, presented in this paper, can help the various stakeholders of a process-driven SOA to overcome two important issues. Firstly, it exploits the concept of architectural view to deal with the complexity of existing process repositories and to adapt the process representations to the stakeholders' needs and focus. Secondly, it provides the ability of integrating diverse process models and offers explicit relationships for understanding and maintaining process models and for propagating changes. Hence, process models at different abstraction levels and different process concerns can be reused to populate the other. This has been achieved by developing a novel concept for a reverse engineering tool chain, based on partial interpreters and view models, and by seamlessly integrating this reverse engineering tool chain into our view-based modeling framework, which also supports means for forward engineering, such as view integration, view extension and code generation. The reverse engineering tool chain enables the reuse of existing process code, e.g. written in BPEL/WSDL, in the view-based modeling framework.

References

1. Bobrik, R., Reichert, M., Bauer, T.: View-based process visualization. In: Alonso, G., Dadam, P., Rosemann, M. (eds.) BPM 2007. LNCS, vol. 4714, pp. 88–95. Springer, Heidelberg (2007)
2. Chebbi, I., Dustdar, S., Tata, S.: The view-based approach to dynamic inter-organizational workflow cooperation. Data Knowl. Eng. 56(2), 139–173 (2006)
3. Chikofsky, E.J., Cross, J.H.I.: Reverse engineering and design recovery: A taxonomy. IEEE Software 7(1), 13–17 (1990)
4. Chiu, D.K.W., Cheung, S.C., Till, S., Karlapalem, K., Li, Q., Kafeza, E.: Workflow view driven cross-organizational interoperability in a web service environment. Inf. Tech. and Management 5(3-4), 221–250 (2004)
5. Eclipse. Eclipse Modeling Framework (2006), http://www.eclipse.org/emf/
6. Evenson, M., Schreder, B.: D4.1 Use Case Definition and Functional Requirements Analysis. SemBiz Deliverable (August 2007)
7. IBM, B. Systems, Microsoft, SAP AG, and Siebel Systems. Business process execution language for web services (May 2003),
   ftp://www6.software.ibm.com/software/developer/library/ws-bpel.eps
8. IEEE. Recommended Practice for Architectural Description of Software Intensive Systems. Technical Report IEEE-std-1471-2000, IEEE (2000)
9. Kazman, R., Carriere, S.J.: View Extraction and View Fusion in Architectural Understanding. In: ICSR 1998. Proc. of the 5th Int. Conference on Software Reuse, Washington, DC, USA, p. 290. IEEE Computer Society, Los Alamitos (1998)
10. Kindler, E.: On the semantics of EPCs: A framework for resolving the vicious circle. In: Business Process Management, pp. 82–97 (2004)

11. Mendling, J., Lassen, K.B., Zdun, U.: Transformation strategies between block-oriented and graph-oriented process modelling languages. Technical Report JM-200510 -10, WU Vienna (2005)

12. Mendling, J., Ziemann, J.: Transformation of BPEL processes to EPCs. In: Proc. of the 4th GI Workshop on Event-Driven Process Chains (EPK 2005), December 2005, vol. 167, pp. 41–53 (2005)

13. OASIS. Business Process Execution Language (WSBPEL) 2.0 (May 2007), `http://docs.oasis-open.org/wsbpel/2.0/OS/wsbpel-v2.0-OS.eps`

14. OMG. Unified Modelling Language 2.0 (UML) (2004), `http://www.uml.org`

15. OMG. Business Process Modeling Notation (February 2006), `http://www.bpmn.org/Documents/OMG-02-01.eps`

16. openArchitectureWare.org (August 2002), `http://www.openarchitectureware.org`

17. Antonini, P., Canfora, G., Cimitile, A.: Reengineering legacy systems to meet quality requirements: An experience report. In: ICSM 1994. Proceedings of the International Conference on Software Maintenance, Washington, DC, USA, pp. 146–153. IEEE Computer Society, Los Alamitos (1994)

18. Recker, J., Mendling, J.: On the translation between BPMN and BPEL: Conceptual mismatch between process modeling languages. In: Eleventh Int. Workshop on Exploring Modeling Methods in Systems Analysis and Design (EMMSAD 2006), June 2006, pp. 521–532 (2006)

19. Schulz, K.A., Orlowska, M.E.: Facilitating cross-organisational workflows with a workflow view approach. Data Knowl. Eng. 51(1), 109–147 (2004)

20. Tran, H., Zdun, U., Dustdar, S.: View-based and Model-driven Approach for Reducing the Development Complexity in Process-Driven SOA. In: Intl. Working Conf. on Business Process and Services Computing (BPSC 2007), September 2007. Lecture Notes in Informatics, vol. 116, pp. 105–124. Springer, Heidelberg (2007)

21. van der Aalst, W.: On the verification of interorganizational workflows. Computing Science Reports 97/16, Eindhoven University of Technology (1997)

22. Völter, M., Stahl, T.: Model-Driven Software Development: Technology, Engineering, Management. Wiley, Chichester (2006)

23. W3C. Web Services Description Language 1.1 (March 2001)

24. WfMC. XML Process Definition Language (XPDL) (April 2005), `http://www.wfmc.org/standards/XPDL.htm`

25. Zdun, U.: Patterns of tracing software structures and dependencies. In: Proc. of 8th European Conference on Pattern Languages of Programs (EuroPLoP 2003), Irsee, Germany, June 2003, pp. 581–616 (2003)

26. Ziemann, J., Mendling, J.: EPC-based modelling of BPEL processes: a pragmatic transformation approach. In: Proc. of the 7th Int. Conference Modern Information Technology in the Innovation Processes of the Industrial Enterprises (MITIP 2005) (2005)

27. Zou, Y., Hung, M.: An approach for extracting workflows from e-commerce applications. In: ICPC 2006. Proc. of the 14th IEEE Int. Conf. on Program Comprehension (ICPC 2006), Washington, DC, USA, pp. 127–136. IEEE Computer Society, Los Alamitos (2006)

A Lightweight Approach to Partially Reuse Existing Component-Based System in Service-Oriented Environment

He Yuan Huang, Hua Fang Tan, Jun Zhu, and Wei Zhao

IBM China Research Laboratory, Building 19 Zhongguancun Software Park,
8 Dongbeiwang WestRoad, Haidian District, 100094 Beijing, China
{huanghey,tanhuaf,zhujun,weizhao}@cn.ibm.com

Abstract. A fundamental derailment factor for reusing today's business applications is the tight coupling among program components. While SOA advocates an architecture with loose coupling among components, the invocation dependencies among components are still tangled with implementation code traditionally. SCA (Service Component Architecture) - an emerging service-oriented component model - uses a standard and declarative way to handle inter-component dependencies. Thus, SCA components have better reusability from this perspective. This paper proposes a lightweight approach to partially reuse existing components by wrapping them as SCA components. Several challenges are identified and addressed in this paper, especially the one of externalizing component dependencies without changing source code. The proposed approach addresses the challenges systematically, with a supporting system implemented. Moreover, an example scenario is given to better illustrate the usage of the approach. Finally, some future directions of the work are pointed out.

Keywords: Software reuse, component-based system, service-oriented architecture, service-oriented environment.

1 Introduction

A fundamental derailment factor for reusing today's business applications is the tight coupling among program components. Service-oriented architecture (SOA) is an evolution of application architectural style in which an application's business logic or individual functions are modularized and presented as loosely-coupled components - services. The service interface is independent of the implementation so that application developers or system integrators can build applications by composing one or more services without knowing the services' underlying implementations. The need for flexible service composition, in turn, requires that inter-component dependencies should not be hard-coded as invocation at the code level.

SCA (Service Component Architecture) [20] - an emerging service-oriented component model – has been jointly created and advocated by major Java EE vendors including IBM, Oracle & BEA, with the objective of enabling a standard and declarative way of

H. Mei (Ed.): ICSR 2008, LNCS 5030, pp. 245–256, 2008.
© Springer-Verlag Berlin Heidelberg 2008

handling inter-component dependencies. SCA introduces service-oriented concepts into a component model and execution environment. The SCA Assembly Model consists of a series of artifacts which define the configuration of an SCA system in terms of service components which implement and/or use services and the connections (wires) and related artifacts that describe how they are linked together. Moreover, SCA aims to encompass a wide range of technologies for service components and for the access methods which are used to connect them. That's why many believe SCA will become the base for building agile business applications in the future.

Today's reality, however, lies in that a huge number of existing business applications are already written in prevailing component-based programming models like EJB, CORBA, and etc. If we cannot effectively & efficiently reuse these component applications and turn them into composable SCA components, the benefits of SCA will only be realized in the newly built applications, and get discounted considerably. The challenges here can be summarized as follows:

♦ Typically, the anticipated reuse granularity is not at the whole system level for various efficiency considerations. We need to selectively extract those needed components and externalize their linkage to other components.
♦ The runtime platform of the existing component-based system is usually different or incompatible with the target SCA platform; platform migration is usually not possible.
♦ The externalization of those inter-component dependencies typically requires knowledge and access to the original source code, while in most cases, only the access to the executable package (e.g., .ear file for EJB) is available.

While there are some existing approaches to address the first two challenges, there still lacks of approach to externalize component dependencies without changing source code.

In this paper, we propose a systematic way to address the above challenges. A set of component proxies called legacy surrogates are automatically generated, from the component architecture extracted from the executable package, as code following the original programming model (e.g., EJB). Note that legacy surrogates for depended components are introduced to replace the depended components and delegate the invocations to SCA components to be assembled. Another Surrogate, called target surrogate will also be automatically generated, following the programming model of the target platform, as representation of the to-be-reused fragments in the new SCA environment. The legacy and target surrogates are designed to be seamlessly integrated so that they can communicate with each other at runtime. Centered around surrogate, we develop an approach to reuse existing component based system in construction service oriented applications in a non-intrusive way.

The rest of this paper is organized as following. In section II, we will present a brief literature study on the existing ways of reusing existing applications for SOA. Afterwards, our overall methodology and architecture will be presented, followed by a detailed explanation of the technical components with an example scenario of reusing components in an EJB based legacy application. We conclude the paper and give outlook for future research directions in the last section.

2   Related Work

2.1   Methods and Tools for Legacy System Integration

The main intention of this approach is to reuse a portion of an existing component-based system into Service-Oriented applications. Adapting existing legacy systems to be integrated with new technologies and platforms is therefore closely related to our approach. The normal way to integrate existing systems in the new application using new technologies is by adding a wrapper or proxy between them. Kulkarni and Reddy's invention [17] wraps the whole Objected-Oriented application as an object facade which will communicate with new components in opposite integrated component-based application through a connectivity bus which can be any standard middleware. Methods in [16] and [19] add a light weight proxy between the legacy system and the applications with advanced technologies. The proxy plays a mediation role between the different protocols which do not force any one counterpart to comply with the other. These methods based on interface wrappers and proxies all intend to reuse the existing systems' certain functionality completely. Our method, however, reuses the components in the existing systems in a partial manner. That is to say, our method reuses the necessary implemented logics of an existing component and meantime leaves its referred components as placeholders which could be replaced with any other possible components, instead of merely the ones in currently processed system. This is actually a distinguished merit in nature of service component architecture which we are pursuing while reusing the existing systems.

2.2   Methods and Tools for Legacy System Migration

In order to acquire the advanced features brought by new technologies, porting legacy systems to new platforms (e.g. from Windows operating system to Linux operating system; from standalone Web server to J2EE application server) or with advanced technologies (e.g. from procedural paradigm to objected-oriented paradigm) is always both a strong desire and a great concern for users of legacy systems. Although this is not a typical reuse scenario, the nature to process existing systems drives a lot of technologies related to reuse. Understanding and transforming the original legacy system and redeploying the newly porting system are not only time-consuming but also error-prone. This is mainly because the software engineers who perform the porting work are not the original developers. To facilitate the transformation of a legacy system, analyzing and discovering its corresponding high level design to guide the source code transformation has been devoted large numbers of efforts in the literature and practiced much in the real world.

There are two main categories of approaches and corresponding automated systems to address this problem. The first kind of approaches focus on source code and documentation itself and employ static analysis technologies to abstract the high level designs of the target systems (see e.g. [1] [2] [3] [5] [6] [7] [8] [9] [10] [11]and [14]). A related invention proposed by Purewal [15] presents the systems and methods to generate open reusable, business components for Service-Oriented Architecture from existing client/server applications through decomposing them into separate user interface, business logic and event management layers. The different layers are wrapped as services and re-assembled to the open-standard based application. The key steps in these methods are analyzing the source code, mining the components and transforming the original source code to component programs.

The other stream of methods to acquire designs of legacy systems are a variety of methods for profiling, testing, and observing systems' behaviors, including actual execution and inspecting execution traces (see e.g. [4] [12] and [13]). Although this kind of methods and the corresponding tools improve the efficiency of the legacy transformation, intensive manual work on source code transformation are not easily avoided.

These work focus on reengineering the legacy systems to the architecture of technically advanced paradigm and automated or semi-automated transforming the legacy source code. Our method focuses on existing systems implemented with the component technology. The target is to reuse these systems to a Service-Oriented Architecture (i.e. Service Component Architecture) with specifically targeted components. As a result, the differences of our method from the current migration approaches lie in three aspects. Firstly, we do not concern the componentization step and we leave the flexibility for end users to choose any possible candidate components to provide a service. This also means we do not focus on reusing the whole existing system rather a designate set of components. Besides, externalizing referred components is the differentiated point of our method. That is to say, if the reused component has referenced components, we will break this fixed linkage through adding the shallow components for those referenced one. In the shallow components, newly added contents decide which components will be referenced finally. This way we make the referenced components not only provided locally by current system but also other possible ways. This is not addressed explicitly in the current literature. Thirdly, our method does not involve any analysis and modification of original source code of existing systems.

3   Approach and Architecture

3.1   Overall Approach

To overcome the limitations of existing approaches, this paper proposes an approach and apparatus to SCAlize (make component SCA compatible) selected component(s) in component-based system without modifying components implementation. The basic idea is to replace depended components with legacy surrogates and delegate the invocations on these legacy surrogates to the references of the target surrogate (SCA surrogate) of the component(s) to be reused. Fig. 1 shows the steps of the approach.

Firstly, people need to identify the component(s) to be reused in the existing component-based system. There are two typical reasons to select the component(s) to be reused. The first one is to see whether the component(s) is/are required in the ongoing development of a SOA system. The second one is to see how often the component(s) might be reused in future. An important result of this step is the names and interface(s) of the component(s) to be reused. There are lots of ways to get the interfaces of the component(s) in a component-based system. For example, people could directly get the interface of an EJB and get the definition of the interface with reflection mechanism.

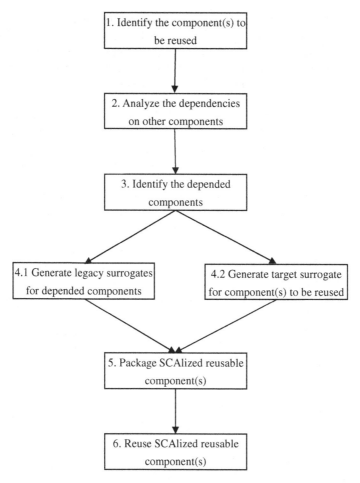

Fig. 1. Approach to Partially Reuse Existing Component-Based System in Service-Oriented Environment

Secondly, people need to analyze the dependencies between identified component(s) and other components in the existing component-based system. There are quite a lot approaches to identify the dependencies at component level, such as analyzing the execution trace.

Thirdly, based on the result of dependency analysis, depended components are identified. Their names and interfaces could be obtained just as the ways to get names and interfaces of component(s) to be reused.

Fourthly, as the component(s) to be reused, depended components, and their dependencies are identified, people could start to SCAlize the component(s) to be reused. There are two paralleled sub steps: generating legacy surrogates for depended components, and generating target surrogate (SCA surrogate) for the component(s) to be reused.

- ◆ The legacy surrogates could be generated with the same names and interfaces in terms of the interfaces of those depended components. The legacy surrogates will delegate invocations on their interfaces to the target surrogate (SCA surrogate). In this way, the component(s) to be reused could work correctly without changing its/their implementation(s) by replacing depended components with legacy surrogates of depended components.
- ◆ The target surrogate (SCA surrogate), which provides services with same functions as component(s) to be reused, could be generated in terms of the interface(s) of component(s) to be reused. This SCA surrogate is actually a proxy to delegate invocations on its services to the component(s) to be reused. Meanwhile, the SCA surrogate has some pending references for functions of depended components. The references will be associated with other SCA components, which really provide the same functions of depended components.

Fifthly, after getting all aforementioned surrogates, people could package SCAlized component(s) for further reuse. This step is relatively easy. Typically, the component(s) to be reused and the legacy surrogates of depended components will be packaged together, while the SCA surrogate will be packaged alone.

Finally, people could reuse the packaged SCAlized component. In terms of the provided functions and required functions of the SCA surrogate, people could assemble it with other SCA components easily and deployed to the target SOA environment. In the meanwhile, the legacy part will be deployed into a runtime which supports the original component model.

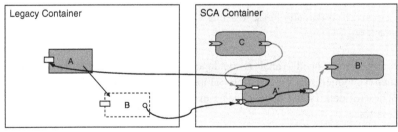

Fig. 2. Abstraction of Resulting Deployment Diagram of our Approach

Fig. 2 shows an abstraction of resulting deployment diagram, where legacy component A is the component to be reused, and legacy component B is the depended component of legacy component A. SCA component C depends on SCA surrogate A', which in turn depends on SCA component B'.

3.2   System Architecture

To enable aforementioned approach, this paper also proposed a surpporting system. As shown in Fig. 3, most of the steps in the approach are addressed in this system.

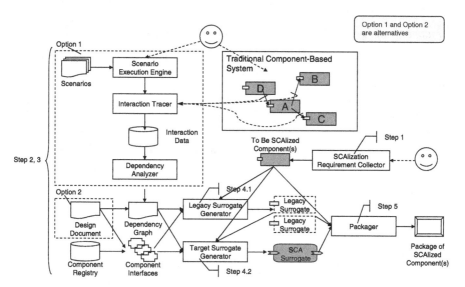

Fig. 3. System Architecture for Partially Reuse Existing Component-Based System in Service-Oriented Environment

The system is composed by a set of components to satisfy the following function:

1) Acquiring the internal structure of the existing component-based system into "Dependency Graph" and "Component Interfaces"

Option1 (Tracing approach): with this approach we will need input of several scenarios for using the original component-based system; these scenarios will be parsed and executed by a scenario execution engine within the original component-based system; through the execution, an interaction tracer (which can be built on top of existing products like Tivoli) will be responsible for capturing all the interaction data among the components of the original component-based system; the interaction data will be sent to a dependency analyzer and generate the dependency graph, which contains a) a set of components with component interface definitions b) a set of dependencies that are mainly representing the invocation relationship among components.

Option2 (Design Document approach): with this approach we assume the design documents and component registry are ready for the original component-based system, and therefore the "Dependency Graph" and "Component Interfaces" can be easily acquired from understanding the design documents.

2) Specifying the requirement to externalize the existing component-based system

SCAlization Requirement Collector: This is a component to help define the requirements for externalizing an original component-based system. The tool will provide UI to visualize all the components within the original component-based system, and the user can use this UI to choose a) SETA: the set of components that will remain in the newly generated package b) SETB: the set of components that need to be externalized as surrogate components c) SETC: the set of components that will become the external dependency of the newly generated package.

3) Automatically generating the "Legacy Surrogates" as well as "Target Surrogate"

Legacy Surrogate Generator: This is a component to generate legacy surrogates that will be combined with the runtime package of the original component-based system saftisfying the following results

♦ With the same names and interfaces of components in SETC, with all the invocations redirected to Target Surrogate.

Target Surrogate Generator: This is a component to generate Target Surrogate (SCA surrogate) satisfying the following results

♦ With the same interfaces of components in SETB, with all the invocation redirected to SETB
♦ Interfaces that will be called by SETC legacy surrogates, and will be redirected to other SCA components as referenced services.

Packager: This component will take the original package, legacy surrogates and SCA surrogate as input and generate two outcomes

♦ A composition package that contains the SCA surrogate that can be used for composition with other SCA components.
♦ A deployment package that contains the original components (SETA, SETB) and legacy surrogates (SETC).

4 Example Scenario

To further illustrate the approach proposed in this paper, we give an example scenario on wrapping reusable components from a legacy EJB-based application. This is an online flower store hosted by a small company. As the company grows, it wishes to extend their business to add all kinds of gifts in their store. Moreover, it wishes to enable more ways of payment than before. Since their bookkeeping application is purchased from third party, the company does not have the source code of the application. In the meanwhile, the company wants to keep the valuable information of customer and their order history. Thus, an ideal way is to reuse the customer and order related components, while developing new catalog, inventory, and payment related components. Furthermore, the company wishes to develop these new components in a SOA way, thus, these components could be easily replaced if needed in future.

Our approach actually provides a good solution for this company. We could wrap existing customer and order related components as reusable SCA component and develop the new components as SCA components. Thus, all these components could be easily assembled in SCA way.

After identifying the scope to reuse, we need to analyze the dependencies among EJBs in legacy application. An instrumentation is introduced in EJB container to log the EJB invocations with details that include the invoked bean name, method name and the invoker, the EJB who made this invocation. Fig. 4 shows the resulting dependency diagram of the legacy application.

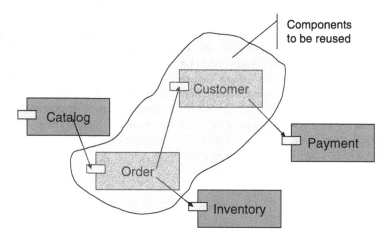

Fig. 4. Dependencies among Components of Legacy Online Store Application

The major components of the legacy application include Catalog, Order, Customer, Inventory and Payment components. After customer selects goods from Catalog, the Catalog will invoke Order component to create an order. Then the Order component will invoke Customer component to get the detailed information of the customer and invoke Inventory component to get and deduce the amount of the item. Furthermore, the customer component will invoke Payment component to interact with some online payment system.

Based on the result of dependency analysis, we could find that the depended components include Payment and Inventory. Thus, the provided interfaces of the components to be reused are Order and Customer, while the required interfaces of the components to be reused are Payment and Inventory. With all these provided and required interfaces, we will generate three types of adapters as shown in Fig. 5.

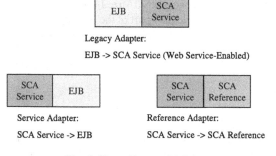

Fig. 5. Three Types of Adapter

With interfaces of Payment and Inventory components, we could generate legacy surrogates for Payment and Inventory components. These legacy surrogates are legacy adapters for invocations on their EJB interfaces to the SCA surrogate through web service. With all these interfaces, we could generate a SCA surrogate, Order&Cutomer', which acts as both Service adapter and Reference adapter. The SCA surrogate provides services with the same functions as Order and Customer and requires the same functions as Payment and Inventory. Moreover, the SCA surrogate delegates invocations on its SCA service to Order and Customer EJB components and delegates invocations on Inventory and Payment functions to its SCA references.

After generating aforementioned surrogates, we could package SCAlized component for further reuse. In this case, we package Order and Customer components, legacy surrogate for Payment, and legacy surrogate for Inventory together as legacy part of the SCAlized component. In the meanwhile, we package the SCA surrogate, Order & Customer', as SCA part of the SCAlized component.

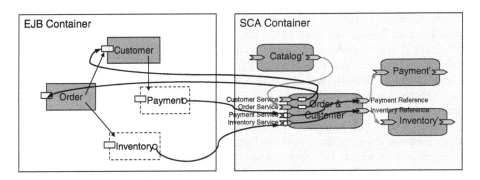

Fig. 6. Deployment Diagram of the New Online Store Application

Finally, we could reuse the packaged SCAlized component in the new online store application. As shown in Fig 6, the legacy part of the SCAlized component is deployed in an EJB container, while the Order & Cutomer' is wired with newly developed SCA components, including Catalog', Payment', Inventory', and deployed in a SCA container.

5   Conclusion

This paper proposes a lightweight approach to partially reuse existing components. The basic idea of this approach is to wrap the interfaces provided by the components to be reused as provided services of a SCA component and externalize the dependency on other components as required services of the SCA component. The resulting SCA component could be easily assembled with other SCA components. Detailed description of the approach is given, while a supporting system is also proposed to enable this approach. Moreover, an example scenario is given to better illustrate the usage of the approach in real world.

Currently, we only apply the approach in an EJB-based application. However, we will try to apply the approach to more applications based on more component models, including CORBA, COM, and etc. While the analysis of component dependency in the example presented in this paper is relatively easy, this analysis will be more difficult in a large component-based application. We are considering leveraging all kinds of static & dynamic analysis approach in the supporting system in the future. Furthermore, while there are cases the to-be-reused part is clearly understand beforehand, there are still cases that people just want to package reusable components in advance, while they have not yet decided where to reuse. In these cases, without design document, we need to unveil the design of the legacy application from the source code or even executable files. Thus, we consider leveraging all kinds of design recovery approaches before we try to identify the scope to reuse.

References

1. Belady, L.A., Evangelisti, C.J.: System Partitioning and its Measure. Journal of Systems and Software 2(1), 23–29 (1982)
2. Chiricota, Y., Jourdan, F., Melancon, G.: Software Components Capture using Graph Clustering. In: Proc. of 11th IEEE International Workshop on Program Comprehension, May 2003, pp. 217–226 (2003)
3. van Deursen, A., Kuipers, T.: Identifying objects using cluster and concept analysis. In: Proc. of 21th IEEE International Conference on Software Engineering, May 1999, pp. 246–255 (1999)
4. Ding, L., Medvidovic, N.: Focus: a Light Weight, Incremental Approach to Software Architecture Recovery and Evolution. In: Working IEEE/IFIP Conference on Software Architecture, Amsterdam, Netherlands, August 2001, pp. 191–200 (2001)
5. Ferrante, J., Ottenstein, K.J., Warren, J.D.: The Program Dependence Graph and its Use in Optimization. ACM Transactions on Programming Languages and Systems 9(3), 319–349 (1987)
6. Harris, D.R., Yeh, A., Reubestein, H.B., Yeh, A.S.: Reverse Engineering to the Architectural Level. In: Proceedings of the 17th International Conference on Software Engineering, Seattle, Washington, April 1995, pp. 186–195 (1995)
7. Hecht, M.S.: Flow Analysis of Computer Programs. North-Holland, Amsterdam (1977)
8. Hutchens, D., Basili, R.: System Structure Analysis: Clustering with Data Bindings. IEEE Transactions on Software Engineering 11(8), 749–757 (1985)
9. Mancoridis, S., Mitchell, B.S., Rorres, C., Chen, Y., Gansner, E.R.: Using Automatic Clustering to Produce High-Level System Organizations of Source Code. In: Proc. of 6th IEEE International Workshop on Program Comprehension, June 1998, pp. 45–52 (1998)
10. Mancoridis, S., Mitchell, B., Chen, Y., Gansner, E.R.: Bunch: A Clustering Tool for the Recovery and Maintenance of Software System Structures. In: Proc. of 15th IEEE International Conference on Software Maintenance, August 1999, pp. 50–62 (1999)
11. Muller, H., Orgun, M., Tilley, S., Uhl, J.: A reverse engineering approach to subsystem structure identification. Journal of Software Maintenance: Research and Practice 5(4), 181–204 (1993)
12. Pagan, F.G.: Partial Computation and the Construction of Language Processors. Prentice-Hall, Englewood Cliffs (1991)

13. Pauw, W.D., Helm, R., Kimelman, D., Vlissides, J.: Visualizing the Behavior of Object-Oriented Systems. In: Proc. of the 8th Annual Conference on Object-Oriented Programming Systems, Languages, and Applications (OOPSLA 1993), pp. 326–337. ACM Press, New York (1993)
14. Schwanke, R.: An intelligent tool for re-engineering software modularity. In: Proc. of 13th IEEE International Conference on Software Engineering, May 1991, pp. 83–92 (1991)
15. Purewal, S.: Systems and Methods for Modeling and Generating Reusable Application Component Frameworks, and Automated Assembly of Service-Oriented Applications from Existing Applications. United States Patent Application Publication, Pub. No.: US 2005/0144226 A1 (June 30, 2005)
16. Moussallam, F., Evelyn, R., Anzizu, M.D., Wilson III, W.W.: System and Method for Migrating Applications from a Legacy System. United States Patent Application Publication, Pub. No.: US 2006/0041862 A1 (February 23, 2006)
17. Kulkarni, V.V., Reddy, S.S.: Method and Apparatus for Reengineering Legacy Systems for Seamless Interaction with Distributed Component Systems. United States Patent Application Publication, Pub. No.: US 2003/0055921 A1 (March 20, 2003)
18. Dyla, W., Gallagher, M.D., Hannay, S.D., Hays, R.L., Lindstrom, D.J.: System and Method for Providing Communication among Legacy Systems Using Web Objects for Legacy Functions. United States Patent Application Publication, Pub. No.: US 2002/0116454 A1 (August 22, 2002)
19. Liang, J., Hodaie, P.: System and Method for Interfacing with a Legacy Computer System. United States Patent Application Publication, Pub. No.: US 2004/0054812 A1 (March 18, 2004)
20. SCA Assembly Model V1.00, http://www.osoa.org/

Towards Variable Service Compositions Using VxBPEL

Chang-ai Sun[1] and Marco Aiello[2]

[1] School of Computer and Information Technology, Beijing Jiaotong University
100044, Beijing, P.R. China
casun@bjtu.edu.cn
[2] Department of Computing Science, The University of Groningen
Nijenborgh 9, 9747 AG, Groningen, The Netherlands
aiellom@cs.rug.nl

Abstract. The Business Process Execution Language (BPEL) is a widely recognized executable language supporting the specification of process-oriented service compositions. However, the language is limited in addressing variable requirements in the description of business processes. We propose to construct variable and maintainable Web services compositions with VxBPEL, an extension to BPEL we developed to define variability in business process specification. We present the main concepts of VxBPEL and show how to achieve better adaptation and variability maintenance of service compositions, which is particularly desired in the context of dynamically changing business goals and processes.

1 Introduction

The growing availability of Web services both on intranets and on the Internet makes attractive to create Web service compositions to provide value-added functionalities [8]. Consider a travel agency service, for instance, which may be composed of flight and accommodation services, provided by third party providers. Since Web services themselves are deployed and executed in open and dynamic environments, the availability of service instances at run-time is an issue by itself. A composition should be flexible enough so that a flight service can be substituted by another one when a given service instance becomes unavailable. Furthermore, the user may have quite different requirements, for instance depending on the type of trip. When a traveler is arranging his/her personal trip to China, he/she would prefer to get the cheapest flight and accommodation. However, if it is a business trip, more expensive solutions may be viable. Obviously, implementing such a business process with a static Web service composition requires a great deal of recoding and manual work.

VxBPEL[7] is an extension of BPEL [4] to deal with adaptation in Web service compositions from the perspective of variability management. VxBPEL addresses the adaptive composition of Web services by providing constructs for explicitly managing variability at the composition language level, and treats the changes as first-class entities. This is a novelty with respect to current approaches [2-3,5-6], particularly those focusing on the implementation level.

In this paper, we propose to construct variable Web service compositions with VxBPEL and show how such compositions are adaptive and maintainable. We use the travel agency example for illustrational purposes. In particular, we focus here on the

H. Mei (Ed.): ICSR 2008, LNCS 5030, pp. 257–261, 2008.

explicit variability management in those cases involving dependent variation configurations, such as dependency between the flights and accommodation, or dependency between flights and frequent flyer programs.

2 Background

Variability is the ability of a software system or artifact to be extended, changed, customized, or configured for use in a specific context [9]. There are two important concepts in variability, namely variation points and variants. Variation points are locations in the design or implementation at which variations will occur, and variants are the alternatives that can be selected at variation points. Variability management includes the design, use, and maintenance of variability [1].

In order to introduce variability management into service compositions, VxBPEL extends BPEL with the constructs for defining and managing the variability. During the development of constructs for variants, variation points, and their associations, VxBPEL employs the COVAMOF variability framework [9] and adapts it to the context of Web services. The choice of COVAMOF is based on its prominent features, including treating variation points and dependencies as first-class citizens, tool support and its validation in industry.

3 Constructing Variable Compositions with VxBPEL

Let us consider the travel agency example again and model the variability with VxBPEL. There are usually several airlines which can provide a flight service required by the customer. This means that there may exist variation with the invocation of flight services. During the service composition design, we need to introduce the variation point at the place where the flight service is invoked. Fig. 1 depicts the modified BPEL process, where the activity <invoke> in the original BPEL process is replaced by the variation configuration. Without loss of generality, we consider two airlines, namely LH and CA. The choice between two variants is determined by the current configuration of the process.

VxBPEL supports complex realization dependencies during the service compositions. For example, an airline may have hotel partners offering discounts to the travelers. In this situation, the travel agency needs to specify the association between airlines and hotels, in order to provide the cheapest travel services to the customers who are concerned with the total travel cost. During the service composition, one can use ConfigurableVariationPoint for specifying the dependencies of such a complex service composition. Fig. 2 depicts the major segments for specifying the dependency realization between airlines and hotels. In the example, CA is the higher level variant and a set of hotel services are lower level variants for providing the discounted accommodation.

With VxBPEL, designers can focus on the main logic of business processes and, at the same time, specify the variable elements during service compositions. The specifications of VxBPEL clearly integrate main business logic and adaptation of process elements. Such service composition specifications are easily adapted, because the variability management will enable the selection of alternative variants at runtime. This is often the

```
<vxbpel:VariationPoint name= "selecting an airline service">
 <vxbpel:Variants>
   <vxbpel:Variant name= "CA">
     <vxbpel:VPBpelCode>
       <invoke inputVariable="FlightRequest" name="processingRequest "
         operation= "processRequest" outputVariable="requestResponse"
         partnerLink="AirlinesCA" portType="AirlinesCA:FlightProcessing">
         <target linkName="Airlines-to-Agent"/>
         <source linkName="Agent-to-Airlines/>
         </invoke>
     </vxbpel:VPBpelCode >
   </vxbpe:Variant>
   <vxbpel:Variant name= "LH">
     <vxbpel:VPBpelCode>
       <invoke inputVariable="FlightRequest" name="processingRequest "
         operation= "processRequest" outputVariable="requestResponse"
         partnerLink="AirlinesLH" portType="AirlinesLH: FlightProcessing">
         <target linkName="Airlines-to-Agent"/>
         <source linkName="Agent-to-Airlines/>
         </invoke>
     </vxbpel:VPBpelCode >
   </vxbpel:Variant>
 </vxbpel:Variants>
</vxbpel:VariationPoint>
```

Fig. 1. The travel agency composition with variant configuration points

```
<vxbpel:ConfigurableVariationPoint id="1" defaultVariant="default">
<vxbpel:Name>... </vxbpel:Name>
<vxbpel:Rationale>...</vxbpel:Rationale>
<vxbpel:Variants>
     <vxbpel:Variant name="default ">
         <vxbpel:VariantInfo> Airline CA and its partner hotels includes the default, hotelA,
                             and hotelB which provide discounts.
         </vxbpel:VariantInfo>
       <vxbpel:RequiredConfiguration>
         <vxbpel:VPChoices>
             <vxbpel:VPChoice vpname="VP1" variant="default"/>
             <vxbpel:VPChoice vpname="VP2" variant="hotelA"/>
             <vxbpel:VPChoice vpname="VP3" variant="hotelB"/>
         </vxbpel:VPChoices>
       </vxbpel:RequiredConfiguration>
     </vxbpel:Variant>
     <!-- Another variant i.e. LH and its dependent services can be defined here. -->
</vxbpel:Variants>
 </vxbpel:ConfigurableVariationPoint>
```

Fig. 2. The illustration of service compositions with complex realization dependencies

case in the world of Web services where requirements change frequently and there is loose control over the components. The variation is supported both at compile-time and at run-time. The latter is achieved by implementing an extension to a BPEL engine to interpret the variability constructs. One may thus claim that service compositions with the VxBPEL achieve better adaptation than those with standard BPEL.

We argue that the variation of service compositions with VxBPEL is easier to understand since one can identify variation points and variants just by their prefixes. A variability management tool can aid the designer to comprehend the variation involved in service compositions. This is particularly useful when the variation of service compositions is complex enough. Additionally, one can change variability management of service compositions by altering the variation configuration. For example, if the airline CA has more than one partner hotel (or needs to change its partner hotels), one just has to alter *vxbpel:VPChoices* to adapt to the new situation. In this sense, we claim that service compositions with VxBPEL have better maintainability than those with standard BPEL in terms of support of variation.

With VxBPEL, one can specify more variable and flexible service compositions, which thereby are able to address various dynamic changes within business processes. VxBPEL consists of BPEL native constructs and variability constructs. For a variable service composition instance, these two parts are seamlessly integrated in a VxBPEL file. Developers use BPEL native constructs for the normal service composition while the latter is used to specify the variable parts within the service composition. When these variability constructs with the prefix *vxbpel* are used, the namespace defining the VxBPEL elements must be included.

4 Concluding Remarks

Constructs provided by the current version of BPEL can be used to define fixed service compositions by specifying activities and interactions between activities. Although some structured activities such as the *switch*, may be used to select different execution paths, the selection is limited to the predefined enumerative choices and hence the configuration supported is static. When a service cannot satisfy a given QoS requirement or is unavailable, it needs to be replaced. When this occurs, the dependent services must be replaced correspondingly. Such replacement is not possible automatically with current standards. VxBPEL, on the other hand, is designed so that new variants can be introduced and managed at runtime. This allows for run-time reconfiguration and significant composition flexibility to be available within a VxBPEL process.

Acknowledgements

We thank all the contributors of the COVAMOF and the VxBPEL platforms, and Elie El-Khoury for comments. The research is partially supported by the Science and Technology Foundation of Beijing Jiaotong Univ. (Grant No. 2007RC099) and the EU Integrated Project SeCSE (IST Contract No. 511680).

References

[1] Bachmann, F., Bass, L.J.: Managing variability in software architectures. In: Proceedings of ACM SIGSOFT Symposium on Software Reusability, pp. 126–132 (2001)
[2] Charfi, A., Mezini, M.: AO4BPEL: An Aspect-Oriented Extension to BPEL. World Wide Web Journal: Recent Advances on Web Services (special issue) 10(3), 309–344 (2007)
[3] Colombo, M., Nitto, E.D., Mauri, M.: SCENE: a service composition execution environment supporting dynamic changes disciplined through rules. In: Proceedings of ICSOC 2006. LNCS, vol. 4292, pp. 191–202. Springer, Heidelberg (2006)

[4] Curbera, F., Goland, Y., Klein, J., Leymann, F., Roller, D., Weerawarana, S.: Business process execution language for Web services, Version 1.1 (2003)

[5] Ezenwoye, O., Sadjadi, S.M.: TRAP/BPEL: A Framework for Dynamic Adaptation of Composite Services, http://www.cs.fiu.edu/~sadjadi/Publications/TechRep-FIU-SCIS-2006-06-02-TRAP-BPEL.pdf

[6] Erradi, A., Maheshwari, P.: AdaptiveBPEL: a Policy-Driven Middleware for Flexible Web Services Compositions. In: Proceedings of Middleware for Web Services (MWS) (2005)

[7] Koning, M., Sun, C., Sinnema, M., Avgeriou, P.: VxBPEL: Supporting variability for Web services in BPEL. In: Information and Software Technology. Elsevier, Amsterdam, http://dx.doi.org/10.1016/j.infsof.2007.12.002

[8] Papazoglou, M.P.: Web services technologies and standards. ACM Computing Surveys (submitted, 2006), http://infolab.uvt.nl/pub/papazogloump-2006-97.pdf

[9] Sinnema, M., Deelstra, S., Hoekstra, P.: The COVAMOF derivation process. In: Morisio, M. (ed.) ICSR 2006. LNCS, vol. 4039, pp. 101–114. Springer, Heidelberg (2006)

Abstract Reachability Graph for Verifying Web Service Interfaces*

Xutao Du, Chunxiao Xing, and Lizhu Zhou

Research Institute of Information Technology,
Tsinghua National Laboratory for Information Science and Technology,
Department of Computer Science and Technology, Tsinghua University,
Beijing 100084, China

Abstract. Web Service Interface Control Flow Automata(WCFA) is presented to model web service interfaces. An Abstract Reachability Graph(ARG) is constructed for the composite web service based on available WCFAs. Nodes in ARG are equipped with a state formula which is an overestimation of the concrete reachable state properties. The algorithm we present to compute the ARG is a variation of the depth first search algorithm. State formulas are computed at the same time with the construction of ARG. Assertions can be made at control points(nodes)to express certain properties. A SAT solver is used to check whether assertions are logical consequences of the state formulas. Then the answer(valid or invalid) will give designers enough information to decide whether the composite web service works as intended.

1 Introduction

Web services provide an effective way for software reuse. They are designed to be packaged software units which can be *called* or *orchestrated* by other applications over the internet. Therefore, the definition of web service interfaces are very important for correctly and effectively reusing of them.

We present Web Service Interface Control Flow Automata(WCFA), which is an extension of control flow automata [1, 2], to describe web service interfaces. In order to capture the global behavior of a composite web service, an *abstract reachability graph*(ARG) is constructed based on the WCFAs of the involved web services. Every node is a control point of the composite web service, and contains a *state formula* which is an overestimation of the *concrete* state properties in real execution. It is the reason our formalism is called *abstract*.

Assertions can be made at every nodes of the ARG. A SAT solver(CVC3) [3] is used to check the validity of the assertions under the assumptions of the state formula of the same node. The result of the SAT solver will tell whether design errors of the composite web service are found.

We will use the example of a trip request application in the following sections. Figure 1 shows the possible interactions of that application.

* This work is funded by the Support Program of the National '11th Five-Year-Plan' of China under Grant No. 2006BAH02A00 and the National High Technology Development Program of China under Grant No. 2006AA010101.

H. Mei (Ed.): ICSR 2008, LNCS 5030, pp. 262–265, 2008.

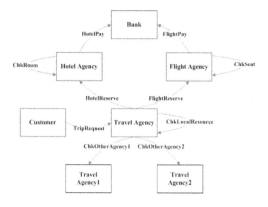

Fig. 1. Composition for TripRequest

2   Web Service Interface Control Flow Automata

Figure 2 gives the WCFA of a travel agency's TripRequest web method, which accepts customer's request to order a trip.

Informally, a WCFA is a directed acyclic graph. Nodes are control points of the web service, which have two fields and are depicted by a tuple <n,t>. The number field n is the unique number for the control point. The type field

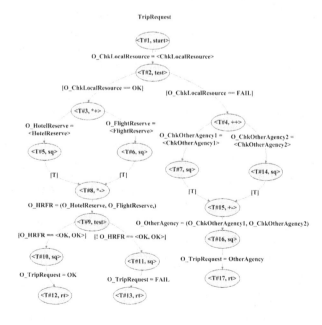

Fig. 2. WCFA for TripRequest

$t\in$ NT={start, sq, test, ++, +-, *+, *-, rt} describes the type of the control point. A start node is the start point of a web service, while rt means return. A sq node has a sequential property and it has one input edge and one output edge. A test node has one input edge and possibly several output edges, only one of which will be chosen according to the label on the edges. A ++(*+) node is the start node for a wait-for-one(wait-for-all) parallel composition. Every *+(++) node has a *collecting* node whose type is *-(+-). A *-(+-) node has several input edges and one output edge. Edges are web method calls, predicate tests or assignments.

3   Abstract Reachability Graph

Abstract reachability graph(ARG) is used to model the global behavior of web services compositions. Every node in ARG is described by a *state formula*, which records information about the paths leading to that node. The algorithm DfARGComp is a variation of the depth first traversal algorithm.

DfARGComp starts from the root of the WCFA of the composite web service. Other relevant information such as the current call stack and state formula also served as parameters. In the trip request application, the search will begin at <T#1,start>. When computing the abstract reachability graph, we need to deal with each of the outgoing edges from the node being processing(say m) to another node, say m'. If m' is not a *collecting* node (the type is not in {*-,+-}), we have two cases to consider. If the outgoing edge is a method call VB=<IMT> with a corresponding WCFA_{IMT}, then we need to *expand* it by recursively calling DfARGComp to get the ARG_{imt}. Then we recursively call DfARGComp to get $\text{ARG}_{m'}$ and create edges to link ARG_{imt} and $\text{ARG}_{m'}$. If the outgoing edge is a method call VA=<EMT> which has not a WCFA, or a predicate test [p], or a normal assignment VN=ST, then we recursively call DfARGComp to compute $\text{ARG}_{m'}$.

When dealing with *collecting* nodes, there are two cases: if there are still other incoming edges to be processed, then we need to wait and only state formulas are updated; otherwise it is the last edge then we call DfARGComp recursively to obtain $\text{ARG}_{m'}$. When we have processed all outgoing edges of m, all children's abstract reachability graphs are computed. What we need to do is just add all the relevant nodes and edges up to get ARG_m and return.

The essence is that when we are constructing an ARG, the state formula of the current node should be correctly computed and passed to DfARGComp as a parameter. Then each node processed by DfARGComp will have their state formulas computed during the search. State formulas are defined as an edge descriptor or an conjunction of several edge descriptors. An edge descriptor describes an edge or a possible junction of several parallel edges.

Generally, when control flows from one node to another through an edge, the state formula of the latter node is just obtained by adding the edge descriptor to the state formula of the former node. The state formula of those nodes that have several incoming edges is obtained by *combining* all the state formulas of the preceding nodes and incoming edges.

Theorem 1. *If a total of k WCFAs is involved in the computation of the abstract reachability graph for a composite web service, Algorithm* DfARGComp *runs in* $O(E)$ *time, where* E *are the total number of edges of the* k *WCFAs.*

4   Verification

Abstract reachability graph is designed for verification. What we want to verify is certain properties at control points. For example, at node <T#13,rt>, the TripRequest service will return FAIL. Although we may not know why it fails, we know the **Travel Agency** should not pay for room reservation for a FAIL request. Thus we require ([!O_RoomPay == OK]) as an assertion. Assertions are quantifier-free propositional logic formulas over the predicate tests in ARG.

Then we fed the state formula of at node <T#13,rt> as assumptions and the assertion ([!O_RoomPay == OK]) as the conjecture to be checked into CVC3. It will return *invalid* because the state formula at that node contains the edge descriptor [O_RoomPay == OK] ∨ [O_RoomPay == FAIL]. Therefore, we have found an error in our design of TripRequest.

5   Conclusion

We present WCFA as a tool for modeling web services invocation behaviors. For the verification of web service compositions, we propose to use the Abstract Reachability Graph(ARG). ARG is computed by exploring involved WCFA(s) in a depth first search manner with necessary WCFA(s) being expanded. Nodes in ARG are equipped with a state formula, which captures an overestimation of concrete states that can be reached in real running of web services.

Quantifier-free assertions can be made on nodes of ARG. Then a SAT solver is used to check whether the assertion is the logic consequence of the node's state formula. Since both the state formula and the assertion are quantifier-free, the SAT solver is a decision procedure. Thus the designers of web services compositions can use the result to decide whether their design is *correct*.

References

1. Necula, G.C., McPeak, S., Rahul, S.P., Weimer, W.: CIL: Intermediate language and tools for analysis and transformation of c programs. In: Computational Complexity, pp. 213–228 (2002)
2. Beyer, D., Henzinger, T.A., Jhala, R., Majumdar, R.: The software model checker Blast: Applications to software engineering. Int. Journal on Software Tools for Technology Transfer (STTT) 9(5-6), 505–525 (2007); Invited to special issue of selected papers from FASE (2004/05)
3. Barrett, C., Berezin, S.: CVC Lite: A new implementation of the cooperating validity checker. In: Alur, R., Peled, D.A. (eds.) CAV 2004. LNCS, vol. 3114, pp. 515–518. Springer, Heidelberg (2004)

Reuse: From Components to Services

Alberto Sillitti and Giancarlo Succi

Center for Applied Software Engineering, Free University of Bolzano,
Piazza Domenicani 3, Italy
{asillitti,gsucci}@unibz.it

Abstract. In these years, a programming paradigm shift is in progress: researchers and developers are moving from component-based to service-based development. This shift is deeply affecting the technology, changing the way of addressing old problems and producing new standards and methodologies to address the new ones. However, even with this shift, some old problems are arising again and their complexity is increasing. One of such problems is the identification of a set of components/services that can be integrated to build a system. This paper proposes an adaptation of a methodology for ranking and selecting components to a service-based environment.

1 Introduction

In this paper, we propose the adaptation to a service-based environment of a methodology to select components for building an integrated system [2]. The approach from which we are starting has been developed in the EU project CLARiFi (CLear And Reliable Information For Integration) (http://clarifi.eng.it/). The project focused on the development of a broker architecture to support the selection of the components suitable for the development of an integrated system. This approach was innovative because it focuses on the problem of selecting a set of components able to work together to build an entire system (or most of it) instead of selecting a single component to address a specific requirement. This work aims at adapting this approach to a service-based environment.

There are many definitions of component in literature [1], we consider the Szyperski's definition: "*A software component is a unit of composition with contractually specified interfaces and explicit context dependencies only. A software component can be deployed independently and it is subject to third party composition*" [6]. According to the W3C (http://www.w3.org/), SOA (Service Oriented Architecture) is defined as a "*set of components which can be invoked, and whose interface descriptions can be published and discovered*".

According to these definitions, a service has all the characteristics of a component and some more: 1) it can be developed using different technologies; 2) it can be executed independently in different run-time environments. This last feature allows the development of systems that result from the run-time integration of several pieces owned and run independently. This new kind of integration generates new problems related to the dynamic composition: the ability to modify (semi)automatically the structure of a system at run-time changing the services involved and/or the integration workflow.

H. Mei (Ed.): ICSR 2008, LNCS 5030, pp. 266–269, 2008.

If a huge set of services is available, the main problem is retrieving the ones that satisfy the requirements of the integrator. Therefore, a requisite for an effective adoption of the service-oriented paradigm is the availability of a smart broker service [4]. A broker is a mediator between service suppliers and system integrators. Technologies such as UDDI – Universal Description, Discovery, and Integration (http://www.uddi.org/), ebXML – Electronic Business eXtensible Markup Language (http://www.ebxml.org/), and their evolutions have been developed to support the creation of public and private directories in which suppliers can deploy the description of their services using a standard language such as WSDL (Web Service Description Language). However, such technologies present several limitations from the points of view of the description and the discovery of the services stored in the broker.

The paper is organized as follows: section 2 presents the proposed process in relation to the state of the art; section 3 draws the conclusions and presents future work.

2 The Process and the State of the Art

The goal of integrators is the inspection of a directory to find services to build a system. The task of the broker is to match the integrator's requirements with internal classification.

Below are illustrated the steps that compose a system selection (Figure 1).

- Understanding integrator's requirements. It means to understand the integrator's "target".
- Definition of integrator's profiles. The broker must understand user profile to understand better the requirements.
- The searching mechanism. The broker "translates" requirements in a query to the directory to find candidate services.
- Ranking a multitude of candidate services. The possible great amount of candidate service can be unmanageable. The broker must help the selection of the most promising ones.
- Compatibility. Services must interact each other to be used in a system. The broker has to check compatibility among them.

This paper focuses on how to describe a service to support its retrieval.

The integrator describes a system through requirements. Natural language is the simplest way to express requirements and it is the ideal notation for human communication. Unfortunately, in software requirements it is not the best solution [3]. Another possible approach to the problem is the usage of facets [4]. In the early definition, facets are a set of pairs key-value that describe properties of a system including both functional qualities (e.g., data formats supported, functionalities offered, etc.) and non-functional ones (e.g., price, reliability, response time, etc.). Facets allow providers to describe in a structured way the relevant aspects of a software system. Moreover, if a common and meaningful set of key-value pairs is defined, potential users can perform advanced searches inside a repository. Such queries can be more complex than the traditional keyword matching in a plain text description and exploit the additional semantic available in the facets such as values in a specific range or in a pre-defined set. In this way, users can design queries specifying conditions such as the support of a specific set of features, the response time below a specific threshold, the price in a certain range, etc.

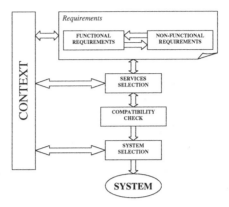

Fig. 1. The ranking and selection process

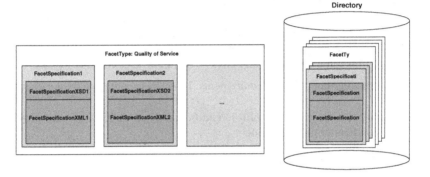

Fig. 2. Example of facet structure and directory

The ability to find a specific service in a large directory is related to: the quality of the taxonomy used to define the keys and the quality of the values inserted in the description by the provider. Taxonomies allow the definition of proper keys in a specific (and limited) domain area. For this reason, the usage of different taxonomies to cover different domains is a suitable solution to provide extensive support to facets. However, taxonomies are useless if the providers do not use them correctly and do not provide a complete description of their services through them. This approach requires a considerable amount of effort from the provider but is extremely useful form the point of view of the user that is looking for a service.

This basic definition of facets is very limited since it is not able to support complex descriptions, relations among the defined attributes, etc. Such definition is usable for the description of software components, but it is not enough flexible to support services. The main extension of the original CLARiFi methodology is in the upgrade of the facet description. In many cases, the usage of a single value or a set is not enough and some properties need to be described in a more expressive way. For this reason, the concept of facet has evolved to include complex structures based on XML technologies [5, 7]. Facets can be described through a set of XML documents. A facet is defined as a set that includes a facet type and one or more facet specifications (Figure 2). A facet type is a label that describes the high-level concept of the facet such as quality of service, interoperability, etc. while the facet specification is the actual implementation of the concept. It is possible that several facet specifications are associated to a single facet type providing different ways of describing the high-level concept. Every facet specification includes two documents: an XML schema that defines the structure and the related XML implementation.

3 Conclusions

In this paper, we have adapted a methodology for retrieving components from a repository to the retrieval of services from a directory. This work introduces a process to improve the identification of services and the selection of a complete system build using them. The main modification to the previous process is the inclusion of the description of the services through XML-based facets that allow a more detailed description and retrieval.

The work intends to support the automated selection of services as a human-driven process. However, some concepts can be extended and applied at run-time when most of the decisions have to be taken by an automated system.

References

1. Brown, A., Wallnau, K.: The Current State of Component-based Software Engineering. IEEE Software 15(5) (1998)
2. Clark, J., Clarke, C., De Panfilis, S., Granatella, G., Predonzani, P., Sillitti, A., Succi, G., Vernazza, T.: Selecting Components in Large COTS Repositories. Journal of Systems and Software 73(2) (2004)
3. Meyer, B.: On formalism in specifications. IEEE Software 2(6) (1985)
4. Prieto-Diaz, R., Freeman, P.: Classifying Software for Reusability. IEEE Software 4(1) (1997)
5. Sawyer, P., Hutchinson, J., Walkerdine, J., Sommerville, I.: Faceted Service Specification. In: Workshop on Service-Oriented Computing: Consequences for Engineering Requirements (2005)
6. Szyperski, C.: Component Software. Addison-Wesley, Reading (2002)
7. Walkerdine, J., Hutchinson, J., Sawyer, P., Dobson, G., Onditi, V.: A Faceted Approach to Service Specification. In: 2nd International Conference on Internet and Web Applications and Services (2007)

Active Binding Technology: A Reuse-Enabling Component Model

Anmo Jeong[1], Seungnam Jeong[1], Yoonsun Lim[2], and Myung Kim[2]

[1] LiberNex, 138-509 ICT, Seoul National University, 151-742 Seoul, Korea
{amjeong,hellojsn}@libernex.com
[2] Dept. of Computer Science & Engineering, Ehwa Womans University,
120-750 Seoul, Korea
lys96@ewhain.net, mkim@ehwa.ac.kr

Abstract. One of the primary obstacles to the reuse of independently-developed binary components on the industrial level lies in that the existing component technologies do not clearly separate component assembly from component development for type safety. To tackle this problem with type safety intact, we propose a new component model, Active Binding Technology, in which each Active Binding component, unlike the conventional one that actually has provided interfaces only, contains independently-defined required interfaces as well. The assembler can later adjust any interface mismatches between pre-produced Active Binding components in the glue component, whose template code is generated from the metadata of the components being combined.

Keywords: Component Model, Component Reuse, CBD.

1 Introduction

UI controls and the components located in the bottom layer of enterprise applications designed according to a multi-layered architecture [1] are autonomous. These autonomous components depend only on their platforms and do not have any dependency upon other components, and so they are reusable without source code change on the existing commercial component technologies such as .NET and Java [2].

But an overwhelming portion of components that have a medium granularity between a typical class and a typical SOA service [3] are designed and developed so as to fulfill their job depending on other components' services. The required interfaces these components use in calling the services of their lower-layer (server) components are in fact the provided interfaces of the server components. The required interfaces of a component based on the existing commercial component technologies are defined outside the component (in its server component obviously) and its metadata has only the identifiers of the required interfaces and/or the identifier of the component that implements the required interfaces [4].

We have judged that these shortcomings are stemming from the fact that software components are not developed as pure parts like in other engineering disciplines, and so have specified three tenets that have to be observed in order to realize the CBD

H. Mei (Ed.): ICSR 2008, LNCS 5030, pp. 270–273, 2008.

ideal of developing software by the reuse/assembly of independently developed binary components [5].

Tenet 1. *Every software component must not include any assumption, metadata, or code concerning the composition with other components.*

Tenet 2. *Component development process and component composition process should be completely separated and independent.*

Tenet 3. *Any new software technology or development process should be in seamless harmony with and complement the latest commercial software technologies.*

2 Active Binding Component

The client component based on the existing commercial component technologies calls a method of its server object using the reference of a provided interface defined in the server component instead of using a self-contained required interface.

This is because the commercial technologies regard interfaces as types and do not allow interfaces with the same identifier (full name) to exist in more than one place, nor allow the instance reference of the object implementing a particular interface to be assigned in a variable of another interface with a different identifier. A client component implemented in this way can hardly be independently reused because it contains the code about the dependence on interfaces defined outside it and thus is tightly coupled with its server component.

By contrast, in order to satisfy Tenet 1, the Active Binding component has a structure in which, when it needs a service from its server component, it actively uses a self-contained required interface when calling the corresponding method of the server object, instead of passively depending on a provided interface defined in the server component. When developing an Active Binding component, the developer only needs to define a required interface if a service from a server component becomes necessary, and use the reference of the required interface to complete the code. This results in a component that self-contains both provided and required interfaces, the specifications of which automatically get included in the component metadata. As this component does not depend on any outside interfaces, it becomes a 'complete part' with no assumption about real component assembly.

3 Active Binding Component Assembly

Fig. 1 shows the structure of two independently developed Active Binding components being combined. When they are combined according to Tenet 2, the mediation between calling/called methods is carried out in the glue component whose template code is generated out of the metadata of the two components, without having to handle the source code of the client and server components.

Active Binding Technology, conforming to Tenet 3, supports the component assembly that utilizes the existing design and development experiences. ABT expresses the holistic view of the behavior of the set of components that concern each use case of the application with an interaction model in a UML sequence diagram, and uses the model in assembling components.

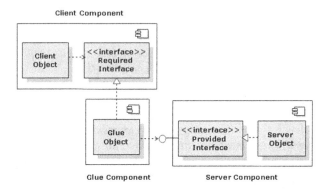

Fig. 1. Active Binding Component Assembly Model

To elaborate this according to what the developer and the assembly tool does respectively, the developer first places the binary components that concern the use case to be assembled in the visual assembly tool, and completes the interaction model by drawing message arrows that represent the calling/called relationships among the components. Each message arrow is mapped to a glue component that adjusts the discrepancies between the calling/called interfaces. When the developer opens the properties window of a message arrow, the assembly tool reads in and shows the required interfaces information of the client component and the provided interfaces information of the server component. When the developer then selects the caller method and the called method to be connected, the assembly tool generates the glue component, class and method that implements the required interfaces, using the metadata read from the components, and also generates the code for calling the called method of the server component and inserts it in the generated method.

Then the developer can edit the generated method code to adjust not only syntactic discrepancies between the two components but also semantic differences that might exist between the parameters/return values of the components. For example, if the client component sends a parameter with Korean currency won to the server component while the server component requires a parameter with US dollar, the developer can solve the problem by inserting in the glue component the code that converts won into dollar.

Detailed descriptions attached to each of the methods in the required and provided interfaces using custom attributes can help the developer select and assemble caller/called methods afterwards. Also, the developer can express the behavioral semantics of the components to be combined by attaching to every service method of a component the identifiers of the required interfaces it depends on, in order of calling.

4 Conclusion

The existing commercial component technologies such as Java and .NET provide high-quality framework functions and excellent development tools to develop complex distributed systems very efficiently. These technologies, however, do not come up with any solution for assembling binary components with different interfaces without changing their source code, making difficult the reuse of non-autonomous components that implement business logic. Against this background, we have proposed an extended version of the existing component models, rather than making a whole new model, to improve reuse rate and maintenance efficiency while maintaining the high development efficiency the existing technologies provide.

Active Binding Technology lays a stepping-stone for reusing independently-developed binary components by providing a practical method to tackle interface mismatches, but if it is to properly realize the CBD ideal of 'Development by Assembly' with COTS components, further studies for the formal expression of component semantics should be conducted. Also, in order to raise the rate of component reuse to a higher level, an additional study to remove the dependency of service components on business data objects, which vary from application to application, ought to be carried out.

References

1. Fowler, M.: Patterns of Enterprise Application Architecture. Addison-Wesley, Reading (2003)
2. De Prince Jr., W., Hofmeister, C.: Analyzing Commercial Component Models. In: Proceedings of the 3rd IEEE/IFIP Conference on Software Architecture, Montreal, Canada, pp. 205--219 (2002)
3. Brown, A., Johnston, S., Kelly, K.: Using Service-Oriented Architecture and Component-Based Development to Build Web Service Applications. Rational Software Corporation (2002)
4. Magee, J., Tseng, A., Kramer, J.: Composing Distributed Objects in CORBA. In: Proceedings of the 3rd International Symposium on Autonomous Decentralized Systems, Berlin, Germany, pp. 257--263 (1997)
5. Clements, P.: From Subroutines to Subsystems: Component-Based Software Development. The American Programmer~8(11) (November 1995)

Collective Reuse of Software Components Speeds-Up Reliability

Iaakov Exman[1,2], Guy Zohar[2], and Yehuda Hassin[2]

[1] School of Engineering, Bar-Ilan University, Ramat-Gan 52900, Israel
exmani@eng.biu.ac.il
[2] Software Engineering Dept., Jerusalem College of Engineering,
POB 3566, Jerusalem 91035, Israel
iaakov@jce.ac.il, guyzohar1@gmail.com, hassin@jce.ac.il

Abstract. Reliable behavior of systems of autonomous agents – such as collections of deployed robots – is difficult to attain. Agents could provide mutual support, but lack of coordination may weaken, rather than increase reliability. We propose *collective reuse* of replaceable software components among autonomous agents, based upon a *shared factory architecture*. Coordinated replacement is achievable on-the-fly, whatever the component status: idle, runnable or actually running. Replacement propagation among agents grows faster with increasing numbers of agents for practical collection sizes, as measured by a reliability *speedup*. The architecture was demonstrated by simulations combining real and virtual robots.

Keywords: Collective Reuse, Software Components, Shared Factory Architecture, Autonomous Agents, Reliability speedup, Design Patterns.

1 Introduction

Predictable and stable behavior of systems of autonomous agents – such as clusters of robots or satellites in orbit – is a hard goal to attain. An individual agent may be deployed in distant places or in dangerous environments, and replacement of faulty physical modules, may be difficult or virtually impossible to perform.

Faulty software is replaceable by components having the same interface, but space constraints within agents prevent storing all imaginable software replacements, say from second source manufacturers. Wireless transmission of software components from a fixed station [1] has been proposed to overcome these constraints.

This paper proposes *collective reuse*, in which exceptions encountered generate events, immediately communicated to the sibling agents, by a *shared factory architecture* taking care of agent coordination. Otherwise, siblings could fail in the same manner as the first agent that detected the fault. Thus all agents benefit from information gathered by anyone of them, mutually reinforcing their reliability, without giving up the flexibility of autonomous agents.

In the remainder of the paper, "Collective Reuse" is defined (Section 2), a shared factory architecture is introduced (Section 3) and the approach is validated by real/virtual robots simulation results (Section 4). A discussion concludes the paper.

H. Mei (Ed.): ICSR 2008, LNCS 5030, pp. 274–277, 2008.

2 Collective Reuse

For a system defined as a collection of autonomous agents, reliability is viewed as a problem of the whole system. Usually a single agent detects the need of a new/ substitute software component. Possible causes are:

- Software faults – when a new fault is detected, a new/replacement fault-free software component is obtained, and retransmitted to all sibling agents.
- Hardware faults – say a sensor fails. A new/substitute software component may bypass the sensor by an algorithm independent of the faulty hardware. This fault must not occur in all siblings, thus retransmission is not automatic.

Now we can define Collective Reuse:

> _Definition_: **Collective Reuse** among a collection of similar autonomous agents [the siblings], is an active reuse mechanism whereby an agent communicates a detected fault, triggering its siblings to do on-the-fly addition or replacement of software components, while preserving their autonomous behavior.

Collective Reuse has two essential roles: a- *Component availability* – to assure that a component is available, creating it if not yet found in a repository; b- *Coordination* – to inform siblings of new faults, and dispatch replacements in suitable times.

3 The Shared Factory Software Architecture

Shared factories perform the two referred roles – factory and coordinator – shown as the upper orthogonal states of the Shared Factory Statechart in Fig. 1.

The coordinator has three orthogonal internal states: a) *Generate event* – catches product execution exceptions and generates replacement events; b) *Handle event* – notifies the factory to trigger a new instantiation cycle, then applies the chosen replacement policy; c) *Replace file* – imports necessary *dlls* (dynamically linked libraries) and swap files to memory, to allow factory production.

The Factory extends the *'factory method'* design pattern [2]. The extension allows events to trigger the factory and notifies the other siblings. It also loads required *dlls*.

The instantiation policy is as follows. For each component C_i, a users' List(i) – which sibling agents j use the component – remembers which objects were created. Users in List(i) are notified of a faulty component before starting its replacement.

To avoid duplicate objects, the factory does not instantiate objects while a component is being replaced. In this case an already loaded component is marked as faulty. A user creation request waits until replacement finishes and the new C_i has no faults. Only then, an object is instantiated. A creation policy pseudo code is seen next.

```
CreatingObject(Uj, Ci)
If Ci Not loaded then /* first time */
       Load Ci;                         Else
       MakeNewList(List(i));                  While (Ci has Fault)  Wait(1);
       MakeNewObject(Ci);                     MakeNewObject(Ci);
       InsertUserList(List(i),Uj);            InsertUserList(Uj);
```

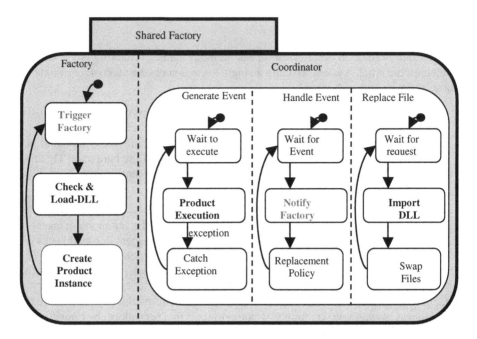

Fig. 1. Shared Factory architecture – The coordinator internal states are orthogonal. Factory and Coordinator interactions are: an event handler triggers the factory (in red); the factory loads a dll only after it was imported by the coordinator (in blue).

4   Results and Validation: Reliability Speedup

Collective reuse was demonstrated in a collection of real three-wheeled mobile robots and virtual robots. Robots perform navigation tasks in a room with obstacles. A laptop carried by physical robots runs an MS.NET environment. The system is written in C#.

For autonomous robots, speedup is a reasonable metric to assess collective reuse efficiency – time spent in the Handle_Event coordinator state. Reliability speedup is defined as the ratio between a single robot time T_1 and the average T_N of N robots:

$$Speedup = T_1 / T_N \qquad (1)$$

Speedup is seen in Table 1 and Fig. 2. A table entry is the mean of tens of single runs.

Table 1. Handle_Event duration and speedup

Number of Robots	Total Duration (sec)	T_N = Average Duration per Robot	Reliability Speedup
1	0.406	0.406	1.000
2	0.398	0.199	2.040
5	0.500	0.100	4.063
8	0.438	0.055	7.429
10	0.953	0.095	4.263
20	2.656	0.133	3.059

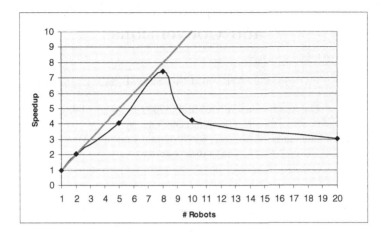

Fig. 2. Collective reuse speedup against robot numbers – Speedup is a trade-off between autonomous processing and communication costs. Almost linear increase up to a point of diminishing returns (curve with points) is compared with strict linearity.

5 Discussion: Related and Future Work

Collective reuse speedup is very intuitive. A single robot must discover the software fault, stop the faulty component, trigger the factory, and do the replacement by itself. None of the activities is spared. A robot collection has a double source of savings:

a. Increased probability of fault discovery by any robot, saves from its siblings the need to trigger the factory;
b. Reduced probability that many robots run the faulty component. Most robots replace the latter in a background mode, while running other tasks.

Representative literature samples refer to component state capture [5], robotic software reconfiguration [3], and to autonomic systems [4].
Future work will deal with variations of replacement policies and multiple shared factories to show the significance of collective reuse for large robot numbers.

References

1. Exman, I., Yermol, S., Hassin, Y.: Run-Time Software Module Swapping Increases Robot Survivability. In: Proc. 1st Israel Conf. on Robotics, Tel-Aviv University, Israel (2006)
2. Gamma, E., Helm, R., Johnson, R., Vlissides, J.: Design Patterns: Elements of Reusable Object-Oriented Software. Addison-Wesley, Boston (1995)
3. MacDonald, B., Hsieh, B.P., Warren, I.: Design for Dynamic Reconfiguration of Robot Software. In: 2nd Int. Conf. Autonomous Robots and Agents, New Zealand (2004)
4. Patouni, E., Alonistioti, N.: A Framework for the Deployment of Self-Managing and Self-Configuring Components in Autonomic Environments. In: IEEE WoWMoM 2006 (2006)
5. Vandewoude, Y., Berbers, Y.: Component state mapping for runtime evolution. In: Int. Workshop on Unanticipated Software Evolution, within PLC 2005, Las Vegas, NE (2005)

Refinement of Component Model Standards and Conventions

Hazleen Aris[1] and Siti Salwah Salim[2]

[1] Universiti Tenaga Nasional, 43009 Kajang, Malaysia
hazleen@uniten.edu.my
[2] University of Malaya, 50630 Kuala Lumpur, Malaysia
salwa@um.edu.my

Abstract. One the research areas in component-oriented software development is component model development. Various component models have been defined and specified, but whether or not they meet the purpose of a component model is still a subject of discussion. This paper presents our effort in refining the standards and conventions of a component model in order to produce components that meet their purpose. Application of the refined standards and conventions to a selection of component models is also presented.

Keywords: Component model, component model standards, component model purpose.

1 Introduction

The success of component-oriented software development largely depends on a clear definition and precise specifications of component model. According to Wallnau et al. [1], to define what a component model is, one has to know the purpose of a component model. Therefore, they have defined the purpose of a component model to comprise the following:

- **Uniform composition**, where two components can interact iff they share consistent assumptions about what each provides and requires of the other,
- **Appropriate quality attributes** of a system, which depend on its software architecture and
- **Deployment of components and applications** where components can be deployed from the developer environment into the composition environment and later into the customer environment.

A set of standards and conventions (referred to as *standards* henceforth at a number of places for readability) that need to be imposed on component developers to ensure the fulfillment of the above purpose is also defined. These are:

- **Component types**, which may be defined in terms of the interfaces implemented by a component,

H. Mei (Ed.): ICSR 2008, LNCS 5030, pp. 278–281, 2008.
© Springer-Verlag Berlin Heidelberg 2008

- **Interaction schemes**, which specify how components are located, which communication protocols are used and how qualities of service are achieved and
- **Resource binding**, which binds a component to one or more resources.

These standards, however, are somewhat generic. Relying on these standards alone will not be of much help to the component developers in making sure that the components developed will achieve the stated purpose. Therefore, in this paper, we describe our effort in refining the standards so that they can provide more information in producing purposeful components. Section 2 describes our approach in refining the standards. Section 3 explains the application of the refined standard to selected component models and section 4 concludes the paper.

2   Refinement of Standards and Conventions

Based on the description of component model purpose and standards in section 1 and their detailed elaboration in [1], we can relate each standard to the purpose that it can fulfill as shown in Fig. 1. Uniform composition of components can be achieved when they share consistent assumptions about what each provides and requires. Consistent assumptions are made possible when each component declares its component types, defined in terms of the interfaces implemented. Standardisation of the types of components used and their interaction schemes ensures the fulfillment of desired quality attributes. Resource binding mechanisms enable the deployment of components into the composition environment to produce applications.

Fig. 1. Standards and conventions that achieve particular purpose of component model

Åkerholm and Fredriksson [2] map the three standards to component definition, component interface and component composition respectively. In our opinion, a better mapping for these three standards and conventions are *component interface*, *contract* and *component composition* respectively, each of which becomes the basis for the refinement of component model standards. Furthermore, our review on other research work on component models discovers that most work indeed contain definitions on component interface, contract and component composition as means to achieve the purpose of a component model, albeit the terms used in describing them differ.

From the elaboration on the component interface, contract and composition in [1], details about each of these three aspects of a component model can be extracted as shown in Fig. 2. Interface of a component is of two types; *provides* and *requires*. Each type of interface should include not only the syntax, but also the semantic for reasons stated in [3]. Contract can be futher divided into two types of contracts, component-component (C-C) contract and component-framework (C-F) contract. C-C contract defines component constraints through its precondition, postcondition and invariant. C-F contract concerns with resource management issues like component lifecycle and protocol between component and its composition framework. For component composition, two aspects can be further looked into; binding mechanism and binding time. Binding mechanism should cater for simple composition between components, deployment of components in its framework and sub assembly of a child component into its parent component. As for the binding time, two types of binding are possible; late and early bindings where late binding is preferred for greater composition fexibility.

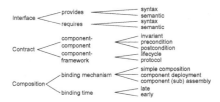

Fig. 2. Refinement of the interface, contract and composition of a component model

3   Application of the Refined Standards

The refined standards were applied to seven (7) research-based component models; SOFA [4], UML [5], CDL [6], Fractal [7], Visual Component [8], Cat One [9] and Formal Model [10]. These component models were selected based on their generic nature and sufficient written information. We did not apply the refined standards to the industrial standard component models for the reason given by [11].

Result of the application shows that the refined standards can be categorised into two; well supported standards and less supported standards. Well supported standards are the standards adhered to by all (or almost all) of the selected component models. These are the interfaces' syntax and semantic, contract's invariant, precondition and postcondition, simple composition and component (sub) assembly. The rest of the refined standards are classified as less supported because the result shows that only a few (less than half) of the selected component models include these standards in their specifications. These are component-framework lifecycle and protocol, component deployment and binding time.

4   Conclusion

Even though component model standards exist, it is discovered that the existing standards are too general and are not able to sufficiently guide component developers in producing component that meets its purpose. Therefore, this paper describes our effort in refining the standards so that the purpose of component model can be better materialised. It makes the standards more distinct in such a way that they can be clearly compared to the description of each component model. Result of the standards application shows that none of the selected component models satisfy all the refined standards with some of the standards are well supported by the component models while some others are less supported. The refined standards can also be used in improving the existing component models or in developing a new component model.

References

1. Wallnau, K., Bachmann, F., Bass, L., Buhman, C., Comella-Dorda, S., Long, F., Robert, J., Seacord, R.: Technical Report on Volume II: Technical Concepts of Component-Based Software Engineering. Software Engineering Institute. Carnegie Mellon University, Pittsburgh (2000)
2. Åkerholm, M., Fredriksson, J.: Technical Report on A Sample of Component Technologies for Embedded Systems. Mälardalen Research and Technology Centre, Department of Computer Science and Electronics Mälardalen University, Västerås Sweden (2004)
3. Crnkovic, I., Hnich, B., Jonsson, T., Kiziltan, Z.: Basic Concepts in CBSE. In: Crnkovic, I., Larsson, M. (eds.) Building Reliable Component-based Software Systems. Artech House, Inc., Norwood (2002)
4. Plášil, F., Bálek, D., Janeček, R.: SOFA/DCUP: Architecture for Component Trading and Dynamic Updating. In: Proceedings of the Fourth International Conference on Configurable Distributed Systems, Annapolis, MA, pp. 43–51 (1998)
5. Cheesman, J., Daniels, J.: UML Components: A Simple Process for Specifying Component-Based Software, 1st edn. Addison-Wesley Professional, Reading (2000)
6. Teschke, T., Ritter, J.: Towards a Foundation of Component-Oriented Software Reference Models. In: Butler, G., Jarzabek, S. (eds.) GCSE 2000. LNCS, vol. 2177, pp. 70–84. Springer, Heidelberg (2001)
7. Bruneton, E., Coupaye, E., Stefani, J.B.: Specification on the Fractal Component Model. The Object Web Consortium. France Télécom S.A (2002-2003)
8. Kent, S., Howse, J., Lauder, A.: Modelling Software Components. In: Proceedings of the 9th International Workshop on Database and Expert System Applications, Vienna, pp. 789–200 (1998)
9. DSouza, D.F., Wills, A.C.: Objects, Components, and Frameworks with UML The CatalysisSM Approach. Massachusetts. Addison Wesley Longman, Inc., Massachusetts (1998)
10. Cox, P.T., Song, B.: A Formal Model for Component-based Software. In: Proceedings of the IEEE Symposia. on Human-Centric Computing Languages and Environments, Stresa, pp. 304–311 (2001)
11. Estublier, J., Favre, J.-M.: Component Models and Technology. In: Crnkovic, I., Larsson, M. (eds.) Building Reliable Component-based Software Systems. Artech House, Inc., Norwood (2002)

Identifying and Improving Reusability Based on Coupling Patterns

Andrea Capiluppi and Cornelia Boldyreff

Centre of Research on Open Source Software – CROSS
Department of Computing and Informatics, University of Lincoln
{acapiluppi,cboldyreff}@lincoln.ac.uk

Abstract. Open Source Software (OSS) communities have not yet taken full advantage of reuse mechanisms. Typically many OSS projects which share the same application domain and topic, duplicate effort and code, without fully leveraging the vast amounts of available code.

This study proposes the empirical evaluation of source code folders of OSS projects in order to determine their actual *internal* reuse and their potential as shareable, fine-grained and *externally* reusable software components by future projects.

This paper empirically analyzes four OSS systems, identifies which components (in the form of folders) are currently being reused internally and studies their coupling characteristics. Stable components (i.e., those which act as service providers rather than service consumers) are shown to be more likely to be reusable. As a means of supporting replication of these successful instances of OSS reuse, source folders with similar patterns are extracted from the studied systems, and identified as externally reusable components.

1 Introduction

Reuse of software components is one of the biggest promises of software engineering [3]. Enhanced productivity, increased quality and improved business performance are often pinpointed as the main benefits of developing software from a stock of reusable building blocks [33].

Recently, practical approaches to commercial software reuse have included both in-house and COTS-based approaches. Many companies have already successfully produced and reused in-house components, in the forms of documentation, system and components design, source code, and so on, which are kept as valuable assets and not made available elsewhere [25,29]. One of the most critical aspects of successful in-house reuse is the long-term commitment of the management [30].

Reuse of small scale components, e.g. functions of programming language libraries, either in-house or externally produced has been common practice since high level languages have been in use. A new possibility for reusability of external components has arisen through the exploitation of both COTS and OSS in what can termed "whole system reuse". New products can be developed based on existing systems, either on a closed-source basis (e.g., commercially available COTS [31]), or by reusing entire OSS systems, such as web-server Apache, the MySQL database management system, or the PHP language [37]. In the latter case, OSS systems also provide the source code

H. Mei (Ed.): ICSR 2008, LNCS 5030, pp. 282–293, 2008.

underlying the system, and the code can be modified before reuse. One of the drawbacks of this approach is that entire systems are reused, even though only a subset of their functionalities may be required in the new system. Commercial companies must address these issues in order to take advantage of the proprietary-COTS shift: *whether to use* COTS, *how to use* COTS, and *what to modify* in their in-house systems to cope with COTS [10] and the same questions apply in the selection of OSS component reuse.

Although much attention has already been focused on the study of reusable COTS, including OSS components in corporate software production, the reusability of software "from" OSS projects "in" other OSS projects has only started to draw the attention of researchers and practitioners in OSS communities [20]. While a huge amount of code is daily created, modified and stored in OSS repositories, software reuse is rarely perceived by OSS developers as a critical factor in their projects, nor is the source code of other projects considered as a potential way to build new OSS systems upon existing ones. For different and composite reasons [34], briefly recounted here in the following Sections, several OSS projects typically address the same software need independently. For example, a search for the *"email client"* topic on the SourceForge site will result in more than 500 different projects being listed, each implementing some features of the same topic. Duplication of coding effort therefore is currently producing similar products with little sharing of the basic building blocks or the larger subsystems.

In order to address this missing "reuse" link in OSS projects, the objective of this paper is to provide OSS communities with a technique for identifying and benefiting from reusable components (under a "design with reuse" perspective [26]).

2 Definitions and Approach

The terminology and definitions used in this paper are extracted from similar studies in the literature, for example, the definition of *coupling* (intended for both

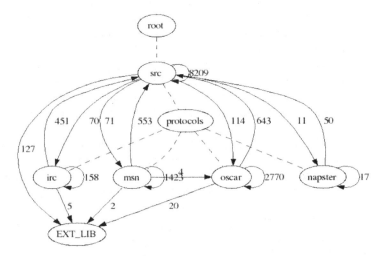

Fig. 1. Couplings among folders in one of the releases of the Gaim system – Dashed lines represent hierarchical connections without involving couplings

object-oriented [1,21] and procedural [13] languages) and the notion of *instability* of source packages [17]. In this section an overview of these terms is given, as they will be used throughout this work.

- *Source function*: basic unit of source code; this term is used to refer to procedures, subroutines, but also OO methods.
- *Source file*: any file with at least one source function.
- *Source folder*: any folder containing at least one source file [9]. The term *module* is used to refer to source code functions, files and folders.
- *Folder structure*: from the perspective of file naming, code organization and storage, this is the tree structure composed of elementary components (source files, source folders). The root of the tree is represented by the parent folder [9,8].
- *Extensibility of a source folder*: following Martin [24] who defines *extensibility* as the number of concrete and abstract classes in a package, we define the number of source files contained in a folder as the *extensibility* of that folder. This attribute serves to characterize the potential usefulness of a source folder. Ideally, one would want to reuse folders with large extensibility, i.e., with a large number of similarly scoped functionalities (in the forms of files or functions), rather than a number of related smaller folders.
- *Coupling*: this is a measure of interconnection among modules in a software structure [33]. In this study, three types of coupling are extracted, based on the definitions of common coupling [36]: these couplings were extracted via the Doxygen engine[1], and, albeit related, they represent different metrics for the links among modules.
  i. The **dependency relationship** is based on source files, and describes, for each file, how many and which other files are currently depending on it. After extracting it, this type of coupling was transformed into a folder-to-folder relationship, i.e. between the folders actually containing the files affected by the coupling.
  ii. The **include relationship** is also based on source files, and describes the number of external files that a specific source file includes in its declarations. Again, this file-to-file coupling was upgraded to a folder-to-folder relationship, as above.
  iii. The **function call relationship** is based on source functions, and describes the relationship among functions or procedures. It produces as a result the representation of calls within functions. This type of coupling was at first upgraded to a file-to-file relationship, and then to a folder-to-folder relationship: this permitted to have all the extracted couplings at the same level of granularity. The result of the extraction and conversion of couplings to folder-to-folder relations is exemplified in figure 1.
- The number of *Afferent Couplings (Ca*, or in-bound coupling) of a source folder represents the sum of other source folders that depend on it, and it is an indicator of the its *responsibility*. [17] used this metrics for OO languages and specifically for packages. In the following, the focus is on source folders as packages of a system, even if the system is written in procedural languages.
- The number of *Efferent Couplings (Ce*, or out-bound coupling) of a module represents how many other modules it depends on, and it is an indicator of the folder's *independence* [17].

---

[1] Doxygen, http://www.stack.nl/~dimitri/doxygen/

– The *Instability (I)* of a module is the ratio of efferent coupling (Ce) to total coupling (Ce + Ca) such that $I = \dfrac{Ce}{(Ca + Ce)}$. This metric is an indicator of the folder's resilience to change [17]. The range for this metric is 0 to 1, with $I = 0$ indicating the lowest instability for a folder and $I = 1$ indicating a completely unstable folder [17]. Since Ca and Ce are measured at the folder level, and couplings among folders may greatly vary due to larger or smaller amount of calls, *weighted* instability factors will be introduced below, termed wCa and wCe.

3   Case Studies – Evolutionary Analysis

The first part of this study has been performed over all the public releases of four large OSS projects[2], and is specifically targeted at understanding the structural relationships among source folders. It was noted that both MPlayer and XMMS share the same functionalities (playing and recording multimedia), yet they are developed by independent teams of developers. The reasons discovered by past works [34] are enough for developers to start their own project and duplicate efforts. This means that the reuse of code written by others has to overcome similar obstacles, apart from the technical ones [20].

In terms of activity and code released, it was observed that the Arla project spans some 8 years of development, Gaim approximately 6.5 years, MPlayer 4.5, while XMMS 5 years. In terms of productivity, a high frequency of releases was observed in the Gaim and MPlayer projects (on average, more than one release per month), while it was lower in the case of Arla (less than one per month). The XMMS case finally shows that a new release has been available on average every two months. This general productivity trend has had a repercussion on size achieved (in LOCs) and overall number of source folders found in the latest observed release.

In terms of developers, it was observed that the MPlayer project was the most successful in forming an OSS community providing code patches, new functionalities and bug fixes (210 developers). A direct link between the community formed and the size achieved was also detected in the overall size at the latest observed release: in the cases of the 4 projects studied here, larger communities usually achieve larger systems, apart from the Gaim case (25 developers, 235 kLOCs), where a smaller community has achieved a larger system than those developed by other, larger communities (Arla – with 83 developers, 215 kLOCs – and XMMS – 43 developers, 110 kLOCs).

From the reuse standpoint, it was noted that recurrent folders are successfully reused across the selected OSS systems. The most notably folders are the following:

1. *Libraries of the C language (libc)*: they provide generic functionalities, like the I/O output (the module "stdio.h"), or the stub functions for socket communication (contained in "socket.h"). In this work, all the connections involving calls to elements of the generic libc libraries are, for simplicity, redirected to a generic "libc" folder. Evaluating the instability of this folder, it was found that throughout the evolution

---

[2] Arla http://www.stacken.kth.se/project/arla/, Gaim http://www.pidgin.im, MPlayer http://www.mplayerhq.hu/ and XMMS http://www.xmms.org/

of all the selected systems, this folder has a constant lowest instability (0): it does not invoke any outside resources, and it just provides services.

2. *Localization/international folder*: the code contained in this specific subsystem translates the messages, or the interfaces, of the application in the local language of the user. OSS projects using code of this subsystem typically include it in a folder named "intl". The evolutionary behavior of the instability of this folder showed a very low instability (between 0 and 0.2), which again denotes a provider of services, rather than a consumer.

3.1 Source Folders as Reusable Units

Empirical findings demonstrated that object-oriented packages show four basic patterns ("*pure client*", "*pure server*", "*hybrid*" and "*silent*"), based on whether they mostly require, or are called by, other packages [23]. The present work expands these findings in two ways:

1. It considers the folders of procedural languages as modules: when asked, the developers of the XMMS case study confirmed that source folders serve to them as place-holders for "similar-scoped" source files[3]. The "wav" folder, for instance, keeps all the source files for the wav audio file format.
2. It evaluates coupling among folders to build an instability index: folders with lowest instability index are identified as candidates for reuse.

Considering the couplings within and outside of source folders, it was noted that all the case studies (apart Arla), show recurring initial values. At least 80% of their couplings are among elements of the same source folder, showing an applied example of modularity [33]: considering only the "function calls" coupling, this value increases to 90%. From an evolutionary standpoint, all the analyzed systems show a growth in number of source folders, but a increasingly problematic coupling pattern: the overall amount of couplings within folders decreases while the systems increase in size. This recalls the results of *architectural erosion* mentioned in [27]; as systems depart from its "*initial architecture's intent and conceptual integrity*", couplings connect many other folders, and the whole architecture becomes much harder to understand and maintain.

The Arla case is an outlier, and shows an intertwined system already from its initial releases, where half of the couplings affect two or more source folders. From the definitions given above, this system is going to experience less reusable folders, since most of the existing folders are already linked into a complex network of couplings.

This initial result shows that, on average, OSS developers actively use source folders as containers of similar-scoped elements, and prefer linking elements in the same folder rather than coupling different folders. However, this result should not be used to statically judge a software system; the Arla system is not inherently worse than the others analyzed, but on average its source folders are more instable, as per the definition given. Based on that, it is likely that selecting reusable folders from this system will be more difficult.

---

[3] Reported from conversations, email correspondence and private communication.

Table 1. Reusable folders detected via the coupling analysis: wCe refers to the product "Efferent folders * Efferent calls", while wCa refers to a similar product of afferent folders and calls

Folder	I	E	wCe	wCa	Calls to self	Calls to libc	Description	False positive
Arla project – reusable folders								
root/lib/ro-ken	0.01	145	11*73	71*1326	395	367	Library handling missing or broken parts	yes
root/rx	0.03	33	13*111	53*1042	495	141	Library implementing the rx protocol	no
Gaim project – reusable folders								
root/src	0.030	139	12*1117	30*14462	9437	868	Common source files of the Gaim system	yes
MPlayer project – reusable folders								
root/liba52	0.02	23	2*21	9*230	196	15	ATSC A/52 stream decoder	no
root/libav-codec	0.03	154	22*155	27*4493	3780	168	Library for coding and decoding video and audio streams	no
root/libaf	0.03	38	7*52	25*464	294	112	Audio filter layer library	no
root/lib-faad2	0.06	86	6*23	2*1063	1096	37	Decoding library for AAC formats	no
root/libmp-demux	0.06	136	21*257	28*2852	2740	353	Demultiplexer Library for MPEG, ASF, AVI formats	no
root/tremor	0.045	29	4*17	4*363	372	34	Tremor integer-only Ogg Vorbis audio codec	no
root/loader	0.054	27	8*203	24*1192	688	75	N/A	yes
root/osdep	0.066	25	6*47	23*174	17	54	N/A	yes
root/loader/wine	0.138	27	5*142	14*318	83	11	Header files for the Microsoft Windows compatibility	yes
XMMS project – reusable folders								
root/lib-xmms	0.003	19	4*20	25*1081	416	86	Generic library for the XMMS project	no
root/xmms	0.091	87	20*277	26*2121	2157	121	Common source files of the XMMS system	yes

3.2 Identifying Reusable Folders

In this section, the data gathered in the evolutionary exploration of the four case studies is used to extract reusable folders. In particular, the coupling patterns of the "libc" and the "Intl" folders will be looked for in other folders. Low values in the instabilities will trigger the definition of reusability of the folder, and a preference will be given to folders with larger extensibility. Tentatively, two thresholds were set: the joint combination of an instability lower than 0.2, and an extensibility larger than 10, highlight a folder as reusable. In table 1, a list of reusable folders per project is given, based on the instability and extensibility thresholds. The table summarizes the following data:

1. Each project has a set of rows, pointing at reusable folders (second column) found in that project. In each set, folders with a small instability (as per the threshold given) and containing a larger amount of source files (i.e. higher extensibility, conforming to the tentative threshold) are preferred as potential reusable folders.

2. Efferent coupling has been evaluated via the product of the number of efferent folders and the number of total efferent calls. Afferent coupling (6th column) is given by a similar product, but involving afferent folders and calls. Intra-folder calls are summarized by the "Calls to self" column, while links to the "Libc" folder are shown in the "Calls to libc" column. In many cases, the amount of calls within source folders are larger than the amount of efferent calls, which confirms the lowest instability of these folders.

3. A description of each folder (last column of table 1) has been extracted either from the description files contained in the folder, or by browsing the documentation. This task is of key importance in order to describe a folder to potential reuses, and it has not been possible to automate this task.

3.3   Validation of the Predictors – Instability and Extensibility

As stated above, and considering the relatively few empirical studies focused on the reuse of OSS components, the practice of reuse of OSS components is not widespread, and it needs further investigation. The implemented algorithm selects folders which are being actively reused by these systems (the "rx" folder, provided by IBM, reused in the Arla system; the folder "tremor" in the MPlayer system, table 1). In terms of validation of the proposed metrics as predictors of external reusability, the following lists the approach used:

– **Detecting reused folders:** The list of reusable folders, as listed in table 1, has been processed in a semi-automatic way, through various engines: the main SourceForge site[4], the Krugle code search engine[5], and the FLOSSmole repository[6] have been searched against each of these folders. The SourceForge site has been searched manually, browsing for the names of each folder, and analyzing whether new projects exist as a spin-off from that folder, or if existing projects include the requested folder; the Krugle engine has also been manually searched, and the existing OSS projects that include the requested folder have been detected; the FLOSSMole repository has been automatically searched for matching names of new projects with the name of the requested folder.
– **Detection of actual reuse:** The folders found in any of the information sources have been detected as such. No further analysis has been performed to check whether their current coupling interaction, or their extensibility, has changed overtime as in the original case studies.

Based on the approach above, it was found that some of the highlighted folders are currently distributed as *independent* OSS projects: the "liba52" folder of MPlayer (7th row of table 1, and the "libxmms" folder of XMMS (12th row of table 1) are currently distributed as separate OSS systems.

In terms of "external" reusability [32], it was also found that some of the folders in the MPlayer project are reused in various OSS projects:

---

[4] http://sourceforge.net/
[5] http://www.krugle.com/
[6] http://ossmole.sourceforge.net/

- the "liba52" folder is currently reused by the "gst-ffmpeg" project;
- the "libavcodec" folder is currently reused by several other OSS projects ("gst-ffmpeg", "xmovie", "quicktime4linux", "mythtv" among others);
- the "libfaad2" folder is reused by the "audacious-plugins" project;
- the "libmpdemux" folder is reused by the "nmm" project.

The algorithm as illustrated above is subject to detecting false positives, i.e. targetting folders as reusable but never reused. Based on the given thresholds (Instability <= 0.2; Extensibility >= 10), the latest analyzed releases of the analyzed projects presented the false positives listed in the last column of table 1. These false positives fit into two main categories, the first contains those folders which currently represent most of the functionalities of the system (*e.g.* the "root/src" folder in Gaim, and the "root/xmms" in the XMMS system). These are typically large-grained components, and in terms of reusability, they should be split into other components before being reusable. The second category contains those other folders which present a reusability potential, but currently are not reused: these false positives represent missed reuse opportunities.

4   Related Work

This work is related to various research areas: reuse of components, empirical studies on software systems, graphic visualizations, software couplings, and software architectures. Since this work is in a larger research context, related to the study of the evolution of OSS systems, from which the case studies presented in this paper have been taken, empirical studies of OSS are also relevant to this research. In the following Section, an overview of the related works is presented, and consideration is given to determining how this work expands upon the related work.

The research with the closest scope to the present work is presented in [20], where a framework is proposed for the reuse of components in the OSS environment. It points out some key aspects to consider carefully, and which could impede its implementation, such as the license types, the ego-boosting problems or the programming languages; these social aspects were previously stressed also in [34]. The technical aspects of incorporating external code are also mentioned, but no in-depth analysis is provided. The present work studies some of the technical details of selecting reusable folders, but the mentioned aspects are all key points which should be given consideration as well.

As mentioned above, many *reuse* research studies (and a set of specific conferences on the topic of "Software Reuse") have been devoted to developing techniques [22,37] and frameworks for globally enhancing reuse [3], establishing state-of-the-art and critical aspects of reuse [25,30]. This present work has been conceived as having the OSS development communities as its main recipients and beneficiaries in order that results and techniques of this academic research can be fed back to the OSS communities and advance the development of their systems.

This work is also related to the study of *software architectures*: previous works ([18,19,38]) have defined and used different views of architecture of a software system. For example, [19] refers to a "4+1" view model to describe a system involving logical, process, physical, development views, and user scenarios. This model defines different perspectives for different stakeholders; the present work uses the concepts of logical ("hierarchical") and process ("coupling") views to establish a comparison between them. Similarly, [18] defines four architectural views of software systems, which in turn focus on coarser degrees of granularity (conceptual, or the abstract design level; module, or the concrete design level; code, or components level; and execution level). As stated above, the present research focuses on the views which are closer to the work of software developers, as, for instance, the folder or the file level. In the selection of attributes, the limit is on those that it is possible to derive from projects found in existing OSS repositories with a reasonable effort. Hierarchical ("abstract design level") and coupling ("component level") views can both provide insight into how developers deal with macro and micro-components of software systems, respectively.

Recently, it has been realized that empirical data for OSS systems is more widely available than that for proprietary systems. A general distinction can be drawn among these studies. In part, research studies are based "on" OSS systems "for" advancing the Open Source Software Engineering body of knowledge; other studies access OSS projects for generating boundary crossing conclusions on software systems in general. Recent studies of the first kind include those examining single OSS projects [2,15,16] [14,35], or those examining several OSS projects [6,7,28]. This work is intended as a means to directly inform OSS developers of the availability of existing potentially reusable folders upon which they can build new applications.

As previously reported, recent work [11,23] has been focused on OO *package analysis*, in order to characterize the roles of specific folders. This work is greatly inspired by these research studies, and focuses the "source folder" as the fundamental unit in a network of couplings. The advances presented in this paper are based on considering interaction coupling within procedural languages as the most representative in an OSS context [7], on providing an evolutionary perspective of these interactions, and on focusing the analysis on the reusability of folders based on their couplings.

Recent work on *code couplings* in OSS has been reported in [1,39], where the analysis used the definition of common and control coupling; two or more modules are commonly coupled when they share a reference to the same variable. Our approach is slightly different, since the source code (mostly C with some C++) is analyzed by considering three different couplings (dependency, and include coupling, and calls among functions). We consider their relevance from the point of view of two different visualizations, in order to define a relationship between code coupling and what we define as the folder structure of a software system at a given stage of its evolution.

5   Conclusions, Further Work and Threats to Validity

This paper has presented an approach to evaluating the source folders of a software system as potentially reusable and shareable fine-grained components. The current state of the art in terms of reusability are two-fold: the commercial internal reuse, which is typically not shared, and the COTS approach, which reuses "black-box" components.

This paper focused its reuse approach on smaller components, the folders (or directories) of a software system. Building on the vast amount of OSS knowledge and the OSS code base, specific source folders were observed as successfully reused across OSS systems. An analysis of the coupling (i.e., the interactions among various other folders) was carried out in order to characterize these specific folders based on patterns of interaction. The approach described above had two objectives. The objective was to look for similar coupling patterns in other folders in order to identify potential candidates for reuse in other OSS projects, based on the coupling patterns observed.

The empirical results are based on literature definitions. It was found that successfully reused folders have a low instability index, i.e., they provide more services to other folders than they ask for from other folders. In a service-based terminology, these folders act mostly as servers for other folders. This coupling pattern was searched for in other source folders, and a list of folders with a similar behavior was provided in table 1: these folders represent potentially reusable components. In terms of external reusability, the algorithm identified some source folders which are already being reused in the OSS community as side projects of existing OSS systems.

Various areas are being evaluated as further work: a key aspect of this research is the extraction of information to characterize the potentially reusable source folders; this should be made automatic and non-invasive. Also, other types of coupling (dynamic and data couplings, inheritance etc.) have been identified in previous works, and should be considered to provide a more complete picture. Finally, it is planned to use a tooling technique to bind and/or resolve external dependencies in order to explore whether even modules with many dependencies could be highly reusable.

Several threats to validity have been identified: first, the usage of instability and extensibility alone could not be enough to categorize a source folder as reusable. Due to transitive dependencies, developing a new module using others, it will automatically becomes less reusable than the ones that were reused (because Ce increases), unless it was manage to create many dependencies to the new module (such that Ca increase as well). Second, only the dependency, inclusion and function calls couplings were studied. Other types such as data coupling [5], or dynamic coupling, [1]), were not considered. Further works will enhance our analysis to consider these types and to examine the use of other characteristics to determine reusability. Finally, other characteristics determine whether a module should be reused in another system. Apart from those already cited by [20], there could be inherent reasons for not reusing a specific module, even if its instability is low at the coupling level. It could be that it is too small, or that it is very complex (in terms of cyclomatic complexity, for instance).

References

1. Arisholm, E., Briand, L.C., Foyen, A.: Dynamic Coupling Measurement for Object-Oriented Software. IEEE Transactions on Software Engineering 30(8), 491–506 (2004)
2. Aoki, A., Hayashi, K., Kishida, K., Nakakoji, K., Nishinaka, Y., Reeves, B., Takashima, A., Yamamoto, Y.: A case study of the evolution of jun: an object-oriented open-source 3d multimedia library. In: Proceedings of the 23rd International Conference on Software Engineering, Toronto, Canada, ICSE, pp. 524–533 (2001)
3. Basili, V.R., Rombach, H.D.: Support for Comprehensive Reuse. IEEE Software Engineering Journal 6(5), 303–316 (1991)
4. Beecher, K., Boldyreff, C., Capiluppi, A., Rank, S.: Evolutionary Success of Open Source Software: an Investigation into Exogenous Drivers. In: Electronic Communications of the EASST: ERCIM Symposium on Software Evolution, vol. 17(8) (2007)

5. Briand, L.C., Morasca, S., Basili, V.R.: Property-based Software Engineering Measurement. IEEE Transactions on Software Engineering 22(1), 68–86 (1996)
6. Capiluppi, A.: Models for the Evolution of OS Projects. In: Proceedings of the International Conference on Software Maintenance, Amsterdam, Netherlands, pp. 65–74 (2003)
7. Capiluppi, A., Lago, P., Morisio, M.: Evidences in the Evolution of OS Projects Through Changelog Analyses. In: Proceedings of the 3rd Workshop on Open Source Software Engineering, Portland, OR, USA, ICSE (2003)
8. Capiluppi, A., Morisio, M., Ramil, J.F.: Structural Analysis of Open Source Systems. In: Madhavji, N.H., Ramil, J.F., Perry, D. (eds.) Software Evolution and Feedback: Theory and Practice, pp. 207–222. Wiley, Chichester (2006)
9. Capiluppi, A., Morisio, M., Ramil, J.F.: The Evolution of Source Folder Structure in Actively Evolved Open Source Systems. In: Proceedings of the 10th International Software Metrics Symposium, pp. 2–13 (2004)
10. Carney, D.: Assembling Large Systems from COTS Components: Opportunities, Cautions, and Complexities. Technical report, SEI Monographs on the Use of Commercial Software in Government Systems (1997)
11. Ducasse, S., Lanza, M., Ponisio, L.: Butterflies: A visual Approach to Characterize Packages. In: Proceedings of the 11th International Software Metrics Symposium (2005)
12. Ellson, J., Gansner, E., Koutsofios, L., North, S.C., Woodhull, G.: Graphviz, Open Source Graph Drawing Tools (2002)
13. Fenton, N.E., Pfleeger, S.L.: Software Metrics: a Practical and Rigorous Approach. Thomson (1996)
14. Koch, S., Schneider, G.: Effort, Cooperation and Coordination in an Open Source Software Project: GNOME. Information Systems Journal 12(1), 27–42 (2002)
15. German, D.M.: Using Software Trails to Reconstruct the Evolution of Software. Journal of Software Maintenance and Evolution: Research and Practice 16(6), 367–384 (2004)
16. Godfrey, M.W., Tu, Q.: Evolution in Open Source Software: A Case Study. In: Proceedings of the International Conference on Software Maintenance, San Jose, CA, USA, pp. 131–142 (2000)
17. Gorton, I., Zhu, L.: Tool Support for Just-In-Time Architecture Reconstruction and Evaluation: an Experience Report. In: Proceedings of the 27th international conference on Software engineering, pp. 514–523 (2005)
18. Hofmeister, C., Nord, R., Soni, D.: Applied Software Architecture. Addison-Wesley, Reading (2000)
19. Kruchten, P.: The 4+1 View Model of Architecture. IEEE Software 12(5), 88–93 (1995)
20. Lang, B., Abramatic, J.F., Gonzalez-Barahona, J.M., Gomez, P., Pedersen, M.K.: GI 1975. In: Mühlbacher, J.R. (ed.) GI 1975. LNCS, vol. 34(12), p. 2. Springer, Heidelberg (1975)
21. Li, W., Henry, S.: Object-oriented Metrics that Predict Maintainability. Journal of Systems and Software 23(2), 111–122 (1993)
22. Llorens, J., Fuentes, J., Astudillo, H.: Incremental Software Reuse. In: Proceedings of the International Conference on Software Reuse, Torino, Italy, ICSR (2006)
23. Lungu, M., Lanza, M., Girba, T.: Package Patterns for Visual Architecture Recovery. In: Proceedings of the Conference on Software Maintenance and Reengineering, pp. 32–41 (2006)
24. Martin, R.C.: Agile Software Development, Principles, Patterns, and Practices. Prentice-Hall, Englewood Cliffs (2002)
25. Matsumoto, Y.: Some Experience in Promoting Reusable Software Presentation in Higher Abstraction Levels. IEEE Transactions on Software Engineering 12(1), 43–60 (2004)
26. McClure, C.: Software Reuse Techniques. Prentice-Hall, Englewood Cliffs (1997)
27. Medvidovic, N., Jakobac, V.: Using Software Evolution to Focus Architectural Recovery. Automated Software Engineering 13(2), 225–256 (2006)

28. Mockus, A., Fielding, R.T., Herbsleb, J.D.: Two Case Studies of Open Source Software Development: Apache and Mozilla. ACM Transactions on Software Engineering and Methodology 11(3), 309–346 (2002)
29. Mohagheghi, P., Conradi, R.: Different Aspects of Product Family Adoption. In: Proceedings of 5th International Workshop on Product Family Evolution, pp. 429–434 (2003)
30. Morisio, M., Ezran, M., Tully, C.: Success and Failure Factors in Software Reuse. IEEE Transactions on Software Engineering 28(4), 340–357 (2002)
31. Morisio, M., Seaman, C.B., Parra, A.T., Basili, V.R., Kraft, S.E., Condon, S.E.: Investigating and Improving a COTS-based Software Development. In: Proceedings of International Conference on Software Engineering, pp. 32–41 (2000)
32. Poulin, J.S.: Measuring Software Reuse: Principles, Practices, and Economic Models. Addison-Wesley Longman Publishing Co., Inc., Boston (1996)
33. Pressman, R.S.: Software Engineering: a Practitioner's Approach, 2nd edn. McGraw-Hill, Inc., New York (1986)
34. Senyard, A., Michlmayr, M.: How to Have a Successful Free Software Project. In: Proceedings of the 11th Asia-Pacific Software Engineering Conference, Busan, Korea, pp. 84–91. IEEE Computer Society, Los Alamitos (2004)
35. Stamelos, I., Angelis, L., Oikonomou, A., Bleris, G.L.: Code Quality Analysis in Open-Source Software Development. Information Systems Journal 12(1), 43–60 (2002)
36. Stevens, W.P., Myers, G.J., Constantine, L.L.: Structured Design. IBM Systems Journal 13, 115–139 (1974)
37. Torchiano, M., Morisio, M.: Overlooked Aspects of COTS-based Development. IEEE Software 21(2), 88–93 (2004)
38. Tu, Q., Godfrey, W.M.: The Build-Time Software Architecture View. In: Proceedings of 2001 International Conference on Software Maintenance, Florence, Italy, pp. 65–74. IEEE, Los Alamitos (2001)
39. Yu, L., Schach, S.R., Chen, K., Offutt, J.: Categorization of Common Coupling and Its Application to the Maintainability of the Linux Kernel. IEEE Transactions on Software Engineering 30(10), 43–60 (2004)

Conquering Fine-Grained Blends
of Design Patterns

L. Sabatucci[1], A. Garcia[2], N. Cacho[2], M. Cossentino[3], and S. Gaglio[1]

[1] Dip. Ingegneria Informatica, University of Palermo, Italy
`sabatucci@csai.unipa.it, gaglio@unipa.it`
[2] Computing Departement, Lancaster University, United Kingdom
`{a.garcia,n.cacho}@lancaster.ac.uk`
[3] ICAR-CNR, Consiglio Nazionale delle Ricerche, Palermo, Italy
`cossentino@pa.icar.cnr.it`

Abstract. The reuse of design patterns in realistic software systems is often a result of blending multiple pattern elements together rather than instantiating them in an isolated manner. The explicit description of pattern compositions is the key for (i) documenting the structure and the behavior of blended patterns and, (ii) more importantly, supporting the reuse of composite patterns across different software projects. In this context, this paper proposes a fine-grained composition language for describing varying blends of design patterns based on their structural and behavioural semantics. The reusability and expressiveness of the proposed language are assessed through its application to 32 compositions of GoF patterns recurrently appearing in three different case studies: the OpenOrb middleware, the JHotDraw and JUnit frameworks.

1 Introduction

Even though design patterns have been widely accepted by industrial and academic organizations, their definition and reuse still impose deep concerns on contemporary software engineers. The pivotal difficulty stems from the fact that pattern solutions are largely sensitive to different contexts where they are reused, especially on how they are combined with each other [1,5]. Patterns often need to be documented as pair-wise blends of patterns' responsibilities rather than as individual and intact entities [2,15]. This phenomenon has been recurrently identified in the design of product lines [8], middleware systems [6], and domain-specific frameworks [7].

Effective reuse of composite patterns is far from being trivial for several reasons. The symbiotic application of design patterns results in the intricate twine of pattern participants and the target application [13]. Pattern composites usually entail significant morphs of the original pattern solutions through the conjunction or merge of structural and behavioral elements. They should be systematically documented so that they can be unambiguously instantiated, traced and reused within and across software projects. The lack of explicit documentation for recurring compound patterns leads to design rationale being irrecoverable [3].

H. Mei (Ed.): ICSR 2008, LNCS 5030, pp. 294–305, 2008.
© Springer-Verlag Berlin Heidelberg 2008

In fact, pattern composition support has been recognized to be a key element for the usability of pattern languages and underlying development tools [4].

However, after twelve years the Gang-of-Four (GoF) pattern catalogue [11] has been published, effective support for documenting recurring composite patterns is still lacking. One of the main gaps is that pattern composition has been restricted to coarse-grained documentation approaches [19, 22] which do not address structural and behavioural blends of inner participant members [13]. Even though contemporary programming techniques, such as aspect-oriented programming [16] and subject-oriented programming [18], have brought advanced mechanisms for enabling improved pattern composability [14], empirical evidence shows that they do not scale much for coping with modular treatment of pattern composites [7, 12].

In this context, the contribution of this paper is twofold. First, a design approach is proposed for addressing varying forms of pattern blends (Section 2). We define a design language for describing fine-grained pattern compositions based on their structural and behavioral semantics. An expressive and simple set of operators is used for *unifying, conjoining, concealing* and *externalizing* pattern elements (Section 3). Second, the proposed approach is assessed through its application to different open source applications, the *OpenOrb* middleware, and the JHotDraw and JUnit frameworks (Section 4). Our analysis is based on the reuse and expressiveness evaluation of 32 GoF pattern compositions. We also discuss the novel features of our technique on the light of a comparison with existing work (Section 5). Some concluding remarks are reported in Section 6.

2 Defining Composable Patterns with POLaR

This section introduces POLaR (Pattern Ontology Language for Reuse), a design language for describing fine-grained pattern compositions based on their structural and behavioral semantics. The language encompass several phases of pattern reuse that are discussed in details in [20]. This paper is mainly focused on the operators that are provided for different categories of pattern blends (Section 2.1). In order to clearly illustrate these operators pattern definition constituents are discussed in Section 2.2.

2.1   Case Study: A Reflective Middleware

Figure 1 shows a design slice of an *OpenOrb*-compliant reflective middleware system [7] in which 21 classical design patterns [11] are used and combined to achieve the middleware requirements of customizability and adaptability [6]. A number of methods and attributes were omitted for simplification reasons. In Figure 1, each number represents a specific pattern, and these numbers are associated with methods and attributes in the ContreteBind class. The goal is to illustrate how various pattern realizations affect internal members of a single class. The attachment of a number implies that the respective method or attribute is part of the implementation of the corresponding pattern.

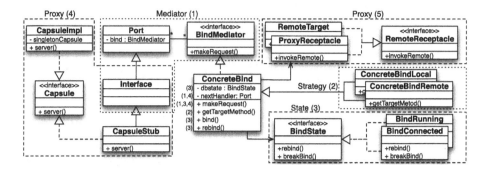

Fig. 1. Design slice of the OpenOrb middleware

For instance, the implementation of the *Mediator* pattern (represented by number 1) includes: (i) all methods defined in the Port, BindMediator, Interface classes and (ii) the attribute nextHandler and the method makeRequest in the class ContreteBind. As a result, a single pattern is blended with other four patterns (Figure 1): *State*, *Strategy*, and two instances of *Proxy*. Figure 1 is a mere representative example of the difficulty in understanding and reusing pattern compositions in realistic scenarios.

Pattern blends can be classified in two conservative and overlapping blends. A conservative combination maintains separate involved patterns by creating loose relationships among the elements. Pattern overlapping occurs when pattern elements are merged in a unifying structure. For instance, Figure 1 shows that the combination of *Proxy(5)* and *Mediator(1)* is conservative since it preserves an intact core structure of both the patterns, whereas the combination of *Proxy(4)* and *Mediator(1)* is an overlapping composition.

2.2   Static and Dynamic Pattern Constituents

The POLaR language is based on a set of constituents that can be combined in order to define the structure and the behavior of the pattern solution. The language syntax combines: (i) elements used to define the pattern, (ii) elements of the programming language for implementing the solution and (iii) elements of the system under development. We consider useful to introduce the definitions of these elements.

Pattern Description Element (PDE). Atomic constituent of patterns that describe the structure or the behavior of the solution. PSEs are: (i) participants, (ii) collaborators, (iii) events and (iv) actions.

Language Element (LE). Element of the programming language that is used for implementing the pattern. For example, Java includes: classes, attributes, methods, constructors, interfaces and the like.

Affected System Element (ASE). Element of the system that is influenced by the pattern application. A typical example of ASE is a business class that is assigned to a participant of the pattern.

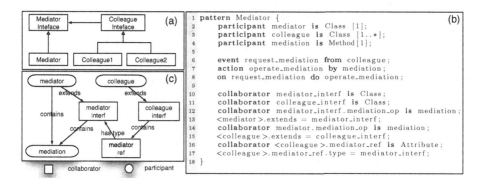

Fig. 2. Formalization of the *Mediator* pattern. (a) The classical structure from [11]. (b) A slice of code used to describe the solution. (c) pattern semantic description diagram.

The definition of patterns encompasses alternant levels of stability: some PDEs (Pattern Description Elements) are precisely described and do not require further details through the pattern instantiation, whereas some others are sketched and their concrete definition is delayed to the pattern instantiation phase. The latter means that the structure and behaviour of those pattern elements are volatile and their final definition depends on the application context and the other patterns to which they are going to be composed.

The description of the static structure comprises two PDEs: participant and collaborator. Both of them are used to assign responsibilities. The main difference is that a collaborator is a concrete element that will be added to the system, whereas a participant is only a placeholder for an ASE (Affected System Element). Both a participant and a collaborator own a type, which refers to a LE (Language Element).

Along this section the *Mediator* pattern [11] (Fig 2.a) is used to illustrate the pattern description language. The *Mediator* pattern description (Fig 2.b, lines 2-4) includes the colleague, the mediator classes and the mediation method as participants. Therefore, differently from role model approach, not only classes can be defined as participants: at line 4 in Fig 2.b, a participant method is defined. The type of a participant indicates what kind of ASE can be assigned to the participant. For instance the Interface class can be a colleague, the ConcreteBind class can be the mediator and the makeRequest method can realize the mediation. Participants are also marked with multiplicities (at the end of each expression) that are constraints for the number of ASEs allowed. In the example only one mediator and one mediation are allowed, whereas many colleagues may exist.

Several collaborators are part of the *Mediator* pattern (Fig 2.b, lines 10-12, 14 and 16). For example, the colleague_interf and the mediator_interf are two classes of the mediator structure that do not depend on the specific application context. During the pattern instantiation phase all the collaborator elements become elements of the system.

Fig 2.c shows the structure of the *Mediator* pattern solution as a typed graph. It is an UML class diagram where a graphical stereotype notation is used in order to obtain a concise description. Participants are shown by using ovals, whereas collaborators are shown by using boxes. Static relationships are used to connect these elements, thereby creating a graph. The diagram focuses on the relationships among participants and collaborators underlining the semantics that is behind the pattern and it is particularly useful in order to illustrate pattern blends in next section.

The description of the behavior of a pattern comprises two PDEs: events and actions. Their use allows for the behavioral description of the pattern semantics. An event encapsulates an abstract circumstance that is the cause of triggering a specific behavior, involving one or more static elements. The *Mediator* pattern description (Fig 2, line 6) includes an example of event definition. The request_mediation is an event that can be originated by a colleague. This event expresses the need of a colleague to communicate with another colleague.

An action encapsulates what happens when an event occurs. Actions are related to events by using cause-effect relationships. The *Mediator* pattern (Fig 2.b) the operate_mediation action is defined at line 7 and it is connected to the request_mediation event at line 8. Actions, as well as events, are abstract elements that require to be detailed in the pattern instantiation phase.

3   Operators for Pattern Composition

This section presents the operators for pattern composition based on the fine-grained pattern elements (Section 2). In general terms, the composition process between a couple of patterns *P1* and *P2* creates a new pattern *P3* that contains all the PDEs of *P1* and *P2*. Fig 3.c shows the result of the composition, before the use of any operators.

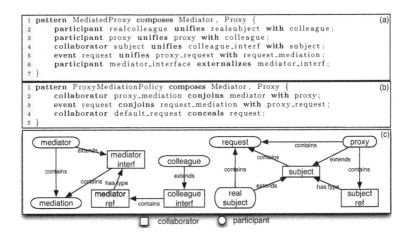

Fig. 3. Two compositions between *Mediator* and *Proxy*. (a) Code for the *Mediated-Proxy*. (b) Code for the *ProxyMediationPolicy*. (c) Composition diagram.

Along all this section we use two examples of composition between the *Mediator* and the *Proxy* patterns: the *MediatedProxy* and the *ProxyMediationPolicy*.

Figure 1 presents the *MediatedProxy* pattern obtained as a composition of *Proxy(4)* and *Mediator(1)*, that is used to implement the connection between the *proxy* and the *real subject* participants of the *Proxy* pattern. This is useful when in order to implement a flexible mechanism to define how *proxy* and *real subject* interact, thus avoiding the direct invocation. The *Mediator* pattern fits this requirement by assigning the responsibility of coordinating a set of colleagues to the mediator. Therefore, this blending requires the unification of some responsibilities of the two patterns: the *proxy* and *real subject* participants must also be colleagues that refer to the same *mediator*.

The *ProxyMediationPolicy* pattern, is a composition of *Proxy(5)* and *Mediator(1)*, (Figure 1). that uses a different approach in order to realize the coordination process encapsulated in the *mediator* participant. Here the mediator object (ConcreteBind) needs a RemoteTarget within its mediation process; these two objects are separated by using a *Proxy* pattern. The *mediator* participant only requires a reference to the *proxy* object thus the structure of the resulting pattern maintains unchanged both the *Mediator* and the *Proxy* original structures.

3.1   Static Pattern Blending

The static operators can be used in order to modify the structure of the pattern solution, represented by a graph in the static description diagram.

Static Unification. The unification operator is used to express overlapping compositions producing strong changes in the resulting pattern: the elements that are unified represent the pivot points for the overlap. The unification can be applied to two operands that must refer to the same PLE and the same LE. The new element will receive all the features of its originators, and these will no more be present in the structure.

Figure 4.a/b show two unifications of participants. The effect is the creation of two new participants, RealColleague and Proxy that get all the relationships that their originators prescribed in the original pattern description. The aim of these two unifications is to create a pattern with the characteristics of the *Proxy* pattern, where both the proxy and realsubject participants are also colleagues of a *Mediator* structure, so they can communicate by using a mediator.

When the unification is applied to two participants, the new participant has a multiplicity that is the intersection of the two original's ones. For instance the unification of a participant with multiplicity [0,2] with a participant [1,*] generates a participant [1,2]. Operations in Figure 4.a/b generate a composition problem when the pattern implementation target is an object-oriented programming language (even though it is easily realisable with aspect-oriented languages). After the unification, both the RealColleague and the Proxy are involved in a multiple inheritance. Therefore, the unification of the colleague_interf collaborator with the subject collaborator solves this problem. The effect of this operation is shown in Figure 4.c and the final structure of the *MediatedProxy* is shown in Figure 4.d.

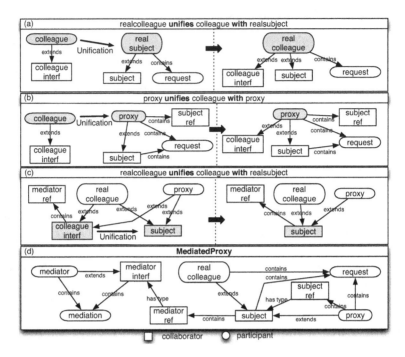

Fig. 4. Effects of the static unification in the *MediatedProxy* pattern. (a-b) Unification of participants. (c) Unification of collaborators. (d) Final structure for the *Mediated-Proxy* after the use of the operators.

Static Conjunction. The conjunction supports a conservative pattern blending. Only marginal changes are visible to the structure of the involved patterns, promoting the traceability of the involved PDEs. The operands continue to exist after the operation. The visible effect is the creation of a new element that is responsible for connecting the two ones in order to realize their collaboration. The language does not put any constraints on the nature of the two operands that is possible to conjoin. They can be indifferently participants or collaborators but syntactic rules of the programming language must be kept. Fo instance it is possible to conjoin a class with an attribute (it becomes an attribute of the class), but it is not possible to conjoin a method with an attribute.

Figure 5 illustrates the composition *ProxyMediationPolicy* that creates a synergy between the two patterns. This is obtained by conjoining the mediator with the proxy participants. The operator introduces a proxy_ref attribute in the mediator class, that refers to a proxy object. The new pattern has all the characteristics of a *Mediator*, which uses the *Proxy* inside the mediation process.

Externalization and Concealing. These two unary operators are conceived in order to modify the nature of collaborators and participants. The externalization is applicable only to a collaborator, changing it to a participant of the pattern. After this operation, ASEs can be assigned to the new participant. The twofold

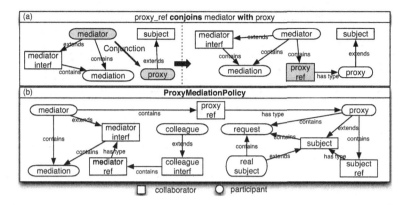

Fig. 5. Effects of the static conjunction in the *ProxyMediationPolicy* pattern. (a) Conjunction of participants. (b) Final structure for the pattern after the use of the operator.

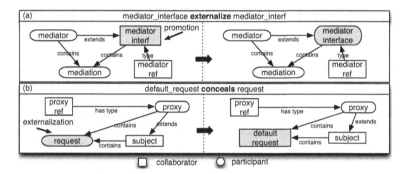

Fig. 6. (a) Effect of the externalization of a participant in the *MediatedProxy*. (b) Effect of the concealing of a collaborator in the *ProxyMediationPolicy*.

goal of externalization is to (i) allow for the unification of a collaborator with a participant, and (ii) delegate some responsibilities (originally delineated inside the pattern) to ASEs. An example of externalization is shown in Figure 6.a, where the operator is applied to the mediator_interf collaborator. The result is the creation of a new participant, named mediator_interface replacing the collaborator.

The concealing operator modifies the nature of a participant delegating its responsibilities to a collaborator of the structure. After the transformation, it becomes a fixed element of the structure and it does not requires further detailing, in the instantiation phase. The aims of concealing are to: (i) allow unification between a participant with a collaborator, and (ii) specialize the pattern, setting some responsibilities. An example of concealing is shown in Figure 6.b, where the operator is applied to the request participant with the introduction of a default_request collaborator. The latter is a method containing a standard code for executing the *proxy* request by the mediator.

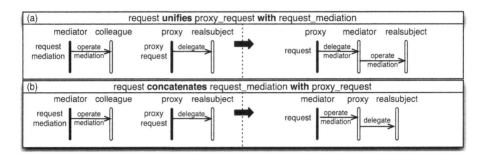

Fig. 7. (a) Effect of the event unification in the *MediatedProxy* pattern. (b) Effect of the event conjunction in the *ProxyMediationPolicy* pattern.

3.2 Dynamic Pattern Blending

Dynamic composition operators complete the language for pattern blends. Only two operators are contained in this category, the unification and the conjunction. Both of them work on pattern events, and as consequence, on their associated actions.

Event Unification. As already illustrated in Section 2, pattern description defines events and actions as expressions of the pattern behavior. The effect of unifying two events is the creation of a new event in the pattern, whereas the two original ones do not exist anymore. The new event is responsible to trigger all the events of its originators. This operation, therefore, produces a blend of the flows of actions related to the two involved patterns. After this blending, new actions can be added to the flow of events, and the order of execution of the existing ones can be rearranged according to new needs.

Figure 7.a shows an unification of events related to the *MediatedProxy* pattern: the request_mediation is unified with the proxy_request. The new pattern uses the *Mediator* logic to allow the communication between the proxy and the real-subject of the *Proxy* pattern. Therefore the delegate action is executed by using the operate_mediation. After the unification a new event request is the trigger for these actions.

Event Conjunction. As for the unification, the effect of the conjunction of two events is the creation of a new event in the pattern, whereas the two original ones do not exist anymore. The difference is that this operation maintains the flows of actions unchanged, treating them as atomic blocks of behavior. The new event is responsible to trigger the first flow of actions. The execution of the second flow of actions is triggered after the end of execution of the first one.

In Fig 7.b a conjunction of events (for the the *ProxyMediationPolicy* pattern) is shown: the request_mediation is concatenated to the proxy_request since the mediation algorithm of the *Mediator* uses a remote invocation encapsulated in the *Proxy*. Therefore the delegate action is executed as a consequence of the execution of the operate_mediation.

4   Evaluation and Lessons Learned

This section discusses some qualitative results obtained by the application of our pattern composition language to the three different case studies: OpenOrb [7], JHotDraw [9] and JUnit [10]. We have chosen these applications because they are from heterogeneous application domains and, as a result, the feasibility of our language constructs and composition operators can be assessed in different contexts. OpenOrb was already introduced and discussed in Section 2. JHotDraw is an open-source software conceived for drawing 2D graphics. It was built with a massive use of design patterns as exercise for demonstrating the reuse process. JUnit is an open source testing software written in Java. It encompasses a pattern-oriented framework design with variabilities for the organization of software tests and testing graphical interfaces.

The activities for the assessment of the language are: (i) analysis of the patterns and their blends from the three target systems; (ii) for each couple of interacting patterns we have analyzed motivations of their collaboration; and, (iii) we have analyzed how to aggregate responsibilities of these patterns by using our operators. Due to space constraints we can not report complete results of the assessment here, but we give some indications about the language expressiveness and pattern composition reusability. We have been able to represent 20 patterns from the GoF's catalogue and to combine them by using 30 pair-wise compositions, and 2 compositions involving more than two patterns. Finally we have instantiated 62 patterns (some of them more than once) in the OpenOrb case study.

We have observed that the expressiveness of our pattern blending language is widely related to the fine-grained nature of the composition operators (Section 3). In fact, the operators covered all the pattern compositions emerging in our three case studies, with some exceptional cases, for instance, in the *Chain of Responsibility* and *Facade* patterns. The problem in representing the *Chain of Responsibility* is related to the implicit relationship among the participants *predecessor* and *successor*. In instantiation phase, apart to assign the classes to these participants, it is necessary to specify the order of these classes in the chain. We are getting around this limitation by instantiating the pattern more than once, every time with only one *predecessor* and one *successor*. Therefore, we are also studying a way to delay the definition of some elements of the pattern in order to better handle these intricate scenarios.

We have also analyzed to what extent each pattern composition has been reused across the three case studies. The evidence of composition reuse was especially high thanks to the fact the analyzed case studies are from very different domains. The result of this experiment is that 13 over 32 pattern compositions have been reused in more than one case study. Two of these combinations, namely (*Adapter+Command* and *Command+Composite*), have been reused in all the three applications.

5   Related Work

Different approaches have been proposed for documenting pattern blends: role composition [19, 13], UML-based composition [22], temporal logic composition [17] and aspect-oriented composition [21, 6].

In [19] role diagrams are used for implementing and documenting object collaboration patterns. These roles are sensibly different from our participants, since only classes can play roles in these patterns, whereas every entity can be a participant (including methods and attributes). In [22] an UML approach for composing patterns is proposed. The main limitations of this work are: (i) this approach is suitable only for OO languages, and (ii) the UML approach is mainly focused on the static composition, whereas dynamic composition are not considered. Mikkonen [17] proposes a formal approach for composing patterns, which focuses on cooperation of behavioral layers. Their composition is based on one operator only: the multiple inheritance. The limitation is twofold: (i) the verbosity and heavyweight precision it requires in defining and combining the pattern elements, and (ii) multiple inheritance is considered difficult to handle in realistic contexts. In [21] a generic composition technique for merging dynamic structures is proposed that is based on state charts. The process considers the diagram meta-model in order to build a graph, to which it is possible to apply several transformations.

6   Conclusion and Future Work

This paper presented an innovative composition technique for describing blends of design patterns, based on their own static and dynamic semantics. The language has been conceived for dealing with heterogeneous pattern compositions, presenting a set of operators to manage different pattern blending styles. The peculiarity of the approach is the fine-grained level chosen for fronting with the composition of pattern elements in the resulting composite patterns. We have applied our approach in three real-life case studies, obtaining encouraging results in terms of reusability and expressiveness. Future work includes the refinement of a visual notation for representing the composition, and concluding our ongoing tool implementation for the pattern composition process.

References

1. Alexander, C., Ishikawa, S., Silverstein, M.: A Pattern Language. Center for Environmental Structure Series, vol. 2. Oxford University Press, New York (1977)
2. Basit, H.A., Jarzabek, S.: Detecting higher-level similarity patterns in programs. SIGSOFT Softw. Eng. Notes 30(5), 156–165 (2005)
3. Bosch, J.: Specifying frameworks and design patterns as architectural fragments. In: Proceedings of TOOLS 1998, p. 268. IEEE Computer Society, Los Alamitos (1998)
4. Budinsky, F.J., Finnie, M.A., Vlissides, J.M., Yu, P.S.: Automatic code generation from design patterns. IBM Syst. J. 35(2), 151–171 (1996)
5. Buschmann, F., Meunier, R.: A System of Patterns. ACM Press, Addison-Wesley Pub. Co., New York (1995)
6. Cacho, N., Batista, T., Garcia, A., Sant'Anna, C., Blair, G.: Improving modularity of reflective middleware with aspect-oriented programming. In: Proceedings of SEM 2006, pp. 31–38. ACM Press, New York (2006)

7. Cacho, N., Sant'Anna, C., Figueiredo, E., Garcia, A., Batista, T., Lucena, C.: Composing design patterns: a scalability study of aspect-oriented programming. In: Proceedings of AOSD 2006, pp. 109–121. ACM Press, New York (2006)
8. Clements, P., Northrop, L.: Software Product Lines: Practices and Patterns. Addison-Wesley, Reading (2002)
9. Gamma, E.: JHotDraw, HTTP (1998), `http://www.jhotdraw.org/`
10. Gamma, E., Beck, K.: JUnit, `http://www.junit.org`
11. Gamma, E., Helm, R., Johnson, R., Vlissides, J.: Design Patterns: Elements od Reusable Object-Oriented Software. Addison-Wesley Professional Computing Series. Addison-Wesley Publishing Company, New York (1995)
12. Garcia, A., Sant'Anna, C., Figueiredo, E., Kulesza, U., Lucena, C., von Staa, A.: Modularizing design patterns with aspects: a quantitative study. In: Proceedings of AOSD 2005, pp. 3–14. ACM Press, New York (2005)
13. Hammouda, I., Koskimies, K.: An approach for structural pattern composition. In: Proceedings of SC 2007, Braga, Portugal (March 2007)
14. Hannemann, J., Kiczales, G.: Design pattern implementation in java and aspectj. In: Proceedings of OOPSLA 2002, pp. 161–173. ACM Press, New York (2002)
15. Izurieta, C., Bieman, J.M.: How software designs decay: A pilot study of pattern evolution. In: 11th International Symposium on Empirical Software Engineering and Measurement, 2007 (ESEM), September 21,(2007)
16. Kiczales, G., Lamping, J., Mendhekar, A., Maeda, C., Lopes, C.V., Loingtier, J., Irwin, J.: Aspect-oriented programming. In: Aksit, M., Matsuoka, S. (eds.) ECOOP 1997. LNCS, vol. 1241. Springer, Heidelberg (1997)
17. Mikkonen, T.: Formalizing design patterns. In: Proceedings of ICSE 1998, Washington, DC, USA, pp. 115–124. IEEE Computer Society, Los Alamitos (1998)
18. Ossher, H., Kaplan, M., Harrison, W., Katz, A., Kruskal, V.: Subject-oriented composition rules. In: Proceedings of OOPSLA 1995, NY, USA, pp. 235–250. ACM Press, New York (1995)
19. Riehle, D.: Describing and composing patterns using role diagrams. In: Mätzel, K.-U., Frei, H.-P. (eds.) 1996 Ubilab Conference, Zürich, Germany, June 1996, pp. 137–152 (1996)
20. Sabatucci, L.: A Framework for Rapid Development of Multi-Agent System. PhD thesis, Dipartimento di Ingegneria Informatica, University of Palermo, Italy (2008)
21. Whittle, J., Moreira, A., Araújo, J., Jayarama, P., Elkhodary, A., Rabbi, R.: An expressive aspect composition language for uml state diagrams. In: Model Driven Engineering Languages and Systems, pp. 514–528 (2007)
22. Yacoub, S.M., Ammar, H.H.: Uml support for designing software systems as a composition of design patterns. In: Gogolla, M., Kobryn, C. (eds.) UML 2001. LNCS, vol. 2185, pp. 149–165. Springer, Heidelberg (2001)

Pattern-Based Transformation Rules for Developing Interaction Models of Access Control Systems

Dae-Kyoo Kim and Lunjin Lu

Department of Computer Science and Engineering
Oakland University, Rochester, MI 48309, USA
{kim2,l2lu}@oakland.edu

Abstract. This paper presents a set of transformation rules for transforming a non-secure interaction model to a secure interaction model using an access control pattern. The transformation rules resolve conflicts, uncertainties and type mismatches that may arise during pattern application. We demonstrate a case study using the Mandatory Access Control pattern and a defense messaging system in the military domain, and discuss about an analysis of the resulting model for pattern conformance.

1 Introduction

Access control provides integrity, confidentiality and availability of shared resources in a system. The development of an access control system involves high complexity due to the cross-cutting nature of access control. The complexity can be effectively managed by systematic use of access control models (e.g., see [2,4,10]) which describe a mechanism for governing access requests to shared resources at a high level of abstraction. We view an access control model as a design pattern that provides a generic solution for access control problems. This view promotes the reusability of an access control model and helps in detecting errors at earlier stages.

In this paper, we present a set of transformation rules for transforming a non-secure interaction model to a secure interaction model using an access control pattern. The transformation rules are used to resolve uncertainties, conflicts and type mismatches that may arise during pattern application. In our work, we describe interaction models in the Unified Modeling Language (UML) [7], a de facto standard language for modeling software systems, and access control patterns in the Role-Based Metamodeling Language (RBML) [5], a sub-language of the UML for precisely specifying design patterns. Use of precise specifications of access control patterns enables systematic reuse of access control patterns.

A major contribution of this paper is the transformation rules that 1) resolve uncertainties in determining the location to add pattern behavior in the model, 2) handle conflicts associated with operator fragments (e.g., *alt, break, opt*) in UML 2.0, and 3) address the problem of type mismatches where the type of a model element is different from that of its corresponding pattern element.

H. Mei (Ed.): ICSR 2008, LNCS 5030, pp. 306–317, 2008.

We demonstrate how the presented transformation rules can be used for transforming a model of a defense messaging system using the Mandatory Access Control (MAC) pattern [7]. The transformed model is analyzed for conformance to the applied pattern and the transformation rules. The remainder of the paper is organized as follows. Section 2 relates our work to other work. Section 3 describes an RBML specification of the behavior of the MAC pattern. Section 4 presents transformation rules. Section 5 demonstrates a case study using the technique, and Section 6 concludes the paper.

2   Related Work

Model transformation has gained great attention in aspect-oriented modeling [1,8,9] where cross-cutting concerns are modeled as design aspects separately from functional aspects. Clarke and Walker [1] proposed composition patterns to decompose and compose cross-cutting aspects based on subject-oriented techniques. The composition patterns are described in UML templates and composed with a functional model through parameter binding. Their work suffers from duplication problem [8] caused by one-to-one binding when a pattern is instantiated multiple times. The concept of roles in our work overcomes this limitation.

Reddy *et al.* [9] proposed a tag-based approach for composing sequence diagrams. Similar to Clarke and Walker's work, they use a variation of UML templates to design a cross-cutting behavior as a design aspect. The sequence diagram being composed can have two types of tags (simpleAspect and compositeAspect) that specify insertion points of the aspect in the model. A composite aspect includes position fragments (e.g., begin, end) which constrain the location of the fragment interactions that are added to the sequence diagram. Aspect parameters are bound to corresponding elements of the sequence diagram based on an implicit binding semantics. Their work has a similar limitation to Clark and Walker's work due to use of templates. The position fragments influenced the position directives in our work for designating insertion points.

Klein and Plouzeau [8] proposed a three-step approach for composing sequence diagrams. In the first step, the sequence diagram to be composed is decomposed into basic sequence diagrams which contain only sending and receiving messages and high-level sequence diagrams which contain fragment operators. In the second step, interface sequence diagrams that capture the common behaviors of the basic sequence diagrams are designed. In the third step, the designer determines if the pattern sequence diagram can be simply added into high-level sequence diagrams, or should be composed with the basic sequence diagrams. They accurately point out the problem of duplicate behaviors with templates when multiple instantiations are made. To address this issue, they use the interface sequence diagrams from the second step to exclude duplicate behaviors. However, use of interface sequence diagrams introduces places for potential errors and makes the composition process complicated. The concept of interface sequence diagrams is similar to the interaction patterns in our work in that they capture a common behavior.

3   Specifying Mandatory Access Control

Mandatory Access Control (MAC) is an access control model that governs access based on security levels [10]. We presented MAC as an access control pattern [7], and henceforth refer to MAC as the MAC pattern. The MAC pattern consists of the following concepts: *User, Subject, Object, Operation, Security Level, Category* and *Reference Monitor* [7]. *User* represents a user or a group of users who interact with the system. A user is assigned a hierarchical security level (e.g., SECRET, CONFIDENTIAL) and a non-hierarchical category (e.g., U.S., Allies). A user may have multiple login IDs which can be active simultaneously. A user may also create or delete one or more subjects. *Subject* represents a computer process which acts on behalf of the user to request an operation on the target object. *Object* represents any information resource in the system that can be accessed by user. Like a subject, an object is assigned a hierarchical security level and a non-hierarchical category. *Operation* is an action invoked by a subject to perform a task on the target object. *Security Level* represents a hierarchical classification assigned to users (subjects) and objects. *Category* represents any value from a non-hierarchical set. *Reference Monitor* checks the accessibility of the user by enforcing the following constraints. Given that $L(s)$ is the security level of a subject s and $L(o)$ is the security level of an object o:

- *Simple Security property*: A subject s can read an object o only if $L(s) \geq L(o)$.
- *Restricted *-property*: A subject s can write an object o only if $L(s) \leq L(o)$.

We use the Role-Based Metamodeling Language (RBML) [5] to specify the MAC pattern. RBML is a UML-based pattern specification language developed in our previous work [5] to precisely specify design patterns. The RBML defines a pattern in terms of roles which are played by UML model elements. Every role has a *base metaclass* in the UML metamodel and *metamodel-level constraints* which specialize the base metaclass to restrict the type of the model elements that can play the role. Every role has a realization multiplicity to constrain the number of elements playing the role. If the realization multiplicity is not specified, the default multiplicity *1..** is used requiring that there be at least one element playing the role.

Interaction Pattern Specifications (IPSs) are a type of RBML specifications capturing the interaction behavior of a pattern in a sequence diagram view. An IPS consists of lifeline roles and message roles whose base is the *Lifeline* metaclass and the *Message* metaclass in the UML metamodel. In the UML metamodel view, an IPS defines a specialization of the UML metamodel which characterizes a family of sequence diagrams. A member in the family is said to conform to the IPS [5]. A conforming sequence diagram must have lifelines that can play the lifeline roles in the IPS. A lifeline conforms to a lifeline role if the lifeline has messages whose sequence of incoming and outgoing messages is the same as that of the incoming and outgoing message roles on the lifeline role.

Figure 1 shows an IPS for the MAC pattern where roles are denoted by the symbol "|", and their base metaclass is shown implicitly by the graphical

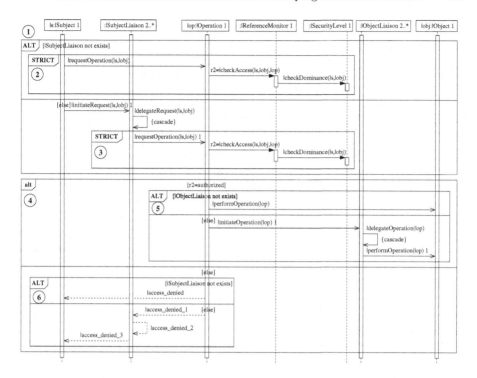

Fig. 1. MAC IPS

notation. The roles that have a realization multiplicity other than the default multiplicity *1..** are explicitly specified. The IPS shows use of two metamodel operators, **ALT** and **STRICT** which are defined in the RBML to constrain the structure of a conforming sequence diagram. The **ALT** operator is used to define alternative scenarios with a guard condition for conforming sequence diagrams. Only one scenario that satisfies the guard condition can appear in a conforming model. The **STRICT** operator preserves the message sequence in the fragment which should not to be disturbed by any other messages in a conforming model. This operator preserves a critical sequence of pattern behaviors. Note that these operators are different from the UML model operators (e.g., *alt*, *strict*) which design the behavior of objects at runtime. The RBML metamodel operators are distinguished in capital letters from UML model operators. An IPS may also have UML model operators as shown in Figure 1 (e.g., *alt*). Use of the *alt* operator requires a conforming model to have a corresponding operator that exhibits lifelines and messages that play the lifeline roles and message roles in the *alt* operator in the MAC IPS.

Given the notational background, the MAC IPS describes the following. A subject requests an operation with parameters including itself and the target object. There are two ways of sending the request as specified in the **ALT** fragment ①. One way is to send the request directly to the operation lifeline, and the other way is to send the request through subject liaisons which are intermediate lifelines delegating the request to the operation object. Only one scenario may appear in a conforming model. It should be noted that the |*SubjectLiaison* lifeline role and its associated message roles (|*initiateRequest()*, |*delegateRequest()*, |*requestOperation()*) are required only in the second scenario of the fragment ①. The message roles have the following dependencies:

- An |*initiateRequest()* operation requires a |*requestOperation()* operation.
- A |*delegateOperation()* operation requires a |*requestOperation()* operation.

The *cascade* constraint on the |*delegateRequest()* role specifies that an *initialRequest()* message is delegated through intermediate lifelines playing the |*:SubjectLiaison* lifeline role until a *requestOperation* message is invoked on the *op:Operation* lifeline. A lifeline role that has a *cascade* constraint must have a realization multiplicity with a lower bound greater than or equal to 2 so as to obtain a meaningful delegation as shown in the |*:SubjectLiaison* role. The request is checked for accessibility by the *checkDominance()* operation which enforces the *simple security property* and *restricted-* property*, as described in the **STRICT** fragments ② and ③. These fragments mandate the interaction sequences not to be interfered by any other interactions in a conforming model. The *alt* fragment ④ describes the authorized case and denied case. If the request is authorized, it can be sent directly to the target object or through object liaisons (intermediate lifelines delegating the requests) as specified in the **ALT** fragment ⑤. If the access is denied, the request is sent back to the subject, which is described in the **ALT** fragment ⑥. A conforming sequence diagram must have an *alt* fragment corresponding to the *alt* fragment ④ with the same relative sequence of interactions as specified in the fragment ④.

4   Transformation Rules

Pattern-based model transformation is a process of transforming a model using a design pattern to improve a certain quality of the system. During transformation, conflicts, uncertainties or type mismatches may occur. To handle these issues, we define the following rules:

Unmapped Message Roles (UMR). Given a mapping, the location of the mapped message roles in the model is automatically determined to be where the mapped messages are present. However, the location for unmapped roles may not be determined. For example, in Figure 2(a) while the location of the |*m1'()* role is determined at the mapped message *m1()* in the transformed model, the location for the unmapped role |*m2'()* is not determined. According to the IPS, an instance (*m2'()*) of the |*m2'()* must be placed after the *m1()* message playing the *m1'()* role. However, the sequence diagram has another message *m2()* after *m1()* which should be taken into account in determining the location of *m2'()*. In consideration of *m2()*, *m2'()* can be placed either before *m2()* or after *m2()*, which is nondeterministic.

To resolve such an uncertainty, we define two position directives, [(*message*|*message role*) **before** (*message*|*message role*)] and [(*message*|*message role*) **after**

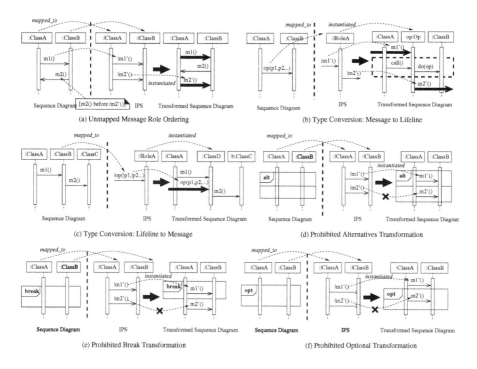

Fig. 2. Transformation Rules

(*message*|*message role*)] to designate a particular location for a message or a role instance. For example, [*a()* **before** |*b()*] stipulates that the message *a()* be placed immediately before an instance of the |*b()* role. Using position directives, the problem in Figure 2(a) can be resolved by specifying [*m2()* **before** |*m2'()*] which places the *m2()* message right before an instance of the |m2'() role (*m2'()*). Note that position constraints should not violate the pattern behavior. For example, having [|*m2'()* **before** *m1()*] would violate the pattern behavior due to the reverse sequence of the messages playing the |*m1'()* and |*m2'()* roles.

Type Mismatches (TM). Given a mapping, an element may be mapped to a role whose base is different from the type of the element. In such a case, a type conversion is required. A concrete example is found in the Visitor design pattern [3] where cross-cutting operations over an object structure are captured as visitor classes. In general, these operations are designed as operations, and use of the Visitor pattern requires transforming them to classes. To handle a message-to-lifeline type mismatch, we define the following rule:

Mapping a message op() *to a lifeline role* |:RoleA *creates a new lifeline* op:Op *(an instance) of the* |:RoleA *role and adds a* call() *message from the source lifeline of* op() *to the new lifeline* op:Op *and a* do() *message from the new lifeline* op:Op *to the target lifeline of* op().

Figure 2(b) illustrates the rule. In the figure, the *op()* message whose type is the *Message* metaclass is mapped to the *:|RoleA* role whose type is the *Lifeline* metaclass. This requires to transform the *op()* message to a lifeline (*op:Op*) that can play the *:|RoleA* role.

The TM rule reestablishes the interaction between the new lifeline *op:Op* and the source lifeline (*:ClassA*) and the target lifeline (*:ClassB*) of the *op()* message in the original sequence diagram using two auxiliary messages *call()* and *do()*. The *call()* message captures the operation call invoked by the source lifeline *:ClassA* and is added between the source lifeline *:ClassA* and the new lifeline *op:Op*. The *do()* message captures execution of the call on the target lifeline *:ClassB* and is added between the new lifeline *op:Op* and the target lifeline *:ClassB*. The *do()* message takes the new lifeline *:op:Op* as a parameter to execute it on the target lifeline *:ClassB*. There are two issues involved in a message-to-lifeline transformation. One is determining locations for the *call()* and the *do()* messages in the transformed model, which requires considering the message sequence in the sequence diagram and the sequence of the unmapped message roles in the IPS. To address this issue, we use the **before** and **after** directives presented in the UMR rule as follows:

$$op() \mapsto :|RoleA\ ([call()\ \textbf{after}\ |m1'()],[do()\ \textbf{before}\ |m2'()])$$

This constraint specifies that the *call()* operation must be placed immediately after an instance of the *m1'()* role, and the *do()* operation immediately before an instance of the *m2'()* role. If there are multiple instances of the *|m1'()* role, the **after** directive places the *call()* message after the last instance. Similarly, if there are multiple instances of *|m2'()*, the **before** directive places the *do()* message before the first instance. The *call()* and the *do()* messages may be specified to play the *|m1'()* and the *|m2'()* roles, respectively, as follows:

$$op() \mapsto :|RoleA\ ([call() \mapsto |m1'()],[do() \mapsto |m2'()])$$

In this case, the *|m1'()* and the *|m2'()* roles are not instantiated. If the message roles mapped to the *call()* and the *do()* messages involve parameter roles, they must be instantiated in the signature of the *call()* and the *do()* messages. The other issue to address is handling the parameters of the message being transformed. In Figure 2(b), the *op* message has two parameters (*p1, p2*). Since the message is transformed to a lifeline, the parameters of the message should be handled in some way. We assume that the parameters are transformed to attributes of the corresponding class of the new lifeline in the class diagram derived from the transformed sequence diagram (not shown in Figure 2(b)). This makes the parameters no longer expressive in the sequence diagram.

The opposite conversion from a lifeline to an operation is also possible. For example, a creator lifeline in a sequence diagram may be mapped to a creator message in a pattern (e.g., the Abstract Factory pattern [3]). To handle such a conversion, we define the following rule:

Mapping a lifeline :ClassA *to a message role* |op() *creates a new message* op() *(an instance) of the* |op() *role and a new lifeline* :ClassB *(an instance) of the target lifeline role of the* |op() *role, and redirects the incoming and outgoing messages of the* :ClassA *lifeline to the new lifeline* :ClassB.

Figure 2(c) illustrates the rule. In the figure, the *:ClassB* lifeline is mapped to the |*op()* message role. The transformation rule creates instances (*op()*, *:ClassD*) of the |*op()* role and its target lifeline role *:|RoleA*, and redirects the messages *m1()* and *m2()* of the *:ClassB* lifeline to the new lifeline *:ClassD*. However, the location of the *op()* message in the transformed sequence diagram is not determined yet. There are three places where the *op()* message can be placed: before *m1()*, after *m2*, in between *m1()* and *m2()*. To designate a location, the following constraint is defined, placing the *op()* message in the third option:

:ClassB ↦ |*op()* ([|*op()* **after** *m1()*],[|*op()* **before** *m2()*])

In a lifeline-to-message transformation, we assume that the properties of the lifeline become properties of the target lifeline of the transformed message.

Operator Fragments (OF). The model being transformed may have fragments of the **alt**, **break** and **opt** operators [11] whose execution depends on a guard condition. If a pattern behavior is composed with a fragment of these operators, the pattern behavior cannot be guaranteed to be executed because of the conditional execution. To prevent this, we define the following rules:

- **alt** Rule. An **alt** fragment describes alternative scenarios determined by a guard condition. If the pattern behavior is split into the two choices of an **alt** fragment, the pattern behavior exhibited in the unselected choice at runtime will not be executed. To prevent this, the following rule is defined:

  A pattern cannot be split into the alternatives in an **alt** *fragment.*

  Figure 2(d) shows a prohibited transformation for an *alt* fragment. In the figure, the *m1'()* instance of the |*m1'()* role is composed with the first choice of an **alt** fragment, while the (*m2'()* instance of the |*m2'()* role is composed with the second choice. This is invalid because either of *m1'()* or *m2'()* in the *alt* fragment will not be executed, which violates the pattern.
- **break** Rule. A **break** fragment describes a terminating scenario for the sequence diagram. If a pattern behavior is composed with a **break** fragment, the pattern behavior will not be executed if the guard condition of the fragment is false. To prevent this, the following rule is defined:

  A pattern cannot be split into a **break** *fragment and the normal scenarios (the scenarios outside of the* **break** *fragment).*

  Figure 2(e) shows a prohibited transformation for a **break** fragment. The transformation shows that the *m1'()* instance of the |*m1'()* role is composed with the **break** fragment while the *m2'()* instance of the |*m2'()* role is composed with the normal scenarios. This should be prohibited because *m2'()* cannot be executed when the **break** fragment is enabled or vice versa.
- **opt** Rule. An **opt** fragment describes a choice of behavior depending on a guard condition. An **opt** fragment is similar to a *break* fragment in terms of

structure, but does not require to break out the normal scenario. As a matter of fact, an option is semantically equivalent to an alternative fragment where the first choice has non-empty content and the second choice is empty [11]. A similar rule to the **break** rule is defined for **opt** fragments as follows:

*A pattern cannot be split into an **opt** fragment and the regular scenarios (the scenarios outside of the **opt** fragment).*

Figure 2(f) shows a prohibited transformation for an **opt** fragment. In the figure, the $(m1'())$ instance of the $|m1'()$ role is composed with the regular scenario, while the $(m2'())$ instance of the $|m2'()$ role is composed with an *opt* fragment. This violates the pattern because the $m2'()$ message will not be executed when the guard condition of the fragment is false.

5   A Case Study

We demonstrate the transformation rules using the MAC pattern applied to a defense messaging system (DMS) in the military domain. The DMS allows a user to create a new message, set up a sensitivity level for the message, and send and receive the message. Only an authorized and uniquely identified user can use the system. A sent message is sorted by the message sorter to identify the recipient. The recipient is checked for accessibility to the message based on MAC policies before receiving. If the sensitivity level of the recipient does not satisfy the sensitivity level set in the message, the recipient cannot receive the message, and the message is sent back to the sender. Every successful and erroneous transaction must be logged in persistence. In this case study, we assume that the security level of the message is same as the sender's. Figure 3 shows a sequence diagram describing sending a message without access control. We apply the MAC pattern to the sequence diagram based on the following mapping:

$(o:MsgSender \mapsto |s:|Subject)$, $(sendMsg\_1() \mapsto |initiateRequest())$,
$(:MsgSorter \mapsto :|SubjectLiaison)$, $(:Delivery \mapsto :|SubjectLiaison)$,
$(sendMsg\_2() \mapsto |delegateRequest())$, $(r:MsgRecipient \mapsto |obj:|Object)$,
$(sendMsg\_3() \mapsto |op:|Operation ([call() \mapsto |requestOperation()],[do() \mapsto |perform-Operation()]))$.

The mapping is given as input to the transformation algorithm [6] to evaluate conformance of the elements to the mapped roles by enforcing the metamodel-level constraints of the roles. If any nonconformance exists, the element is transformed to be conformant by the algorithm. The only metamodel-level constraint in the MAC IPS is the base metaclass which requires type matching. The only violating mapping of this constraint is $(sendMsg\_3() \mapsto |op:|Operation)$ where the type of $sendMsg\_3()$ is the *Message* metaclass, while the type of the $|op:|Operation$ role is the *Lifeline* metaclass. The transformation algorithm applies the TM rule to this pair to convert the type of $sendMsg\_3()$ to the *Lifeline* metaclass.

Applying the rule results in creation of a lifeline *op:sendMsg_3* and two messages *call()* and *do()*. The mappings of $(call() \mapsto |requestOperation())$ and $(do()$

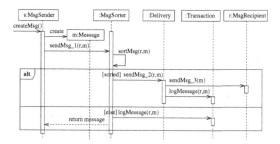

Fig. 3. Defense Messaging System

$\mapsto \lfloor performOperation()\rfloor$ require the parameter roles ($\lfloor s$, $\lfloor obj$, $\lfloor op$) of the *requestO-pration()* and *performOperation()* roles to be instantiated into the signature of the *call()* and *do()* messages.

The mapping determines which scenario in the **ALT** fragments ①, ⑤ and ⑥ in Figure 1 the DMS model should conform to. The mappings (*:MsgSorter* $\mapsto$ *:*$\lfloor SubjectLiaison$) and (*sendMsg_2()* $\mapsto$ $\lfloor delegateOperation()$) determine the second scenario in the **ALT** fragment ① which describes delegation of the request through subject liaisons. This also determines the second scenario in the fragment ⑥. Similarly, the mapping (*do()* $\mapsto$ $\lfloor performOperation()$) determines the first scenario in the **ALT** fragment ⑤ which describes sending the request directly to the target object. These require the DMS model to have message sequences conforming to the second scenario of the **ALT** fragment ① and the first scenario of the **ALT** fragment ⑤.

The unmapped roles (*:*$\lfloor ReferenceMonitor$, *:*$\lfloor SecurityLevel$, $\lfloor requestOperation()$, $\lfloor checkAccess()$, $\lfloor checkDominance()$, $\lfloor access\_denied\_1$, $\lfloor access\_denied\_2$, $\lfloor access\_denied\_3$) in the MAC IPS are instantiated to be added into the model. The UMR rule is applied to determine the location of the unmapped message roles in the transformed model. In Figure 1, the $\lfloor requestOperation()$, $\lfloor checkAccess()$ and $\lfloor checkDominance()$ roles are specified in a **STRICT** fragment which requires their sequence to be preserved. Thus, instances of the roles are treated as one block. The location of the block can be determined relative to the locations of the messages mapped to the $\lfloor delegateRequest()$ and $\lfloor performOperation()$ roles which are immediately before and after the block. The above mapping shows that the two roles are mapped to the *sendMsg_2()* message and the *do()* message, respectively. This determines that the instance block must be placed between the *sendMsg_2()* and the *do()* messages. The return message roles in the second scenario of the fragment ⑥ are instantiated according to the mapping for the $\lfloor s$:$\lfloor Subject$, *:*$\lfloor SubjectLiaison$ and $\lfloor op$:$\lfloor Operation$ roles. Note that the unmapped roles in the unselected scenario in ①, ⑤ and ⑥ should not be instantiated unless they participate in the selected scenario.

The DMS model has one **alt** fragment for which the OF rule should be applied. The OF rule prohibits the MAC IPS from being split into the two different scenarios in the **alt** fragment. Given the mapping and enforcement of the *UMR* rule, the OF rule is observed.

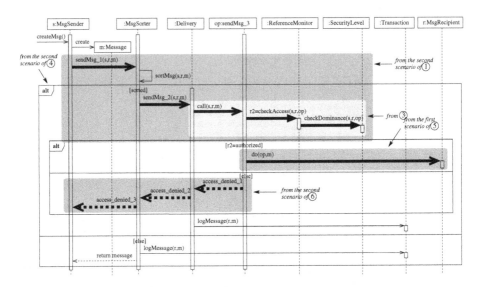

Fig. 4. Case 1: Defense Messaging System with MAC

Figure 4 shows the resulting sequence diagram where the pattern behaviors are highlighted. In the model, the MAC pattern intercepts the request from *Delivery* to the recipient to check dominance of the recipient's security level over the security level set on the message. If the recipient's security level is higher than the message's security level, the request is authorized, and the message is delivered to the recipient. Otherwise, the request is denied, and the message is sent back to the sender. The outer *alt* fragment is added by the **alt** fragment ④. The sequence of the *call()*, *checkAccess()* and *checkDomination()* messages in the outer *alt* fragment preserves the sequence in the *STRICT* fragment ③.

The transformed model should be checked for conformance to the pattern to ensure correct incorporation of the pattern behavior. We have conducted a conformance evaluation for the transformed model using logic programming. In the evaluation, we implemented the MAC pattern as a query and the transformed model as a logic program. The logic program is executed with the query to compute all feasible mappings by enforcing the conformance rules described in Section 4. The details of the approach are beyond the scope of this paper.

6   Conclusion

We have presented a set of transformation rules for developing interaction models using design patterns and demonstrated the application of the transformation rules via a defense messaging system and the MAC pattern. In addition to the case study presented in this paper, we have conducted two other case studies for a healthcare system and a database access system. The presented transformation rules are developed based on these case studies. We expect the rules to be extended as more case studies are conducted. A possible extension would be converting an operation parameter to a lifeline or vice versa. Rigorous transformation rules presented in this paper together with a precise RBML specification of an access control pattern provides a solid foundation for mechanical pattern application. Also, the metamodeling design of a pattern facilitates the development of a prototype. We are currently developing a prototype tool for the proposed technique. Such a tool would enable not only automatic pattern application, but also automatic rollback of an applied pattern when necessary.

Acknowledgements

This material is based upon work supported by the National Science Foundation under Grant No. CCF-0523101.

References

1. Clarke, S., Walker, R.: Composition Patterns: An Approach to Designing Reusable Aspects. In: Proceedings of International Conference on Software Engineering, Toronto, Canada, pp. 5–14 (2001)
2. Ferraiolo, D.F., Sandhu, R., Gavrila, S., Kuhn, D.R., Chandramouli, R.: Proposed NIST Standard for Role-Based Access Control. ACM Transactions on Information and Systems Security 4(3) (2001)
3. Gamma, E., Helm, R., Johnson, R., Vlissides, J.: Design Patterns: Elements of Reusable Object-Oriented Software. Addison-Wesley, Reading (1995)
4. Harrison, M.H., Ruzzo, W.L., Ullman, J.D.: Protection in Operating Systems. Communications of the ACM 19(8), 461–471 (1976)
5. Kim, D.: The Role-Based Metamodeling Language for Specifying Design Patterns. In: Taibi, T. (ed.) Design Pattern Formalization Techniques, pp. 183–205. Idea Group Inc. (2007)
6. Kim, D., Gokhale, P.: A Pattern-Based Technique for Developing UML Models of Access Control Systems. In: Proceedings of the 30th Annual International Computer Software and Applications Conference, Chigaco, IL, pp. 317–324. IEEE Computer Society Press, Los Alamitos (2006)
7. Kim, D., Mehta, P., Gokhal, P.: Describing Access Control Patterns Using Roles. In: Proceedings of Pattern Languages of Programming Conference (PLoP), Portland, OR (2006)
8. Klein, J., Plouzeau, N.: Transformation of Behavioral Models Based on Compositions of Sequence Diagrams. In: Proceedings of Model-Driven Architecture: Foundations and Applications 2004 (MDAFA), Linkoping, Sweden, p. 255 (2004)
9. Reddy, R., Solberg, A., France, R., Ghosh, S.: Composing Sequence Models using Tags. In: Proceedings of MoDELS workshop on Aspect Oriented Modeling, Genova, Italy (2006)
10. Sandhu, R., Samarati, P.: Access Control: Principles and Practice. IEEE Communications 32(9), 40–48 (1994)
11. The Object Management Group (OMG). Unified Modeling Language: Superstructure. Version 2.0 Formal/05-07-04, OMG (August 2005), http://www.omg.org

Balancing Quantification and Obliviousness
in the Design of Aspect-Oriented Frameworks

Linda Seiter

John Carroll University, Department of Mathematics and Computer Science
University Heights, Ohio, United States
lseiter@jcu.edu

Abstract. Aspect-oriented languages support modular programming by providing powerful referencing mechanisms that allow programmers to make quantified assertions about their programs. An aspect selects a set of program elements using a reference called a *pointcut*. An aspect also defines *advice methods* that transform the control flow surrounding the selected program elements. It is difficult, however, to define a reusable aspect when the advice methods require access to the local context of the program elements, as the bindings of the advice parameters may vary in each application. This leads to a breakdown of the modularity, quantification and obliviousness properties of aspect-oriented programming. This paper presents a model for modularizing the crosscutting references found in aspect-oriented frameworks. An extension to AspectJ is presented that utilizes Java annotations to implement polymorphic advice method parameters.

1 Introduction

Aspect-oriented programming (AOP) is a powerful mechanism for achieving software reuse, particularly when implementing *crosscutting* concerns. A concern is crosscutting if it is not easily encapsulated within a single object-oriented construct such as a class or a method. Filman and Friedman propose that the distinguishing feature of AOP is the ability to make quantified assertions about programs that were written by programmers oblivious to such assertions [3]. At a minimum they require that an aspect-oriented language supports the expression of statements of the form [3]:

In programs P, whenever condition C arises, perform action A.

Quantification involves the reuse of the functionality encapsulated in action A without requiring the programmer to explicitly list all of the places in program P where condition C arises. Thus, a quantified reference encapsulates a description of condition C in a single program expression. As an example, assume we wish to make the following global assertion:

In program P, whenever a constructor is called, record the call to a log file.

There may be many statements in program P that involve a constructor call. The condition "all constructor calls" is crosscutting in an object-oriented language since it can not be encapsulated in a single class, method or expression. An AOP language

H. Mei (Ed.): ICSR 2008, LNCS 5030, pp. 318–329, 2008.

such as AspectJ allows all such statements to be referenced by a *pointcut* [2]. The condition "all calls to a constructor" can be expressed by the pointcut:

$$call(*.new(..))$$

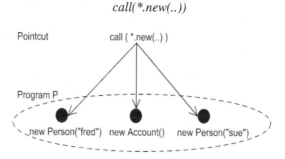

Fig. 1. Quantification: One to Many Binding

A pointcut describes one or more join points, which are points of execution in a program. The constructor calls in Figure 1 represent three separate join points. When a join point is reached during program execution, an aspect can specify code to execute before, after or in place of the join point, thus transforming the normal flow of control. In AspectJ, the control flow transformation is encapsulated in an *advice method* [2]. The pointcut describes the join points representing the condition C, while the advice method represents the action A to perform as each join point is reached. Quantification occurs when a pointcut describes a set of join points as in Figure 1. Obliviousness is preserved since the application source code does not directly reference the aspect code. It is the pointcut that establishes the reference to the application join points. However, consider the following situation:

In programs P, whenever condition C arises, perform action A with object O.

Specifically, action A must reference an object O that exists within the scope of a program element specified by condition C. In AOP terms, the advice method requires a reference to an object in the current join point scope. Object O may be referenced through a method parameter at one join point, or it may be referenced as the target of the method at another join point. The modularity of program P may be broken and the ability to make quantified assertions may be diminished when action A is not completely independent of the context in which condition C arises [11].

This paper presents a solution for supporting quantified, polymorphic references to join point contexts within AspectJ advice methods. Section 2 first illustrates the problem with an example framework. Section 3 demonstrates the use of Java annotations to support polymorphic aspect advice parameters, and discusses the tradeoff the programmer must consider in balancing the goal of aspect reuse with the goal of application-level obliviousness. Section 4 includes a discussion of related work. The paper concludes with a description of tool support for implementing polymorphic advice parameters.

2   Aspect-Oriented Framework for Thrashing Detection

Consider the design of a framework for detecting signs of thrashing in multi-agent swarm applications [10]. The framework is illustrated with two problem domains, vertex coloring and Sudoku puzzle, which are both abstractions of common resource allocation and scheduling problems.

In the vertex coloring problem, each vertex must have a color that differs from its adjacent vertices. The general case of vertex coloring for non-planar graphs is NP-Complete. The goal is to find the minimum number of colors required to color the graph. The Sudoku puzzle requires the digits 1 to 9 to appear exactly once in each column, each row, and each of the nine 3×3 blocks. The Sudoku puzzle problem is also intractable. The goal in a swarm application is to enable emergence, where a global solution to a complex problem arises out of the simple interactions of many agents. For vertex coloring, each vertex is an agent that checks for color conflicts with neighboring vertices. If a conflict exists, the vertex picks a new color. Partial solutions in the form of a conflict-free sub-graph will spread through the graph over the course of a simulation. However, the partial solutions dissolve when a vertex on the border of the conflict-free sub-graph changes its color due to a neighboring conflict. The color change may cause a new conflict with a neighboring vertex. This has a trickle effect that causes the dissolution of the partial solution. The frequent dissolution of partial solutions can be viewed as a sign of agent thrashing. Similar behavior arises in the Sudoku puzzle, where an agent is assigned to each cell, as well as other multi-agent applications.

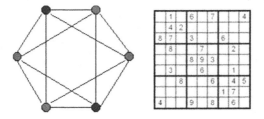

Fig. 2. Vertex Coloring and Sudoku Puzzle Problems

2.1 Stability Monitoring with Singleton Aspects

Thrashing detection and management is a crosscutting concern that can not be modularized in a single class. The first step to implementing this concern is to intercept the execution of the agent's conflict detection method in order to maintain a history of agent stability. This paper presents a simplified model for maintaining the history. It does not discuss conflict resolution and thrashing management. The framework implements the following global assertion:

When a conflict test occurs, update the agent's stability based on the result of the conflict test.

The condition is the execution of an agent's conflict test method. The action to perform is the update of the agent's stability. The action requires two references to objects that are in the local context of the test method: (1) the agent under test and (2) the result of the test. Each agent must be extended with state and behavior for monitoring its stability. Static crosscutting defines a set of changes to be made to a class [2]. It is depicted

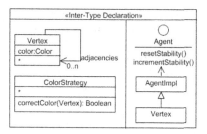

Fig. 3. Inter-Type Declaration Diagram for Vertex Stability Monitoring Aspect

visually in an Inter-Type Declaration Diagram (ITDD) [4]. Figure 3 contains an ITDD for an aspect that adds stability monitoring to the vertex coloring application. The left-hand side of the diagram shows the classes that will be altered, *Vertex* and *Color-Strategy*. The *ColorStrategy.correctColor* method detects color conflicts for the vertex parameter and returns a value indicating whether the vertex is conflict free. The right-hand side of the diagram describes how to transform the model using inter-type declarations, which add new fields, methods, super-classes or interfaces to a class [2]. The right-hand side introduces a new interface *Agent* and new class *AgentImpl* that realizes the interface. The *Vertex* class is altered by weaving in a new superclass *AgentImpl*, which adds state and behavior for recording stability.

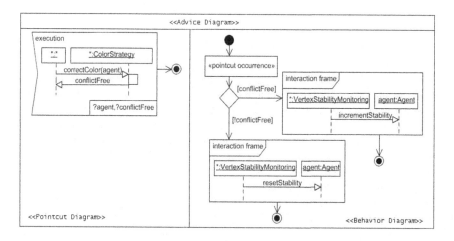

Fig. 4. Advice Diagram for Vertex Stability Monitoring Aspect

Dynamic crosscutting describes the changes made to the application's control flow and is depicted in an Advice Diagram. The left hand side of the Advice Diagram in Figure 4 declares a pointcut that will intercept the conflict detection method *ColorStrategy.correctColor*. The pointcut binds two variables at the join point: *agent* and *conflictFree*. The *agent* variable is bound to the vertex object that is passed as a parameter to *ColorStrategy.correctColor*. The *conflictFree* variable is bound to the boolean value that is returned from the method. The right hand side of the diagram in Figure 4 describes what happens when the method execution join point is reached. It updates agent stability based on the conflict test result.

```
@Aspect
public class VertexStabilityMonitoring {
  @DeclareParents(value="Vertex",
                  defaultImpl=AgentImpl.class)
  public Agent agent;

  @Pointcut("execution( args(agent) &&
          Boolean ColorStrategy.correctColor(Vertex))")
  void conflictTest(Agent agent) {}

  @AfterReturning (pointcut="conflictTest(agent)",
                  returning="conflictFree")
  public void afterConflictTest(Agent agent,
                                Boolean conflictFree){
    if (conflictFree)
      agent.incrementStability();
    else
      agent.resetStability();
  }
}
```

Fig. 5. AspectJ5 Implementation of Vertex Stability Monitoring Aspect

Figure 5 contains the AspectJ5 implementation of the stability monitoring aspect. AspectJ5 is an annotation-based version of AspectJ [2]. The *@DeclareParents* annotation performs static crosscutting by altering *Vertex* to subclass *AgentImpl* and to implement the *Agent* interface. The pointcut intercepts the *ColorStrategy.correctColor* method execution and binds the variable *agent* to the method's vertex parameter. This variable is then passed as a parameter to the *afterConflictTest()* advice method, which is executed after the *ColorStrategy.correctColor* method. Note that static crosscutting makes it possible for a *Vertex* object to be assigned to an *Agent* variable. The advice method's *conflictFree* parameter is bound to the value that was returned after execution of the *ColorStrategy.correctColor* method.

Figure 6 contains an aspect that implements stability monitoring for the Sudoku puzzle; the Advice Diagram is omitted. *SudokuCell.checkCell* tests if a cell's number is unique among the other cells in its row, column or block. The result is stored in the *isUnique* instance variable. Static crosscutting alters the *SudokuCell* class to extend *AgentImpl*. The pointcut captures the execution of *SudokuCell.checkCell*, binding *agent* to the method's self reference. While the aspect in Figure 5 was able to bind both advice parameters, the aspect in Figure 6 can only bind the *agent* parameter at the method execution join point. The result of the conflict test is stored in the instance variable *isUnique*, which is not accessible through a join point signature or return value. The binding of *conflictFree* is performed within the advice method body.

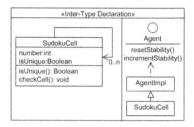

```
@Aspect
public class SudokuStabilityMonitoring {
  @DeclareParents(value="SudokuCell",
                  defaultImpl=AgentImpl.class)
  public Agent agent;

  @Pointcut("execution(void SudokuCell.checkCell())
            && this(agent)")
  void conflictTest(Agent agent) {}

  @AfterReturning(pointcut="conflictTest(agent)")
  public void afterConflictTest(Agent agent) {
    Boolean conflictFree=((SudokuCell)agent).isUnique();
    if (conflictFree)
      agent.incrementStability();
    else
      agent.resetStability();
  }
}
```

Fig. 6. Sudoku Stability Monitoring Aspect

2.2 An Aspect-Oriented Framework for Stability Monitoring

The aspects presented in Figures 5 and 6 both define a custom implementation for a particular swarm application. Each aspect binds a specific application class to its new super-class, defines a unique pointcut for referencing the conflict test method, and implements unique bindings for the variables used in the advice method. The aspects are examples of the singleton pattern and are not reusable. AOP frameworks are traditionally structured using the *template advice* design pattern [6]. A template advice method is implemented in an abstract aspect that defines an abstract pointcut. The advice method invokes abstract methods for the parts of the algorithm that vary.

Figure 7 contains an AOP framework for stability monitoring. The abstract aspect *StabilityMonitoring* contains a template advice method to update agent stability. The advice method supports the flexible binding of the agent and conflict result by invoking the abstract methods *getAgent* and *getResult*. Both methods take a reference to the join point as a parameter in order to allow join point specific bindings.

Figure 7 also contains a concrete aspect *VertexStabilityMonitoring* that extends the abstract aspect for the vertex coloring application. *VertexStabilityMonitoring* overrides the abstract pointcut to intercept the *ColorStrategy.correctColor* method execution. The concrete aspect also overrides the role binding methods *getAgent()* and *getResult( )*, which will be called from the inherited advice method upon execution of *ColorStrategy.correctColor*. *VertexStabilityMonitoring* also defines an inter-type declaration to extend the *Vertex* class. The Sudoku application would require the implementation of a separate concrete aspect, which is omitted.

```
@Aspect
public abstract class StabilityMonitoring {
  @Pointcut("")
  public abstract void conflictTest() {}

  @AfterReturning(pointcut="conflictTest()",
                  returning="jpReturn")
  public void afterConflictTest(JoinPoint jp,
                                Object jpReturn)  {
    Agent agent = getAgent(jp);
    Boolean conflictFree = getResult(jp,jpReturn);
    if (conflictFree)
      agent.incrementStability();
    else
      agent.resetStability();
  }
  public abstract Agent getAgent(Joinpoint jp);
  public abstract Boolean getResult(Joinpoint jp,
                                    Object jpReturn);
}

@Aspect
public class VertexStabilityMonitoring
            extends StabilityMonitoring {

  @DeclareParents(value="Vertex",
                  defaultImpl=AgentImpl.class)
  public Agent agent;

  @Override
  @Pointcut("execution(
          Boolean ColorStrategy.correctColor(Vertex))")
  public void conflictTest() {}

  @Override
  //bind to ColorStrategy.correctColor 1st parameter
  public Agent getAgent(Joinpoint jp)
  { return (Agent) jp.getArgs()[0]; }

  @Override
  //bind to ColorStrategy.correctColor return value
  public Boolean getResult(Joinpoint jp,
                           Object jpReturn)
  { return (Boolean) jpReturn; }
}
```

Fig. 7. AOP Framework Design for Stability Monitoring

The framework shown in Figure 7 demonstrates little improvement in code reuse. Each swarm application still requires a concrete aspect for the join point specific bindings. Figure 7 also demonstrates an issue involving the modularity and maintainability of AOP frameworks. Code is considered modular if it is textually local, if there is a well-defined interface that describes how it interacts with other components, and if the interface is an abstraction of the implementation in that it is possible to make changes to the implementation without violating the interface. The concrete *Vertex-StabilityMonitoring* aspect in Figure 7 violates these conditions. Its pointcut is fragile in that a change to the *ColorStrategy.correctColor* signature may require pointcut maintenance. The *agent* and *conflictFree* bindings are also fragile.

3   A Reusable Aspect-Oriented Component

This section presents an extension to the AspectJ5 language that supports the polymorphic binding of advice method parameters. The solution relies on Java annotations to serve as the interface between an aspect and an application.

```
@Retention(RetentionPolicy.RUNTIME)
@Target(ElementType.METHOD)
public @interface ConflictTest {
   String agent();
   String conflictFree();
}
```

Fig. 8. @ConflictTest annotation

```
public class Sudokuell {
   ...
   @ConflictTest(agent="this",
                 conflictFree="this.isUnique()")
   public void checkCell() { ... }
}
public  class ColorStrategy {
   ...
   @ConflictTest(agent="vertex",
                 conflictFree="return")
   public Boolean correctColor(Vertex vertex) { ... }
}
```

Fig. 9. Adding the @ConflictTest annotation to the application methods

The *@ConflictTest* annotation in Figure 8 modularizes the crosscutting references required for implementing stability monitoring. A Java annotation is similar to an interface in that it declares a set of method signatures. However, an annotation can be used to extend methods and other program elements with additional type information. The *@ConflictTest* annotation will be added to each conflict method. Its members will be assigned values to reference the agent and test result. Java restricts the return type of an annotation member to primitive types, String, Class, enumerations, or other annotations. Therefore, the *@ConflictTest* members will store a string to be evaluated at runtime using the join point's context to produce a reference to the agent and result.

Figure 9 demonstrates how to add the @ConflictTest annotation to a method. The object that represents the agent in the *SudokuCell.checkCell* method is accessible through the method self reference, thus the *agent* member is set to *"this"*. The result of the test is stored in the instance variable, the *conflictFree* member is therefore set to *"this.isUnique()"*. The agent in the *ColorStrategy.correctColor* method is referenced by the parameter, thus *agent* is set to *"vertex"*. The result of the test is returned out of the method, the *conflictFree* member is therefore assigned the value *"return"*.

```
@Aspect
public   class StabilityMonitoring {
  @Pointcut("execution (@ConflictTest * *.*(..))")
  void conflictTest () {}

  @AfterReturning(pointcut="conflictTest()",
                  returning="jpReturn")
  public void afterConflictTestExecution(
        @Mixin(AgentImpl.class)
        @AnnotationRef("ConflictTest.agent()")
        Agent agent,

        @AnnotationRef("ConflictTest.conflictFree()")
        Boolean conflictFree )   {

    if (conflictFree)
        agent.incrementStability();
    else
        agent.resetStability();
  }
}
```

Fig. 10. Reusable Stability Monitoring Aspect

Figure 10 contains the implementation of a single reusable aspect for stability monitoring. AspectJ5 supports join point matching based on Java annotations [2]. The pointcut captures the execution of all *@ConflictTest* annotated methods. However, the pointcut is still not powerful enough to bind the advice parameter, as the binding differs per join point. Figure 10 introduces two new annotations *@Mixin* and *@AnnotationRef* that extend AspectJ5 to support polymorphic advice parameters. *@AnnotationRef* dynamically binds an advice parameter by evaluating the annotation member at the join point. JEXL is a tool that evaluates a Java string within a given context [7], it can be used to evaluate the expression contained in the annotation in order to produce an object reference. The *@Mixin* annotation performs static crosscutting. Each object referenced by the *agent* parameter will be extended with the *AgentImpl* functionality.

Figure 11 depicts the quantified, polymorphic references utilized by the aspect. The pointcut binds to multiple *@ConflictTest* methods. The advice parameters bind to local context through different references per join point. The *@Mixin* annotation wraps multiple classes with new structure and behavior.

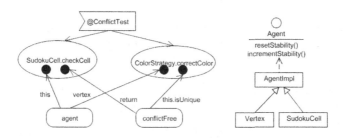

Fig. 11. Polymorphic context reference and role extension

What does it take to reuse this aspect in a new application? The programmer simply adds the *@ConflictTest* annotation to the appropriate application method. The annotation can either be added directly to the method as shown in Figure 9, or the annotation can be added by an aspect that contains annotation declarations, shown in Figure 12. The annotation declarations add the *@ConflictTest* annotation to the application methods without altering the application source code, thus supporting application-level obliviousness. However, modularity and maintainability are negatively impacted since the annotation declarations directly reference the application method signatures. The approach from Figure 9 is preferable. It may also require maintenance if the signature changes, however, the changes are local and potentially easier to automate.

```
declare @method :
public * SudokuCell.checkCell(..) :
@ConflictTest(agent="this", conflictFree="this.isUnique()");


declare @method :
public * ColorStrategy.correctColor(Vertex) :
@ConflictTest(agent="vertex", conflictFree="return");
```

Fig. 12. AspectJ Annotation Declaration

An additional question to consider is how the addition of the *@ConflictTest* annotation to an application method differs from making a direct call to a library method. First of all, the *@ConflictTest* annotation is part of the method signature rather than a method call in the method body. This allows the method body to remain consistent with implementing the primary application concern. The code related to the crosscutting concern is encapsulated as an annotation on the method signature, which makes crosscutting part of the explicit interface of the method. Note also that there may be numerous aspects that crosscut *@ConflictTest* annotated methods. Static crosscutting defined by the @*Mixin* annotation prevents typing issues that may arise with an explicit call to a library method. Finally, the crosscutting class model is not tangled into the primary class model and issues with multiple inheritance are avoided.

4 Related Work

Obliviousness was marketed as a key property when AOP was first proposed. It was argued that designers could develop a software component without requiring knowledge of how the component might be integrated with an aspect. However, the lessons learned by the software community over the past several years have shown that obliviousness does not necessarily improve the software development process and in fact may lead to programs that are difficult to develop, understand and evolve. Obliviousness prevents a programmer from understanding how simple program modifications may impact existing aspects, leading to inconsistencies during maintenance.

Several researchers have proposed the use of explicit crosscutting interfaces as a means of restoring modularity and reusability in AOP. Each proposal involves some reduction of obliviousness. Kiczales and Mezini propose aspect-aware interfaces to describe how aspects and non-aspects crosscut [8]. Aspect-aware interfaces update the traditional model of interfaces to include information concerning how a particular pointcut affects the class model. The approach computes aspect dependencies and shows the dependencies as annotations on the explicit interfaces of application methods that are crosscut by an aspect.

XPIs (Crosscut Programming Interfaces) represent another approach to improving modularity in AOP systems [5]. Their goal is to allow for separate and parallel evolution of aspects and advised code by decoupling aspect code from the unstable details of advised code. Unlike a regular interface that abstracts a procedure, an XPI abstracts a crosscutting behavior. The pointcut itself is abstracted to an XPI rather than embedded directly into an aspect. The XPI also defines *required* and *provided* obligations, thus serving as a contract between aspect and advised code.

Kulesza et al present a model for improving extensibility in frameworks through a mechanism called Extension Join Points (EJPs) [9]. EJPs define a contract between the framework classes and a set of aspects that extend the framework. The emphasis with EJPs is their use in documenting the hotspots in a framework, exposing a set of events for crosscutting composition and supporting the implementation of optional features in a framework through the definition of predefined execution points.

The model of polymorphic advice method parameters that has been presented in this paper goes beyond the approaches of aspect-aware interfaces, XPIs and EJPs to abstract not only the pointcut-related interfaces but also the context-related interfaces that are required by the aspect advice.

5 Conclusion

Aspect-oriented programming is a promising new technique for encapsulating crosscutting concerns. However, it can be challenging to implement aspect components that are adaptable to different application contexts. In this paper, Java annotations were presented as the adaptive connector between software components. The annotation serves to clearly define the boundary between the aspect and the application, across which control and data flow. AspectJ5 has been extended with two annotations, *@AnnotationRef* and *@Mixin*, which together support polymorphic advice parameters. This allows the programmer to develop aspects that are reusable in a variety of applications. The modularity of the aspect and application code is also improved when compared to a traditional AOP framework implementation. It can be argued that the direct addition of an annotation to an application method causes a reduction in application-level obliviousness. However, it also leads to the development of reusable, modular aspects.

Acknowledgements

Peter Kovacina, Matthew Kucera and Lester Eliazo developed an annotation processor to transform an aspect that contains *@AnnotationRef* bindings into one that utilizes JEXL to evaluate and bind the advice parameters. The tool also transforms an aspect that uses the *@Mixin* annotation into one that relies on wrapper objects to simulate the static crosscutting. These three outstanding undergraduate students were supported by a Huntington/Codrington Foundation scholarship.

References

1. Aldrich, J.: Open Modules: Modular Reasoning about Advice. In: Black, A.P. (ed.) ECOOP 2005. LNCS, vol. 3586, pp. 144–168. Springer, Heidelberg (2005)
2. AspectJ, http://www.eclipse.org/aspectj/
3. Filman, R., Friedman, D.: Aspect-Oriented Programming is Quantification and Obliviousness. In: Workshop on Advanced Separation of Concerns, OOPSLA 2000, ACM, New York (2000)
4. Grassi, W., Sindico, A.: UML Modeling of Static and Dynamic Aspects. In: Nierstrasz, O., Whittle, J., Harel, D., Reggio, G. (eds.) MoDELS 2006. LNCS, vol. 4199, Springer, Heidelberg (2006)
5. Griswold, W., Sullivan, K., Song, Y., Shonle, M., Tewari, N., Cai, Y., Rajan, H.: Modular Software Design with Crosscutting Interfaces. IEEE Software 23(1), 51–60 (2006)
6. Hanenberg, S., Schmidmeier, A.: Idioms for Building Software Frameworks in AspectJ. In: AOSD Workshop on Aspects, Components, and Patterns for Infrastructure Software (2003)
7. JEXL, http://commons.apache.org/jexl/
8. Kiczales, G., Mezini, M.: Aspect-oriented programming and modular reasoning. In: Proceedings of the 27th international Conference on Software Engineering, ICSE 2005, St. Louis, MO, USA, pp. 49–58. ACM, New York (2005)
9. Kulesza, U., Alves, V., Garcia, A., de Lucena, C., Borba, P.: Improving Extensibility of Object-Oriented Frameworks with Aspect-Oriented Programming. In: Morisio, M. (ed.) ICSR 2006. LNCS, vol. 4039, pp. 231–245. Springer, Heidelberg (2006)
10. Seiter, L., Palmer, D., Kirschenbaum, M.: An aspect-oriented approach for modeling self-organizing emergent structures. In: Proceedings of the 2006 international Workshop on Software Engineering For Large-Scale Multi-Agent Systems, SELMAS 2006, Shanghai, China, pp. 59–66. ACM, New York (2006)
11. Steimann, F.: The paradoxical success of aspect-oriented programming. SIGPLAN Not 41(10), 481–497 (2006)

Lightweight, Semi-automated Enactment of Pragmatic-Reuse Plans

Reid Holmes and Robert J. Walker

Laboratory for Software Modification Research
Department of Computer Science
University of Calgary
Calgary Alberta, Canada

Abstract. Reusing source code in a manner for which it has not been designed (which we term a *pragmatic-reuse task*) is traditionally regarded as poor practice. The unsystematic nature of these tasks increases the likelihood of a developer pursuing one that is infeasible or choosing not to pursue a feasible one. In previous work, we demonstrated that these risks can be mitigated by providing support to developers to help them systematically investigate and plan pragmatic-reuse tasks. But planning is only a small part of performing a pragmatic-reuse task; to enact a plan, the developer would have to manually extract the code they want to reuse and resolve any errors that arise from removing it from its originating system. This paper describes an approach that semi-automates the process of pragmatic-reuse plan enactment, automatically extracting the reused source code and resolving the majority of compilation errors for the developer through *lightweight* (i.e., computationally simple but analytically unsound) transformations. By reducing the number of low-level compilation issues (which are typically trivial but copious) that the developer must resolve, they are able to focus on the higher-level semantic and conceptual issues that are the main barrier to the successful completion of the reuse task. The efficacy of our approach to save developer effort is evaluated in a small-scale, controlled experiment on non-trivial pragmatic-reuse tasks. We find that our approach improves the likelihood of a pragmatic reuse task being successful, and decreases the time required to complete these tasks, as compared to a manual enactment approach.

Keywords: Pragmatic software reuse, lightweight source code transformations.

1 Introduction

As developers write code, they encounter situations where the functionality they are developing is familiar to them; either they have developed something similar before, or they know of some existing software that provides similar functionality [1]. Unfortunately, the existing functionality is often not designed in a way that permits its reuse in a black-box manner (e.g., as a framework, component, or product line) [2]. The developer is then left with few choices: re-implement the functionality, which is expensive and does not leverage existing mature code; re-modularize the existing code, which can be expensive and may not make sense for the original system; or to reuse the existing code in an

H. Mei (Ed.): ICSR 2008, LNCS 5030, pp. 330–342, 2008.

ad hoc copy-and-modify process, which can lead to poor decisions being made [3,4]. Copy-and-modify is often the *pragmatic* choice for software reuse in real scenarios.

Industrial developers undertake pragmatic-reuse tasks as a means to save time and leverage the testing effort put into existing source code; however, traditional approaches to pragmatic reuse can lead the developer to make poor decisions: they can commit too early to completing infeasible tasks; or they can avoid feasible reuse tasks due solely to superficial complexities. In previous research we addressed the shortcomings of traditional pragmatic-reuse approaches by supporting a lightweight means for simultaneously investigating and planning pragmatic-reuse tasks [5]. While planning can greatly increase the developer's comprehension of a pragmatic-reuse task, a plan remains an abstract artifact; for a plan to be useful, it must be followed ("enacted") to successfully complete the pragmatic-reuse task. Without tool support to enact pragmatic-reuse plans, three shortcomings remain: (1) the developer has to manually locate and integrate reused source code; (2) the abundance of low-level compiler errors during integration can obscure more complex high-level semantic and conceptual issues; and (3) investigating different options in the reuse plan can be expensive due to the costs of repeatedly manually modifying the source code.

Previous research has examined means for automatically or semi-automatically making adaptive modifications to source code. Much research requires that the source being adapted must be designed for reuse [6,7,8,9] or at least be compilable before adaptation [10,11]; these requirements are not met in pragmatic-reuse scenarios. Some work has considered means for automatic adaptation, but requires that the adapted entities be formally specified [12,13]; such formal specifications are not typically available in pragmatic-reuse contexts.

While pragmatic-reuse plans can help the developer to understand the reuse task at a high-level, it removes him from the realities of the source code; without enacting the plan it is difficult to tell if a decision in the plan makes the reuse task infeasible. To reduce the effort needed to enact a pragmatic-reuse plan, we have designed an approach for the semi-automatic enactment of these plans. Key to our approach is the application of lightweight (i.e., computationally simple but analytically unsound) transformations to the reused source code. We have implemented this approach in a tool called Procrustes[1], a plug-in to the Eclipse integrated development environment (IDE)[2]. Procrustes copies the code to be reused to the developer's project, and then modifies the code to be reused to minimize the number of dangling references the developer must inspect and correct; dangling references that cannot be transformed easily are flagged for the developer's attention. By semi-automating the enactment phase, the developer can instantly receive feedback on the implications of the plan and focus on the higher-level semantic problems that may inhibit the reuse task. This feedback loop makes it practical to quickly consider alternative decisions for a particular reuse task, thereby allowing the developer to create a higher-quality result.

We have performed an initial evaluation of our approach through two investigations into pragmatic-reuse tasks on two medium- to large-scale systems: a comparative case

---

[1] The name comes from a figure in Greek mythology who would invite passersby to lie in a bed, whereupon he would force them to fit by stretching or amputation.

[2] http://eclipse.org (v3.2.1).

study to determine the minimum necessary effort for these tasks; and a controlled experiment involving 8 developers enacting pragmatic-reuse plans manually and with our semi-automated approach.

The remainder of the paper is structured as follows. Section 2 provides additional background about pragmatic-reuse plans. Section 3 describes our lightweight approach for semi-automating the enactment of pragmatic-reuse plans. Related work is considered in Section 4. Our evaluation is presented in Section 5. Remaining issues are discussed in Section 6.

Our previous work contributed a method for investigating and planning pragmatic-reuse tasks. In contrast, this paper contributes a lightweight approach for the semi-automatic enactment of pragmatic-reuse plans; this is evaluated by comparing the success rates of pragmatic-reuse tasks with and without our lightweight approach.

2   Background: Pragmatic-Reuse Plans

Developers currently perform pragmatic reuse tasks manually. They identify some fragment of source code they want to reuse and integrate with their project. They then successively traverse through compilation errors that have arisen and resolve them one at a time (integrating more code as necessary). Unfortunately, for large reuse tasks it is difficult to tell at the outset if the task will be successful. We introduced the concept of the pragmatic-reuse plan to help developers understand the scope of pragmatic-reuse tasks before the investment of integrating the reused code [5].

A pragmatic-reuse plan consists of a list of tagged program elements. Classes, methods, and fields can be marked as as **accepted** ("I want to reuse this code"), **rejected** ("I don't want to reuse this code"), or **remapped** ("I want to redirect dependencies on this code to be on something within my own system"). Special cases exist for **injecting** code into classes and **extracting** fields by reusing only specific fields from a class.

3   Procrustes: Semi-automating Enactment

Procrustes bridges the gap between the conceptual intent of a pragmatic-reuse plan and the realization of the task. To do this, Procrustes copies the source code fragments that the developer intends to reuse from the originating project into the target project (see Section 3.1) according to the pragmatic-reuse plan. Using the plan, Procrustes integrates the reused code with the target project by resolving the dangling references that arose from removing the code from its originating environment (see Section 3.2).

3.1   Extraction

After the developer activates Procrustes (by pressing the "enact plan" button in the IDE), it locates all of the source code corresponding to accepted nodes in the reuse plan and first copies this code into the target project. The original package hierarchy is maintained within the extracted code, for ease of comprehension.

After Procrustes has copied the code into the target project, dependencies between the reused classes will remain valid as the package structure was maintained. Any dependencies to structural entities outside those being reused would normally cause compilation problems; however, the integration portion of Procrustes resolves many of these (see Section 3.2).

3.2 Integration

During this phase, the source code that has been migrated from the original system to the target system must be manipulated to resolve any compilation problems that have arisen. When source code is removed from the context for which it was written and placed into a foreign environment, many of its dependencies can be unfulfilled. The unfulfilled dependencies in the reused code are manifested as dangling references to classes, methods, and fields that were not reused (and do not exist in the target project).

Using the model that represents the pragmatic-reuse plan, Procrustes can pre-compute each of the changes that the tool should perform to repair many dangling references. The integration process proceeds in four main steps:

Managing Source Code Additions. The code addition step adds new code to those entities previously migrated to the target project in Section 3.1. There are two cases that must be handled: code injection, and field extraction. For code injection, any fragment provided by the developer is inserted into its target class (as specified in the reuse plan).

For field extraction, any fields in the plan that have been marked for extraction are copied from the class in which they were declared into the target class specified in the pragmatic-reuse plan. Moving the field only updates its declaration, not its references in the reused code (this happens in the next step). Again, the import statements are also updated to reflect this addition to the target class.

Managing Dangling References. The management of dangling references is the most complex step in the integration phase. Two primary classifications of dangling references are managed: (1) references to fields, calls to methods, and references to super-types that were rejected in the reuse plan; and (2) calls to methods and referenced fields that have been injected, extracted, or remapped in the reuse plan.

Procrustes searches each accepted source element for dependencies on other elements that have been rejected. If a dependency on a rejected field or method is found, it is managed by commenting-out the entire statement containing code corresponding to the dependency within the accepted code. Procrustes comments-out rejected dependencies, rather than remove them completely, rather than remove them completely, as their details could still be informative to the developer. These comments are accompanied with a tag to indicate that the change was made by Procrustes. This also allows the developer to easily locate each change to the source made by Procrustes using traditional search tools. For the sake of simplicity, Procrustes rejects field references and method calls only at the statement level; despite the inherently unsound nature of such a lightweight approach to transformations, in practice we have found it to be effective (Section 5).

If the pragmatic-reuse plan has reused a class but not some subset of its supertypes, the tool must remove references to those supertypes. This often occurs as developers trim the functionality they are interested in from an inheritance hierarchy. Any number of supertypes can be removed. If the subclass was dependent on a method within a rejected supertype this would be shown as a dependency between a method in the subtype and a method on the supertype during the planning process. This dependency would have been resolved at the beginning of this step.

Finally, any accepted element with a structural dependency that has been remapped is handled. These cases are simpler than in the rejected-element case as code does not disappear; it is simply redirected. This step handles 5 cases: calls to injected and remapped methods and references to injected, extracted, and remapped fields.

Managing Unnecessary Code. This step removes methods and fields marked as rejected in the reuse plan that are declared within accepted classes and interfaces. For code readability, rejected fields and methods are completely removed from the source code by removing them from their containing class, rather than just being commented out. The tool only needs to remove methods and fields that are children of classes that have been accepted, i.e., if a type is completely rejected or remapped Procrustes does not need to delete any code as it would not have been integrated to the target system.

Finalizing Source Code Modifications. Each of the changes made by the three previous steps were made to an intermediate representation of the code, not directly to its text. This separation minimizes the chances that one change will cause another alteration to fail. After all the steps are complete, Procrustes applies the changes to the files and writes them to disk, collecting statistics about the scope of the changes it has made.

3.3   Implementation

Procrustes is implemented as an Eclipse plug-in. By creating the tool as a plug-in we are able to leverage many of the features that Eclipse provides for parsing, compiling, and manipulating Java files. Each of the nodes in the reuse plan matches a specific structural element in Eclipse's Java abstract syntax tree (AST). All of our changes are recorded using the Eclipse `ASTRewrite` class. This class aggregates the changes made during each of the steps of the integration phase; the source files are all changed and written to disk only at the end of this phase.

4   Related Work

Previous work in a variety of areas bears similarity to the problem we address; however, none meets all the requirements for (semi-) automating the enactment of pragmatic-reuse plans.

Most reuse literature emphasizes designing for reuse, for example, in object-oriented programming [14], frame-based reuse [7], domain-specific language-based approaches [6], and component-based approaches [8,9]. Such approaches are inappropriate in our context, as pragmatic reuse entails situations where the original design did not anticipate the desired reuse scenario.

Transformation-based approaches to reuse were prevalent in the 1980s, for example, that of Feather [10]. Such approaches were based on the notion of formally correct refinement, thus requiring compilable programs and (usually) formal specifications; neither is available in our context. Jackson and Rinard recognize the continuing value of unsound analyses [15], for both their usefulness and ease of efficient implementation.

Several systems have been developed to identify reusable components. Lanubile and Visaggio developed a technique based on program slicing to identify reusable source code [16]. The CARE system [17] identifies and extracts reusable components using a metrics-based approach; the applicable components must have no or few external dependencies. These systems do not allow the developer to specify which detailed entities are to be reused, or how to deal with problematic dependencies.

Various approaches attempt to adapt code for use in a novel context. The Adapter object-oriented design pattern [11] adapts classes or objects to conform to a required interface, but maintains all the dependencies of the original classes or objects; in our context, we need to be able to eliminate or replace such dependencies. Approaches like that of Gouda and Herman [12] and of Yellin and Strom [13] automatically adapt components to new contexts; however, they require complete, formal specifications to operate that are not typically available or appropriate for pragmatic-reuse tasks.

5   Evaluation

The intent of our approach is to greatly reduce the effort required to enact a pragmatic-reuse plan. By reducing this effort, developers can better judge the merits of their reuse tasks to maximize their chances of having desirable outcomes. To evaluate Procrustes we set out to answer two questions: (1) How much effort can semi-automating the enactment of pragmatic-reuse plans save developers? (2) Does semi-automating the enactment of pragmatic-reuse plans affect the outcomes of pragmatic-reuse tasks performed by developers? Each question was addressed with its own evaluation.

In both evaluations, "completion" was defined as the successful execution of a test suite that we provided for the purpose. One test suite was implemented as an Eclipse plug-in, while the other was a standalone application; we henceforth refer to both as test harnesses.

5.1   Task Descriptions

Both evaluations used the same two tasks. Each of these tasks involved extracting specific functionality from an existing system and integrating it into a new system. Each task operated on a different open-source Java system from a different domain.

Metrics Lines-of-Code Calculator. The Metrics Eclipse plug-in[3] can compute 23 different metrics (e.g., lines of code, cyclomatic complexity, efferent coupling, etc.) for resources inside Eclipse projects. This plug-in contains 229 classes comprising 14.5 thousand lines-of-code (kLOC). The goal of this task was to reuse the lines-of-code (LOC) calculator from this project; however, the system was not designed to enable individual metrics to be reused without the remainder of the Metrics plug-in.

The reuse plan for this task involved reusing portions of 8 classes. Successful completion of this task involved reusing 392 LOC. For the task to be a success, the reused code had to compute the LOC for every class in every project in the Eclipse workspace when activated by the test harness.

---

[3] http://metrics.sf.net v1.3.6.

Azureus Network Throughput View. Azureus[4] is a client application for the Bit-Torrent peer-to-peer file-sharing protocol. Azureus contains 2,257 classes comprising 221 kLOC. It contains a view that visualizes its network throughput for the user. The goal of this task is to extract this network throughput view from Azureus and integrate it into a new system. This feature was not designed to be reused outside of Azureus.

The reuse plan for this task involved reusing portions of 6 classes. Successful completion of this task involved reusing 366 LOC. To succeed at the task, the reused code had to be able to correctly display a data set provided in the test harness.

5.2   Analysis of Minimum Required Effort

Our first evaluation considered how much effort Procrustes can save a developer by semi-automating the enactment of a pragmatic-reuse plan. We performed both tasks both manually and using Procrustes. The number of compilation errors present after copying all of the required code (in the manual case) or pressing the "enact plan" button in the Procrustes-supported case is given in Table 1. These numbers are the first indicator to the developer of the amount of work facing them before they can complete the task.

Table 1. Compilation errors for each task and treatment

Case	Procrustes	Manual	Error reduction
Metrics	3	62	95.2%
Azureus	11	32	65.6%

Compilation errors alone are not always a good indicator of required effort. Often, making one small change in the source code can remedy (or create) several errors. To get a true sense of the minimum amount of effort the developer would need to expend to successfully complete each reuse task, we investigated each task in terms of "edits". An edit represents a single conceptual change the developer makes to the source code. The minimum number of edits required to successfully complete each task with each treatment is given in Table 2.

Table 2. "Edits" required for each task and treatment

Case	Procrustes	Manual	Edit reduction
Metrics	2	60	96.7%
Azureus	4	25	84.0%

Some edits require more thought and investigation on the part of the developer to resolve than others. These difficult edits arise due to conceptual mismatches between the original and target systems [2]. For the Metrics task, only one of the edits represented a conceptual mismatch that arose from removing the reused code from the system for which it was designed. Three edits in the Azureus task represented conceptual mismatches; these were common between the two treatments. While Procrustes does not

---

[4] http://azureus.sf.net v2.4.0.1.

resolve any of the conceptual mismatch errors, it helps the developer to quickly identify them by resolving all of the trivial compilation errors that occlude them. This difference is especially evident when a developer repeatedly iterates on a reuse plan.

5.3 Task Effectiveness Experiment

Our second investigation sought to determine if developers performing pragmatic-reuse tasks had better outcomes using Procrustes. We performed a controlled experiment with eight developers. Four of these were industrial developers (I1 through I4) and four were software engineering graduate students (G1 through G4). The participants had between 6 years (an industrial developer) and 12 years of experience (also an industrial developer). Each participant was randomly assigned a task–treatment pairing. Each task–treatment pairing was completed by two graduate students and two industrial developers. Each participant used Procrustes for one task and performed the other task manually. We created a reuse plan for each task and provided identical versions for each treatment. A time limit of one hour was set for each task; we chose this time limit as it seemed like a reasonable amount of time for a developer to invest in this kind of task. We recorded whether or not the participants succeeded or failed for each task, how long they spent performing the task, and collected their final code for later analysis. After completing both tasks the participants completed a follow-up questionnaire (see the website cited earlier for details).

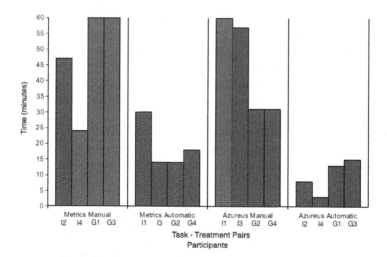

Fig. 1. Results of the task effectiveness experiment. Green/hatched bars indicate success. Red/solid bars indicate failure.

The results of the experiment are shown in Figure 1. The figure depicts successful task–treatment pairings in green (diagonal hatching in greyscale). Those task–treatment pairings that were failures are indicated in red (solid in greyscale). The graph clearly shows that the participants successfully completed more tasks using Procrustes (8 out of 8) than with the manual treatment (4 out of 8). It is also clear that, for these tasks, developers were able to complete the tasks in less time using Procrustes than when undertaking them manually.

Manual Treatment. The four participants who manually enacted the Metrics LOC reuse task were the least successful. By examining their resulting code and reading their comments in the questionnaire, it became clear that they knew they had a problem to fix, but they did not know where this problem was. At the outset of this manual task, each participant (I2, I4, G1, G3) had 62 compilation errors to resolve; in the process of resolving these errors, they seemed to become disoriented. While each of them ended up with code that compiled, only I2 successfully completed the task (in 47 minutes). One of the participants became so frustrated with this task that after 24 minutes he gave up. One of the participants who failed at this task (I4) reported, "The manual approach was mostly drone work; it took longer to get the target project into a state where interesting problems could be solved." Even I2, who was successful, stated, "[The manual task was] not hard, very tedious though. I was sitting there going 'this should be automated.'"

The other 4 participants undertook the manual version of the Azureus task. Only one of these developers (I1) failed to complete the task (after 60 minutes); the rest managed to finish in an average of 40 minutes.

Automated Treatment. Each of the participants who undertook the Metrics LOC task using Procrustes managed to successfully complete the task (in an average of 19 minutes). In the questionnaires, these developers mentioned that they were able to concentrate on the 3 compilation errors that remained after Procrustes ran. Since two of these errors were trivial, they were able to focus on the single remaining error (which was a conceptual mismatch). While this error was tricky to solve, each of them was able to get the code to work successfully with the test harness.

All the participants also completed the Azureus task using Procrustes (in an average of 10 minutes). These developers did not seem to have any trouble changing the reused code to use the specific fields for blue rather than the `blues` array. For this task, I4 said, "There where still some syntactic mismatches, but what I found was that the problems that remained were more directly related to the actual misalignments between use contexts; they were more directly related to the reuse I was trying to achieve."

5.4 Lessons Learned

The first evaluation demonstrated the amount effort that Procrustes can save the developer. The second evaluation showed that this savings can translate into an increased rate of success for pragmatic-reuse tasks. The controlled experiment showed that Procrustes enabled the developers to quickly locate the conceptual mismatches that were the real barrier to completing the tasks; these mismatches could not be found by looking at the reuse plan alone.

6 Discussion

In this section, we consider a number of issues regarding our claims, evidence, and conjectures about the current work, and where the work should go from here.

6.1 Does Semi-automating Enactment Matter?

A pragmatic-reuse plan remains an idealization until it is enacted to complete a pragmatic-reuse task. Semi-automation aids the developer by eliminating the most trivial issues so that the developer can focus on addressing non-trivial problems. In contrast, Participant G1 failed at the manual treatment of the Metrics task because he could not resolve the conceptual mismatch between the source and target environments; he reported spending 40 of 60 minutes resolving low-level compilation errors. This pattern recurred: in all 4 of the unsuccessful manual treatments, the developers were able to get the code to compile without error; however, in 3 of the 4, the developers also used their full 60 minutes without completing the task.

We believe this time-savings also matters from an industrial perspective; developers are only willing to invest a limited amount of time into these kinds of tasks before building the functionality from scratch. As Participant I2 states, "I wouldn't use [a pragmatic-reuse plan] on its own... I don't care that the model is nice, it's running code that counts. The automation provided by Procrustes gives me the bridge I need to make the model valuable." And, "[The manual approach] gives me a jigsaw puzzle where I've opened the box and have all the pieces. [Procrustes] gives me a 90% complete puzzle and I just have to put in the last pieces. It's what makes the tool usable to me."

6.2 Do Lightweight Transformations Suffice?

We have developed Procrustes specifically to minimize the number of compilation errors associated with reusing source code that was not designed for reuse. As such, it applies only the most basic of transformations. Significant conceptual mismatches [2] will not be repaired by these transformations. However, in our experience we have found that the vast majority of mismatches encountered are trivial in nature, but copious, and that the transformations applied by Procrustes suffice to repair these.

As Participant I4 states, "The automatic enactment brought the target project into a state where I could more immediately start working out the higher-level mismatches between contexts. The remaining compilation errors were more directly related to these [higher-level] mismatches. In contrast, the manual enactment involved a lot more iterations of compile/fix and the errors [were] more low-level."

Using a more complex means of specifying the transformations could allow the enactment task to be fully automated. We suspect that the cost of using a fully-expressive transformation language would be significantly greater than the cost of manual enactment. Procrustes provides an alternative to these two approaches.

6.3 Representativeness of Participants and Tasks

The number of participants was fairly small, at only eight. We have not attempted to quantify the relative effort of the treatments with statistical significance and have reported times only to give a sense of scale and trends. Half of our participants were industrial developers and half were experienced graduate students. While there was some variation between these two groups, the trend in the results is unambiguously in favour of Procrustes.

Our first evaluation also considered the "ideal" developer who could complete her tasks with the minimum amount of work. While this developer is also not representative, she does represent the lower-bound that the best developers could strive to achieve. Even this developer had to perform considerably more work with the manual treatment than with the semi-automated one.

Only two tasks were performed on two systems. Each of these tasks were non-trivial, being taken from real development scenarios and not synthesized for the sake of the research; each involved the reuse of functionality that had not been designed to be reused in the way we needed. The systems were of medium- to large-scale from two disparate domains.

For the sake of experimental control, we provided the participants with pragmatic-reuse plans for their tasks. While this control enabled us to compare the effectiveness of multiple developers performing the same tasks with different treatments, future evaluations will involve developers creating and enacting their own reuse plans.

6.4   Net Cost of Pragmatic Reuse

One might question how much effort must be expended to create or to interpret pragmatic-reuse plans, and whether this effort would overwhelm the reported benefits of semi-automated enactment. In our experiment, each pragmatic-reuse plan required less than 30 minutes to construct by us, despite our lack of experience with the original systems. The 30 minute investment required to create the plans involved gaining an understanding of the originating system, something that developers would need to do in both manual and tool-supported scenarios.

While our evaluation indicates that Procrustes can help with pragmatic-reuse tasks, going forward we will have to evaluate the relative performance of three different cases: (1) a developer creating functionality from scratch; (2) a developer manually reusing similar functionality from a pre-existing system; and (3) a developer creating a pragmatic-reuse plan, and enacting it with Procrustes. With such an evaluation, we would like to gain an insight into the relative merits of tool-supported end-to-end pragmatic-reuse scenarios compared to more traditional unanticipated-reuse approaches.

7   Conclusion

This paper has described Procrustes, a tool for semi-automatically enacting pragmatic-reuse plans. By resolving the bulk of the compilation errors that arise from reusing a piece of source code out of the context it was designed for, Procrustes allows the developer to focus their effort on resolving errors that represent conceptual mismatch between the source and target systems.

We performed two evaluations to determine the efficacy of Procrustes. In the first evaluation we found that a putative developer doing the least amount of work possible would have to perform significantly more work to enact a pragmatic-reuse plan manually than with Procrustes. The second evaluation found that participants using Procrustes were far more likely to successfully complete a pragmatic-reuse task (8 out of 8 cases) than those performing the same tasks manually (4 out of 8 cases). Additionally, in all successful tasks, the use of Procrustes reduced the time needed for the enactment process to between 25% and 40% of the times for the manual treatments, on average. The implication of these studies is that semi-automation can make it feasible for the developer to iterate on their reuse plan, allowing them to explore the concrete realization of different plan alternatives, leading to higher-quality reuse plans and more successful reuse tasks.

Procrustes utilizes computationally simple but analytically unsound transformations to enact a pragmatic-reuse plan. Because of their simplicity, these transformations are fast to perform. Despite their lack of soundness, they can effectively filter out trivial mismatches from the developer's attention, allowing them to focus on whether and how to address non-trivial mismatches. The lightweight nature of our approach, coupled with our appreciation of the needs of the developer, are key to its success.

Acknowledgments

We wish to thank Brad Cossette, Rylan Cottrell, Jonathan Sillito, and the other members of the Laboratory for Software Modification Research for their helpful comments. This work was supported in part by the Natural Sciences and Engineering Research Council of Canada and in part by IBM Canada.

References

1. Sen, A.: The role of opportunism in the software design reuse process. IEEE Transactions on Software Engineering 23(7), 418–436 (1997)
2. Garlan, D., Allen, R., Ockerbloom, J.: Architectural mismatch: Why reuse is so hard. IEEE Software 12(6), 17–26 (1995)
3. Garnett, E.S., Mariani, J.A.: Software reclamation. Software Engineering Journal 5(3), 185–191 (1990)
4. Krueger, C.W.: Software reuse. ACM Computing Surveys 24(2), 131–183 (1992)
5. Holmes, R., Walker, R.J.: Supporting the investigation and planning of pragmatic reuse tasks. In: Proceedings of the International Conference on Software Engineering, pp. 447–457 (2007)
6. Neighbors, J.M.: Draco: A method for engineering reusable software systems. In: Biggerstaff, T.J., Perlis, A.J. (eds.) Software Reusability. Concepts and Models of ACM Press Frontier. ACM Press Frontier, vol. 1, pp. 295–319. Addison–Wesley, Boston, United States (1989)
7. Bassett, P.G.: The theory and practice of adaptive reuse. In: Proceedings of the Symposium on Software Reusability, pp. 2–9 (1997)
8. Mezini, M., Ostermann, K.: Integrating independent components with on-demand remodularization. In: Proceedings of the Conference on Object-Oriented Programming, Systems, Languages, and Applications, pp. 52–67 (2002)
9. Estublier, J., Vega, G.: Reuse and variability in large software applications. In: Proceedings of the Foundations of Software Engineering, pp. 316–325 (2005)
10. Feather, M.S.: Reuse in the context of a transformation-based methodology. In: Biggerstaff, T.J., Perlis, A.J. (eds.) Software Reusability. Concepts and Models, vol. 1, pp. 337–359. Addison-Wesley, Reading (1989)
11. Gamma, E., Helm, R., Johnson, R., Vlissides, J.: Design Patterns: Elements of Reusable Object-Oriented Software. In: Adapter design pattern, Addison-Wesley, Reading (1994)

12. Gouda, M.G., Herman, T.: Adaptive programming. IEEE Transactions on Software Engineering 17(9), 911–921 (1991)
13. Yellin, D.M., Strom, R.E.: Protocol specifications and component adaptors. ACM Transactions on Programming Languages and Systems 19(2), 292–333 (1997)
14. Johnson, R.E., Foote, B.: Designing reuseable [*sic*] classes. Journal of Object-Oriented Programming 1(2), 22–35 (1988)
15. Jackson, D., Rinard, M.: Software analysis: a roadmap. In: Proceedings of the Conference on The Future of Software Engineering, pp. 133–145 (2000)
16. Lanubile, F., Visaggio, G.: Extracting reusable functions by flow graph-based program slicing. IEEE Transactions on Software Engineering 23(4), 246–259 (1997)
17. Caldiera, G., Basili, V.R.: Identifying and qualifying reusable software components. Computer 24(2), 61–70 (1991)

Constructing Flexible Application Servers with Off-the-Shelf Middleware Services Integration Framework*

Yan Li, Minghui Zhou**, Donggang Cao, and Lu Zhang

Software Institute, School of Electronics Engineering and Computer Science,
Peking University
Key Laboratory of High Confidence Software Technologies (Peking University),
Ministry of Education, Beijing 100871, China
{liyan05,zhmh,caodg,zhanglu}@sei.pku.edu.cn

Abstract. With the ever increasing complexity and scale of application server and the emergence of reliable OTS middleware service components, more and more application server vendors are inclined to reuse OTS middleware services in the construction of the application server. However, in conventional OTS middleware service integration, flexibility is sacrificed by hard coding concrete OTS middleware services. This paper proposes CAC (Contract, Adapter, and Configuration), a framework to integrate OTS middleware services in a flexible way. The evaluations show that our framework effectively reduces the cost of application server maintenance and OTS products customization.

1 Introduction

The complexity and scale of J2EE application servers are constantly increasing over the past decade. Until now, there have already been 23 items in Java Enterprise Edition 5, and there are more than 15 complex middleware services constituting the application server. Enabling all the features makes it a significant challenge for the vendors to evolve the application server completely, correctly and quickly. Meantime, reliable Off-the-Shelf (OTS) middleware services, also called, OTS products, have been provided by some communities, such as Apache Tomcat for Web container. Thus, more and more vendors are inclined to selectively integrate some OTS middleware services into the application server, such as Web container and transaction service, and so on, which is called *OTS middleware service integration.*

Flexibility relates to the range of possible changes supported by a platform [1]. In OTS middleware service integrations, flexibility can be refined into the requirements supported by application servers: (1) ease of modification for the evolvement of OTS middleware services; (2) ease of substitution of OTS middleware services.

In conventional OTS middleware service integrations, flexibility is sacrificed by hard coding a concrete one, as different OTS products' APIs are various. However, OTS products are continually evolving by third-parties, and application server

---

* The research was sponsored by the National Grand Fundamental Research 973 Program of China under Grant No. 2002CB312003, the National Nature Science Foundation of China under Grant No. 60603038, 60503029, and the National High-Tech Research and Development Plan of China under Grant No.2007AA01Z133, No.2006AA01Z156, No. 2006AA01Z189.
** Corresponding author.

H. Mei (Ed.): ICSR 2008, LNCS 5030, pp. 343–346, 2008.
© Springer-Verlag Berlin Heidelberg 2008

vendors prefer to integrate different third-parties' product for a kind of middleware service to best meet user requirements. No matter a minor change of the integrated OTS product or the vendors' need to substitute the existing OTS product, application server developers have to review and modify all the related codes scattered in the application server, and furthermore either the large scale of the related codes or the deficiency of development documents make the modification and substitution harder.

To achieve flexibility, any concrete logic of OTS products should be decoupled from that of application servers. We propose CAC (Contract Adapter Configuration), an OTS middleware services integration framework to address this problem. The main contributions of this framework are as follow. First, it effectively reduces the cost and the time of the OTS middleware services-based application server maintenance. Because once the contract is defined, the maintenance workload of the integration is limited to the adapter rather than scatter around the complex application server codes whenever OTS middleware services evolve. Second, it allows application server vendor rapidly customize the application server to better meet the diverse requirements through configuration. Besides, we implemented CAC in a J2EE application server to demonstrate its feasibility and effectiveness.

In the rest, Section 2 introduces the framework. Section 3 evaluates the framework.

2 Integration Framework of Middleware Services (CAC)

To avoid tangling the concrete logic of OTS middleware services with that of application server, the framework is constructed as in Fig.1: Contract defining the abstract interaction logic between the application server and a kind of middleware services, adapter implementing the contract for a candidate OTS product to eliminate the mismatches between the product and the contract, and configuration acting as a glue to stick a specific OTS product to be used.

There are four steps when the application server invokes an OTS product (Fig. 1):

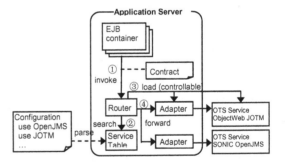

Fig. 1. CAC framework overview

1. Some parts of the application server (e.g., EJB container) invoke the middleware service through the predefined contract. The invocation is sent to the router which is responsible for loading and invoking the required OTS products.
2. When the router receives an invocation, it searches the service table for the appointed OTS product. The type of the middleware service is used as keyword.
3. The router checks the status of the found OTS product. If it is unloaded, the router loads this OTS product and its corresponding adapter.
4. Finally, the router dispatches the invocation to the appointed OTS product via the adapter and returns the result to the invocating part. Java reflection mechanism is employed to operate on the appointed OTS product.

The details of the three main elements are given below.

Contract. As the basis of the integration framework, the contract is composed of a set of operations. These operations exactly cover the functionalities required by the application server to invoke and control this kind of middleware services. If the Service Provider Interface (SPI) has existed in the specifications, the contract should be consistent with it. Then, application server developers define the application server specific operations. Developers should be careful when defining specific operations, considering it may not be supported by all OTS middleware service.

Adapter sits between OTS middleware service and the application server to compensate for the differences between the API of OTS product and the contract. One or more adapters are employed according to the mismatches between API and the operations in the contract into three kinds (Table 1).

Table 1. Three kinds of mismatch

Kind	Definition
Name mismatch	The API rightly corresponds to the operation M in the contract, but only the names of the operations do not match.
Function mismatch	The API is incomplete to the operations in the contract, e.g., application server has to do pre or post processing for the operations in the contract. Or operation M in the contract should be implemented by a sequence of the operations in the APIs.
Function deficiency	No operation in the API supports operation M in the contract.

Configuration describes OTS products used by an application. For each kind of middleware service, the configuration should specify the middleware service type, the adapter name, the load time (e.g., immediate representing loading at bootstrap or lazy representing loading when invoked), and the middleware service properties (e.g., the timeout for transaction). The application server will parse the configuration and store it in the service table at the bootstrap before deploying the applications.

3 Evaluation

Due to the inflexibility leaded by hard coding way, we restructured PKUAS [3], an open source J2EE-compliant application server, with CAC framework (Fig. 2). There are different OTS products for each middleware service in the OTS repository. The contract layer is composed of all the contracts for each kind of middleware services.

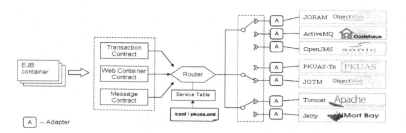

Fig. 2. The CAC Framework in PKUAS

pkuas.xml acts as the configuration. Below, we will present an evaluation of CAC with respect to the flexibility and the performance overhead in PKUAS.

Flexibility, here, is the requirements of easy modification for the evolvement of OTS products and easy substitution of OTS products. So we employ N_C, the number of classes to be changed when modifying or substituting an OTS product, to measure the flexibility. We count the N_C of three OTS products in CAC-based PKUAS (PKUAS^C), the hard coding version of PKUAS (PKUAS^H) and a well-known open source application server ObjectWeb JOnAS v4.8 [4] (Table 2).

Table 2. Numbers of classes

	ObjectWeb JOTM	ObjectWeb JORAM	Apache Tomcat
PKUAS^C	5	3	1
PKUAS^H	53	9	14
JOnAS	40	11	18

Table 3. Experimental results

OTS Service	Response time (with CAC)	Response time (without CAC)	Performance overhead
Apache Tomcat	540 ms	532 ms	1.5%
ObjectWeb JOTM	133 s	129s	3.1%

As shown in the Table 2, the N_C has been greatly reduced. Because the contract layer separates application server from concrete OTS products, only the adapters will use the specific OTS product's APIs, thus N_C in the CAC-based version is decreased to the number of adapter-related classes. Consequently, the application server developers just need to maintain the adapters whenever the OTS products evolve, and can substitute an OTS product by simply modifying the configuration. Comparably, in the hard-coding way, developers have to review and modify each part depending on OTS products in the application server, which is time-consuming and error-prone.

As CAC inserts an intermediary layer into the middleware service invocation process, we compared the original PKUAS with the CAC-based version by some tests to analyze the performance overhead of CAC (Table 3). For testing the integrated web container (Tomcat), we used Orientware XLinker [5]'s TestEcho web service as the server-side program; For testing the integrated transaction service (JOTM), we used the JOnAS test suite [6]. Comparing with the benefits CAC brings, we believe 3% performance lost is affordable.

References

1. Parlavantzas, N., Coulson, G.: Designing and constructing modifiable middleware using component frameworks. The Institution of Engineering and Technology, pp. 113–126 (2007)
2. ObjectWeb JOTM, http://jotm.objectweb.org/
3. PeKing University Application Server, http://forge.objectweb.org/projects/pkuas/
4. JOnAS, http://wiki.jonas.objectweb.org/xwiki/bin/view/Main/WebHome
5. Ge, S., Hu, C.M., Du, Z.X., Wang, Y., Lin, X.L., Huai, J.P.: A Web service-based application supporting environment. In: Proceedings of the National Software and Application, pp. 97–102 (2002)
6. JOnAS Transaction Service conformance test suit, http://www.easybeans.org/doc/testguide/en/integrated/testguide.html

SAM: Simple API for Object-Oriented Code Metrics

Adam Edelman, William Frakes, and Charles Lillie

Virginia Polytechnic Institute and State University
Northern Virginia Center
7054 Haycock Road
Falls Church, Virginia 22043, USA
{edelman,frakes}@vt.edu, clillie@nc.rr.com
http://www.nvc.vt.edu

Abstract. This paper introduces the Simple API for Object-Oriented Code Metrics or SAM. SAM has two distinct advantages over current application generators for metrics. First, SAM can collect a much larger set of metrics since it maintains context during metrics analysis. Second, SAM is completely language independent since it specifies the types of events a parser must generate, but not how to generate those events. Through examples, we will demonstrate how our API allows us to collect metrics not possible with application generators. We will also demonstrate how SAM can reduce the lines of code per metric by up to 90 percent when measured against some of today's most popular standalone tools.

Keywords: Software metrics, source analysis, code inspection, parsing, generators, code metrics, object-oriented metrics, static analysis.

1 Introduction

Currently, there is no standard framework for software metrics. Definitions are nebulous and even metrics that appear simple, such as lines of code, are measured differently from application to application. In addition, new metrics continue to be released claiming better, more accurate measurement of software products and processes. To keep pace, new metric tools are created and current tools must be updated. By contrast, the process of parsing a programming language does not change as frequently. It would therefore be beneficial to separate the relatively static task of language parsing from the more dynamic task of metrics analysis.

Parsing is the first step in creating metrics tools. Since programming languages have become increasingly complex, building a parser from scratch is time consuming, with developers usually taking advantage of a parser generator. A parser generator takes as input an annotated language description in the form of a grammar. From the grammar, the parser generator generates a parser consisting of a syntactic parser or recognizer augmented with semantic actions that are triggered by the recognizer [1].

H. Mei (Ed.): ICSR 2008, LNCS 5030, pp. 347–359, 2008.
© Springer-Verlag Berlin Heidelberg 2008

For metrics, adding code to the parser means correctly identifying each metric event of interest. This can be difficult for complex programming languages. For example, the grammars for the Java language that come with JavaCC [2] and ANTLR [3], two of the most popular parser generators currently used in many metrics tools [4]-[7], are both over 1000 lines. Within the grammars, there are 29 separate locations of non-comment source lines (NCSLs). Consequently, when parsing and metrics are tightly coupled, the complexity of even simple tasks increases relative to the complexity of the grammar.

We propose a model that decouples parsing from metrics analysis. Several other works have explored this idea [8]. Most can be classified as application generators since metric tools are created using domain specific languages. We refer to these methods collectively as the generative methods.

GENOA [9] is a framework based on the GEN++ analyzer generator. GEN++ parses C++ code and creates parse trees decorated with additional information useful for code metrics. Users then describe how GENOA should use the decorated parse trees using a GENOA specific language known as GENII. This allows users to create customizable applications abstracted from the parser. However, in this approach the user must use GENII specifications to create applications, which requires in-depth knowledge of the parse tree structure. In addition, GEN++ only works with the cfront C++ complier.

CIA++ (C++ Information Abstractor) [10] is another tool built on the GEN++ analyzer generator. The system extracts all information form the decorated parse tree and stores it in a text database. Command line tools perform specialized queries on the database. This requires information about the structure of the database to determine what data can be obtained and how to obtain it. In addition, CIA++ also relies on the cfront compiler. ARMA (Ada Reuse Measurement Analyzer) [11] uses its own parser to parse Ada source code and create decorated parse trees. A metric analyzer then calculates reuse metrics from the parse trees. Although the system separates parsing from metrics analysis, ARMA is used to calculate a specific set of metrics from Ada source code and cannot be customized by the user.

WebMetrics [12] is a platform independent metrics tool that uses JavaCC to parse object oriented source files and store source attributes in a MySQL [13] database. A user queries the database with SQL queries to retrieve information. WebMetrics improves upon previous work by using a SQL database that allows developers to hook into the code analysis database without knowledge of a specialized query language. However, WebMetrics suffers the same shortfalls of other previous work. While separating parsing from metrics, all these approaches also separate code attributes from the actual code. Users queries are limited to a static collection of attributes. Although the queries may be flexible, a user is ultimately limited by the data.

SAM has two distinct advantages over generative methods. First, SAM can collect a much larger set of metrics since SAM maintains context during metrics analysis. Generative methods bind code attributes at compile time, performing analysis on the static set of attributes. SAM pushes data binding from compile time to runtime, performing parsing and analysis concurrently. This allows us access to the underlying source code, or context, during analysis. SAM relies on an event driven model for metrics where the parser sends notifications of metric related events as it traverses the source code. Events that are of interest to object-oriented metrics collection include the occurrences of lines, methods, and classes in a source file. In addition to notifications, the parser provides context sensitive attributes related to the notification. Using attributes, we can obtain the line text for every occurrence of a line and reconstruct the entire source code. Since an object-oriented code metric is by definition any metric derived from object-oriented source code, we will be able to obtain any object-oriented code metric with SAM.

The second advantage of SAM is language independence. SAM specifies the types of events a parser must generate, but not how to generate those events. Consequently, a compiler or a parser generator can be used to build a SAM parser without altering the metrics analysis module. Any object-oriented language that contains the events can be modeled in SAM.

SAM also provides advantages over many of the methods currently used to build metrics software. We will show how, using SAM, we can reduce the lines of codes required to create metrics applications by up to 90% compared to some of today's most popular metric tools. In the next section, we describe the system model for SAM. Section III compares SAM with current generative methods and standalone tools. In Section IV, we show through examples that SAM can collect metrics not possible with generative methods and more efficiently than current standalone tools. Section V is the conclusion.

2   System Model

Our API adheres to many of the principles in the Simple API for XML (SAX) [14], since it recognizes the elements of source code similar to how SAX recognizes XML elements. In SAX, an application consists of a SAX parser and a registered SAX listener. The parser, which implements the XMLReader interface, handles the XML document as a single stream of data. The data stream is unidirectional such that previously accessed data cannot be re-read without re-parsing. The parser generates callback methods as it traverses the XML document.

An event listener, which implements the ContentHandler interface, can register with the parser and receive the callback notifications. The main callback methods are startDocument, endDocument, startElement, and endElement. Fig. 1 illustrates the interaction between SAX components while parsing an XML document.

In addition to providing event notification, the methods also return attributes such as element name, namespace URI, and other useful attributes. The attributes provided by the callback methods depend upon the parser used since there is little guidance describing what attributes a SAX parser should provide. Since creating a parser from scratch is time consuming, a developer usually takes advantage of a pre-existing implementation of a SAX parser. By separating

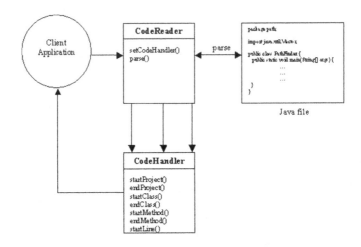

Fig. 1. High level architecture for SAM

information extraction from information use, we can easily swap parser in and out of applications without having to change the business logic of the application. If a parser does not contain the right attributes for an application, a developer can select any number of SAX parsers freely available on the Internet that suit the needs of the application better. The spectrum of parsers range from the extremely portable to blazing fast, and a choice can be made depending on the priorities of the project. If further customization is required, the developer has the option of building a SAX parser so long as it implements the XMLReader interface. This guarantees there will be a parser that meets the requirements of any application, and all interactions with the event listener occur according to a predefined specification.

We would like to apply this idea to metrics by creating an API flexible enough for use in any OO metrics application. SAX focuses on the well-defined concept of an XML element. In metrics, an element is not as clearly defined. To help us determine the elements of source code analysis, we performed domain analysis on several of the most popular open source metrics tools using the DARE [15] methodology. From our domain analysis, we were able to group metrics into five distinct categories. The categories are line, method, class, documents and project. As in SAX, there is the notion of a multi-leveled hierarchy of events, such that events do not occur independently of each other. For example, a method will start and end inside of a class. A class will start and end inside of a file. While each system used different terminology, architecture analysis revealed that each divided the metrics into similar categories and recognized the hierarchical relationship among the categories. With the metric elements defined, we describe the components of SAM.

Code Reader: Code Reader is the Java interface that SAM parsers must implement. CodeReader contains the following methods: parse(InputSource) and setCodeHandler(CodeHandler). The parse method takes an InputSource, which is any input capable of being serialized to character or data stream. This is usually a source file. The CodeReader converts the input into a stream of events corresponding to structural features of the input, namely, lines, methods, classes and the project. The events are sent to the CodeHandler specified by the setCodeHandler method. The parser used in Section III is for the Java language.

CodeHandler: The CodeHandler is the interface implemented by classes that wish to receive event notifications. These classes are where metrics analysis occurs. The classes implement the start and end methods for each metric event, which will be called by the parser. Each method also contains an Attributes class passed in as a parameter. The instantiated class of the Attributes interface is specific to the generated event and populated by the parser during source code traversal. In our Java SAM implementation, the JavaMethodAttributes class contains the parameters, exceptions and return type of a method. By not forcing developers to implement a large number of mandatory attributes, we allow developers the flexibility to customize their parsers in ways that suits their need with creating unnecessary overhead.

Using this model, we can measure almost any object-oriented code metric. In the next section, we will demonstrate some of these capabilities.

3   Comparing SAM to Current Methods

3.1   Generative Methods

SAM has two distinct advantages over current generative methods. First, compared to generative methods SAM is able to collect a much larger set of metrics. Current generative methods are limited because they perform metric parsing and metric analysis as two distinct procedures (Fig. 2). For parsing, the front end of a compiler or a parser generator is used to parse the source code and collect a specific set of attributes that are useful for later metrics analysis. This can include inbound/outbound method calls, number of lines, or nesting level. Attributes are stored in a decorated parse trees, text file or database for later use during metrics analysis. By parsing and storing the information in a metrics oriented data structure, generative methods abstract parsing from metrics analysis. We save development time by reusing the parsing module and allow ourselves to focus on metrics analysis. However, the set of metrics we can compute is limited by the attributes collected. For example, if we wanted to calculate cyclomatic complexity [16] we would need to know how many branches exist in the source code. If we cannot find the necessary attribute in the database, it will not be possible to calculate the metric. We could build a very large database to store every imaginable metric related attribute, but inevitably, this approach falls short since it is impossible to collect all the attributes for every metric we would want to calculate now and in the future.

SAM preserves the abstraction of parsing and analysis, but uses a different model, presented in Fig. 3, to collect a far larger set of metrics. Instead of relying on a static set of attributes, we report attributes as they happen, which

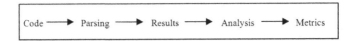

Fig. 2. Generalized process flow for generative methods

allows us to examine the context in which the metric event occurred. Context is guaranteed by the LineAttributes class, which when implemented must contain the text of the current line. Going back to our cyclomatic complexity example, if no branch attributes existed in our LineAttributes class we could examine the line to determine the existence of a branch. Context allows us to collect metrics even when the attributes needed for analysis do not exist in our database.

Fig. 3. Process flow for SAM

The second advantage to SAM is language independence. Most generative methods use the front-end of a complier, which only parses a single language. A notable exception is WebMetrics, which relies on the JavaCC parser generator to populate an attributes database. The JavaCC parser generator contains a library of language grammars, which WebMetrics uses to parse different languages.

SAM is language independent since the events it generates are common to all object oriented languages. The CodeReader class can use the front-end of a compiler or a parser generator to convert the input source code into a stream of events. In the following section, we used the JavaCC parser generator for parsing and generating the metric event for Java code. JavaCC maintains a free repository of parsing specifications for many languages and we could have just as easily used any of the other languages to do the parsing tasks required by the CodeReader class. After modifying the grammar to generate SAM events, we could swap it into our application without having to make any other changes. The level of abstraction in SAM provides us with true language independence not found in the generative methods. Therefore, our hypothesis is that collection ability is a function of the number of attributes a generative system provides, although context allows us to collect any code metric regardless of attributes. In addition, language independence is a function of how many languages an application can accept as input.

3.2   Standalone Methods

We refer to a metrics tool as standalone if it takes as input a file or files and, without any user interaction, outputs a set of metric results. Currently, almost all open-source standalone tools are built using parser generators. This entails modifying a parsing grammar by adding code to perform metrics analysis. The generated parser works in conjunction with additional classes written from scratch to create a functional standalone tool. In order to leverage a parser generator, a developer must become familiar with the language of the grammar specification. This can be a difficult process as every parser generator has its own grammar specification language. Once familiar with the language, it is necessary to go through the entire grammar for a specific language to determine where to add metric analysis code. Since the metrics analysis code is spread throughout the grammar file, the parsing process is tightly coupled to analysis. As a development approach, combining parsing and metrics analysis removes the abstraction we saw in the generative methods, significantly increasing the code required for an application and decreasing the readability and maintainability. The benefit to this approach is we now have access to context, which allows us to collect an unlimited set of metrics, not bound to an attributes database. Consequently, we have traded ease of use for analysis flexibility.

SAM aims to combine the flexibility of parser generators with the ease of use of application generators. Since SAM uses metric events, we do not need to examine an entire language grammar. In addition, all the metric logic is completely separate from the parsing, which means less code and makes the system more readable and more maintainable. As previously mentioned, we can collect any code metric with SAM, so there is no reduction of analysis flexibility. For these reasons, SAM is an ideal API for developers looking to quickly develop and deploy metric software.

Our hypothesis states that as we increase the number of classes required to derive a metric, the amount of code also increases. In the next section, we will demonstrate the capabilities of SAM and show how we can significantly reduce the amount of code compared to standalone tools while collecting a range of metrics not possible with generative methods.

4   Numerical Methods

For our experiments, we tested how effective SAM is in reducing the amount of code required to build a metrics application. To test this, we compared the lines of code required to obtain a metric in a standalone tool against the lines of code required by a SAM version. Since we needed access to source code, we limited our comparison to open source metrics software written in Java. We chose the ten most popular tools, ranked by activity, available on SourceForge [17]. We then used the DARE methodology to build a feature table listing which metrics each tool collected. The five most collected metrics are shown in Fig. 4. We chose these metrics as the focus of our experiments.

To compare SAM to standalone tools we measured the number of classes and lines of code per metric for each of the five metrics. Determining a NCSL total was especially difficult task since all the tools measured several metrics. In addition, most tools included a user interface that we did not want to count as

	CCCC	EMP	CA	Jmove	DF	JNCSS	IntoJ	Dep	Jrefactory	Jdepend	Total
Number of Classes	X			X		X		X	X	X	6
Efferent Coupling		X		X				X		X	4
NCSLs	X		X			X					3
CSLs	X		X			X					3
Cyclomatic Complexity		X	X				X				3

CCCC: C and C++ Code Counter   Dep: Dependometer
EMP: Eclipse Metrics Plugin   JNCSS: JavaNCSS
CA: Code Analyzer
DF: Dependency Finder

Fig. 4. Top five metrics as ranked by popularity

part of the metrics analysis code. We decided not to include any class primarily dedicated to the user interface. For any classes containing interface and analysis code, we only counted the analysis lines. We included code common to the analysis of multiple metrics in the NCSL count for each of those metrics. We did not include any code added to the parser generator grammar, even though in many cases it contained analysis logic. While the results are not an exact count, we believe our approach gives a conservative estimate of the number of NCSLs required for each metric.

Next, we built application with SAM to compare against the standalone tools. This required a CodeReader class capable of parsing the Java language. Ordinarily, a developer does not write this class, instead choosing the class from a library. However, since no SAM library exists we wrote our own. Once written, our CodeReader class can be used in any Java SAM application. We built our CodeReader class (JavaSAMReader) by leveraging the JavaCC parser generator. To get JavaCC to work within the SAM model, we modified the Java language grammar with code that populated the Attribute classes and generated our SAM events. A CodeReader for C++ or Smalltalk would be built in much the same way since JavaCC grammars exist for those languages as well. The parse method of JavaSAMReader generates a JavaParser class from our modified JavaCC grammar. We use the setCodeHandler method to tell the JavaParser where to send the attributes and event notifications. JavaSAMReader required 376 lines of additional code in the JavaCC grammar and 16 lines in the class itself for a total of 392 NCSLs. For our results, we did not include the lines required to build the JavaSAMReader class since we did not count lines from parsing modules in the standalone tools. In addition, a developer usually chooses the CodeReader from a library rather than building one from scratch.

Once we have our CodeReader class, we can begin building metrics applications. To demonstrate how an application is built using SAM we will build a simple application that measures NCSLs and CSLs (comment source lines). Our SAM application will consist of two classes. A main class instantiates our CodeReader and CodeHandler, and calls the parse method on the CodeReader to begin parsing. A class implementing the CodeHandler interface handles the events generated from the CodeReader.

```
package edu.vt.cs.sam.examples;
import edu.vt.cs.sam.*;
import edu.vt.cs.sam.readers.*;

public class LineCounter {

  public static void main(String[] args) {
    CodeReader codeReader = new JavaSAMReader();
    CodeHandler codeHandler = new LineHandler();
    codeReader.setCodeHandler(codeHandler);

    try {
      System.out.println("Line Count for File: " + args[0]);
      codeReader.parse(args[0]);
    } catch (SAMException e) {
      System.out.println("A problem occurred during parsing.");
      e.printStackTrace();
    }

  }

}
```

Fig. 5. LineCounter.java

Fig. 5 shows the LineCounter class, main class of our application, which instantiates the JavaSAMReader and LineCountHandler. We call the setCodeHandler method to tell JavaSAMReader where to send the events and then call the
parse method to begin parsing the specified file. The parse method throws a
SAMException if any errors occur during parsing.

Fig. 6 is the LineCountHandler, which implements the CodeHandler interface. For our application, we only need the endLine and endFile methods. Each
time the endLine method is called, we check the JavaLineAttributes to determine which counter to increment. When we reach the end of the file, we print
the counts to screen. It is important to note that an implementation of LineAttributes does not have to distinguish comment from non-comment lines. In
fact, the only required field for classes implementing LineAttributes is line text.
However, those developing Attributes classes are strongly encouraged to include
as many helpful fields as possible.

This simple application demonstrates how to quickly build metrics tools using
SAM. Our application required only 2 classes and 31 lines of code. Compared
to standalone tools, this represents a code savings of over 90 percent. Results
for other metrics are equally impressive. Fig. 7 compares SAM with some of the
standalone tools. The reason our results are so dramatic is not that the SAM
model does anything radically different from these standalone tools. In many
ways, their design actually mirrors that of SAM. For instance, JRefactory [5] has
MethodMetrics, TypeMetrics, and ProjectMetrics classes, which are functionally
equivalent to the Attributes classes in SAM. The MethodMetrics class contains
attributes such as method name, parameter count and block depth.

These attributes might appear in an implementation of MethodAttributes,
and in fact do appear in our JavaMethodAttributes implementation. The
difference between our model and the standalone methods goes back to the abstraction between parsing and metric analysis. In JRefactory, the MethodMetrics

```
import edu.vt.cs.sam.attributes.JavaLineAttributes;
import edu.vt.cs.sam.helpers.DefaultHandler;

public class LineCountHandler extends DefaultHandler {

  private int csl = 0;
  private int ncsl = 0;

  public void endLine(JavaLineAttributes jla) {
    if (jla.isComment()) {
      csl++;
    }
    else {
      ncsl++;
    }
  }

  public void endFile() {
    System.out.println("CSL: " + csl);
    System.out.println("NCSL: " + ncsl);
  }
}
```

Fig. 6. LineCountHandler.java

	SAM		JNCSS		Dependometer		Jrefactory		Jdepend	
	Classes	NCSLs	Classes	NCSLs	Classes	NCSLs	Classes	NCSLs	Classes	NCSLs
Number of Classes	2	30	4	495	10	869	8	582	5	492
Efferent Coupling	2	50			11	1060			5	492
NCSLs	2	31	4	518			8	635		
CSLs	2	31	4	518			8	635		
Cyclomatic Complexity	2	37	3	448						

Fig. 7. Number of Classes and Non Comment Source Lines Required to Obtain Metrics in Various Tools

class calculates lines of code per method and performs other analysis that breaks this abstraction, increasing the number of classes needed to build an application, which in turn increases the lines of code. As we can see in Fig. 7, as the number of classes increases so do the lines of code. Since our parsing module is well abstracted, we only require analysis related classes, which translates to fewer classes and less code.

Now let us look at a different example to understand how context helps us collect metrics otherwise impossible with generative methods. Efferent coupling measures the dependence of one class on others. High coupling may indicate brittleness since the class is dependent upon the stability of the classes to which it is coupled [4]. We measure efferent coupling by determining the number of types directly referred to anywhere in a given class. A direct reference means we do not include all the classes or interfaces of an inheritance tree, rather just the class or interface referred to in the class we are measuring. Fig 8 shows our EfferentCouplingHandler, which implements the CodeHandler interface. At the start of a class, we add any types the class extends or implements to a list

```
package edu.vt.cs.sam.examples;

import java.util.Vector;

import edu.vt.cs.sam.attributes.JavaLineAttributes;
import edu.vt.cs.sam.attributes.JavaMethodAttributes;
import edu.vt.cs.sam.attributes.JavaClassAttributes;
import edu.vt.cs.sam.helpers.DefaultHandler;

public class EfferentCouplingHandler extends DefaultHandler {

  private Vector knownTypes;

  public void endLine(JavaLineAttributes jla) {
    if (jla.getLineType().equals("fieldDeclaration") ||
        jla.getLineType().equals("localVariableDeclaration")) {
      addKnownType(jla.getLineText());
    }
  }

  public void startMethod(JavaMethodAttributes jma) {
    Vector v = jma.getParameterList();
    v.addAll(jma.getExceptionList());
    for (int i = 0; i < v.size(); i++) {
      addKnownType(v.get(i).toString());
    }
  }

  public void startClass(JavaClassAttributes jca) {
    knownTypes = new Vector();
    Vector v = jca.getExtendsList();
    v.addAll(jca.getImplementsList());
    for (int i = 0; i < v.size(); i++) {
      addKnownType(v.get(i).toString());
    }
  }

  public void endClass(JavaClassAttributes jca) {
    System.out.println("Known Types for Class: " + jca.getClassName());
    for (int i = 0; i < knownTypes.size(); i++) {
      System.out.println(knownTypes.get(i));
    }
  }

  private void addKnownType (String type) {
    type = type.replaceAll("public|protected|private|static|final|transient|volatile|\\[|\\]","").trim();
    int endIndex = type.indexOf(" ");
    if (endIndex == -1) {
      endIndex = type.length();
    }
    type = type.substring(0,endIndex);
    if (!knownTypes.contains(type)) {
      knownTypes.add(type);
    }
  }
}
```

Fig. 8. EfferentCouplingHandler.java

of known classes. We use JavaClassAttributes to retrieve these types with the getExtendsList and getImplementsList methods. As we encounter lines within the class, we check to see if they are declarations by using the getLineType method of JavaLineAttributes. If the line is a declaration, we get the line text and check it for types not that do not exist in the list of known types. We print the list to the screen when we reach the end of the class.

This example shows how we can use a combination of attributes and context to gather metrics that are unobtainable with methods based strictly on static attributes. Our JavaClassAttributes contains the list of types a class implements or extends, so we use these attributes. There is no attribute for referred type in JavaLineAttributes. Thus, we must examine the line text. If this were a generative tool with the same set of attributes, determining efferent coupling would simply not be possible. In SAM, the attributes serve as a helpful starting place for an application instead of a strict limitation.

Through our examples, we have shown that SAM can collect metrics not possible with generative tools and more efficiently than current standalone tools based on parser generators.

5   Conclusion and Future Work

This paper detailed SAM, a simple and reusable API for the development of object-oriented code metrics software. SAM has two distinct advantages over current application generators for metrics. First, SAM can collect a much larger set of metrics since it maintains context during metrics analysis. Second, SAM is completely language independent since it specifies the types of events a parser must generate, but not how to generate those events. Due to the limit application generators place on metrics collection, most of today's standalone metrics tools rely on parser generators. Although, parser generators provide flexibility in metrics collection, they remove the abstraction between parsing and analysis, which increases the amount of code required to obtain a metric. By combining the abstraction of generative methods with the flexibility of parser generators, we demonstrated significant improvements over either single approach. In our examples, we showed how our API allows us to collect metrics not possible with application generators by combining attributes with context. We also compared SAM to some of the most popular open source metrics tools to determine how much of a code savings we could get by using SAM. Our results proved that SAM could reduce code significantly, up to 90 percent for some metrics.

Our future work focuses on growing the SAM library. As we have seen, one of the major benefits of SAM is the abstraction that exists between parsing and metrics analysis. Specifically, developers can focus on analysis when libraries of parsers exist for their use. Currently, there is no such library. This is why SAM is freely available on SourceForge at http://simpleapimetric.sourceforge.net/. We encourage everyone to download the API and make suggestions to help us grow and improve SAM.

References

1. Parr, T.J., Quong, R.W.: LL and LR translators need k 1 lookahead. ACM SIG-PLAN Notices 31(2), 27–34 (1996)
2. JavaCC Website: https://javacc.dev.java.net/
3. ANTLR Website: http://antlr.org/
4. Eclipse Metrics Plugin Website: http://www.teaminabox.co.uk/downloads/metrics/
5. JRefactory Website: http://jrefactory.sourceforge.net/
6. JDepend Website: http://www.clarkware.com/software/JDepend.html
7. JavaNCSS Website: http://www.kclee.de/clemens/java/javancss/
8. Succi, G., Liu, E.: A Relations-Based Appproach for Simplifying Metrics Extraction. In: ACM Applied Computing Review, pp. 27–32. ACM Press, New York
9. Devanbu, P.: GENOA - A Customizable, Front-End Retargetable Source Code Analysis Framework. ACM Transactions on Software Engineering and Methodolgy 8(2), 177–212 (1999)

10. Grass, J.E., Chen, Y.: The C++ Information Abstractor. In: The Second USENIX C++ Conference, San Francisco, CA (1990)
11. Bieman, J.M., Karunanithi, S.: Measurement of Language-Suppported Reuse in Object-Oriented and Object-Based Software. Journal of Systems and Software 30, 271–293 (1995)
12. Scotto, M., Sillitti, A., Succi, G., Vernazza, T.: A Relational Approach to Software Metrics. In: 2004 ACM Symposium on Applied Computing, pp. 1536–1540 (2004)
13. MySQL Website: http://mysql.com/
14. SAX Website: http://www.saxproject.org/
15. Frakes, W., Prieto-Diaz, R., Fox, C.: DARE: Domain Analysis and Reuse Environment. Annals of Software Engineering 5, 125–141 (1998)
16. McCabe, T.J.: A Complexity Measure IEEE Transactions on Software Engineering, 2 (1976)
17. SourceForge Website: http://sourceforge.net/

Leveraging Source Code Search for Reuse*

Hans-Jörg Happel, Thomas Schuster, and Peter Szulman

Forschungszentrum Informatik (FZI), Haid-und-Neu-Str. 10-14,
D-76131 Karlsruhe, Germany
{happel,schuster,szulman}@fzi.de
http://www.fzi.de

Abstract. The importance of search as a central support activity for information handling and software reuse has been highlighted by several authors. Although it is one of the most dominant daily activities of developers, it is not a first order concern of most development tools. Recently a number of specialized search engines for source code emerged that enable access to reusable assets from both the web and within organizations. We argue that those source code search engines can play a key role for information access throughout the software development lifecycle. In this paper we present an analysis of existing approaches and tools. Furthermore we point out several shortcomings and provide a roadmap for future enhancements.

1 Introduction

Software engineering is a knowledge-intensive activity, which requires developers to deal with a large set of information of various sort - ranging from descriptions of the application domain, software engineering techniques, the software project itself and its development artifacts. Additionally, software development today is characterized by distributed team work, often involving several parties, for instance in outsourced or Open Source development settings. Hence, good communication and coordination of information within the software development team is crucial [8].

The importance of search as a central support activity for information handling has been highlighted by several authors. In an empirical analysis of developers' daily work activities, Singer et al. [22] found out that searching for information was the most dominant daily activity of the participating developers. Henninger [9] reports that searching and accessing different types of information, accounts for around 40% of the time of people in software organizations. A more recent observation of developers using the Eclipse integrated development environment (IDE) by Murphy et al. [19] shows that search is an important activity even just inside the IDE.

While this notion of *search* is rather fuzzy, and subsumes several different activities (c.f. section 2), the reuse of existing artifacts is considered a major

---

* This work has been partly supported by the TEAM project, which is funded the EU-IST program under grant FP6-35111 and the BMBF-funded project WAVES.

H. Mei (Ed.): ICSR 2008, LNCS 5030, pp. 360–371, 2008.

issue in terms of productivity [7]. However, widespread artifact reuse remains difficult for several reasons.

First, the software development process is typically driven by requirements given by involved stakeholders [3]. Many companies therefore fail to realize synergies or to reuse artifacts and development knowledge from prior or simultaneous projects. Secondly, the retrieval of reusable assets requires an appropriate description [18]. However, it turned out that it is difficult to define and maintain suitable metadata especially for binary artifacts [7].

In this paper, we argue that the recently emerging technology of source code search engines can be an important enabler for searching reusable components in particular and for any kind of information need in the software development process in general. However, we identified that most source code search engines are focussed on retrieving lines of code and often lack possibilities to explore further connected information.

The remainder of this paper is organized as follows: Section 2 summarizes situations in which a developer or a development team might need to seek for further information on functional and non-functional details of a software system. Section 3 describes current state of the art in terms of searching facilities for software systems. In Section 4 we catch up with the preceding section and demonstrate our vision on capabilities a development supporting search engine has to cover. Finally the paper will close up with our conclusion of the problem domain furthermore we will give an outlook on next steps in this field of study.

2   Use Cases

With shortening release cycles in mind recent years have shown that Software Engineering demands that developers get information on implementation details as quick as possible. Since software also raises in complexity the need to exchange information amongst development and project management increases as well. From a development perspective two needs for involved teams can be distinguished. The first one is to know which functionality (**what**) has to be implemented. The second question is the way (**how**) these requirements (again: **what**) might be implemented. Both issues contain several facets and can be addressed in a diversity of means. In the remainder of this section we focus on the **how** of these engineering aspects. So far we figured out five main issues in this field of studies which are comprised in the table below.

Issue	Topic
Software reuse and enhancement Software maintenance	Software re-engineering
Information about reuse	Insight information and understanding
Project properties and relevance License compliance	

In larger projects a software engineer has to deal with one or more of these aspects. As the table displays it the topics can be arranged under two super topics; the first two can be summarized as questions concerning **software re-engineering** whilst the last three can be aggregated as topics dealing with **insight information and understanding**. Both of our next two sub sections will therefore address these questions in detail.

2.1 Software Re-engineering

The process of re-engineering is usually deeply integrated in many phases during attention handling of common software development processes. This is what is also considered as refactoring which is mainly driven by changing requirements, but also during maintenance re-engineering is often needed to incorporate new features.

Software Reuse and Enhancement. In general a software engineer might raise the question if a given problem demands a complete new development or if it is possible to make use of other solutions. If that is not the case a subsequent question could be if the problem domain can be further divided into smaller parts. For each of these parts the original question could be raised again or otherwise the problem might be divided again and so on. Related to this approach an engineer could also ask if an existent solution does cover part of the problem domain and therefore might be used partially to build up a new piece of software. Independent of the mode of search - partial or complete solutions - this domain can be further divided into four aspects of search:

- Search of feature
- Search of algorithm
- Search of component
- Search of Library

Depending on the decomposition grade one of these categories will be applicable for search queries.

Software Maintenance. Software maintenance involves task such as defect repair, which requires developers to locate code relevant to a maintenance task. Also it demands developers to grasp the internal structure and design rationale (program understanding). Therefore developers often need to seek inside the project for certain artifacts, methods or code snippets. As far as extensions to given functions are spotlighted an engineer has to answer questions described in the previous paragraph.

2.2 Insight Information and Understanding

Reuse, which strives to find existing artifacts that might be reused partially or as a whole in a new context, always also demands developers to grasp insight details of the software artifacts that are part of the search results as well as those that belong to the software that has to be extended. Besides understanding the problem domain another need is to know that the software complies with applicable laws and does not interfere with rights of other parties.

Information About Reuse. Whenever other solutions are reused there is a need to understand at least how this reuse can be accomplished. That means that an engineer has to know how to bind or integrate the solution to the current project. Therefore it is at least necessary to know about those parts in a black box manner (comparable to the knowledge of a common api, e.g. Java 2 SE). To get this done a software engineer might be looking for code samples using the same solution whilst in a second step common test cases might also be searched in order to check functionality or correct binding of the elements found in first place. More information might be interesting from an evaluation perspective wherein it can be desirable to know if there are any projects related to the current development project. Concerning related projects again there might be two different questions. The first one is dealing with competing projects in the project's problem domain. The other one is related to similar projects - that might also be competing - that are running on other platforms or are written in different implementation languages.

Project Related Information. Besides search for solutions and how to integrate those it might also be relevant to get an idea of elements found in terms of their quality. This question is not only related to foreign products but also to the own solution or other solutions the team might have developed before. Code quality in this sense can be interesting out of different points of view like metrics according to quality assurance models (e.g. ISO 9126, FURPS, FCM or FS Model) or relevance for other projects. Regarding relevance in other projects a developer is interested if a project is referenced by others which might be an indicator of quality also. Regarding the own project, references and dependencies, e.g. of classes can also reveal failures in system design (like common anti patterns).

License Compliance. Another problem that appears in the process of software development independent of the usage of foreign projects is the question of compliance. If other projects are used the question is if a certain license is applicable or if some references have to be removed before this license can be used. Also it is definitely important for companies that use third party software that this software does not violate other rights. Even if there is no cross reference to other libraries the question remains if a certain piece of code could be claimed by other third parties as their own property. Summarizing these questions the complete code including all used libraries needs to be checked for license compliance.

3   Code Search Process

In this section, we describe and analyze existing approaches and tools for searching in source code. Therefore, we first introduce a number of paradigms, before we do a systematic comparison according steps in the search process. Finally, we describe some open issues of state-of-the-art implementations.

3.1 Overview of Approaches

This section shortly describes three different paradigms of code search: keyword-based search, structured search and search in an IDE.

Keyword-Based Search. As known from common web search, keyword-based search is a convenient retrieval method for end users. It requires them to express their information need by plain text keywords and returns a set of matching documents. There are various extensions to the basic concept of keyword-based search, such as Boolean queries (combining keyword terms by Boolean operators), fuzzy queries (allowing results for similar terms) or phrase queries. Recently a number of web search engines specialized on source code, which adopt the keyword-based paradigm, have been created. Accordingly, the user enters a set of keywords to retrieve a list of source code files.

Those source code search engines, such as Koders[1], Krugle[2] or Google Code-Search[3] index freely available Open Source code which is available throughout the internet or from platforms such as SourceForge[4]. Besides that, some vendors offer their software for enterprise internal usage.

Structured Search. While keyword-based search is considered to be an intuitive and fast model that can be applied to all resources that have a plain text representation, its approach suffers from low semantic precision (due to synonyms and homonyms) and does not allow for sophisticated expressions of an information need. Structured search approaches in turn, define special query languages, which allow users to express more complex queries. Database queries in SQL are an example of this.

Accordingly, structured search is not applicable to any kind of information, since information items must also comply with a formal schema, against which the structured queries can be matched. Source code can be used for structured search, since it complies with a formal schema. In recent years a number of approaches have applied these techniques, mainly in the domain of software maintenance. Work such as of Welty and colleagues [25,5] or in the QBench project [21] extract facts from source code to build a formal knowledge base. Users could then run queries against this knowledge base such as "give me all classes which call this class". While structured search allows for more powerful and precise expressions of an information need, this requires either skilled users or advanced search interfaces which hide the query formulation complexity from the user.

Search Inside an IDE. Searching inside and for certain source code artifacts is relevant in reuse and maintenance scenarios. The default tool environment for these tasks is typically an integrated development environment (IDE). Searching

---

[1] http://www.koders.com
[2] http://www.krugle.com
[3] http://www.google.com/codesearch
[4] http://www.sourceforge.net

functionality of such tools, like the popular Eclipse IDE, has improved over the last years. While based on keyword-based search [10], Eclipse allows restricting queries to certain syntactical structures of the source code. Thus, Eclipse provides some kind of combination of keyword-based and structured search.

3.2 Comparison of Approaches

In this section, we describe the features and state-of-the-art of source code search engines in detail. Therefore, we present our analysis according to the major steps in the information retrieval process:

– The search starts with the information need of a user. This need triggers the user to formulate a query to a search engine (Query Formulation)
– The search engine retrieves - based on an appropriate algorithm - the search results by analyzing the query and the indexed documents. The search results are ordered according to a ranking algorithm (Relevance Ranking)
– The ranked result set is presented to the user based on a presentation concept, which includes aspects that allow the user to quickly assess whether a search result meets the information need (Result Presentation)
– If no search result fulfills the information need of the user, users typically refine (or vary) their original query in several iterations to find some that meets their information need (Result Interpretation)

In the following, we will further characterize existing approaches. Basis for our analysis was our comparison of six web-based source code search engines (c.f. [4]) as well as research papers submitted on that topic.

Scope. The majority of approaches concentrate on raw source code. While most actual systems focus on popular programming languages such as Java, some engines index up to 45 different languages. Some systems, such as Krugle go beyond source code and also allow searching for open source projects and related technical information.

Query Formulation. The vast majority of approaches offer a plain search box in order to express a simple keyword-based query. However, when compared to web search, source code search engines typically offer a broader range of extended search options. This means that they allow for restricting the search to source code of a specific Open Source software license or some structural elements inherent to the code such as class names, method names, method calls or interface names.

As already pointed out, the LaSSIE [5] and QBench [21] systems offer to formulate complex structured queries according to a pre-definied model [24]. Furthermore, the web-based engines Merobase[5] and Codase[6] allow specifying object abstractions consisting of combined class and method information which can be matched.

[5] http://www.merobase.com
[6] http://www.codase.com

Relevance Ranking. With relevance ranking, search engines try to order the set of matching results according to their relevance for the querying user. Classic information retrieval approaches such as TF-IDF [1] use statistical information for this ranking. TF-IDF computes a higher score for a result document the more often a queried term occurs in a result document and the more seldom this term is in the overall set of documents. Most keyword-based approaches use this kind of algorithms to compute their relevance ranking.

An exception from this is the ComponentRank approach [17], which applies the Google PageRank concept in a software engineering context. The original PageRank roughly computes a single page rank value for each page based on the page rank values all of pages which link to that page. ComponentRank accordingly equates single Java files with pages and their use relations in the code (i.e. function calls) with hyperlinks. The ComponentRank of a file is thus computed by aggregating the ComponentRanks of its calling files. Similar to Google, the authors report that often used and probably more generic components are ranked high.

For approaches offering structured search, ranking is a different issue. Since precise formal queries allow for a logical comparison with the result representations, a result is either a match or not. Ranking is thus often done alphabetically, or can be manually specified by the user as part of the query.

Presentation of the Search Results. As described so far, many source code search engines adopt the basic concepts of classic web search. Result presentation is no exception from this. Most source code search engines use a list-based result presentation, which shows the name of the matching classes and a preview of the containing source code. Some search engines, such as the search inside the Eclipse IDE, use a tree-based model, which displays matches in kind of an abstract-syntax tree, which shows its surrounding elements. Similarly, search results in Krugle are presented at the correct hierarchical position of the files belonging to a certain open source project.

Result Interpretation. Web search engines employ various techniques to guide and leverage user interaction, once a first list of results is displayed. One example are query refinements, which suggest similar queries or terms which seem more appropriate (e.g. in the case of typos). Another example are feedback mechanisms which allow deriving users relevance rating for the given results. Such relevance rankings can either be collected explicitly (e.g. manual rating by the user) or implicitly (e.g. by interpreting user behaviour) [13].

While some source code search engines provide some basic query refinement mechanisms (e.g. Google CodeSearch), no system is reported to leverage any relevance feedback.

4   Open Issues and Potential Improvements

While our description shows, that there have been remarkable achievements in terms of code search in the past years, we also observe a number of open issues, which need improvements in order to further improve code search.

4.1   Query Formulation

Let's go back to our introductory example: A developer has to extend an already existing CMS solution by time recording mechanism which allow users to tag their working time in the CMS system. First the developer might look for existing components realizing the required functionality. Usually he doesn't know in advance, what properties the required code has. Probably he types only some keywords like "time", "record" in the query field of the search engine and lets the search engine find the "best" match. Of course we can not expect from a search engine to read the thoughts of a developer and compute the best matches; therefore some additional hints are necessary. The developer might have already been working on this task for a while. He could have also prepared the code for the new time tagging functionality by modification of some classes or methods of the CMS solution. He could have at least localized that part of the system by browsing through the packages of the system in an IDE, where the time tagging component should be plugged in. These kinds of working context information may imply some interesting information for a search engine. For example there may exist several time tagging components, but not all suitable for a CMS context. Classic information retrieval talks about the notion of *context*, when it comes to contextual information, which can help to disambiguate synonymous queries. However, when only considering implicit context information, at least web-based search systems are limited to data that is transmitted with the request, such as the browser language or the IP address. Source code search however, could possibly benefit even more from contextual information, at least when triggered from within an IDE. In general all kind of context information may be incorporated in the search, like task context (which tasks is the developer currently working on?) or even the role of the user (for example a tester may rather search for examples how a piece of code is used, than for the functionality itself. Techniques to find out developer's working context are already addressed by tools like mylyn [14] or Strathcona [11]. The Strathcona tool demonstrates, how this contextualized information from the code editor can be used to restrict the result set. However, Strathcona is limited to find related artifacts for a given context, and does not allow for free-form queries from the user.

Additionally there are also some more aspects of the query, which influence the accuracy of the matches as also described in section 2.1: Does the developer search for an algorithm, a component or for an example how a certain component is used? They have different characteristics, which may be exploited by the search engine as heuristics like: a component has usually a strong internal cohesion and usually has a lot of references from other projects. A code example may be rather a small piece of code in a method body and has references to a certain component.

4.2   Ranking

Statistical ranking methods like used by most source code search engines perform rather badly. This may be due to the fact, that source code – in contrast to normal text – usually shows a skewed distribution of index terms. This, statistical measures do not well discriminate among results. The ComponentRank approach [12] has shown to perform well tackling that issue.

While ComponentRank does well in highlighting highly-reused framework code, it neglects less "popular" non-framework code, which might be a better fit. Above we described the need to extend the code search by using heuristics to differentiate between such cases. Of course heuristics do not guarantee perfect results, however based on them an appropriate ranking is possible.

Also a high reuse factor (and thus a high CodeRank) nor the heuristics above do necessarily imply a high software quality. Developers do not aim to find *a* solution, but rather a *good* solution regarding software quality. Software quality itself can be divided into internal and external quality. External quality characteristics are those parts of a product that face its users, where internal quality characteristics reflect the developers' perspective onto quality like maintainability of code. However it is not proven, in the practice we can observe that good internal code quality leads to good external quality. That is why we suggest focusing on the developers' perspective and rank results based on their internal quality properties. Techniques to measure internal code quality of software systems are already available [21], however they have to be adapted to the needs of the code search.

4.3   Result Presentation

Result presentation is one of the weakest points of current source code search engines. First, code seems to be placed redundantly on the web, such that search engines return a lot of duplicate results. Using code duplicate detection techniques [2,20,6] it is possible to eliminate exact duplicates and group similar code fragments. Furthermore results often show semantic differences (e.g. a keyword matching in a method body vs. in a method signature) which are not self-evident for the user.

As said many approaches focus on a list-style representation of code search results. We claim that due to its inherent interconnection, source code requires contextual information to interpret its suitability. Research in software maintenance has shown that dependency diagrams can be very helpful to analyze code structures [23]. If developers operate on such diagrams they usually gather a fast overview of software without reading the code. Thus, we consider graph-like representations, visualizing the context of a search result, as a worthwhile alternative [16,15].

Once a piece of code was found, a developer should be able to interactively navigate over the structure of the software starting from the piece of code found. This way he would be able to navigate through methods calls, to parents or children in the inheritance hierarchy, or browse over the package hierarchy around the match. By ensuring navigation through the code starting from the matches, the developer might judge easier the relevance of the matches.

4.4   Result Interpretation

In order to improve the efficiency of follow-up queries, relevance feedbacks provided by the developer can be used to evaluate the accuracy of previous matches of the code search. Besides tracking subsequent searches and result clicks, web-based search engines can not derive much information about what the user does with a search result. In source code search, when it is executed from within an IDE, search systems can track far more user interaction, which can help to improve the system. As an example, a search plugin could monitor if result code was directly adapted by the user. In this case, a much stronger (implicit) relevance rating can be derived compared to when a result is just "clicked".

5 Conclusion

In this paper, we have described the phenomenon of source code search engines in the context of software engineering. We therefore identified software reuse, maintenance, the retrieval of insight information and understanding as main use cases for the usage of these tools. In our opinion source code search engines can play a major role to discover not only directly reusable lines of source code, but also larger components and artifacts from related projects.

With the analysis of the current state-of-the art of source code search engines it became obvious that some of these tools offer interesting features, while all of them mainly follow very similar concepts. In this case that means that the tools are based on classic information retrieval techniques, which are not perfectly suitable when dealing with source code.

Among those shortcomings the lack of possibilities to leverage the formal, structured nature of source code artifacts and the list-based paradigm of result representation are the most severe ones. As one of the most critical items we figured out that all source code search approaches so far do not offer advanced interaction mechanisms on the search results and moreover do not implement quality ranking algorithms. Thus, we suggest a number of concrete approaches to leverage source code search in the context of software engineering. Mainly we base our ideas on the combination of source code search process and well-known technologies from software engineering research. Currently we are working on the integration and evaluation of those approaches in our own source code search engine.

References

1. Baeza-Yates, R.A., Ribeiro-Neto, B.: Modern Information Retrieval. Addison-Wesley Longman Publishing Co., Inc., Boston (1999)
2. Baker, B.S.: A Program for Identifying Duplicated Code. Computing Science and Statistics 24, 49–57 (1992)
3. Cheng, B.H.C., Atlee, J.M.: Research directions in requirements engineering. In: FOSE 2007: 2007 Future of Software Engineering, pp. 285–303. IEEE Computer Society, Los Alamitos (2007)
4. David, J., Happel, H.-J., Kleb, J., Maalej, W., Schmidt, R., Volz, R.: D6: Report describing state-of-the art in search mechanism and context similarity. Project deliverable. ist-project team 35111, 03 (2007)

5. Devanbu, P.T., Brachman, R.J., Selfridge, P.G.: Lassie: A knowledge-based software information system. Commun. ACM 34(5), 34–49 (1991)
6. Ducasse, S., Rieger, M., Demeyer, S.: A language independent approach for detecting duplicated code. icsm, 00:109 (1999)
7. Frakes, W.B., Kang, K.: Software reuse research: Status and future. IEEE Trans. Software Eng. 31(7), 529–536 (2005)
8. Cernosek, E.N.G.: The value of modeling. developerworks (2004)
9. Henninger, S.: Case-based knowledge management tools for software development. Autom. Softw. Eng. 4, 319–340 (1997)
10. Hermann, B., Muller, C., Schafer, T., Mezini, M.: Searchbrowser: An efficient index-based search feature for the eclipse ide. In: Eclipse Technology eXchange workshop (eTX) at ECOOP 2006 (2006)
11. Holmes, R., Walker, R.J., Murphy, G.C.: Approximate structural context matching: An approach to recommend relevant examples. IEEE Transactions on Software Engineering 32(12), 952–970 (2006)
12. Inoue, K., Yokomori, R., Fujiwara, H., Yamamoto, T., Matsushita, M., Kusumoto, S.: Component rank: relative significance rank for software component search. In: ICSE 2003. Proceedings of the 25th International Conference on Software Engineering, pp. 14–24. IEEE Computer Society, Washington (2003)
13. Kelly, D., Teevan, J.: Implicit feedback for inferring user preference: a bibliography. SIGIR Forum 37(2), 18–28 (2003)
14. Kersten, M., Murphy, G.C.: Using task context to improve programmer productivity. In: SIGSOFT 2006/FSE-14: Proceedings of the 14th ACM SIGSOFT international symposium on Foundations of software engineering, pp. 1–11. ACM, New York (2006)
15. Lewerentz, C., Noack, A.: CrocoCosmos - 3D Visualization of large object-oriented programs, pp. 279–297
16. Lewerentz, C., Simon, F.: Metrics-based 3d visualization of large object-oriented programs. In: VISSOFT 2002. Proceedings of the 1st International Workshop on Visualizing Software for Understanding and Analysis, p. 70. IEEE Computer Society, Washington (2002)
17. Matsushita, M.: Ranking significance of software components based on use relations. IEEE Trans. Softw. Eng. 31(3), 213–225 (2005); Inoue, M.-K., Yokomori, M.-R., Yamamoto, M.-T., Kusumoto, M.-S.
18. Mili, A., Mili, R., Mittermeir, R.T.: A survey of software reuse libraries. Ann. Softw. Eng. 5, 349–414 (1998)
19. Murphy, G.C., Kersten, M., Findlater, L.: How are java software developers using the eclipse ide? IEEE Softw. 23(4), 76–83 (2006)
20. Rieger, M., Ducasse, S.: Visual detection of duplicated code. In: Ducasse, S., Weisbrod, J. (eds.) Proceedings ECOOP Workshop on Experiences in Object-Oriented Re-Engineering, number 6/7/98. Forschungszentrum Informatik Karlsruhe (1998)
21. Simon, F., Mohaupt, T., Seng, O. (eds.): Code Quality Management. Dpunkt Verlag (2005)
22. Singer, J., Lethbridge, T., Vinson, N., Anquetil, N.: An examination of software engineering work practices. In: CASCON 1997. Proceedings of the 1997 conference of the Centre for Advanced Studies on Collaborative research, p. 21. IBM Press (1997)

23. Stasko, J.T., Brown, M.H., Price, B.A. (eds.): Software Visualization. MIT Press, Cambridge (1997)
24. Trifu, M., Szulman, P.: Language independent abstract metamodel for quality analysis and improvement of oo systems. In: Proceedings of the 7th German Workshop on Software-Reengineering (WSR 2005), Bad Honnef, Germany (2005)
25. Welty, C.A.: Software engineering. In: Baader, F., Calvanese, D., McGuinness, D.L., Nardi, D., Patel-Schneider, P.F. (eds.) Description Logic Handbook, pp. 373–387. Cambridge University Press, Cambridge (2003)

An Experimental Evaluation of Documentation Methods and Reusability

Martin Blom, Eivind J. Nordby, and Anna Brunstrom

Computer Science, Karlstad University, Sweden
{Eivind.Nordby,Martin.Blom,Anna.Brunstrom}@kau.se

Abstract. This paper presents an experimental evaluation carried out in an academic environment. The goal of the experiment was to compare how different methods of documenting semantic information affect software reuse. More specifically, the goal was to measure if there were any differences between the methods with regard to the time needed to implement changes to existing software. Four methods of documentation were used; executable contracts, non-executable contracts, Javadoc-style documentation and sequence diagrams. The results indicate that executable contracts demanded more time than the other three methods and that sequence diagrams and Javadoc demanded the least time.

1 Introduction

Code is an indispensable deliverable of all software based products and all over the world code is reused, modified and maintained. One area where quality and maintainability are addressed is in the handling of semantic aspects, by which we mean semantic information on the class and method levels. Promising and often-used methods in this area include executable contracts [1], non-executable contracts [2], Javadoc [3] and sequence diagrams as in UML [4]. Neither of these methods is new and much interesting research on the theoretical side has been done, see for instance [5] for contracts or [6] for UML. What seems to be lacking, though, is empirical studies to verify what benefits can be obtained by using the methods. The intention of the experiment presented in this paper is to provide one step in the process of empirically verifying the effects of using a particular documentation method for improving software quality.

2 Experimental Setup

The experiment compared the four documentation methods mentioned above. It used 15 students as test subjects who implemented change requests to four programs written in C++. The experiment was performed over a period of four consecutive days where each day contained one three-hour work session in which the test subjects worked on one assignment. After the four days, all students had solved all assignments and worked with all methods.

H. Mei (Ed.): ICSR 2008, LNCS 5030, pp. 372–375, 2008.

2.1   Documentation Methods

The aim of the experiment was to compare different documentation methods that focus on semantic aspects in the software. Since neither of the methods selected for evaluation give any structural or syntactic help, this was supplied to the test subjects independent of the documentation method as class diagrams and comments in the code. It is very important that the methods being compared actually are comparable, i.e. that they have the same area of application. In our experiment, the area of application is semantic documentation, and all methods must therefore focus on that area. *Executable contracts* are either written as executable commands in the same language as the actual program code or in a meta-language and later compiled into the code [7,1]. A contract is written for every method comprised of a precondition expressing what should hold before calling the method and a postcondition expressing the effects of the method. *Non-executable contracts* are similar to executable contracts, but are written as comments that can be program code, plain English or combinations of both [2]. Since non-executable contracts have a less formal structure, they are less exact but more easily read and can also express conditions that are not executable. *Javadoc* is a technique using special comments and is separately compiled to generate the documentation. It is used extensively by Java [3] developers and is an easy way of producing documentation. Since the application language in the experiment was C++, some of the features of Javadoc had to be emulated. *Sequence diagrams* are used in UML [4] as a way of documenting interactions between software parts. They contain information on methods and their invocations as well as conditions and call sequences.

2.2   Assignments

In the experiment, we needed four assignments that could be combined with the documentation methods such that the subjects never had to solve the same assignment twice. These assignments had to be solvable by the test subjects within the given time interval, but in order for the documentation methods to have any effect on the time needed for implementing the changes, the assignments still needed to be non-trivial. One assignment, Coffee Machine, was found in an article by Alistair Cockburn [8] and the other three assignments were constructed by the authors. The *Coffee Machine program* (550 LOC) emulates a coffee machine that accepts coins and produces coffee and other beverages. The change request was to implement functionality to change the concentration of the beverages. The *ATM program* (450 LOC) was a simple implementation of a money dispenser where the user can insert a card, enter a pin code and withdraw money. The change request was to add functionality to handle more than one account. The *Address Book program* (700 LOC) was a simple implementation of an address book containing people and addresses that could be edited in various ways. The change request was to add handling of two or more address books. The *Booking System program* (800 LOC) handles resources such as rooms, persons and times and the change request was to check for double bookings and to add extraction of available times and rooms.

2.3   Experiment Design

The test subjects were computer science students in their third year with a decent background in programming using C++. They had all been exposed to all four documentation methods in previous courses, although not extensively. The main metric was time for completion of the assignments since it is a good indication on how easy or hard the different methods made implementing the changes. The quality of the resulting software was controlled by test cases, as we wanted all subjects to produce software of roughly the same quality. To avoid the problem of diversity among test subjects, all test subjects were subjected to all methods in random order according to a Graeco-Latin square design [9]. Since no test subject can solve the same problem more than once without serious learning effects, the number of assignments needed was equal to the number of methods used, i.e. four in this case. This experimental setup is hence a factorial design with individual subjects and assignment as blocking variables and documentation method as treatment. The analysis for a factorial experiment such as this is an ANOVA-test [9], a test that makes it possible to analyze the effects of both treatments, blocking variables and noise in an experiment with a limited number of data points.

3   Results and Conclusions

This section presents the results derived from the experiment. Not all subjects managed to complete their assignments within the given time frame. These subjects were removed from further analysis, leaving eight subjects who managed to solve all their assignments within time. Table 1 contains the figures on not completed assignments for each method. The table shows that 25% of all assignments were not completed on time and that the non-completed assignments were reasonably well distributed between the methods except sequence diagrams. The rest of the analysis includes only the eight subjects who completed all assignments on time. This reduction imposes a threat to the validity of the experiment. Table 2 shows the average values of the time needed to complete the assignments for the different documentation methods and their diversions from the grand average. As can be seen in the table, the average for executable contracts is 27 minutes more than the grand average. This indicates that the test subjects demanded more time to reuse software where the semantic information was documented using executable contracts. This might be expected, since the syntax is

Table 1. Methods and number of not completed assignments

	Not completed	%
Total	15	25%
Executable contracts	5	33%
Non-executable contracts	4	27%
Javadoc	4	27%
Sequence diagrams	2	13%

Table 2. Completion time for methods and their diversions from grand average

	Average	Div. from GA	Div. from GA (%)
Grand average (GA)	101.6 min	–	–
Executable contracts	128.5 min	27.0 min	26.6%
Non-executable contracts	98.8 min	−2.7 min	−2.7%
Javadoc	89.5 min	−12.0 min	−11.8%
Sequence diagrams	89.1 min	−12.3 min	−12.2%

more formalized and expressive than the other methods and thus might be more difficult to read and understand. Javadoc and Sequence diagrams were seen as the two methods of documentation that demanded the least time to read and understand and had average values close to 12 minutes below the grand average. This might be explained by their informal nature. As for the last method, non-executable contracts, the average is close to the grand average. Since there were differences between methods, a more detailed analysis was conducted using an ANOVA-test that showed *treatment* to be significant on the 10%-level, thus indicating that the differences initially found between methods are statistically significant, although on a rather low level. The statistical evaluation thus supports the initial findings that executable contracts demanded more time than the other methods and that Javadoc and sequence diagrams demanded less time.

References

1. Meyer, B.: Object Oriented Software Construction, 2nd edn. Prentice-Hall, Englewood Cliffs (1997)
2. Blom, M., Nordby, E.J., Brunstrom, A.: An experimental evaluation of programming by contract. In: Proceedings of the Ninth Annual IEEE International Conference and Workshop on the Engineering of Computer-Based Systems, Lund, Sweden (2002)
3. Gosling, J., Joy, B., Steele, G.: Java Language Specification. Addison-Wesley, Reading (1996)
4. Jacobson, I., Booch, G., Rumbaugh, J.: The Unified Software Development Process. Addison-Wesley, Reading (1999)
5. Findler, R.B., Felleisen, M.: Contract soundness for object-oriented languages. In: Proceedings of OOPSLA 2001, Tampa, Florida, USA, pp. 1–15 (2001)
6. Song, I.-Y.: Developing sequence diagrams in uml. In: Kunii, H.S., Jajodia, S., Sølvberg, A. (eds.) ER 2001. LNCS, vol. 2224, pp. 368–382. Springer, Heidelberg (2001)
7. Kramer, R.: iContract - the Java Design by Contract Tool. In: Proceedings of the TOOLS 1998 Conference, Santa Barbara, USA (1998)
8. Cockburn, A.: Object-oriented analysis and design, part 2. C/C++ Users Journal (1998)
9. Box, G., Hunter, W., Hunter, J.: Statistics for Experimenters. John Wiley and sons, Chichester (1978)

An Empirical Comparison of Methods for Reengineering Procedural Software Systems to Object-Oriented Systems

William B. Frakes, Gregory Kulczycki, and Natasha Moodliar

Computer Science Department, Virginia Tech, Falls Church, VA, 22043, USA
frakes@cs.vt.edu, gregwk@vt.edu, natasham@vt.edu

Abstract. This study empirically compared two methods for reengineering a procedural system to an object-oriented system. Our hypothesis was that it is possible to support this process with a repeatable method. The first method was manual and was used as a baseline for evaluating the second method, which was repeatable and based on analysis of procedure coupling. The repeatable method was found to be effective for identifying objects. It produced code that was much smaller, more efficient, and passed more regression tests than the manual method. Analysis of object-oriented metrics indicated both simpler code and less variability among classes. Particularly striking was the order of magnitude difference between the average cohesion metric (LCOM) for the manual and repeatable methods.

Keywords: Reengineering, coupling metrics.

1 Introduction

The main goal of our research is to define a method and tools to assist in the process of converting code in a procedural language, such a C, to an object-oriented language such as C++ or Java. Our hypothesis is that it is possible to support this process with a repeatable method. This study builds on a previous paper presented at ICSR9 [7].

The history of programming and software engineering demonstrates the continual evolution towards larger grained programming constructs and more human focused languages [8]. One aspect of this evolution is the development of more reusable systems based on object-oriented design and programming. One way of achieving this is by reengineering existing procedure-based systems to object-oriented systems. Companies sometimes use the migration from C to C++, for example, as opportunities for better reuse [5][13][15].

Many companies have large inventories of legacy code written in procedural languages. When these companies migrate to new object-oriented architectures, they do not want to start from scratch. Therefore, a need exists for a methodology that can analyze existing procedural code and identify related functions and data that can be encapsulated into reusable objects in the application domain. Since the study by Pole [15] there have been many studies of the procedural to object-oriented reengineering process [1][6][12][13][14][19].

H. Mei (Ed.): ICSR 2008, LNCS 5030, pp. 376–389, 2008.

The current study compares the result of two previous studies, in which we reengineered the ccount metrics tool, written in C, to object-oriented programs written in C++. In the first study, a professional programmer reengineered the procedural code using a manual method [18]. The programmer inspected the C code and designed the object-oriented code based on principles that he considered appropriate. In the second study [7], we used a repeatable method to analyze the procedural code and aid the programmer in determining how to create classes from groups of functions. The method used various coupling metrics to determine how strongly any two procedures were related, and therefore, whether they belonged in the same class in an object-oriented design. The method used the premise that program elements that exhibit certain kinds of coupling can be grouped together to form classes.

In this study, we present an empirical comparison of the C++ code produced by the manual method with the C++ code produced by the repeatable method. Section 2 of this paper briefly describes the manual and repeatable methods that we used in our comparison, and section 3 compares the code using several different metrics. In section 4 we make some concluding remarks.

2 Methodology

We have conducted two studies of reengineering procedural to object-oriented code [7][18]. The procedural system used in the studies was ccount, a metrics tool for the C language that calculates the number of commentary and non-commentary source lines in a C program, and their ratio. It was developed as a simple programming quality tool and was used as an example program in [9].

The original version of ccount was written in K&R C on AT&T Unix. An ANSI-C version of ccount was subsequently created and this is the version that was used in our studies. The ANSI version of ccount consists of 749 non-commentary lines of code in seven files containing seventeen functions, including the main function. The ccount metric tool was used because it is tractable for a small case study, but non-trivial, so the studies are relevant.

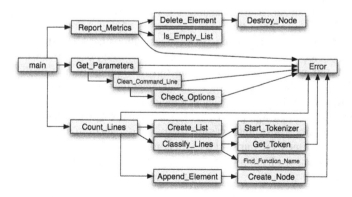

Fig. 1. A call graph for the original procedural code

In both studies, cflow was used to identify the flow of control (call structure) of ccount. The output from cflow is in text format, which we then converted to the call graph shown in Figure 1.

2.1 Manual Reengineering Effort

In the first study, ccount was reengineered to C++ using standard reusable components and a singleton design pattern [11] to capture utility classes. There is more than one way to convert a software product from one language to another. A very simple approach would be to take the modules or functions in the existing language and wrap them in modules or functions from the other language. This ensures that the resulting product is in the target language while not changing the functionality and the results by much. This is not optimal since, even though the conversion is complete, the new product does not use all the benefits and features of the new language. This is especially true when the source language is C and the target language is C++. Since C++ is backwards compatible to C, a very simple conversion would be to change the extensions on the files to .cpp and change printf's to cout's and be done. But, the resulting product would still be C in C++ clothing.

A second option would be to use a C to C++ reengineering effort such as that described in the Pole method [15], which we discuss in more detail in the next subsection. A third option is to start from first principles. This involves looking at the problem statement, identifying the objects that stand out in the problem, and designing and developing the product from the ground up. The process involves defining attributes and methods for the various objects and creating classes for these objects. This option produces better code with most utilization of the features of the destination language than the first option. Also, since this design is from the ground up, one can take advantage of various optimizations from the beginning and support quality and maintainability from the start. This approach, however, is poor reuse because it requires a from-scratch development effort. This approach takes much longer for the conversion.

The first study used a combination of the second and third options. We started from first principles in identifying objects and, once the objects were identified, the existing functions were remapped into methods that were appropriate for those objects. By doing so, we eliminated some functions, added new ones, and replaced existing ones with those from the standard C++ libraries. Sometime we replaced the functions with simpler ones that took advantage of the progress made in software platforms, and the portability of code that comes with using ANSI standards.

Since we decided to use the existing functionality and not rewrite from the ground up, we were left with some functions that did not belong to any of the objects we identified. Some of these needed to be global since they maintained state information within the function between calls. These functions were packaged into a utility class. We used the singleton design pattern [11] to achieve a single instance of the object. In addition, due to time constraints, we left the parsing algorithm used for the classification of a line the same as it was in the C version.

From the statement of the problem and first principles, we identified three distinct objects:

- File – An object that needs to be analyzed, and one in which CSL (comment source lines), NCSL (non-comment source lines), and the ratio of CSL to NCSL must be determined. At least one file must be analyzed during any invocation.

- Func – An object at the lowest granularity that needs to be analyzed and whose metric must be reported. Every function belongs to one file, and a file can contain one or more functions. Code external to a C function is treated as belonging to a function named *external*.
- Line – An object that needs to be classified as either external or belonging to a function. It may be a comment, non-comment, neither, or both. Every line belongs to only one function and a function has one or more lines.

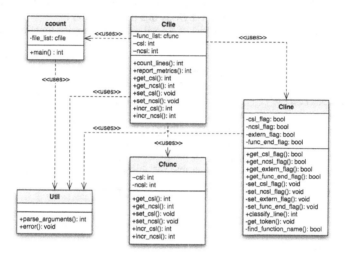

Fig. 2. A UML class diagram of the code produced by the manual method

These objects have certain attributes, and we find a very good match of C functions with methods of these objects, though with a few changes. In addition, there are other functions and modules such as error checking and reporting, and command-line parsing that are either external to these objects or are not confined to one object. Finally, the sturdier, more generic and more optimal list container from the C++ Standard Template Library can safely replace the C code for linked-list generation, maintenance, and deletion.

Figure 2 gives a UML class diagram of the reengineered code. The diagram represents all of the classes in the resulting code, but it omits some of the methods due to space constraints. Since the reengineering in this study was done by a professional programmer, this serves as a baseline for the repeatable method.

2.2 Repeatable Method

In the second study [7] we extended the Pole method by defining coupling metrics and using them to identify potential reusable objects in the ccount metrics tool. This study forms the foundation of the proposed research. In this subsection, we will briefly describe the steps in the method along with the various metrics used. We then demonstrate how objects are identified by using one of the metrics—the direct invocation metric—and following it through the object identification process for the ccount metrics tool.

Table 1. Notations and definitions for the eight coupling metrics used in [Frakes 2006]

Name	Definition
Direct Invocation Metric	The number of times that one function is statically referenced in the body of another function.
Recursive Invocation Metric	The number of times one function f_2 is statically referenced in another function f_1 plus number of times f_1 is statically referenced in f_2.
Indirect Invocation Metric	The number of times that a function f_1 statically references a function f_2 by way of a third function f_{mid}.
Shared Parameter Metric	The number of formal parameters in two functions that have the same type and same name.
Shared Variable Metric	The number of variables shared between two functions. Two variables in different functions are considered shared if they can be traced back to a common source (declaration).
Shared Variable Tokens Metric	This metric counts the static occurrences of all variables in two functions that share a common source.
Shared Type-Name Variable Metric	This metric considers functions to be related if they share variables with the same type and the same name.
Shared Type-Name Variable Tokens Metric	This metric counts the static occurrences of all formal parameters, global variables, and local variables that are common between two functions.

The method starts with the premise that program elements that exhibit certain kinds of coupling can be grouped together to form objects. The steps in the reengineering process are as follows:

1. The domain expert creates a function stop list. A stop list contains functions identified by the domain expert as utility functions that do not perform tasks specific to the domain.
2. A call graph is generated. A tool or manual scanning of the code base is used to generate a call graph (as in Figure 1) that shows the flow of control in the legacy code.
3. Dependency and context lists are created. A dependency list identifies all the functions invoked from a given function. A context list does the reverse—it identifies the functions that invoke or use a given function.
4. Objects are identified. In this step the metrics are calculated and the potential objects are identified. This step turned out to be the most involved step in the process. For clarity, we break its description into three sub-steps.
   - Summary data is collected. The summary data contains information for each function that is not in the stop list, such as the types and names of parameters, variables, and functions used in the given function.
   - Metrics are calculated. Different coupling metrics describe different relationships between functions, such as how many times one function invokes another or how many parameters are shared by the functions. In this study we used eight different coupling metrics (described in Table 1) and evaluated each one individually for its effectiveness in identifying objects.
   - Candidate objects are identified. The software engineer determines a threshold for each metric. If the metric for a pair of functions is above the threshold, those functions are candidates to appear as methods in the same class.

5. Domain expert chooses objects. The domain expert examines candidate objects and determines whether they are reasonable for the domain. Variables common to two or more functions are examined for their appropriateness as object attributes. Left-over functions, including the functions in the stop list, can be converted into individual objects or packaged as utility objects.

Each metric used in this methodology describes a distinct relationship between any two functions in the legacy system. We call them coupling metrics because they are based on various forms of module coupling, such as those given in [9], and because they indicate the dependency and the amount of communication that takes place between functions. A brief description of each metric used is given in Table 1.

The metrics can be divided into three broad categories based on the kind of coupling.

1. Invocation metrics. These metrics are based on routine call coupling as described in [16]. They rank functions based on how often one function invokes another.
2. Shared parameter metrics. This category currently contains only one metric—the shared parameter metric. It is based on data element coupling as described in [9], which exists when data is passed from one function to another through a disciplined interface such as a parameter list.
3. Shared variable metrics. These metrics are based on data definition coupling as defined in [9]. Data definition coupling occurs when functions manipulate data of the same type.

Our goal was to use these metrics to determine if any two functions in the legacy system belong together in the same class when we move to an object-oriented system. In [7], we looked at many metrics because we did not know which ones would be the most effective in identifying objects

An interesting result of this research was that, for the ccount metrics tool, the two most successful metrics turned out to be the simplest—the direct invocation metric and the shared parameter metric.

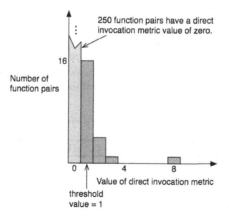

Fig. 3. Distribution of values for the direct invocation metric

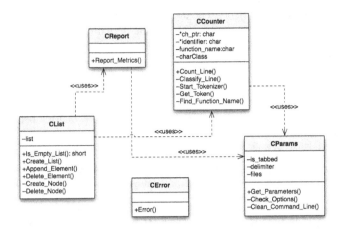

Fig. 4. Class diagram of objects selected using the repeatable method

Figure 3 gives the distribution of values obtained for the direct invocation metric. There are 17 functions in the ccount metrics tool, which means there are $17 \times 16 = 272$ function pairs to consider. Out of those, there were 250 function pairs where no invocation occurred, 16 function pairs where one invocation occurred, four where two invocations occurred, and one each where three invocations occurred and eight invocations occurred. The decision of which threshold to use was empirical to ensure that functions did not cluster in one object. In the case of the direct invocation metric, the vast majority of function pairs had a metric value of zero, so a threshold value of one was chosen—a value of anything greater than one would have meant that too many functions would be in classes by themselves.

Based on the above observations and using the candidate objects as references, we chose the classes shown in Figure 4 for coding the object-oriented version of ccount. The list data type is identified and encapsulated in its own class. The functions main, Error, and Report_Metrics were each placed in their own class.

The study found that coupling metrics provide a good starting point for identifying objects, although the metrics used in the study had limitations. For example, they were not able to completely identify the list data type in ccount. Hence domain expert analysis is an important step in the process. It is necessary for finalizing the optimal objects from the candidate objects identified from the coupling metrics.

Table 2. Process variables

Step	Time taken
Create stop list	1 hour
Create flow graph	1 hour
Dependency list	2 hours
Identify objects	48 hours
Domain expert analysis	16 hours
Coding	23 hours
Total	93 hours

As seen in Table 2, the largest amount of time spent in the process was in identifying objects. The total time taken for the process was 93 hours. Though we did not record the times it took to calculate each metric in the identify-objects step, we estimate that we did not spend more than six hours calculating the direct invocation metric and the shared parameter metric—the two metrics that seemed to give the best results.

This case study presented a good first step in determining how to reengineer a legacy procedural system into an object-oriented system. The methodology examined was found to be helpful in identifying objects. Though most of the calculations for the repeatable method were performed by hand, many of these can be automated. The calculations for the metrics can be automated, and some level of automation may be possible for the translation from the procedural to the object-oriented code. We intend to investigate these possibilities in future research.

3   Comparison of Results: Metrics Summary

In this section we compare the manual and repeatable method on several metrics. First we compared the two methods in terms of regression testing. As can be seen in Figure 5, the repeatable method passed more of the ANSI C version regression tests, 11 tests passed, than did the manual method, which passed eight. One key difference between the two methods is in total code size (commentary code + source code). As summarized in Figure 6, the manual method produced 2,481 lines of code, an increase of 61% over the C version. The repeatable method, on the other hand, was virtually the same as the C version producing 1,547 lines of code. As can be seen in Figure 7, the execution speed follows a similar pattern, with a small increase in execution speed for the repeatable method, and a much larger one for the manual method. The differences in execution speed may be partially caused by the increase in code size.

The increase in code size was also reflected in numbers of methods. The manual method produced 59 methods vs. 20 for the repeatable method. The manual method produced four custom classes and reused the List class from the C++ standard template library. The repeatable method produced five custom classes. The average number of methods per class was therefore 14.75 for the manual method and four for the repeatable method.

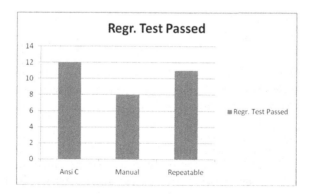

Fig. 5. Number of regression tests passed by the original procedural code, the OO code developed using the manual method, and the OO code developed using the repeatable method

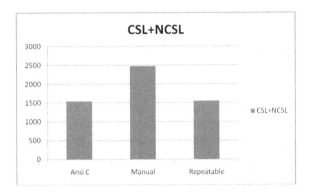

Fig. 6. Difference in code sizes of the original procedural code, the OO code developed using the manual method, and the OO code developed using the repeatable method

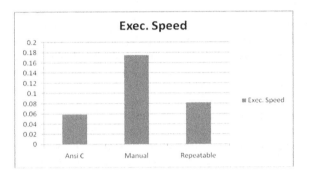

Fig. 7. Difference in execution speed of the original procedural code, the OO code developed using the manual method, and the OO code developed using the repeatable method

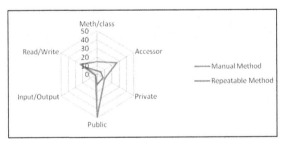

Fig. 8. Spider graph comparison of metrics related to numbers of methods in code generated using the manual and repeatable method

Of the 59 methods in the manual method, 49 of them were public and 10 were private. The programmer using the manual method included a large number of accessor methods in his code (27 in total), so this increase may in part be due to his design decision to make heavy use of accessor methods. Of the 20 methods produced in the repeatable method, 12 were public and 8 were private. This is much closer to the 16 functions in the procedural code. The repeatable code had 5 accessor methods, while the procedural code had 2. The manual method also had an equal or greater number of I/O and read/write methods than the repeatable method. The manual method produced 2 I/O methods and 23 read/write methods, while the repeatable method also produced 2 I/O methods, but produced only 17 read/write methods. The original code contained 3 I/O methods and 12 read/write methods. The number of I/O and read/write methods is suggested as a predictor of good reuse components in [17]. The spider graph in Figure 8 gives an overview of these method numbers.

3.1 Evaluation Using Object-Oriented Metrics

We evaluated the manual and repeatable versions of the code using object-oriented metrics found in [4]. The metrics were weighted methods per class (WMC), coupling between object classes (CBO), response for a class (RFC), and lack of cohesion in methods (LCOM). The other metrics associated with this set, depth of inheritance tree (DIT) and number of children (NOC), were not used since neither method produced code with inheritance. The object-oriented metrics are designed to work on a per class basis. We report them here for each class and also give the average over all classes in each system. Interpreting these metrics is not always straightforward, though extreme numbers indicate a possible need to redesign the class [4]. There is also some indication that higher numbers can lead to more problems [3].

The weighted-methods-per-class metric gives the number of methods in each class. Weighting certain methods higher than others can change this number. For example, one might decide to give a lower weight to accessor methods or private methods. We have given equal weight to all methods since we have already reported numbers of accessor and private methods. Table 3 gives the weighted methods per class, which in this case is the same as the number of methods per class. The methods per class in the code produced with the manual method are almost always higher than those in the code produced with the repeatable method.

Table 3. Weighted methods per class (WMC) for the manual and repeatable methods

Manual method		Repeatable method	
Class	**WMC**	**Class**	**WMC**
Cfile	19	CCounter	6
Cfunc	15	CError	1
Cline	21	CList	6
Util	5	CParams	6
		CReport	1
Mean	15	Mean	4
Median	17	Median	6
Range	16	Range	5

For the coupling-between-object-classes metric, a class is considered coupled to another class if it uses attributes or methods from the other class, or vice versa. Therefore, if class A is coupled to class B, then class B must be coupled to class A. Note that the coupling metrics used in the repeatable method were based on many different forms of coupling. In this study both the manual method and repeatable method produced code in which all the attributes were private, so coupling occurs if one class uses the methods of another. Table 4 gives the CBO metrics for each class produced under the different methods. The numbers for the repeatable method are slightly higher.

Table 4. Coupling between object classes (CBO) for the manual and repeatable methods

Manual method		Repeatable method	
Class	**CBO**	**Class**	**CBO**
Cfile	3	CCounter	2
Cfunc	1	CError	4
Cline	2	CList	3
Util	1	CParams	1
		CReport	2
Mean	1.75	Mean	2.4
Median	1.5	Median	2
Range	2	Range	3

The response for a class is the number of methods in a class plus the number of methods it calls from other classes. For example, if class A has one method that invokes two other methods, both from different classes, then the response for class A is three. All methods are counted only once. Table 5 gives the response for each class produced by the manual and repeatable methods. The RFC values for the manual method are decidedly higher than those for the repeatable method. The manual mean is more than triple that of the repeatable method, and the range is more than double.

Table 5. Response for a class (RFC) for the manual and repeatable methods

Manual method		Repeatable method	
Class	**RFC**	**Class**	**RFC**
Cfile	28	CCounter	9
Cfunc	17	CError	1
Cline	23	CList	7
Util	6	CParams	7
		CReport	3
Mean	18.5	Mean	5.4
Median	20	Median	7
Range	22	Range	8

The lack-of-cohesion-in-methods metric tries to measure the cohesiveness of a class. The higher this number, the less cohesive a class is. The *most* cohesive classes have an LCOM value of zero. The LCOM value is based on the notion that in a cohesive class, most methods will use most of the attributes of the class. If most methods do not use many attributes, the lack of cohesion is higher. The exact formula is LCOM = $\max(n \cdot m - 2 (A_1 + A_2 + \ldots + A_m))$ where n is the number of attributes in the class, m is the number of methods in the class, and A_i is the number of attributes used by method i. Table 6 give the LCOM values for each class produced by each of the methods. As shown in the table, most of the LCOM values for the classes in the manual method are significantly higher than the values for the classes in the repeatable method. The value for the Cline class is particularly extreme.

Table 6. Lack of cohesion in methods (LCOM) for the manual and repeatable methods

Manual method		Repeatable method	
Class	**LOCM**	**Class**	**LOCM**
Cfile	40	CCounter	8
Cfunc	17	CError	0
Cline	138	CList	0
Util	4	CParams	14
		CReport	0
Mean	49.75	Mean	4.4
Median	28.5	Median	0
Range	134	Range	14

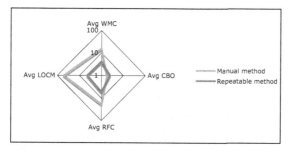

Fig. 9. Spider graph summarizing the object-oriented metrics on a logarithmic scale

Figure 9 summarizes the object-oriented metrics using a spider graph. The average metric values for the manual method are higher than those for the repeatable method for all metrics except the CBO metric.

4 Conclusion

This study examined two methods for reengineering procedural software systems to object-oriented systems. Our hypothesis was that it is possible to support this process

Table 7. Summary of metric contained in this paper

Metric	ANSI C	Manual	Repeatable	See
Regression tests passed	12/17	8/17	11/17	Figure 5
CSL + NCSL	1542	2481	1547	Figure 6
Execution speed	0.0582 sec	0.175 sec	0.0816 sec	Figure 7
Public methods	N/A	49	12	Figure 8
Private methods	N/A	10	8	Figure 8
Accessor methods	2	27	5	Figure 8
Read/Write methods	12	23	17	Figure 8
Input/Output methods	3	2	2	Figure 8
Avg. WMC	N/A	15	4	Table 3
Avg. CBO	N/A	1.75	2.4	Table 4
Avg. RFC	N/A	18.5	5.4	Table 5
Avg. LOCM	N/A	49.75	4.4	Table 6

with a repeatable method. We empirically evaluated our method to determine its utility, and found that the repeatable method produced more compact and efficient code, and passed more regression tests than did the manual method. Analysis of object-oriented metrics indicated both simpler code and less variability among classes. Particularly striking was the order of magnitude difference between the average cohesion metric (LCOM) for the manual and repeatable methods. Table 7 summarizes our findings.

Our analysis raises an interesting issue regarding the use of the repeatable methods. In general, we expect more variability in the manual method, and we observed this. Programmers using the manual method are redesigning the code from scratch, so their different design philosophies will be more apparent than they would be if using the repeatable method. Since the goal of the repeatable method is to provide the programmer with a suggested set of methods for each class, different programmers are more likely to produce similar code.

References

1. Achee, B., Carver, D.: Creating Object-Oriented Designs from Legacy Fortran Code. Journal of System Software 39, 170–194 (1997)
2. Chen, Y.F., Nishimoto, M.Y., Ramamoorthy, C.V.: The C Information Abstraction System. IEEE Transactions on Software Engineering 16(3), 325–334 (1990)
3. Chidamber, S.R., Darcy, D.P., Kemerer, C.F.: Managerial Use of Metrics for Object-Oriented Software: An Exploratory Anaylysis. IEEE Transactions of Software Engineering 24(8) (August 1998)
4. Chidamber, S.R., Kemerer, C.F.: A Metrics Suite for Object-Oriented Design. IEEE Transactions of Software Engineering 20, 476–493 (1994)
5. Dunn, M., Knight, J.: Software Reuse in an Industrial Setting: A Case Study. In: Proceedings 13th International Conference on Software Engineering, pp. 329–338 (1991)
6. Fanta, R., Rajlich, V.: Reengineering Object-Oriented Code. In: Proceedings of the International Conference on Software Maintenance (1998)
7. Frakes, W.B., Kulczycki, G., Saxena, C.: Case Study of a Method for Reengineering Procedural Systems into OO Systems. In: Proceedings of the 9th International Conference on Software Resue, pp. 184–202 (2006)
8. Frakes, W.B., Kang, K.: Software Reuse Research: Status and Future. IEEE Transactions on Software Engineering 31(7), 529–536 (2005)
9. Frakes, W.B., Fox, C.J., Nejmeh, B.A.: Software Engineering in the UNIX/C Environment. Prentice Hall, Englewood Cliffs (1991)
10. Frakes, W.B., Pole, T.P.: An Empirical Study of Representation Methods for Reusable Software Components. IEEE Transactions on Software Engineering 20(8), 617–630 (1990)
11. Gamma, E., Helm, R., Johnson, R., Vlissides, J.M.: Design Patterns: Elements of Reusable Object-Oriented Software. Addison-Wesley Professional, Reading (1994)
12. Gui, J.: Software Reuse through Reengineering of Legacy Systems. In Information and Software Technology (2003)
13. Lanza, M.: Object-Oriented Reverse Engineering, PhD Theses, University of Bern (2003)
14. Newcomb, P., Kotik, G.: Reengineering Procedural into OO Systems. In: Proceedings, 1995 Working Conference on Reverse Engineering (1995)
15. Pole, T.P.: Pole Method for C to C++ Reengineering. Personal Communication (1991)

16. Pressman, R.S.: Software Engineering: A Practitioner's Approach, 6th edn. McGraw-Hill, New York (2005)
17. Selby, R.W.: Quantitative Studies of Software Reuse. In: Software Reusability: Applications and Experience, vol. 2, pp. 213–233. ACM, New York (1989)
18. Suryanarayanan, L., Frakes, W.B.: Re-engineering with Reuse: A Case Study. Virginia Tech. project report, Computer Science department (2003)
19. Valasareddi, R., Carver, D.A.: Graph-Based Object Identification Process for Procedural Programs. In: 1998 Working Conference on Reverse Engineering (1998)
20. Whitney, M., Kontogiannis, K., Johnson, J.H., Bernstein, M., Corrie, B., Merlo, E., McDaniel, J., De Mori, R., Muller, H., Mylopoulos, J., Stanley, M., Tilley, S., Wong, K.: Using Integrated Toolset for Program Understanding. In: Proceedings of the CAS Conference (CASCON 1995), pp. 262–274 (1995)

Appendix: Workshop and Tutorial Abstracts

Jianjun Zhao and Jeff Poulin

Workshops

First Workshop on Domain Specific Analysis and Design for Reuse (DSADR 2008)

Wenyun Zhao[1], Haiyan Zhao[2], Xin Peng[1], Wei Zhang[2],
Seok-Won Lee[3], and Yijun Yu[4]

[1] Computer Science and Engineering Dept., Fudan University, Shanghai, 200433, China
[2] Insitute of Software, Peking University, Beijing, China
[3] The University of North Carolina at Charlotte, Charlotte, NC 28223-0001, USA
[4] Dept. of Computing, The Open University, Walton Hall, Milton Keynes, MK7 6AA, UK

1 Motivation

Software reuse is a promising and attractive concept for improving software productivity, quality and time to market. However, a series of problems will often be encountered when considering reuse in a completely general context, including incompatible variability assumption, architecture mismatch, inability for more specific problem, etc. So a more promising way is to practice reuse based product development within specific domain in a prescribed way, as in the area of domain engineering and software product line.

Reuse oriented analysis and design is the premise of successful reuse based development within specific domain. Problems to be solved include commonality and variability analysis, domain model, domain specific architecture design and description, design for variability, DSL (domain specific language), etc.

2 Topics

DSADR 2008 is the first time to be held in conjunction with ICSR, to bring together interested practitioners and researchers to exchange ideas and experiences, and

H. Mei (Ed.): ICSR 2008, LNCS 5030, pp. 390–399, 2008.
© Springer-Verlag Berlin Heidelberg 2008

discuss current and emerging practices. The workshop will include a keynote speech and a series of presentations and discussions on relate issues.

DSADR 2008 seeks contributions from researchers and practitioners interested in all aspects of analysis and design for domain specific software reuse. To this end, we solicit research papers related to, but not limited to, the following principal topics: domain analysis and modeling; domain specific software architecture; domain specific reuse repository; variability analysis and implementation; DSL (domain specific language); tools for domain specific reuse; experience report on domain specific reuse; other topics on domain specific reuse.

All submissions will be peer-reviewed by 3 PC members and accepted papers will be published by the Journal of Computer Science and Frontiers (http://www.ceaj.org/wes) after the workshop.

First Workshop on Knowledge Reuse (KREUSE2008) Summary

Anabel Fraga[1], Juan Llorens[1], Rubén Prieto-Díaz[2], and José Miguel Fuentes[3]

[1] Universidad Carlos III de Madrid, Departamento de Informática,
Av. Universidad 30, Leganés,
28911 Madrid, Spain
{llorens,afraga}@inf.uc3m.es
[2] James Madison University, Computer Science Department,
Virginia, USA
prietodiaz@cisat.jmu.edu
[3] R&D Dept., The Reuse Company, Virginia, USA
josemiguel.fuentes@reusecompany.com
http://www.kr.inf.uc3m.es/KREUSE2008.htm

The main purpose of Software Reuse is to improve software production by reusing previously created assets. Due to well known historical reasons, its industrial application has been based on the systematic application of domain engineering. The most important weakness of this approach has been the huge investment needed to be accomplished by practitioners. Low or negative return of Investment (ROI) ratios became one of the key problems for its wide-spreading. New approaches try to solve this problem by *going back* to the origins, reducing the need of previously modeled assets by improving indexing, classification and searching of assets on the fly. Knowledge Reuse is at the moment, one of the most advanced, active and modern research areas in the Reuse field. It deals with the application and integration of reuse methods, processes and tools within Knowledge Management processes. It is important for industry because it increases the productivity benefits. Currently, a significant problem that companies have, is the variety of information available, and thus it is a challenge for them to transform information into knowledge, to represent any kind of knowledge within a common repository, and finally offer reuse methods to users. In some measure, the Knowledge Reuse field needs to cope with the fact that knowledge may be anywhere, used by anyone and in any situation. Knowledge is very difficult to accumulate, be sought and be integrated for new needs. One of the basic problems with different types of knowledge is that reusers do not always get what they need from repositories, for reasons that have to do in part with how repositories are created, in part with not up-to-date retrieval techniques, and with almost not existing solutions for smart merging and integrating knowledge within other knowledge. This is a big part of the *window* to be covered by the Knowledge Reuse area.

Topics of the workshop include: Formal representations of different kind of knowledge, Ontology-based representations and their application to Reuse, Universal Knowledge Representation, Knowledge Modeling, Innovative Techniques for Knowledge Representation, Knowledge extraction, indexing and mining, Knowledge Classification, Knowledge Retrieval, Knowledge transformation, Application of MDA/MDD/MDE to Knowledge Reuse, Knowledge Visualization, Knowledge Traceability, Knowledge Reuse Metrics.

Model Reuse Strategies: Software Case Reuse

Michał Śmiałek[1] and Kizito Mukasa[2]

[1] Warsaw University of Technology, Poland
[2] Fraunhofer IESE, Germany

Abstract. The MoRSe workshop is a response to the new reuse possibilities started with the advent of model-driven development. MoRSe tries to find ways to reuse whole "software cases" instead of just pieces of code or individual model fragments.

Model-driven development (MDD) is an approach to software engineering that tries to overcome complexity of systems through building their models. More and more software developers use modelling languages like UML to formulate requirements and design software. Models associated with producing software are used in a typical path from business processes, through requirements, architectures and detailed design to code. This gives us new, model-related strategies for reusing past knowledge about software systems. The Model Reuse Strategies (MoRSe) series of workshops has been started to respond to these new possibilities. MoRSe has a major objective to find ways for comprehensive model reuse. This includes seeking for understandable yet precise requirements models, methods to link requirements with design models and code, and retrieval languages that allow for reuse of models. With these methods we hope to find ways to reuse more than just pieces of code or individual model elements. We hope to be able to reuse whole "software cases" which combine requirements with design and code thus giving complete problem-solution artefacts.

The MoRSe'08 concentrates on topics associated with organisation of comprehensive model-based reuse frameworks including model repositories and tool support for such repositories. This includes presentation of approaches from requirements engineering, metamodelling, model transformation and querying and inference techniques. Specifically, the workshop focuses on the topics: modelling languages (including requirements modelling) and model transformation languages suitable for reuse, techniques for determining and marking similarity of models, model query languages, model reuse engines, software development methodologies based on model reuse and reuse as applied to user interfaces.

The workshop results should be of interest to researchers working on reuse frameworks, tool producers seeking for novel approaches to reuse and software development teams that want to find ways to reuse their past knowledge based on models. The workshop discussions bring us closer to organising comprehensive frameworks (including a language, a tool and a methodology) that support reuse of models starting from models of requirements and ending with models of code. The workshop proceedings, published by Fraunhofer IRB Verlag, were edited also by Markus Nick from empolis GmbH, Germany and Juergen Falb from Vienna University of Technology, Austria.

International Workshop on Software Reuse and Safety (RESAFE 2008)

Bill Frakes[1] and John Favaro[2]

[1] Department of Computer Science, Virginia Tech,
7054 Haycock Rd., Falls Church VA 22043
frakes@cs.vt.edu
[2] Consulenza Informatica, Via Gamerra 17,
56123 Pisa, Italy
john@favaro.net

In the software engineering community at large, reuse has come of age, and in its various manifestations - component-based development, generative languages, domain engineering and others - it is one of the most popular and important paradigms. But there is one domain in which software reuse is looked upon with suspicion: the domain of safety critical systems. This workshop (http://www.favaro.net/john/RESAFE2008/) addresses the issues.

1 Safety Is Different

In her book *Safeware*, Leveson observes that a common problem in much current work in the area is the tendency to consider safety together with other nonfunctional properties such as reliability, availability, and dependability, leading to the impression that improvement in any of the other areas will automatically lead to improvements in its safety-related characteristics. Yet it is easily demonstrated that a less dependable system can be safer than another, more dependable one, for example. A strong case is made for considering safety on its own merits, separately from other RAM characteristics.

2 A Roadmap for Research in Software Reuse and Safety

The software reuse research community has largely ignored the major issues in safety, although the recent interest in "wrappers" and similar technologies holds promise for addressing some of the issues around reuse of COTS (including entire operating systems) in safety critical systems. One contribution of this workshop is the identification of areas in which researchers can work to advance the state of the art with respect to reuse and safety. A concrete output of the workshop is envisioned to be a roadmap and paper to publish in a suitable journal and on appropriate websites such as the *IEEE Software Engineering* website.

Tutorials

Variability Management for Product Lines with a Generative Technique: Reuse beyond Components by Exploiting Software Similarity Patterns

Stan Jarzabek

National University of Singapore
stan@comp.nus.edu.sg

Component-based and architecture-centric techniques are the basic means to achieve reuse via Software Product Line (SPL) approaches. Component platforms providing various mechanisms for component reuse gain popularity.

Advanced platforms (e.g., .NET or JEE) also start incorporating unconventional generative mechanisms for injection of aspect code that affects (crosscuts) many components. Aspect code seamlessly extends functionality of base components with extra, context-specific functionality such as logging, synchronization or persistence.

In this tutorial, we show how much higher levels of reuse can be achieved by applying XVCL [1] (http://xvcl.comp.nus.edu.sg) that supports not only aspects, but also other powerful mechanisms for handling variability in software, such as change propagation and generic design. These generative mechanisms allow us to streamline non-local customizations with system-wide impact, that spread over component configurations. They also help us unify multiple similar component versions with generic, adaptable meta-components. These strategies can replace labor-intensive manual customizations for reuse with semi-automated customizations, increasing productivity during derivation of custom systems from a reusable component base (a Product Line Architecture, PLA). XVCL approach can reduce the complexity of a PLA, and simplifies its evolution by orders of magnitude as compared to conventional component-based PLAs. The approach works for common services such as aspects, as well as at application domain layers of user interfaces or business logic, which are particularly difficult to componentized for reuse.

References

1. Jarzabek, S.: Effective Software Maintenance and Evolution: Reuse-based Approach. Taylor & Francis, CRC Press (2007)
2. Pettersson, U., Jarzabek, S.: Industrial Experience with Building a Web Portal Product Line using a Lightweight, Reactive Approach. In: ESEC-FSE 2005, European Software Engineering Conference and ACM SIGSOFT Symposium on the Foundations of Software Engineering, Lisbon, pp. 326–335. ACM Press, New York (2005)

Managing Software Reuse: A Case-Based Tutorial

Wayne Lim

Lero, the Irish Software Engineering Research Centre, University of Limerick, Ireland
malibaba@lero.ie

Utilizing the case method, attendees will be provided an overview and analysis of effective methods in several key areas. Specifically, they will learn:

- How to initiate a reuse program, reuse adoption and institutionalization models, the possible roles of a corporate reuse program, and how to select pilot projects.
- How to investigate reuse, what the benefits and costs of software reuse are, how to conduct a cost/benefit analysis for reuse, and some economic results from applying the cost/benefit model in several organizations.

- How to plan for reuse, how to organize and staff the reuse program, how to fund a reuse program, why organizations should measure
- How to implement the reuse plan: technology transfer and change management issues and choosing a conversion strategy.

This tutorial is an interactive, case-based seminar on establishing a software reuse program for your organization. Prior to the seminar, attendees are asked to read a case of an organization attempting to implement reuse.

Mapping Product Line Requirements to a Product Line Architecture

Mike Mannion[1] and Juha Savolainen[2]

[1] School of Engineering & Computing, Glasgow Caledonian University, Glasgow
m.a.g.mannion@gcal.ac.uk
[2] Nokia Research Center, Helsinki
Juha.Savolainen@nokia.com

In the consumer product market space a commercial challenge is to offer personalization of products and services for individual customers at a mass production price. Product line development is a compromise between customer requirements, existing product line architectural constraints and commercial needs. Managing variability is the key to a successful product line development. As a product line evolves selections of requirements for new products are often constrained by the design of the existing product line architecture and the cost of making these changes. This tutorial discusses techniques, experiences and open issues about managing the transitions back and forth between product line requirements and architectural components as products evolve.

One approach to managing these problems is to establish a pool of reusable requirements and to construct the requirements for a new product by making a selection from the pool. We present a set of rules that map the selection constraint values of requirements on to the selection constraint values of architectural assets. The impact of changes made to either set of selection constraint values can be seen and evaluated in the other set. We examine the challenges of these techniques, present results of using them for real-world applications, and describe some software tools that can be used to support them.

References

1. Mannion, M., Kaindl, H.: Using Parameters and Discriminants for Product Line Requirements. Systems Engineering 11(1) (Spring 2008)
2. Savolainen, J., Oliver, I., Myllärniemi, V., Männistö, T.: Analyzing and Restructuring Product Line Dependencies. COMPSAC (1), 569–574 (2007)

Metrics and Strategy for Reuse Planning and Management

Bill Frakes[1] and John Favaro[2]

[1] Department of Computer Science, Virginia Tech,
7054 Haycock Rd., Falls Church VA 22043
frakes@cs.vt.edu
[2] Consulenza Informatica, Via Gamerra 17,
56123 Pisa, Italy
john@favaro.net

Key to planning and managing a systematic reuse program is the formulation and evaluation of a competitive strategy, and subsequent monitoring and measurement of progress against the goals elucidated by that strategy. This tutorial provides a succinct introduction to software reuse metrics, and principles of strategic planning and economic evaluation of reuse-oriented investments. The two parts of the course provide a comprehensive overview of current practice and recent developments in reuse project planning and management. Topics include an introduction to management of reuse projects, basic concepts and terminology in reuse measurement, principles of strategy, and fundamentals of economic evaluation of proposed investments in reuse.

1 Metrics for Managing with Reuse

Topics covered include *Reuse motivations* (Role of reuse in improving productivity and quality, Types of Reuse); *Software Reuse Failure Modes Model*; *Cost Benefit Analysis* (Cost/Productivity Models); *Quality of Investment* (Business Reuse Metrics, Relation of Reuse to Quality and Productivity); *Maturity Assessment* (SPC Reuse Capability Model); *Amount of Reuse* (Reuse Level, Reuse Metrics for Object-Oriented Systems, Reuse Predictions for Lifecycle Objects); *Reusability Assessment*.

2 Value-Based Software Reuse Investment

Topics covered include *Principles of Strategy* (Economic value maximization as the governing objective for a reuse-oriented business strategy, strategy as a bundle of projects); *Principles of Valuation* (Present value concepts, pros and cons of traditional approaches to valuation); *Recent approaches to valuation of software investments* (Projects as bundles of options, option-driven software development).

Designing Software Product Lines with UML 2.0: From Use Cases to Pattern-Based Software Architectures

Hassan Gomaa

Department of Computer Science, George Mason University, Fairfax, Virginia, USA
hgomaa@gmu.edu

This tutorial addresses how to develop object-oriented requirements, analysis, and design models of software product lines using the Unified Modeling Language (UML) 2.0 notation. During requirements modeling, kernel, optional, and alternative use cases are developed to define the software functional requirements of the system. The feature model is then developed to capture product line requirements and how they relate to the use case model. During analysis, static models are developed for defining kernel, optional, and variant classes and their relationships. Dynamic models are developed in which statecharts define the state dependent aspects of the product line and interaction models describe the dynamic interaction between the objects that participate in each kernel, optional, and alternative use case. The object-oriented software architecture for the product line is then developed, in which the system is structured into component-based subsystems. Structural architecture patterns and communication patterns are also used in designing component based distributed product lines. The tutorial is illustrated by means of several examples.

This tutorial is divided into two self-contained parts: the first part addresses Requirements and Analysis Modeling for Software Product Lines with UML 2.0, which covers how to develop requirements and analysis models for software product lines, including use case modeling, feature modeling, static modeling, dynamic interaction and state machine modeling. The second part addresses Design Modeling for Software Product Lines with UML 2.0, which covers how to develop component-based product line software architectures, including software architectural patterns for software product lines, design of distributed autonomous components, designing kernel, optional, and variant components, and designing component interfaces, including ports, connectors, provided and required interfaces.

References

1. Gomaa, H.: Designing Software Product Lines with UML: From Use Cases to Pattern-Based Software Architectures. Addison Wesley Object-Oriented Technology Series (2005)

Author Index

Lecture Notes in Computer Science

Sublibrary 2: Programming and Software Engineering

For information about Vols. 1– 4344
please contact your bookseller or Springer

Vol. 4652: D. Georgakopoulos, N. Ritter, B. Benatallah, C. Zirpins, G. Feuerlicht, M. Schoenherr, H.R. Motahari-Nezhad (Eds.), Service-Oriented Computing ICSOC 2006. XVI, 201 pages. 2007.

Vol. 4640: A. Rashid, M. Aksit (Eds.), Transactions on Aspect-Oriented Software Development IV. IX, 191 pages. 2007.

Vol. 4634: H. Riis Nielson, G. Filé (Eds.), Static Analysis. XI, 469 pages. 2007.

Vol. 4620: A. Rashid, M. Aksit (Eds.), Transactions on Aspect-Oriented Software Development III. IX, 201 pages. 2007.

Vol. 4615: R. de Lemos, C. Gacek, A. Romanovsky (Eds.), Architecting Dependable Systems IV. XIV, 435 pages. 2007.

Vol. 4610: B. Xiao, L.T. Yang, J. Ma, C. Muller-Schloer, Y. Hua (Eds.), Autonomic and Trusted Computing. XVIII, 571 pages. 2007.

Vol. 4609: E. Ernst (Ed.), ECOOP 2007 – Object-Oriented Programming. XIII, 625 pages. 2007.

Vol. 4608: H.W. Schmidt, I. Crnković, G.T. Heineman, J.A. Stafford (Eds.), Component-Based Software Engineering. XII, 283 pages. 2007.

Vol. 4591: J. Davies, J. Gibbons (Eds.), Integrated Formal Methods. IX, 660 pages. 2007.

Vol. 4589: J. Münch, P. Abrahamsson (Eds.), Product-Focused Software Process Improvement. XII, 414 pages. 2007.

Vol. 4574: J. Derrick, J. Vain (Eds.), Formal Techniques for Networked and Distributed Systems – FORTE 2007. XI, 375 pages. 2007.

Vol. 4556: C. Stephanidis (Ed.), Universal Access in Human-Computer Interaction, Part III. XXII, 1020 pages. 2007.

Vol. 4555: C. Stephanidis (Ed.), Universal Access in Human-Computer Interaction, Part II. XXII, 1066 pages. 2007.

Vol. 4554: C. Stephanidis (Ed.), Universal Acess in Human Computer Interaction, Part I. XXII, 1054 pages. 2007.

Vol. 4553: J.A. Jacko (Ed.), Human-Computer Interaction, Part IV. XXIV, 1225 pages. 2007.

Vol. 4552: J.A. Jacko (Ed.), Human-Computer Interaction, Part III. XXI, 1038 pages. 2007.

Vol. 4551: J.A. Jacko (Ed.), Human-Computer Interaction, Part II. XXIII, 1253 pages. 2007.

Vol. 4550: J.A. Jacko (Ed.), Human-Computer Interaction, Part I. XXIII, 1240 pages. 2007.

Vol. 4542: P. Sawyer, B. Paech, P. Heymans (Eds.), Requirements Engineering: Foundation for Software Quality. IX, 384 pages. 2007.

Vol. 4536: G. Concas, E. Damiani, M. Scotto, G. Succi (Eds.), Agile Processes in Software Engineering and Extreme Programming. XV, 276 pages. 2007.

Vol. 4530: D.H. Akehurst, R. Vogel, R.F. Paige (Eds.), Model Driven Architecture - Foundations and Applications. X, 219 pages. 2007.

Vol. 4523: Y.-H. Lee, H.-N. Kim, J. Kim, Y.W. Park, L.T. Yang, S.W. Kim (Eds.), Embedded Software and Systems. XIX, 829 pages. 2007.

Vol. 4498: N. Abdennahder, F. Kordon (Eds.), Reliable Software Technologies - Ada-Europe 2007. XII, 247 pages. 2007.

Vol. 4486: M. Bernardo, J. Hillston (Eds.), Formal Methods for Performance Evaluation. VII, 469 pages. 2007.

Vol. 4470: Q. Wang, D. Pfahl, D.M. Raffo (Eds.), Software Process Dynamics and Agility. XI, 346 pages. 2007.

Vol. 4468: M.M. Bonsangue, E.B. Johnsen (Eds.), Formal Methods for Open Object-Based Distributed Systems. X, 317 pages. 2007.

Vol. 4467: A.L. Murphy, J. Vitek (Eds.), Coordination Models and Languages. X, 325 pages. 2007.

Vol. 4454: Y. Gurevich, B. Meyer (Eds.), Tests and Proofs. IX, 217 pages. 2007.

Vol. 4444: T. Reps, M. Sagiv, J. Bauer (Eds.), Program Analysis and Compilation, Theory and Practice. X, 361 pages. 2007.

Vol. 4440: B. Liblit, Cooperative Bug Isolation. XV, 101 pages. 2007.

Vol. 4408: R. Choren, A. Garcia, H. Giese, H.-f. Leung, C. Lucena, A. Romanovsky (Eds.), Software Engineering for Multi-Agent Systems V. XII, 233 pages. 2007.

Vol. 4406: W. De Meuter (Ed.), Advances in Smalltalk. VII, 157 pages. 2007.

Vol. 4405: L. Padgham, F. Zambonelli (Eds.), Agent-Oriented Software Engineering VII. XII, 225 pages. 2007.

Vol. 4401: N. Guelfi, D. Buchs (Eds.), Rapid Integration of Software Engineering Techniques. IX, 177 pages. 2007.

Vol. 4385: K. Coninx, K. Luyten, K.A. Schneider (Eds.), Task Models and Diagrams for Users Interface Design. XI, 355 pages. 2007.

Vol. 4383: E. Bin, A. Ziv, S. Ur (Eds.), Hardware and Software, Verification and Testing. XII, 235 pages. 2007.

Vol. 4379: M. Südholt, C. Consel (Eds.), Object-Oriented Technology. VIII, 157 pages. 2007.

Vol. 4364: T. Kühne (Ed.), Models in Software Engineering. XI, 332 pages. 2007.

Vol. 4355: J. Julliand, O. Kouchnarenko (Eds.), B 2007: Formal Specification and Development in B. XIII, 293 pages. 2006.

Vol. 4354: M. Hanus (Ed.), Practical Aspects of Declarative Languages. X, 335 pages. 2006.

Vol. 4350: M. Clavel, F. Durán, S. Eker, P. Lincoln, N. Martí-Oliet, J. Meseguer, C. Talcott, All About Maude - A High-Performance Logical Framework. XXII, 797 pages. 2007.

Vol. 4348: S. Tucker Taft, R.A. Duff, R.L. Brukardt, E. Plödereder, P. Leroy, Ada 2005 Reference Manual. XXII, 765 pages. 2006.

Vol. 4346: L. Brim, B.R. Haverkort, M. Leucker, J. van de Pol (Eds.), Formal Methods: Applications and Technology. X, 363 pages. 2007.